The Compulsion to Confess

FROM THE WORKS OF THEODOR REIK

The Compulsion
to Confess

On the Psychoanalysis of Crime

and Punishment

by THEODOR REIK

Essay Index Reprint Series

071770

 BOOKS FOR LIBRARIES PRESS
FREEPORT, NEW YORK

Library of Congress Cataloging in Publication Data

Reik, Theodor, 1888-1970.
    The compulsion to confess.

    (Essay index reprint series)
    At head of title: From the works of Theodor Reik.
    Translation of Geständniszwang and Strafbedürfnis,
and other works.
    CONTENTS: The unknown murderer.--The compulsion to
confess.--The shock of thought. [etc.]
    1. Criminal psychology. 2. Criminal investigation.
3. Confession (Law) I. Title.
[HV6080.R393 1972]   364.3   72-1146
ISBN 0-8369-2856-3

Contents

Publisher's Preface

T*he Compulsion to Confess* is the third of a series of volumes of selections from Theodor Reik's works, of which *The Search Within: The Inner Experiences of a Psychoanalyst* was the first, and *Of Love and Lust: On the Psychoanalysis of Romantic and Sexual Emotions* was the second. The first volume showed the development of his own philosophical attitudes, his personal story, and frank accounts of his training and his work. The second volume, as its sub-title indicates, deals with the love and sex life of men and women, and with differences in the emotional and behavior patterns of the sexes. This new third volume studies the psychology of crime and the deep forces propelling the criminal and the opposing power of unconscious conscience.

As I have pointed out in the other volumes, Dr. Reik did not wish to edit these books himself and since our publishing relation has been close, dating back to 1938, he asked me to do so.

In editing the earlier volumes there was the problem of cutting and of some re-arrangement. This has not been true of this volume. All three books included in it are presented complete, and the short final essay on capital punishment is as it was originally written. The editor's problems have been slight. Dr. Reik's own note explains the contents. The first part, "The Unknown Murderer" (translated by Mrs. Ernest Jones) has been out of print for some time. The rest of the book has never before appeared in English. Dr. Reik, himself, went over the translation by Dr. Norbert Rie and has added material here and there to emphasize certain points.

To me, it is most remarkable that these books, published so long ago in the early days of analysis, are fresh, original and seem to present many insights and facts that have not yet been absorbed by the public interested in psychological literature. This is Reik, the courageous pioneer, and shows as well as any of his books the importance of the man both as a thinker and as something of a prophet.

JOHN FARRAR

Author's Note

THIS volume comprises books and papers written and published in German in the years 1926 to 1928 and—with the exception of *The Unknown Murderer*—until now not translated into English. *The Unknown Murderer*, long out of print, introduced a new subject into the area of psychoanalytic research: the criminal investigation, its motives, its nature and its aims. The problems of circumstantial evidence and the history and technique of trial, the emotional processes in the murderer and in the detectives and the judges were seen here in the new light of psychoanalysis. The way from magical criminology, from oracle and ordeal, oath and torture, to circumstantial evidence was followed and illustrated with the histories of many criminal cases. *The Harvard Law Review* saw in this book a new approach to the psychology and psychopathology of the criminal the understanding of whom "has to go hand in hand with the inquiry into the psychology of those whose duty it is to detect the culprit and to sit in judgment over him." Freud wrote me (September 9, 1932) that he shared my doubts concerning certain planned applications of psychoanalysis in the field of criminology. He took a special interest in the historical aspects of investigation and appreciated "the skill with which you discover the decisive ancient and primal forms behind the modern" (same letter).

Geständniszwang und Strafbedürfnis (Compulsion to Confess and Need of Punishment), published in Vienna in 1925, deals with problems of criminology in a different manner. It is the result of lectures given in the Vienna Psychoanalytic Association and, I hope, retains something of the vivacity and flexibility of the spoken word in presenting a new psychological factor in the emotional life. Comparable to the discovery of a new chemical compound, the hypothesis here presented emerged first in the psychoanalysis of neurotic patients, in the laboratory of analytic practice, so to speak. I had observed that the primal tendency of instinctual expression was subjected to a transformation under the influence of guilt and self-punishment. Freud had already stated that we mortals cannot keep secrets and that "self-betrayal oozes out from all pores." The symptoms and manifestations of neurotic disturbances showed not only the power of our unconscious wishes, but also the intensive influence of forbidding and condemning tendencies, most of which are also unconscious. An abundance of clinical experiences and repeated observations convinced me that most symptoms also have the character of an unconscious confession and that their purpose is to mitigate the pressure of guilt feeling. They are at the same time a kind of unconscious verbal repetition of an unconsciously desired, forbidden deed in action. Transgressing the area of neurosis and character deformation, I tried to prove that the unconscious compulsion to confess plays an important and until now undiscovered role in religion and myth, in art and language and in other social activities. I demonstrated the importance of this tendency for the criminological and penal theories and presented many instances showing its operation in the emotional life of children and adolescents. Modern criminology, especially in the area of juvenile delinquency and pedagogics, will, I am sure, make use of these new insights in the near future as soon as the resistances to original points of view are conquered. They, as well as dynamic psychology, will come to the conclusion that the unconscious need for self-punishment has to be considered one of the most important emotional forces shaping the destiny of men and that the future of mankind will depend on it, on whether we succeed in reducing the power of this unconscious force that threatens us all with extinction. From the exploration of the individual emotional life, the investigation proceeds to the discussion of a collective unconscious compulsion to confess. I picked up this thread of a universal guilt feeling and need of punishment thirty years later in a psychoanalytic exploration of the historical and emotional roots of the belief in an

original sin in which mankind confessed to a universal crime.*
Paul Reinwald, the Swiss scholar, was perhaps the first, in his
treatise *Society and Its Criminals,* who appreciated the impact of
the new points of view here presented. Freud at first had the impression that my conclusions were founded on too slight a basis
but, as he wrote me in a letter on January 13, 1925, the following
presentation "makes your thesis increasingly plausible as you ex-
pand upon it." My attempt "to demonstrate the role of the superego in all neuroses seems as legitimate as it is fruitful." The fact
that he considered this book "thoughtful and extremely important" encouraged me to include it in this collection, especially
since it remained almost unknown to American psychoanalysts
and psychologists. I hope that the subject, whose content must be
of interest to a wide circle of educated readers, will prove fruitful
in future research in many fields of individual and collective
psychology.

The last part of this book contains several new contributions
to the main subject, gleanings of several years. In these psychoanalytic essays, such important psychological problems as fright
and anxiety, the connection between sexual urges and guilt feelings and between hate and fear, the relation of revenge and forgiveness are analytically explored. Social success and unconscious
moral anxiety, the faith in a higher justice and similar questions
are investigated here from psychoanalytic viewpoints and new
insights are gained into the operating of the unconscious forces
that shape the destiny of us all.

The last contribution is a paper on capital punishment from a
symposium published and edited by the judge of a German High
Court. This well-known official asked Thomas Mann, Jacob
Wassermann, Freud and many other prominent personalities
about their views on capital punishment and published their
answers to his questions in a booklet, *Für und wider die Todes-
strafe.* Freud asked me to answer in his place and discussed with

* *Myth and Guilt, The Crime and Punishment of Mankind;* George Braziller, Inc., New York, © 1957. Section VIII of Part Two includes an excerpt from
Myth and Guilt.

me the kind of contribution that psychoanalysis can make to the solution of this important problem. It is, as far as I know, the only expression of Freud's view on this subject and I do not doubt that it will interest all people who have thought about the moral and psychological question of capital punishment.

New York, Summer 1958. THEODOR REIK

PART ONE

The Unknown Murderer

Translated from the German
by DR. KATHERINE JONES

1. THE INTEREST IN CRIME

WHEN WE HEAR of an unsolved crime the first question we ask is not a psychological one. It is: Who did it? And in cases which are accompanied by mysterious circumstances other questions follow. We want to know how a murder was committed, what plan the unknown criminal followed, how he escaped discovery, etc. The psychologist will also direct his attention in such cases to the elucidation and interpretation of certain clues rather than to the unknown motives of the criminal. The conclusions the police draw from such clues, the investigations to which they give rise, how the circle of the persons concerned widens and narrows, all this will occupy us much more than, for instance, the question of the degree in which the ego was involved in the psychogenesis of the crime.

The method of elucidation, the finding out of actual facts by the police, especially making use of all clues, of actual circumstantial evidence, excite our interest. When we ask ourselves the reason for this interest we discover that we do not know the answer. Our interest follows devious routes. Strange, since we thought our interest in criminology centered on the discovery of the unknown motives and aims of the crime and of avenging society. Several questions concerning the psychology of the criminal, the prevention of crime and its therapy, punishment and the reform of penal law have been dealt with in psychoanalytical literature, but the treatment of these problems supposes that the criminal is known. One cannot examine an unknown man psychologically.

The discovery, interpretation and use of clues and the investigation of circumstantial evidence in order to prove the crime lead

3

us far away from psychology. Our interest would be understandable if it concerned methods of examining free associations, such
as were tried in the finding of the actual facts, if it concerned
psychical happenings as they appear to the neurologist who is
called in as an expert. But fingerprints, matches, a scrap of paper,
carelessly dropped cigarette ash? These are things that might
be important for practical criminologists; they concern chemistry,
microphotography, etc., but certainly not scientific psychology.
The clues at the place where the deed was done, which are generally pieces of inorganic matter, are certainly outside the sphere
of that science.

Another interest, that seems more familiar to us, must slowly
take the place of interest in material clues, which lead us away
from psychology into a far-removed land. This is astonishment at
one's own psychic phenomenon. We ask ourselves what such an
interest means psychologically, and where it comes from. We have
returned to our own realm of psychology. The following investigation will start from this question which we have put to ourselves, or which has put itself to us, and will return to it.

It will not be possible to conceal the traces of my tentative and
discursive attempts to solve these problems. I realize how far they
fall short of a conclusive, scientific demonstration. I have not
tried to cover up the inevitable gaps, obscurities and uncertainties.
One might perhaps prove that another way would have been better
than this genetic one which shows how a problem at first emerged,
how it presented its many aspects, and how the attempts to solve
it fared. I cannot dispute this. Maybe there is a hidden inner link
between content and form, and it is this subterranean connection
that my exposition follows. The material, brittle to the touch, has
shown itself in its contents more extensive, more complicated and
richer in connections than one would have guessed from its point
of departure. That happens often in life and science. It soon proved
impossible to abide by the problem as originally defined and to
keep within its frontiers. The initial problem had to take second
place, because new ones which could not be avoided kept cropping
up like hurdles on a racecourse.

I shall be able to show, I hope, that the value of psychoanalysis for criminology is by no means limited to the questions that have so far been discussed by psychoanalysts. A new, undiscovered territory of analytic research opens out. In the following pages I have tried to show whether and what psychoanalysis has contributed to the problem of the unknown criminal; indeed, what this problem means psychologically. In the beginning there was the deed. The criminal's deed, however, rarely has witnesses; and the magistrates, judges and juries have to fall back upon clues that have a certain value in respect to the accused person's guilt or innocence. The whole sum of these clues forms proof; it speaks for or against the guilt of the accused, even when, and especially when, these clues are mute and dead.

2. FROM THE DEED TO THE DOER

WHAT are clues? According to Glaser[1] "all that serves such as proof, but is not proof by itself." In general, one calls clues such facts as allow the conclusion that there must be another fact, one yet to be proved. In penal law the term has come to mean facts that lead to conclusions about the guilt or innocence of the accused. The importance of this conception becomes clear when one realizes that it is through clues that we form our opinion about the facts of a case. There is only one alternative: to catch the culprit red-handed. This and his confession, which used to be considered the crowning proof, are the exceptions in criminal investigation.

Before clues become valuable as links in the chain of proof they serve as suggestions, indications for the detection of the crime. They are in the center of criminological tactics that discover the traces of the deed and deduce such facts from them as will lead to the final stage—a judicial conviction.

Within the clues we clearly distinguish one group: the evidence from material objects. A German expert[2] defines clues as "all that the criminologist can observe and make use of." Observation in this sense is not limited to visual observations: the smell of gasoline in a gutted house is also a clue. Nor need one restrict one's clues to the spot where the deed was done. Apart from these clues there are others, far from the spot, as, for instance, blood on the clothes of suspected persons. Modern criminology distinguishes between the establishment of evidential facts, the investigation of their meaning, and the weighing of their value as proof. The proof value of tangible clues has become so extensive that the laboratory has been called the antichamber of the law courts.[3] Criminologists of our time have left Sherlock Homes far behind; how poor was his method, how primitive his technique of detection! He did not know the automobile, the telephone, the radio, not even photography, let alone fingerprints and measurements.[4] It is interesting to compare the methods of Conan Doyle's detective with the ways and means used by modern criminology, the results he could obtain within a certain time with those we can reach now. In one of his stories[5] a male corpse is found in a little house. Next to the corpse lies a gold ring; on the wall is the word *"Rache,"* written in blood. Holmes starts by saying that the murdered man entered the house accompanied by a tall man—the distance between his footprints shows the man's height—and that the tall man left the house alone. Then he sees that the murdered man had not been injured. He recognizes that he was poisoned. There are no indications of a struggle. The culprit also is probably uninjured. Where does the blood on the wall come from? Perhaps the culprit was bleeding from the nose. This presupposes that he is full-blooded and red-faced. The first provisional description of the murderer is a tall man with a red face.

Compare this result with that of the medical jurist Pfaff in a certain case.[6] The culprit had left his cap behind; in it were two fair grayish hairs. The doctor found under the microscope several cells of pitch-black pigment. The section-planes were quite sharp, the roots atrophied. In the epithelial layer several warts, caused by sweating, could be observed. Dr. Pfaff could say: "The culprit is a sturdy, fattish, middle-aged man; his hair is getting gray, was cut recently and he is going bald."[7]

Fingerprints, the progress of microphotography and microchemistry, of medicine and other branches of knowledge have helped criminology considerably. Naturally, also, the criminal has benefited by the richer and more elaborate techniques available and one can talk of a technical race between criminology and crime. The police have not always won this race.

The interpretation and use of clues lead in two directions: to the objective facts—and there all centers in the question "What has happened and how has it happened?"—and to the determination of the subjective problem for which the answer to the question "Who is the culprit?" is decisive. It stands to reason that investigations have to go in both directions; very often they are conducted quite independently of each other.

Practice often shows that the objective facts can easily be established, sometimes at first glance, whereas there are very few clues to clear up the mystery of the subjective facts. Perhaps the best way of showing the number and variety of aspects is to give some examples. As early as 1889, Dr. Jeserich could prove in a case before the Court of Aurich that a murder had been committed and that arson followed in order to conceal the murder. From the absence of any trace of carbon dioxide in the blood taken from the lungs of the charred body, it could be deduced that there was no breathing during the fire.[8] This shows at the same time how important it is to find out all there is to know about the facts of the case. The plain facts decide whether we have to deal with a crime or an accident. In one case there was a revolver lying at the right side of the corpse. Suicide was assumed, but the dead man was left-handed. It was this fact that made people suspect a murder. On the precise and conscientious examination of detailed facts depends whether and where to search for a culprit. By such means the problem very often solves itself. Here is a famous example: two gentlemen farmers went for a drive in the same carriage; the horses bolted. One of them was thrown out and fatally injured. A more careful examination—it was considered almost superfluous—revealed a splash of blood between the back wheels of the carriage. That could not have happened through the fall from the carriage. The result of the examination was that the second man was proved guilty of murder. He had induced his friend to get out of the carriage and had killed him behind it.

Criminologists have invented a kind of catechism to be applied in every mysterious and complicated case. It is called "The seven golden W's." In other words, correct answers to seven particular questions will provide a sufficient explanation of every crime. The questions are: What? Who? When? Where? In what way? What with? Why? A man is found dead, apparently murdered. What has happened? Who is the victim? When did it happen? Where has it happened? In what way has it happened? With what was the crime committed? Why was it done? If one succeeded in answering all these questions, the case would be completely solved. Very often half of these questions can be answered at once; sometimes, however, a case remains completely unsolved because a single question remains unanswerable.

It is clear that the first question "What has happened?" is the cardinal one for the beginning of the investigation. We have seen that it often depends on this whether such an investigation takes place or not. The question "Who is the murdered person?" is often difficult to answer, either because the mode of death or the murderer have made the corpse unrecognizable. A fraud on an insurance company was perpetrated the other day in the following way: the criminal was driving in his car on a lonely road and gave a lift to a workman. He killed the man and furnished the corpse with his own possessions (passport, watch, etc.); then he set fire to the car and the corpse. People were to suppose that the owner of the car, who in fact was fleeing abroad, was the victim.

The answer to the trivial question: "When did it happen?" has often involved the solution of a difficult case. An expert medical opinion establishing when death took place can be of all-important significance in a murder case. Small details like a stopped watch or a block calendar can help materially towards finding the culprit. Weingart mentions the following case:[9] the day after a theft had been committed, some money, wrapped in newspaper, was found on a suspected person. He maintained that he had had the money for four weeks and had kept it wrapped up in the same newspaper all the time. It was proved, however, that the newspaper had been printed on the day before his arrest. The significance of time and of clues pointing in this direction may be seen in a case which the well-known American criminologist Albert S. Osborn quotes in his book, *The Problem of Proof:*[10] a letter, meant to prove that a mortgage on several thousand acres of land was genuine, was dated 1892 and written with a Remington typewriter. But the Remington typewriter had changed certain details of type in 1898. The letter produced in evidence exhibited these alterations. This example, in which the measurement of the type was the "controlling fact," shows at the same time how the criminal's tool sometimes turns against him. The great significance of time needs no further proof when one remembers the conviction a good alibi carries. The criminologist Karl Stieler maintained that there existed three necessities to make a good poacher: a sawed-off gun, a blackened face and a reliable alibi.

The place where the crime was committed ("Where was it done?") may seem to the layman of less importance; but to find the place very often means finding the culprit. This happens not only through direct clues like fingerprints; the place itself may allow important conclusions. For instance the dead victim is transported to a lonely spot in order to destroy all clues. Here are two examples that show in what different ways the finding of the place was important for the detection of the crime.[11] After a case of arson, the bicycle of a suspected person was found to have attached to it the fragment of an ear of wheat, of the same kind and degree of ripeness as on the wheat field near the fire. The man had used his bicycle to get there and back more quickly and, while committing the act of arson, he had put his bicycle in the wheat field. The place of the crime was known; its immediate neighborhood betrayed the man. In other cases the place of the crime is unknown, and finding it may furnish the most important indications regarding the crime, as in the following case. On a railroad in northern Germany, a postman's moneybag had been emptied and subsequently filled with sand. The train had stopped at approximately twenty stations. To find out where the robbery was committed, a geologist was consulted. He had a sample of sand from each station brought to him which he compared carefully with the sand in the postbag and found that the sand came from a particular station. It was there that the robbery had taken place.

The next question, "How did it happen?" necessitates the investigation of circumstances remotely connected with the act. Here clues often come to light that point unmistakably to the culprit. The "how" very often provides the answer to our inquiries about the criminal. Everything a man does and does not do, what he is and what he wants to be, can find its expression and leave its trace in the way he commits a crime. Certain activities which are not immediately connected with the crime often tell us more about the man than do witnesses. Here is an example of the criminological value of such an accessory clue.[12] Early in 1923 Dr. W. Schatz was asked by the owner of a cereal business to help him in tracing certain thefts—a suspected workman could not be proved guilty. In the room from which several sacks had disappeared no clues could be found. Schatz noticed the end of a ball of string that had been cut quite recently. A search in the workman's home yielded another piece of string, about two yards long, of the same kind. One end matched the freshly cut end of the string found in the room from which the sacks had disappeared. This was proved by microscopic examination. The thief had tied the stolen stacks together with string and thrown them out of the window into a neighboring garden from which he fetched them later. From the nature of his find, Schatz deduced that not one person, but two, had committed the thefts. The string was not cut straight, but obliquely. One person as a rule would cut a thick string by making a loop and cutting it straight through with his knife. But when there are two people, the cutter would cut away from himself, so that the cut would be oblique. The workman confessed that his son had helped him to cut the string and tie the sacks. It is pre-eminently in the examination of such clues and in the deductions which competent and scientific investigation make possible that juridical medicine, microchemistry and microphotography celebrate their greatest triumphs. Trivial things become pieces of proof that carry extraordinary conviction.[13]

In the place where a crime was committed, a workman's coat was found which externally did not furnish any clue in regard to its owner. The coat was put in a bag of strong paper and this parcel was beaten with sticks as long and violently as possible without tearing the paper. Then the bag was opened; the dust which had collected under the coat on the paper was carefully collected and examined under the microscope. The examination proved that the dust which had come out of the coat consisted mainly of finely ground wood; it was inferred that the coat belonged to a joiner, carpenter or worker in a sawmill.

Clues that originate through the culprit's presence in the place of crime are either caused by his person on his surroundings (fingerprints or footprints and impressions) or by the surroundings on his person (on his clothes or things he handles). The traces that were left by the pattern of a corduroy jacket on a dusty marble slab were responsible for the conviction of a man who had committed a murder near Tours.[14] In another case, a thief fell to his knees while climbing a wall; he wore corduroy trousers that were patched with some material of another pattern. Thanks to this detail he left a very characteristic trace which assisted in his discovery.[15] In the case of a St. Petersburg banker,[16] who was found murdered in his office, a cigar was picked up near the corpse which plainly showed teeth marks, and it could be proved that they were not those of the victim. These clues gave the case away: the murderer was the banker's cousin. Similarly other objects which show teeth marks—like a pipe—become important aids for the identification of the culprit. The kind of injury inflicted often indicates a certain person as the murderer. A girl was killed by two workmanlike cuts into the carotid arteries. This suggested a butcher and the suggestion was correct. A. Griffith tells in his *Mysteries of Police and Crime* the interesting case of Mme. Henri, which happened about 1830 in France. A sack containing parts

of a male body was found in the river. The sack was sewn together
at the top and this warranted the conclusion that a woman had
done it; a man would have tied the sack. This observation pointed
to Mme. Henri as soon as the body was identified as her husband's.

With what instrument was the deed done? The importance of
settling this question is obvious. At Dresden a butcher's assistant
had stabbed a woman in the breast with a long knife, and had left
it there when fleeing in a panic. The knife had been in use for
years and had been ground repeatedly. By many sharpenings, it
had taken on a characteristic shape, rather like a sickle. The suspected man denied that the knife was his. His other knives were
compared with this one; all of them had the same shape. A great
number of much-sharpened knives, belonging to other butchers,
were examined; in all these cases the sharpening had altered the
shape in a different way. The murder of Schmoller, a cashier in
a motion picture theater in Berlin, which took place in 1931, was
detected through a clue used by the experts in firearms. The cartridges which were found came from the American munition firm
of Colt and had only been on the market for six months. The
suspected man, an artist, Urban, had only recently returned in
January, 1931, from America, where he had been touring for
two years. Hermann Zafita has given particular attention to the
way in which tools used are characteristic of the user. He insists
upon the importance for criminal psychology of examining the
instruments used in committing a crime.[17]

Apart from these points, which have so far not gone beyond
general observations, the following example will show the significance of tools and instruments in detection. It is given by the
police of Thuringia. In a certain village a farm was burned down.
The police, in searching a stable, found a small printed strip of
paper which had probably been used by the culprit in lighting
the fire. It had been hidden and preserved by a fallen brick. The
police ascertained that the strip of paper was torn out of a school-
book; and they found the unlucky owner.

It has been said that the criminal's worst traitor is his hand.

That was true even at a time when there was no fingerprint system. A peasant scratched the word "miser" with a piece of wood in a neighbor's field, and strewed cornflowers in the groove. The expert employed had the word photographed. The handwriting was recognized as that of an unfriendly neighbor.[18] It is a truism that all we do leaves a trace that tells of our personality.

This example leads us to the last question of the seven golden W's. Why was the deed done? The nature of the act itself often gives the answer, but often much ingenuity is needed to discover it. We shall return to this point and the part which it plays in criminal detection. We do not propose to give any more examples or deal in greater detail with particular criminological views. Classifications of clues, according as they are subsidiary or conclusive, can only have one meaning or are ambiguous, determining a number of questions or only one question, are not all important.

The layman does not realize how much trouble, thought and work, is needed in certain cases where the expert is held up by the criminal's cunning or by unlucky accidents. This is the place to consider false clues, which often lead to tragic errors. A knife which an innocent tramp had lost was actually found near a murdered person. Blood traces the medical jurist thought most significant turned out to be from the bleeding nose of an entirely innocent person. The criminologist has to discriminate most carefully as to whether a given clue is connected with the deed or not. In a murder case, traces of blood were found outside the house; various conclusions were drawn from this fact. But it turned out that the blood came from a dogfight.[19] False clues are of course also staged by the culprit for the purpose of deception. Criminologists agree that often a remarkable amount of intelligence is shown in the fabrication of false clues. The criminal has to anticipate the probable conclusions of the examining experts, and must arrange things so that they fit in with the supposed facts. The success of such efforts is sometimes undeniable. Often the victim has been' buried without suspicions, and only very much later has it turned out by accident or unforeseen circumstances that he died an unnatural death. On the corpse of a murdered keeper, who had for days been on the track of a well-known poacher, an open notebook was found in which a trembling hand had written: "S. has shot me." As other clues pointed in the same direction S. was sentenced to death, but reprieved. A long time afterwards, a boy, the son of a certain man G., made remarks about some strange expressions his parents had used while quarreling. G. was examined and in the end confessed that he had killed the keeper. In doing so he had put on a false beard to resemble S. The note in the book he had written himself, purposely "in a trembling hand."[20]

False clues are not easily detected; often enough they deceive the detective. The expression "crime does not pay" rises from an optimism that, in spite of its businesslike style, underestimates the caution and cleverness of many criminals. But once the investigator has succeeded in detecting deception and false clues, they give the most valuable assistance in reconstructing the crime—and in a very different way from that which their originator planned and desired.

Finally, the discovery of counterclues must be mentioned, i.e., signs that the suspect is not the guilty man. To give an idea of the kind of case with which we are concerned, one interesting example out of many that could be quoted must serve. This time we find astronomers as experts in a criminal case.[21] In the spring of 1910 a man in Nebraska was suspected of having caused an explosion. At the critical moment, two witnesses had seen the man carrying a suitcase. But it so happened that someone had taken a snapshot of people coming out of a church, which was half an hour distant from the site of the explosion, and that the two witnesses were in the photograph. In this photograph there was a man's shadow thrown on a wall, and by means of this astronomers calculated within a few minutes the time at which the snapshot had been taken. By comparing this time with the time of the explosion, it could be proved that the accused could not be guilty. He had already been sentenced to five years' penal servitude, but was acquitted at the retrial.

Scientific investigation has shown the unreliability of witnesses and the superiority of facts as evidence. This trust in "technical proof" is still growing and science attaches increasing importance to the improvement of methods dealing with facts and clues. It is thought to provide the most effective antidote to "the poison of witness's evidence."[22] The introduction of scientific methods into criminal investigation has certainly weakened this poison. But there is some hidden poison in the investigation itself.

"Indirect proof through material clues," as it is called in the criminologist's terminology, does not by itself prove a man guilty. It presupposes the strict, methodical use of the material; the clues must be interpreted, compared with each other, and examined over and over again. Poison found in a body proves poisoning, but not necessarily a crime. A fingerprint in the place of crime proves the presence of a certain person, but not his guilt. The meticulous and precise verification of what happened is the first task of the criminologist, and must precede the examining and interpreting of clues. In an English cookbook, the chapter dealing with the different ways of cooking hares starts with the good advice: "First catch your hare."

3. Begin with Logic

A clue is a fact that must be co-ordinated with others to be of value in finding out what actually happened. In other words: a clue derives its value from a certain psychological process in the examiner. Of what kind is this? To bring facts in relation to each other, to connect them in such a way that their functional significance becomes visible, to separate the essential from the accidental, to draw conclusions from certain premises—all these are logical operations. It is logic, therefore, that must have the first word. Or the last?

Logical reasoning, it would appear, accounts for the criminologists' success; it is this intellectual achievement which we admire in their work. Manuals for judges and detectives insist upon the necessity of logical thinking and the danger of false conclusions in criminal investigations; and this is comprehensible. By drawing a single false conclusion one might lose one's way and find oneself in a maze. This holds true of the process of perceiving the connection between clue and criminal. A footprint, a shadow, a cigar butt—to bring these clues into causal connection with the movements of the suspected man is already a logical operation. Hans Gross says in his famous *Criminal Psychology:* "Simple though this statement about causal connection seems, it is important, because continually to ask and reask the question 'What is effect and what cause?' remains our real and most important task. Whoever keeps on asking himself that question until he gets tired of it cannot make a bad mistake."

Sherlock Holmes is held up to young criminologists as an example of correct logical reasoning. It is true that this is fiction, that the means he employed are out of date, but the gifts of observation and deduction which he made his own are still enviable.[23]

This detective keenly observes trivial details, unimportant to others, thinks about them, connects them with each other, bases his deductions on them. He observes the shape of a man's hands, his nails, his scars, the way he holds himself, the details of his clothes, the sleeves of his coat, it may be, or the knees of his trousers, or his boots. Worn places in a suit often lead him to the most amazing conclusions, and enable him to show with certainty the details of the crime and accurately reconstruct the hidden course of events. These observations of disregarded detail give him an insight into the work, the habits, the present and past life of a given person. To this gift of observation is due the unerring accuracy of his deductions. Lothar Philipp,[24] who insists upon a special kind of reasoning for the criminologist, recommends Sherlock Holmes' method of observation as an example to be followed.

If the method of this detective were not so purely external, and aimed at sudden effect, we could compare many things in his technique with psychoanalytical observation and interpretation. Is it, perhaps, precisely the likeness of the method that has roused our interest? In both methods, observation, interpretation, and the correlation of these lead to the discovery of hidden facts. Certainly, there exist similarities in method,[25] but we must not overlook the great differences. Even if we look away from the dissimilarity in the hypotheses and aims of the two intellectual processes, enough decisive differences remain.

In the criminologist's reasoning a strictly logical process is in question: there is a major premise, one or more minor premises, and a conclusion. The analyst who wants to find out hidden processes works differently. He has little to do with conscious logic; he uses different ways and means. The object of the criminologist's reasoning is knowledge of a material event and the finding of an unknown person. Analytic work aims at discovering a psychological process or a series of such processes. In psychoanalysis, everything except psychological insight is unessential, while, to the criminologist, psychological events are accidental or unimportant compared with the reality which he has to elucidate. In both, clues are observed, made use of and interpreted, but the difference lies in the kind of clues and in the way they are used. The objective clues are aften pieces of inorganic nature. A speck of dust, a fingerprint, a collar, tell a tale to the criminologist, allow him to make certain *a posteriori* conclusions; the objects as such speak. The analyst obtains his conclusions in the great majority of cases only through observation of what a person is doing. An inanimate objects as such tells him little if nothing is done with it, if it is not moved or handled, unless it becomes the object of activity of the person who interests him. The analyst might agree, in one sense, with the criminologist's saying, "A man's worst traitor is his hand." The criminologist has in mind, for instance, the method of identification by fingerprints. The print he finds on a drawer where the crime was committed is of the greatest significance for him; perhaps it gives conclusive evidence regarding the criminal. For the psychonalyst the fingerprint as such has no value, but he could draw certain conclusions by observing a man thoughtlessly playing with something or handling something unconsciously. As we see, the similarities are limited to specific characteristics in the meth-

ods and result, partly from the fact that both are trying to bring
to light a hidden fact.[26]

We must now return to a statement that did not seem quite
right at the time we made it. We said that criminologists obtained
their results by pure logic. Criminologists themselves would like
to hear that said. Many, especially the younger ones, maintain
that the work of logic and combination is the essence of their
activity. They relate their experiences, show the nature of different methods, their successes and their failures, caused by false
conclusions, and try to prove the absolute necessity of logical reasoning in criminal investigation. Cool, objective thought, re-examination of facts according to the rules of logic, *raisonnement*
(Locard) is the pivot of the detective's mental process. Reading
their manuals one gets the impression that exact knowledge of the
different ways of reasoning determines success or failure in a case.
The possibilities of false inferences are carefully distinguished and
classified; the various degrees of probability and the implications
of the major and minor premises are examined; the laws of drawing right conclusions are taught and the significance of the cir-
cular argument and the undistributed middle is explained.[27]

To distinguish premises as demonstrative, categorical, and hypothetical should be, according to this view, as easy for the criminologist as is the theory of logical fallacies or syllogisms. The
doctrine of the excluded third, the sufficient reason, the contradiction, etc., must be as familiar to him as the position of the
middle term and the specific modes or figures. It is strictly en-
joined[28] that "criminologists must know the laws of logic and must
learn to think logically."[29]

I am skeptical enough not to overestimate the value of such
training in logic; indeed, I sometimes think that such training can
be indirectly prejudicial in the solving of certain cases by dis-
tracting the attention from essentials. In estimating the value of
clues, I am afraid, it will be of little use to be able to distinguish
between the hypothetic-disjunctive and the categorical conclusion, as described in Lothar Philipp's book. Suppose a detective
has to clear up a burglary; it will avail him little to know "that

the number of possible events is in inverse proportion to the number of clues; the former decrease proportionately as the latter increase."[30] We have already pointed out how limited the value of warnings against false conclusions may be. The danger is not so great as one might suppose from reading criminological theory.[31] Fieldworkers tell us that the Hupa Indians have to cook, serve and eat their game in a certain prescribed way; they believe that otherwise no more game would cross the hunter's path. The ethnologist Preuss maintains that this habit could not have originated in cooking and eating customs; its basis is the superstitious belief that the parts or remains of the dead animal attract living animals of the same species. One is reminded of this when one realizes the degree of importance attached in criminological theory to strictly logical reasoning as the means for the finding of unknown criminals.[32]

Let us take an example of false conclusion which the criminologists present to us as illustrating the absolute necessity of logical knowledge.[33] A cellar was broken into. The accused A. alleges that it was probably done by his enemy M. In fact, there was M.'s fingerprint on a bottle of beer that the burglar was supposed to have drunk. This print is evidence against M., but—says the criminologist—misleading evidence. In our case A. had taken the bottle from M.'s house into his cellar and staged the burglary. The conclusion "M. did it" is wrong; it does not follow the laws of logic—or so we are told. Actually, the error is caused by not knowing enough about the fingerprints, not through lack of logic. Everyone without bias would say that this print only proves that M. has touched the bottle, not that he has committed a burglary. "There needs no ghost" out of the grave of formal logic to teach us that. Mistakes of this kind come from false, hasty or insufficient observation, or, logically expressed, they are already implied in the premise. They have nothing to do with faulty reasoning. In actual detective work, the inferences often show astounding shrewdness, but the premises rest on insufficient knowledge or observation. For instance, the conclusion is arrived at in a certain case that the criminal must have escaped' in such or such a way. Then circumstances make this idea seem impossible; it is given up as logically untenable. But soon it turns out that this "impossibility" actually happened. The scheme of major premise, minor premise, and conclusion does not work in these cases. They remind us of Edgar Allan Poe's sarcastic remark that the Paris police, reputed to be so clever, proceeded according to a fixed number of rules for detecting crime: but those rules often served their purpose so badly that they reminded him of the man who asked for his dressing gown to hear the music better.

The following case remained unsolved for a long time, it was alleged, through applying false logical methods. Several years ago a butcher was shot in a lonely street, early in the morning, on his way to work. His wife had a lover, a young Polish workman; but he proved that he had been at home all the time, from the previous evening until they found the dead man. Respectable and trustworthy people who lived with him confirmed this. His flat was a good way from the site of the crime. Actually the murder had been done in the following way. The young man had calculated exactly the way the butcher had to go. He had sent him a message, purporting to be from his employer, to be at work at six o'clock precisely. A few minutes before the butcher, according to the young man's calculations, had to pass the house, the latter went to the lavatory on the landing; then, quick as lightning, he darted into the street, followed the butcher some distance in his stocking feet, shot him, and then hurried back to the lavatory. A few moments later his brother-in-law was abusing him at the lavatory door for having been inside so long.

This case, quoted by Anuschat,[34] shows how carefully one must examine the data of time and place, but not how well logic works. It was not a logical error that held up this case, but rather lack of skepticism. The witnesses' statements confirming the alibi were not sufficiently examined in regard to their objective truth; they were accepted because the people were trustworthy.

Again and again on studying manuals of criminology, one finds how greatly reasoning is overestimated. This is true positively and negatively; failures are ascribed to faulty reasoning when faults of knowledge and observation are responsible for them. Reason gets the credit for successes which are really due to other psychological processes. Here is an example of the second kind, the solution of a recent difficult case. A taxicab smeared with blood was found in a suburb of Berlin. One window was broken, on the running board lay a cartridge-case. Almost at the same time, the corpse of a chauffeur was found at Ferch near Berlin. The man had been shot. The connection between the two discoveries was easily established. The dead man was recognized as the owner of the cab, Fritz Ponick. The case seemed to be wrapped in mystery; no useful clues could be found. The cartridges were of a very ordinary kind and without any special mark. The only clue proved to be misleading. Ponick had been instrumental in costing a workman his job; there was a possibility that the man had shot him. The clue was followed, but without result. The number of letters and accusations was unending, but they contained nothing of value. One fact was clear: the murder was done on the highroad to Ferch. The two officials who worked on the case asked themselves why that spot had been chosen. They supposed that the criminal knew the road well. Berlin people knew that road, but the inhabitants of Ferch knew it better; best of all those inhabitants who had a car or at least could drive. Now detailed work began, starting from the question: Who drives at Ferch? It took twelve days to examine the alibi of all Ferch towns-people who could drive; then the people who had moved from Ferch to Berlin were interrogated. Among the latter was a Johann Kahlitz who could not prove his alibi, and he turned out to be the author of the crime. A small part of this solution, which was claimed as a victory for reasoning, is due to logical conclusions. The train of inference "the murder was done at Ferch—a man from there knows the road best—best of all he who has driven there—the murder was done by a Ferch man who drives" is certainly logical, and its value and reliability must be examined by logic. But its real nature is of a different kind. To put it differently, it was not logical judgments but psychological preconceived opinions that pointed the way to the criminal. Already the guess why the man chose the highroad to Ferch contains an unconscious psychological factor. I do not wish to deny the value of logical thinking, especially as a control. But it cannot be denied that the overwhelming majority of successes in detection derive from different psychological processes. That does not prevent them from making use of a screen of logic. It is easy to mislead the reason—our minds are only too willing, led on as they are by anonymous forces. With the most seemingly faultless logic one can come to the falsest conclusions.

Often errors in reasoning are put forward as an excuse when experts have caused a miscarriage of justice. In reading the reports of doctors and chemists upon which so many court sentences have been based, and which do not go back more than a hundred years, one is surprised to find on what grounds people have been found guilty of the most serious crimes. And why go so far afield when falsehood, perversity, and superficiality lie so near? As we read psychiatric or psychological reports of our day we can imagine their importance for the guilt or innocence of a given person.[35] It needs no prophet to foretell that the future reader will be shocked at some reports of our present authorities. It is not the logical mistakes we mind,[36] but the superficial and false premises that lead to such fatal consequences. The erroneous statement of facts based on false premises is in reality a much greater danger than deficiencies of deductive powers.

I have already said that the criminologist's thinking is only rarely purely logical, but that he often boasts of its purely logical character and likes to hear it said that his work is based on pure intellect. This is true both of the detective and of the examining magistrate, of the public prosecutor and the counsel for the defence. It very often happens that weight is attached to a proposition as a logical conclusion whereas reason played a very small part in the thinking and considering which led up to it. This is true also in a negative sense: people try to prove what logical mistakes led to a false proposition. Gross stresses the point in his *Criminal Psychology,* and points out that an important source of error in establishing cause and effect lies in the universal, ingrained assumption that cause must have a certain similarity to effect. As an example of such a wrong connection, he quotes a quite intelligent man who suspected a person of murder because that person's mother had died a violent death. The witness stuck to his point. "The man has been mixed up in a murder before; he probably was in this one."[37] This is certainly a wrong conclusion, but what is interesting and instructive is not the logical error, but the reason of the psychological connection. The establishment of the error is merely a preliminary to the essential question as to why the man thinks such a connection a necessary one. This question is psychological and can only be solved by psychological investigation. Criminologists and criminal lawyers, because they take the purely intellectual point of view of observers, completely neglect this side. I recently happened to read a book by Professor von Liszt,[38] *Kriminalistische Beurteilung;* it tries to show how careful the criminologist must be in his logical reconstructions. There is nothing to be said against such care if it does not involve the neglect of other factors. Liszt quotes two examples of wrong conclusions, one made by a public prosecutor, the other by a judge. Here is the first:

"I defended a man who had been arrested for theft one night in a park in Vienna. The accused man and the place where theft was committed were searched for the stolen property, but in vain. At the trial the Crown Counsel maintained that an unknown accomplice must have escaped with the stolen notecase, and said emphatically: 'Why should the accused have gone to the park at night, if not to steal? Nobody goes there at night unless he wants to steal.' And he looked surprised when I replied: 'Hitherto, in my experience, it has only been criminals who have had recourse to the great unknown; the Crown Counsel should think that beneath his dignity. And if the only thieves go to that park at night, why should a thief go there when he could only meet colleagues? And how and why did the victim get there?' "

This reproof was justified, though its triumphant tone and belligerent manner are suspicious, considering that operations of pure logic were solely in question. Was the Crown Counsel's error

really a logical one, a wrong conclusion, as the defending counsel
made out? The assertion that the accused went to the park to steal
and that nobody went there unless he wanted to steal contains a
psychological judgment. It is the business of psychology and not
of logic to examine the view that people go to a park at night for
the sole purpose of stealing. The rejection of that view—be it good
or bad psychology—is made on psychological grounds. The counsel asks: "Why does a thief go to a place where he can only find
colleagues?" That is a psychological problem, not a logical one.
He inquires into human aims and objects, certain mental processes. The form of the judgments expressed is logical, its content
psychological.[39] That often happens in criminal cases. Beneath
the regular and often over-formal surface one sees psychological
questions everywhere. Wherever false reasoning is revealed, one
is justified in looking for concealed motives, conscious or unconscious; under the false flag of logic many things are smuggled
in which people do not want to see declared.

Liszt's other example is similar; this time it is an instance of
the "judicial art of reasoning," as Liszt calls it sarcastically. "A
landlady stopped at the open door of a flat in her house, where the
weekly washing was being done. A quarrel with the tenant ensued.
Suddenly the landlady rushed at the other woman, tore a piece
of wet linen from her hand, hit her in the face with it and then
threw it on the floor. The other woman stooped and picked up
the piece of linen. At that moment the landlord joined in and
advanced towards the stooping woman with raised fist. She rose
quickly to avoid the threatening fist. While doing so, she was supposed to have hit the landlady's face with the piece of washing.
The belligerent landlady brought an action. I was able to prove
through two witnesses that the woman had not hit the landlady;
at the worst she had accidentally touched her face with the wet
piece of washing. But the judge found the defendant guilty with
the following reasoning which I took down in shorthand: 'Two
witnesses have, it is true, said the defendant did not hit the other
party. But the sympathies of those witnesses are not with the

landlady. And it is psychologically probable that a woman who is attacked hits back.' "

There is no doubt that the author is again mistaken. The judge himself explicitly refers to the psychological character of the grounds for his judgment. Here the values are psychological and not logical.[40]

These two cases are not especially representative; there are some much more effective and convincing ones. What matters here is to show that the finding of objective and subjective facts is a psychological process. At this point a challenge imperiously presents itself as a postulate of criminal law, nay, of humanity: if this is so, then it is more important to know something about criminal psychology than to know about the rules of logic. Is it not better to understand what passes in the minds of the detective and the magistrate than to know one's way about in the manuals of logic? The criminologist is warned against false conclusions, hasty deductions, wrong reasoning of every kind. Who warns him against psychological mistakes? If the finding of facts is a psychological process, is not the danger of making wrong psychological judgments greater than that of wrong reasoning?

4. PSYCHOLOGICAL EVIDENCE

ONE of the most important ways of discovering the unknown culprit is to look for the motive. There can be no doubt that this is the province of psychology. The judge has no obligation to bring to light the motive or, rather, the motives of a crime, but the crime remains obscure as long as the motive is not clear. This obscurity is much more serious than any connected with place or time. The complete lack of motive in a murder has something very strange about it that stimulates the investigator to ever renewed efforts to elucidate the case. The importance of clearing up the motive for establishing the evidence rests not merely on the fact that the motive is in itself such important evidence. Often other evidence cannot be used at all or not to its full effect as long as we do not know the motive for a crime. This question of motive is often the starting point for the work of detection. It seems easy to answer from the point of view of the untutored psychologist. The nature of the crime itself seems to give us the solution. It is clear that here we have a murder for revenge, there a case of housebreaking for the purpose of robbery, there a forgery in order to obtain money. But this fine assurance may be shattered by two objections. The first, that crimes are often staged only to deceive. A house is broken into; all the drawers are searched, money and valuables stolen. But the theft is a blind. What the man wanted was only certain letters of which the police knew nothing. The second objection is this. In deducing the intention from the result the criminologist often goes wrong because his deduction is based on his ability to identify himself with the culprit. This appears to him to be a conscious mechanical process which he can perform or not, as he pleases.[41] The result of an act may very well allow us to infer one of its real motives, but this conclusion presupposes that we have to do with psychological processes similar to our own. It does not hold good, for instance, in a case of psychosis. A paranoiac may attack a man because he sees in him his persecutor. We look for the unknown criminal, with whom we are familiar, and presume a motive like jealousy or political enmity. We have presumed only motives due to delusions common to all men; we have not conceived of one which can be explained only by a psychopathology belonging to the man's special delusion.

An attempt to discover the real motive may also fail because we do not understand the mental processes of a foreign race. I remember a mysterious murder which occupied the attention of the Austrian courts in Montenegro during the war. Our understanding of the case was prejudiced by the fact that we did not grasp the psychological meaning of the blood-feud for certain Albanian families. Again, the immense practical importance of motive for criminal investigation was shown by the outrages on the railways at Jüterbog und Bia-Torbagy as well as those at Anzbach and Neulengbach. Those terrible catastrophes seemed to suggest the political activities of an international gang. A paper found on the spot threatening further outrages confirmed this view; it pointed to communist action. Long and troublesome investigation on this hypothesis led to nothing. The criminal, Silvester Matuschka, who was found much later, was a highly pathological individual who found sexual gratification in explosions and other catastrophes and longed for a kind of fame like Herostratus.

One sees how much depends in solving criminal problems on psychological knowledge and gifts. We recognize how little we know of psychological conditions and motives in the psychogenesis of capital crimes. That terrible description of the crime "First it lay before me, then it was past, there was nothing in between" deals a severe blow to the psychologist's pride. We have to admit how little we know of mental processes in the criminal for all our labors. It is still not sufficiently realized that the criminal at the moment of the act is a different man from what he is after it —so much so that one would sometimes think them two different beings. In some of the worst crimes one is reminded of the medieval belief in possession (Nietzsche observed in his *Genealogie der Moral* that the future development of criminal law must learn to isolate the deed from the doer). Our psychological judgment, our instinct as well as our experience, seem to tell us sometimes that the deed does not belong to the doer nor the doer to the deed. Nevertheless the act must be an expression of the criminal's mental tension, must spring from his mental condition, must have promised gratification to his psychological needs. We are faced by a riddle as long as we do not know what motive actuated him. Does he knows it any more than we do? In many cases, and especially in the most serious crimes, he can, with the best will in the world, give us but inadequate information; he is unable to establish a connection between the deed and his personality.[42]

Doubts have been thrown, and rightly so, on the adequacy of the psychological knowledge and understanding of judges in problems of this kind. It is like trying to get to the deepest layers of the earth with a child's spade. Do not let us speak of common sense which guides the judge in his examinations. Stupid things with tragic consequences are still done in the name of common sense. The way in which the judge, the public prosecutor and the defending counsel learn to know the accused is the most cursory that can be imagined, the material at their disposal is the scantiest, the method they employ the most superficial. It is like hearing a foreigner say he knows London well because he has been round it on a conducted tour. In truth, he has seen some remarkable sights which are shown to tourists, including some dismal-looking streets in Chinatown.

The question of the motive is difficult, even if we know the culprit. It is more so, sometimes unanswerable, when we have to guess the motive and from it the unknown criminal. Here the criminologist's psychology shows itself sometimes in an embarrassing manner. The question of motive is very misleading as a help for finding the probable criminal. If one were to judge from the motive only, the situation would soon become grotesque. If everyone who had a motive committed a murder there would be few cases of natural death.

Apart from the search for the motive the primitiveness of criminological psychology becomes obvious to any unbiased person, for instance, when the dangerous question arises whether A. or B. is capable of the crime—that is to say in the evaluation of evidence from character. In the attempts to answer this question we find a psychological naïveté which reminds one of the little girl's question: "Mummy, what does a thief look like?" Just as in early days it was assumed that there was a definite criminal physiognomy and a regular cult of ear lobes grew up, so now people profess to be able to tell from the general impression or special characteristics whether a man can be credited with a murder or a robbery. It is a question of psychological clichés, "standardized" psychology, so to speak. Characterological indications of this kind are often uncertain and misleading. The famous poisoners of Louis XIV's time looked like angels and were particularly meek.

For many years a man named Denke used to kill his victims in his house situated in the middle of a Silesian village, and used to pickle them in tubs. He was generally regarded as an honest, harmless character, law-abiding and religious. The same was true of Angerstein, who exterminated his family; of Matuschka, who was especially admired for his piety, and who sent whole train-loads of men to death and destruction. Similar examples could be given of mass murderers. Middle-class society likes to represent the gulf between itself and the lawbreakers as unbridgeable, and is frightened to find that even mass murderers are made of the same stuff and behave in all walks of life like the rest of us—your very neighbor might be a murderer. The complacency of conscious psychology and the superficiality of psychological observation in crminal investigation are nowhere clearer than in the treatment of the question of whether a person is capable of a crime or not. What a contrast to this primitive outlook is in Goethe's self-portrait: "There is no crime of which I do not deem myself capable."

Evidence from character played an important part in the case of the agricultural laborer Josef Jakobowski. The man, a former Russian prisoner of war, was accused of having killed his own three-year-old child. Again and again the poor man protested: "I innocent—nothing done—why talk?" Even this behavior was considered suspicious. In the summing up we find the sentence, "The accused is a cunning, crafty fellow, without scruples, whom one might believe capable of murder." He was executed on February 15th, 1929; afterwards his innocence was proved conclusively. The Government of the Free State of Mecklenburg-Strelitz had refused to reprieve him. In this case, which relied entirely upon circumstantial evidence, the psychological element was of the utmost evidential importance. How often are these psychological reasons not mentioned in the summing up, though they are the basis of the judgment! Over and over again the attempt to prove something from the evidence would be recognized to have miscarried or failed if the accused had been cleverer and had known how to appear in a more sympathetic light. One must not underestimate the influence of unconscious unfavorable impressions on judge and jury; they diminish suspicion against evidence which would otherwise have been more carefully examined.

The kind of psychological thinking which dominates the law-courts becomes most dangerous when it is thrown as a weight into the scales of Justice. The scales are, indeed, falsely weighted whether it is a question of the "expert's" opinion about a witness's capacity for remembering, or of making a judgment about the nature of a suspect's impulses so as to arrive at a conclusion as to his guilt or innocence. It is not my business to show in how many thousands of cases the naïve trust in one's own psychological insight or in the understanding of other people's mental processes has led to the most terrible miscarriages of justice.[43] I am concerned to show the state of affairs by typical examples and not to describe it exhaustively. One example must stand for many hundred, one case for many.

In the seventies of last century a rich farmer was sitting in an inn of a little Austrian town. It was a public holiday. He explained in front of everyone to a young gamekeeper, who was in love with his daughter and had wooed her passionately, that a marriage between them was out of the question. The young man sat at a table, glumly staring at nothing. Suddenly he shouted so that everyone in the noisy room could hear him, "I'll show that dog what's what. He'll see. It will be he, not I, who will suffer." Then he returned to his drinking. The farmer went home. The next day his corpse was found in the well-lit street. Two tramps gave evidence that they had seen the young keeper pulling a knife with which the murder had been committed out of the murdered man's back. The knife was examined, the keeper arrested. He protested his innocence again and again. He was confronted with the damning evidence; he was cross-examined. But he insisted that he was innocent. He was sentenced to death; the sentence was commuted to twenty years' penal servitude. After he had been in prison for twelve years the real murderer confessed on his deathbed. The case became clear. There was a man in the village, who was in debt, and he knew that the farmer, the girl's father, had on him a notecase full of money. While the keeper sat drinking, this man, un observed, pulled his knife out of its sheath and with it stabbed the farmer in the street when he was going home. The keeper, finding the corpse on the road, recognized with terror his own knife. Now he knew he would be accused; his knife would be the strongest proof against him. To save himself he pulled the knife out of the wound, dried it, and in that situation he was seen by the two tramps. Apart from their testimony the most important element in the case was psychological: the significance to be attached to the fury and despair of the young, rejected suitor against the rich farmer. His threats in the inn were sufficient proof of his hatred; they pointed unequivocally to an intention to attack. But, in summing up the psychological situation, the poverty of criminal psychology was shown again as in so many other cases. That the keeper threatened the farmer with death was not absolute proof of guilt; from the psychological point of view it might even tell against it. The spoken word, calling people names, cursing and threatening, often act like a safety valve, provide an outlet for mental tension. ("His bark is worse than his bite.") We know in how many cases verbal action takes the place of motor action. It is true that this reasoning is not conclusive on the other side; in spite of cursing and threatening, a man may proceed to action and commit murder. We have no means of estimating the effectiveness of individual inhibitions.

Dostoevski said of the use of psychology in interpreting evidence, that it was a stick with two ends.[44] It can be used for the prosecution or for the defence. It is for the psychologist to show clearly this misunderstanding of his science and to repudiate it. Abuses would remain even if the misunderstanding was less obvious, the methods of examinations less gross, the criminologists' psychological assumptions more justified. The interpretations of human actions in such cases are often shamefully naïve, the psychological experiments in the examination sometimes childish, the observations inaccurate and unverified; and the conclusions often show a terrifying lack of worldly knowledge. That the lawyer's understanding of psychological facts is so elementary need not be fatal, but it may become so if it has a say in the decision of guilt or innocence. The edifice of criminal law may be cracking in every joint, but as long as it stands, the judge, whether he strikes or spares, must see men with the eyes of a man. Everywhere in penal procedure the inadequacy of criminal psychology becomes obvious. If the accused is silent it is interpreted as a proof of guilt; if he talks excitedly that shows that he is guilty, too.

In the Hilsner case of ritual murder the Crown Counsel referred to the fact that some witnesses spoke of noticing signs of uneasiness, worry, and blushing in the accused. He laid stress on this and said: "I need not tell you that there was a mental struggle of that kind and anguish of spirit in Hilsner, for you have had the opportunity to watch him during the proceedings. . . .The convulsive movements of his fingers, the change of color—these do not belong to a good conscience." Even if we assume that the remark implied that Hilsner's behavior did not testify to a good conscience, that represented the interpretation of a public officer, and many people might interpret these signs in the opposite sense, as Dostoevsky pointed out. Here we see the ambiguity of psychological speculation in penal law, the danger of false and one-sided interpretation of psychological evidence. Very often the guilty man is throughout quiet and self-assured, whereas a man wrongly accused gives the impression of having a guilty conscience.[45] The accused stutters, is confused and muddled, talks in incoherent sentences; what he says seems like stupid excuses; his voice is uncertain and breaks; in cross-examination he seems to be inventing details because he cannot find his words, and yet he is innocent. The guilty man appears clear-eyed before the court, full of calm assurance; he answers frankly, in short, precise, reasonable sentences, and keeps his head. One's impression is that the matter does not concern him. Cases are known in which the accused collapsed when shown the blood-stained weapon, and who was none the less innocent.

The relevance of psychological evidence as to guilt is still overestimated, although it is known that excitement can spring just as often from endocrine processes as from real guilt. Let us suppose an accused man has lied and has been found out. What psychological conclusions are drawn from this! But how many and what different motives the accused may have for his lie—even assuming that he recognizes it himself as such. To take a lie as a proof of guilt or at least as a reason for suspicion is so common that it seems almost obligatory. In the Hilsner ritual murder case, which a well-known counsel calls "a most shameful miscarriage of justice," sexual motives were suspected in the murder and the accused was questioned about his sexual life. He maintained that he was impotent, and this was contradicted by a woman witness. He also said he had never seen the corpse of the murdered woman, and that was not true. It was clear that he feared to make his position worse by an affirmative answer to these questions. The conclusions drawn from these two lies were absolutely erroneous. The naïve analogies which judges sometimes draw in their psychological reasoning are amazing.

Emile Zola described how puzzled a judge was when he came across a man who was not in the least ashamed of a theft, but over-whelmed with shame when asked to admit that he kept a stocking of the woman with whom he was in love. Criminologists are surprised when they meet with psychological contradictions, and their surprise easily turns into resentment. This resentment results in a wish to brush aside such intolerably contradictory statements. In Zola's novel, *The Human Beast*, Roubaud killed a man out of jealousy. The examining magistrate Denizet could not believe that jealousy was the motive. Mme. Roubaud had a second lover. Why did he kill the first and not the second? "I don't know," the man answers, "I killed the one and not the other." Denizet, who is very proud of his psychological gifts, and the way he uses them, shouts angrily: "Don't continue to tell me that you were jealous and killed out of revenge. I advise you not to tell the judges that fantastic story. They will shrug their shoulders. . . . Believe me, alter your system. Only the truth can save you." But it was the truth he spoke.[46] Similar scenes occur every day in the courts. It is remarkable that the position of an accused person unconsciously influences even the magistrate unfavorably. If he is found to have lied, then the judge has, so to speak, tasted blood. Obstinate denial unconsciously enrages him as though it were a personal offence; it is as if the accused thought him stupid, wanted to deceive him, and the judge reacts accordingly.

Most people think that psychological facts are self-evident; to the criminologist the mind is no "far-flung country," but rather a minutely mapped-out police district. It is in the character of the magistrate not to like psychological surprises.

The judge's moral outlook does not allow him to neglect the connection between the deed of which the accused may be guilty and his behavior in other matters. In a murder case in Austria, the public was particularly incensed against a man who had eaten his supper in the same room where the corpse was lying. In another case where the wife and the servant had killed the peasant together, they received a bad mark for having had sexual relations immediately after. They had, so to speak, misbehaved in front of the corpse. People deplored the murderers' lack of good feeling, and thought they should have observed a respectful interval after the act. It happens often that the accused's past—respectable people have no "past"—appears as a special reason for suspicion. Not only is the man's crime judged, but his character, and a criminal act is more easily credited to the man who has, it may be, made cynical remarks about God or marriage or laughed at the police than to the humble citizen. How much these moral opinions influence the magistrate and the jury, in the question of guilt or innocence, is well-known.[47]

I do not mean to complain of the absence of psychological training and the lack of psychological understanding in the ordinary way. This training is certainly most desirable, but not in the sense in which it is carried by the theorists of penal law, i.e., to perfect the system of psychological evidences against the accused and to make judges and detectives surer in adducing proof of guilt. I would rather wish the contrary: to make them less sure. That is to say, the officers who have to find out the truth in a criminal case should gain enough insight into scientific psychology to see how unreliable and unsuitable psychological evidence and evidence from character is in criminal detection, and how rarely and cautiously it should be used.

Nevertheless, we think the acquisition of psychological knowledge by officers of the court highly necessary. It would not only serve as a corrective to naïve psychological opinions, but it would make judges, public prosecutors, etc., skeptical about their own judgment. It would help the criminologist to have a better understanding of the origin and nature of a criminal act when the author of the act has been found. As proof, as evidence for or against guilt, psychology is useless. Its abuse confronts us every day in court. The many hundred examples in criminal history are still, it would seem, not convincing enough to discredit psychological observation. The most concrete warning, given by Dostoevski in his *Brothers Karamazov*— a much more penetrating illustration than can be found in any manual of penal theory—has fallen on deaf ears. We read with horror in the reports of witches' trials what evidence was produced for the guilt of those poor wretches. In the not so very far future, people may think the same of our present methods of using psychological evidence and of judging character in court.

Psychology is not able, it would seem, to prove people guilty of a crime by any suitable scientific process. Is there no hope of a reliable psychological method of discovering the author of a crime? Is no help from psychology for solving this problem within sight? I think not. It is no concern of the laws of mental life whether society calls certain unhappy creatures criminals or not.

5. Circumstantial Evidence and Psychoanalysis

THERE is no longer any doubt that the coming of analysis must slowly alter the administration of criminal law. These changes will probably not occur in the way some hope for and others dread. They are hard to predict, although there have been apodeictic predictions made recently both by criminologists and psychoanalysts. The student of criminal law and its changes in these troubled times will be in a difficult situation when asked his opinion, the more so because he will have to face not two different groups—criminologists and analysts—but as many opinions as there are minds. It is not my intention to enter into a discussion of the significance of psychoanalysis for criminology. I should only like to say that we analysts are not always innocent when grotesque misunderstandings of our intentions occur. I think we have been too ready to serve criminology without making it clear that we thought our services of questionable value. Alexander and Staub assumed it was right and important to "introduce" psychoanalysts into the courts of justice.[48] They prophesied that psychoanalysis would never again leave these courts.[49] In a review of their book, whose merits for criminal psychology I stressed, I expressed a doubt as to the desirability of psychoanalysis in the law court. I was afraid that the functionaries of the law would misunderstand psychoanalysis and would teach the criminal that what he used to do by instinct was done in accordance with certain rules.

No sooner were those sentences written than they proved correct. During the trial of the parricide, Philipp Halsmann, the medical faculty at Innsbruck thought it probable that he had an Oedipus complex and considered this mental attitude—regarded in Innsbruck as the peculiarity of only a select few—as a reason for suspecting the accused. Freud himself has shown how irrelevant and misleading the introduction of the question of the Oedipus complex in such a case must be.[50] The admission of analysis into court in the near future foreshadows bizarre and terrible happenings—a witches' sabbath of common sense, where the Oedipus complex is used as evidence against the accused, and his unconscious motives as a proof of his guilt. No, I do not wish for the "introduction" of psychoanalysis into court. I had rather it stayed outside. I think a law court is not the right place for psychoanalysis. Its influence goes deeper; its research into criminology will lead to a recognition of the many problems involved in criminal justice.

It seemed for a time as if analytical points of view might serve aims that ought to precede every consideration of the uses of punishment, its extent and execution. Is psychoanalysis fitted to contribute to the question of who the unknown criminal is or even to solve it?

The problem of ascertaining the facts by psychological means appears again and again; judges and laymen, jurymen and counsel have always wanted to know whether a process could not be found that would force the accused to admit his guilt or innocence by objective, involuntary signs. If there were such reliable psychological methods, criminal proceedings would undergo a revolution. Wertheimer and Gross sought a method that should show through free association—independent of the depositions of the person under examination—whether a matter is known to him or not. The method of discovering hidden mental acts was to be used for the involuntary self-betrayal of the accused. In Freud's paper, "Psycho-Analysis and the Ascertaining of Truth in Courts of. Law," the general considerations which might make such a process possible were clearly demonstrated.[51] In it, to be sure, he stressed the point that the experiment could have no influence whatsoever on the decision of guilt or innocence. The differences in the mental situation of the criminal and the neurotic, of the examining magistrate and the psychoanalyst are so pronounced that there could be no thought of a practical use of psychoanalysis for the question of guilt or innocence. Experiments have shown some cases where it has been possible to find facts against the will of the accused by such psychological methods. But there are other cases where the reactions obtained do not admit of such a certain and unequivocal conclusion. In the present state of our science, psychoanalysis is neither suited nor competent to solve the question of guilt or innocence. But one cannot tell how the next generation will answer the question of the practical use of analytic method.

The rising generation of analytical research workers seem to be most confident in this respect. Their optimism would be heartening if it were based on new knowledge. Fromm[52] thinks "that psychoanalysis will contribute more especially to the question of the diagnosis of facts, that is to say in cases where psychology can help to clear up the facts, and assist in deciding whether a man is guilty or not." According to him psychology plays a part similar to chemistry or medicine. He says: "The number of cases in which psychology is important for the question of guilt or innocence is very large. They are especially the cases where there is no confession and where the finding of a plausible motive decides whether a man can be held to have committed the deed or not. Then there are other cases where it is not the deed which is doubtful, but its place in criminal law. In all these cases analytic psychology could be used also *de lege leta,* because its views of the problems of guilt, responsibility and correction stand in no opposition to the present system of criminal law. It works inside this domain in the same way as, say, chemistry, which determines whether a stain is human or animal blood; or like graphology, which identifies the author of two handwritings."

This view shows an optimism that will probably remain quite unshaken by the fact that its statements are incorrect. The only correct observation relates to the number and increase of the cases where psychological considerations have become important for the question of guilt. It remains questionable how far these considerations are reliable and whether they are not inappropriate. Apart from this, Fromm's claims are very misleading. The comparison of psychoanalysis with chemistry or medicine is quite wrong. The decisive difference is obvious; for the field of application of these two sciences is completely different. Chemistry and medicine belong to an apprehensible, though not always comprehensible, world; it is material. Psychology is on a different plane. In chemistry there are hard and fast reactions which are recognized by the sense of smell, taste and vision. The proof of whether a substance is of a certain kind can be seen in the test tube. Psychological reactions do not point to any such material facts and, even if they did, this would not be what is essential for psychological research. For instance, a certain behavioristic reaction "as an expression of the emotions," as one used to call it, may occur because a man has committed a crime—but also because he wished to commit it. Mental reality is the only decisive criterion for psychology; material reality has to take second place.

One should bear these observations in mind when raising the question of whether an individual is "capable" of a crime. Analysis cannot answer it, nor is it a question which analysis is desirous of answering. Rather will it enlighten us about a criminal who has committed the deed and who seems hardly capable of having done so.

In contradistinction to Fromm and many other analysts and psychologists, I believe psychoanalysis quite unsuited to help in discovering the material facts, as the judge has to do. Nor do I see a way of changing our scientific methods so that they could serve criminology in following the traces of the unknown criminal. Let us once more consider Fromm's comparison of the part played by psychoanalysis and by chemistry. Let us suppose a child has been raped. A tramp is arrested on suspicion. His trousers show suspicious stains which are examined and found to be stains of semen. These traces are certainly clues that, together with others, may prove the deed. Can psychology really play a part similar to chemistry in such a case? By no means. The analyst may experiment with disconnected ideas, free associations, interpretation of dreams and faulty acts or other mental reactions; he will contribute nothing of value to the question of actual fact. His endeavors will point to certain mental experiences, but they will not help to answer the question of whether the observed reactions refer to definite physical events. This is true in the most favorable case where the subject is willing to answer questions about his mental life. And now consider the situation of a person accused of a crime. The analyst, acting as an expert in the question of whether the man is capable of the crime or not, enters the cell; will he be welcome?

Is the difference in application between the two above-mentioned sciences and psychoanalysis clear? It lies not in a greater or lesser degree of exactitude, or a difference of reliability and security, in the methods employed, but in the essential difference of the subject-matter under examination. Fromm says that analysis could exercise the same function as chemistry or graphology. But blood-stains and handwriting belong to material reality. Fromm's opinions are fully discussed here, not because they are important, but because they and kindred opinions are apt to favor dangerous misunderstandings about the application of psychoanalysis. Every psychologist interested in this question—and this means every psychologist—must wish to dispel the darkness enveloping this problem and to present it as clearly and unequivocally as possible. It is no service to analytical psychology to enlarge its field of application to imaginary proportions; to do so would only divert attention from its true province.[53] In criminology, particularly, there are tasks awaiting psychoanalysis which have as yet not even been perceived, let alone begun upon.

The judge who asks: "Is this man (or woman) guilty?" expects the answer from psychological experts to be yes or no. But the psychoanalyst can say nothing about that, even after an examination of a man's instincts, conducted under the most favorable circumstances. He might perhaps say: "I have found that this man, who is a model of consideration and altruism, has to deal with severe sadistic impulses of an unconscious nature." The road from such an impulse to the corresponding deed is long and indirect. In most of us the reaction to such forbidden impulses has become so strong that it excludes external, real satisfaction. The existence of such strong forbidden impulses has called forth all our powers of mental defence, so that the former can only express themselves in dreams and unconscious thoughts. I don't know where I read this sentence so pregnant with meaning: "The girl was poor, but clean; her phantasies were the reverse."

If it were a simple truth that repression of instincts of a certain strength provided a kind of guarantee against antisocial instinctual satisfaction, then the psychological situation would not be difficult to grasp. But this is by no means so. These repressed instinctual impulses can break through suddenly and in unsuspected situations with the whole strength of their dammed-up energy and can lead to sadistic scenes and to brutal, perverse and criminal acts.[54] We cannot let psychology decide whether or not a person has committed a crime in obedience to his instincts. Not only the intensity of his instinctual impulses but also that of the contrary forces in him (the anti-cathexes) are decisive. The whole dynamics of instinctual life, which are based on the relative strength of the several factors involved, must be considered here as well as the topography of the psychical processes. Quantitative factors are also concerned; they connect the wish and the intention with the actual executions of the deed; and we have no means of measuring them.

Perhaps we may be allowed to return to the quotation from the trial scene in *The Brothers Karamazov:* "Psychology is a stick with two ends." Freud,[55] who quotes this sentence repeatedly, notes that it represents a grandiose screening of facts. Not psychology, but the judicial methods of ascertainment deserve this sarcasm. "It does not matter who has really done the deed; it only matters to psychology who has willed it emotionally and welcomed it when it was done." These words not only determine the extent of psychological interest, but also the limits of its competency.[56] The solution of guilt lies beyond its scope; it has different aims and problems, but their range is hardly less extensive.

6. SELF-BETRAYAL

THERE is one class of clues that impresses the observer in a special way. It consists of apparently incautious or even careless actions that give the criminal away while his attention is concentrated on wiping out all traces of his guilt. Such clues, which observers try to connect with the criminal's so-called "stupidity," often bring down his sentence upon him. These self-betraying clues can be discovered in the manner of the crime, in the tools, the time, the locality in which the deed was committed and in all the accompanying circumstances.

On December 4th, 1924, the newspapers reported that a gang of burglars had raided the country house of a man called Angerstein, the director of some chalk-works at Stegen. All those present were killed except Angerstein himself who was severely injured. The reason for the raid, it was supposed, was the theft of the workmen's wages. The house itself was set on fire. This report was founded on what Angerstein, who lay severely wounded in hospital, said. However, it was found that the deed must have been done much earlier than Angerstein declared; the *rigor mortis* of the victims fixed the hour of their death approximately. This possibility Angerstein had not considered in planning his terrible murders.

Another example: Dr Erdély, husband of the beautiful Budapest actress Anna Forgács, took his young bride to Millstatt in Carinthia shortly after their wedding. Soon after it was learned that Mrs. Erdély had fallen into a deep abyss near that place. She was conveyed to the hotel where she died. The physician stated that death was due to heart failure and wrote a death certificate. The husband seemed heartbroken. Nevertheless, he telegraphed to the insurance company to send him at once the 20,000 dollars for which Mrs. Erdély's life was insured. The company grew suspicious and insisted on a post-mortem. Dr. Erdély had not considered that marks of strangulation were not usually to be found on victims killed by a fall.

When the criminal tries to be particularly cautious and wants to take every possibility into consideration it often happens that he becomes overcautious and betrays himself by this love of detail. Some criminologists maintain that the only safe way to commit a crime is under the sway of a strong impulse. If the perpetrator is favored by circumstance he may never be discovered. Crimes carefully planned and calculated in advance are often betrayed by a "stupid" chance. For instance, the criminal provides a faultless alibi, but it is *too* carefully prepared. Urban, a case I have mentioned before, who killed a man at Neukölln, said that he was having a telephone talk with his fiancée at Leipzig at the time of the murder. This was almost true, but the exact time of the call could be verified through the telephone office with such correctness and precision that Urban's doom was sealed.

A third example: a garage man at Wannsee, near Berlin, was found unconscious in his garage one September night. His breath came in gasps, the drawers in his room were in disorder, the money was gone; everything pointed to a burglary. The next day the injured man could describe how two men had come on a motorcycle, stunned him and robbed the cashbox. But he had forgotten one thing: a large quantity of gasoline was missing, and that amount could not have been taken away on a motorcycle. He had himself stolen the gasoline and the cash.

Criminologists tell us that such clues, which they call "the establishing of proof by the criminal himself" often occur precisely in the most serious crimes. Take, for instance, the notes written by the mass murderers Haarmann and Denke. The carelessness of these self-betraying clues contrasts strangely with the great caution exercised in the execution of the deed itself.

In a case reported by Wulffen,[57] a housepainter, who had killed a boy, used as a paint pot a fragment of an enamel jug which the child had been carrying. He placed this fragment so carelessly on the window-sill that it was seen by a passing police officer. Nobody thinks it strange that criminals do not leave their visiting cards behind. It is much stranger that they sometimes do so. The *Berliner Tageblatt* reports, for instance, under the headline "Things that Should not Happen" (July 30th, 1931) that the tailor Paul Kneisel was no problem for the police. He and two others broke into a men's outfitting shop on the night of July 7th. The three friends dressed in new suits and took away three more which they sold afterwards. But Kneisel not only left his old jacket behind, but forgot to take his police registration out of it.

We can find material of this sort everywhere without having to consult the annals of crime. Everyday happenings are sufficient. Examples of negligence, carelessness and what is commonly called "criminal stupidity" are frequent in the very crimes where each detail has been carefully planned and considered; and these cases are especially striking and instructive.

There was the case of Consul-General von Barckhausen whose mysterious death in July 1931 was much discussed. Dr. Bar hausen, who had had a brilliant career, led a happy family life and was very popular and much respected. Nobody suspected that this happy man had sustained heavy material losses and that his appearance of wealth could not conceal his ruin for long. He determined to secure at least his family's future. His life was insured for 200,000 marks, which his family was to receive at his death, except in the case of suicide. He carefully prepared a plan which should lead people to the conclusion that he had been surprised and murdered at his house. When he was found shot in his study everything bore out this supposition. The scene was laid so as to make it appear certain that he had been murdered by unknown persons who had entered through the window. Only much later did the investigation discover certain details that excluded this possibility and pointed to disguised suicide. They were only a few trivial matters, minute faults in the masterpiece of calculation that had gone to construct the insurance fraud.

But it was just these little faults that spelled failure. Barckhausen wanted to give the impression of having heard burglars on the Sunday night, of having run out to meet them and having been killed by them. This was well thought out and all the details in the room pointed to a struggle of this sort, but the fountain pen with which he had been writing his suddenly interrupted letter was unopened. When his body was found he had in his right hand a club and a torn tie. The reconstruction of what had happened was meant to be obvious: Barckhausen had fought one of the burglars and had torn off his tie. But in this calculation, too, there was a small, but striking, mistake. The dead man held the tie inside out. If he had grasped his murderer's tie and turned it, his palm would have been under the tie and he would have dropped the club. These two details hinted at the improbability of an attack. The temporary disappearance and ultimate finding of the deceased's notecase made matters clear. When the corpse was found the notecase had disappeared. Next day a postman called who had found the case in a letter box attached to the neighboring house. But at the time when the postman emptied the box Barckhausen was still alive; just at that time he was having his last talk with his servants. The missing notecase was meant to hint at a burglary, and its discovery next day to confirm the supposition. The criminal would apparently have thrown the emptied notecase into the nearest letter box to get rid of it. But Barckhausen had forgotten to ascertain when the box would next be emptied. He supposed that the last Sunday collection had already been made. The time of collection showed that he himself had thrown the notecase in. Here, as in many other cases, we find a number of betraying details in a deed that was most carefully planned and considered. Are there special reasons for this?

The criminal seems to fear the envy of the gods, like the builders of the temple of Nihko. The portal of this sanctuary in northern Japan was of such perfect beauty, its rich relief carvings so wonderfully wrought, that the builders supposed it had evoked the envy of the gods. The consequences would have been terrible; so the builders made a clumsy mistake in one of the columns to appease the angry gods.

Often a criminal provides some of the traces to be expected after a crime, but he fails to carry them through. A house in a large garden was burgled. On the garden wall were marks showing that someone had climbed over; also the gravel paths leading to the house showed footprints. A closer examination revealed that the wall showed traces of a person having slid down it, but on the outside there were no signs of anyone having climbed up it. The perpetrator must, therefore, have been a member of the household.[58] Intelligence and shrewdness are no protection against this "avenging chance" which has often helped the police. A will forged with the utmost skill was dated 1868, but the watermark on the paper had the coat of arms of the German Empire, and so the clever effort was in vain. Subsequent attempts to obliterate traces are also subject to unlucky chances. A man was being detained for perjury. He was also suspected of a number of thefts committed a long time ago. Fingerprints had been found on the scenes of action. He wanted to discredit the evidential value of these fingerprints. So, in prison, he made new ones on pieces of glass and some prisoners who were being discharged took these pieces with them. At a new burglary, these helpful friends left the pieces underneath some windowpanes which they had broken. The man, whose fingerprints appeared, could not possibly have been concerned in this burglary, because he was in prison. Incidentally, had this ruse succeeded, it would have proved the whole system of finger-prints unreliable and inefficient. But it failed; the gods had de-creed the man's doom. The piece of glass with the fingerprints on it was, unfortunately for him, thinner than the broken window-panes.

There are enough examples to show that the very man whose shrewdness and cleverness have unmasked the most cunning of false clues himself meets the same fate and commits the same mistakes and "stupidities" which he has detected in other people, when he in his turn becomes a criminal. Colonel Redl, who was Chief of the Austrian Intelligence Department, had discovered many spies and shown great skill in doing so.[59] For years the dis-covery of spies working against Austria had been his department. He kept specially prepared cigarette cases and chocolate boxes to offer visitors, so as to obtain their fingerprints; guests were photo-graphed without being aware of it, their words were secretly taken down. Many spies were cleverly trapped. Redl proved the Polish Major von Wienskovsky guilty of spying in this way. A commission searched the major's house. His six-year-old daughter was playing in the nursery with her German governess. Redl won the child's confidence, took her hand in his and chatted with her in Polish. He asked her little sums and pretended to be surprised by her correct answers. "You are clever. Are you clever enough to know where Daddy hides his letters?" "Of course," said the child, ran into her father's study, crept under the writing desk and pointed to the left-hand corner. The heavy desk was turned over and a hidden spring found that opened a drawer with incriminating documents in it.

But the same man who knew how to gain and abuse a child's confidence was childish enough when he tried to hide his own secret. Nobody suspected that the Chief of the Intelligence Bureau was himself a spy for Russia. In 1913, in view of the danger of war, private letters were being opened. Two letters under the cipher "Opera Ball B" arrived at the chief post office in Vienna from Eydtkuhnen. The address was typwritten; the letters contained large sums of money. Redl called for the letters late on May 24th, 1913, and escaped unperceived, in a car. The car was identified and its route traced to a well-known hotel. In the car the police found the case of a penknife, made of light gray cloth. Presumably the unknown man who had fetched the letters had used the penknife to open them. The case was given to the hotel porter with orders to find out who had lost it. At that moment Redl came downstairs and put the key of his room on the table. "Have you lost the case of your knife, sir?" asked the porter. "Yes," answered the colonel, putting the case in his pocket, "where did I——?" He stopped in the middle of the sentence. He noticed the stranger sitting at the same table reading some letters; he knew he was lost.

We have given enough examples to ask: "What are these dark powers that thwart the criminal's designs?" There must be a psychological explanation for those typical mistakes and oversights that provide such important clues. Criminal psychology has summed this up in the doctrine of "the one stupid mistake" committed in almost every serious crime.[60] In spite of widespread agreement, we cannot believe that a typical instance of stupidity occurs in every serious crime. Criminological history records a number of perfectly executed crimes where earthly justice, with a heavy heart, has had to resign the perpetrators to divine judgment.

7. THE CULPRIT'S IMPROVIDENCE

CRIMINOLOGISTS describe these symptoms of carelessness, negligence and improvidence by the word *Verbrecherpech* (criminals' bad luck), and consider that the occurrence of such bad luck is "self-evident." Wulffen, in his large book on criminal psychology, thinks that it is a question of the "culprit's improvidence."[61] He seems to have no difficulty in regarding this label as a psychological explanation. The above-mentioned case of Colonel Redl clearly shows an improvidence of this sort; but our investigation begins rather than finishes at this point. How could a man, so experienced in dealing with guilty people, forget his knifecase, and how could he give himself away when he was shown it? How does this improvidence, to use Wulffen's expression, go along with the maximum of caution, shrewdness and calculation which the colonel showed on other occasions or with his clever methods of proving other people's guilt and his extraordinary knowledge of the ways in which spies betray themselves? We have chosen this case especially because it cannot be doubted that the colonel was a very "provident" person, and because both the criminal and the criminologist were combined in him. Hans Gross agrees with Wulffen in thinking that criminologists are often put off the scent because they say to themselves: "No, the culprit could not have been as stupid as all that,"[62] whereas many a criminal case has proved that he *had* been as stupid. Gross goes on to say, "I once even asked myself whether the essence of a criminal did not consist precisely in his inability to avoid making blunders."

We see that criminologists think "criminal's bad luck" is the outcome of common or garden stupidity, an intellectual inferiority due physiological causes. That may be so in certain cases, but not in the great number of crimes planned with forethought and caution which are nevertheless betrayed by some small mistake. One has to seek other explanations and the best science has given us so far is the psychoanalytic one. It assures us that "morals cannot hide a secret" (Freud) and that self-betrayal oozes out of every pore. These trifling mistakes are indications of hidden mental processes, unknown to the ego, which find expression.

Here the contradistinction between the lawbreaker's extreme caution and forethought and his "improvidence" becomes clear. It is not a question of intellectual failure, as such, or of unavoidable mistakes; it is a question of mental compulsion, none the less compelling because its motive is anonymous. If one considers the endless number of such cases one cannot deny that in the great majority of them the mistakes have been unconsciously determined.

The criminal's improvidence is therefore an unconscious piece of providence which aims at self-betrayal and is dictated by dark intentions unknown to himself. His secret is stronger than his will. A counter-will, more powerful than his conscious intentions, destroys his caution. The man who commits a crime without witnesses is the only one who knows about it and it seems as if he were obliged to share this knowledge, even to impart it, as if he were unable to keep it to himself because of the growing mental tension urging him to betray it at any cost—even at that of his head. Children play a game in which one says: "I know something which you don't; guess what it is." And then follow hints about its nature, its place, its peculiarities, etc. The other players guess the answer by the help of such clues. There must be a similar tendency in the criminal which finds expression in these mistakes. It is as if he, like the child, puts a riddle to the law, saying: "I know something you do not know." When anyone says that, especially if he boasts of his knowledge, it will not be long before his secret is out. Secret knowledge clamors to be revealed. The unconscious urge for self-betrayal often finds expression in ambiguous words. But when the mental tension becomes unbearable then the word which allows of only one interpretation breaks through.

One night in 1887 a merchant called Kreyss was murdered in his shop in Berlin.[63] The crime was discovered late next morning. The same morning, just after six o'clock, a woman newsvendor met a man to whom she sold a paper. Seeing him again soon afterwards she inquired if he had already read it. "Oh," replied the man, "there is nothing in it, nothing about the murder." "Another murder?" she asked. "Yes," was the answer, "in Adalbert Street." The man who said this was the murderer.

What is it that urges the murderer to make a veiled disclosure of his deed? Why does murder talk in a thousand strange tongues?[64] It is clear that in the criminal two mental forces are fighting for supremacy. One tries to wipe out all traces of the crime, the other proclaims the deed and the doer to the whole world. (I will not explain in detail here the essence of this second tendency, because my book discussing this matter, is included in this volume.[65]) It is impelled by the unconscious desire for punishment which expresses itself in faulty acts of this kind. Of course, there are criminals who do not react to their deed in this way, but in some cases this unconscious need for punishment becomes so strong that it overwhelms the culprit and from the very outset seals his fate.

Here are some examples of "criminal's bad luck" or "stupidity" given by Wulffen: an epileptic burgled a doctor's house. On finding himself face to face with a skeleton he had an epileptic attack and was discovered. Another case quoted by Wulffen is so strange that he should have hesitated to attribute the criminal's misfortune merely to improvidence. Franz Gal, from Kaposvar in Hungary, heard that his neighbor Josef Varga had sold his oxen for 900 kronen. He waited till Varga and his wife had left the house, then he stole the money. Their little girl of six was alone at home, and Gal determined to do away with the unwelcome witness. He tied a rope to a beam in the ceiling, made a noose, and asked the child to put her head into it. She asked him to show her how to do it, so he climbed on a chair and showed her. Suddenly the chair slipped from under him and he was caught in the noose. The frightened child ran out of the house. When the parents returned the man was dead. This is an instance of a faulty act (*parapraxis*) appearing as an accident, of suicide disguised as clumsiness. The tendency to self-punishment preceded the forbidden deed, as is sometimes the case in an obsessional neurosis, and drove the ego to the death it had unconsciously willed.[66]

Similar examples indicate a mental development which may be described as an internalization of the law of talion, "eye for eye, tooth for tooth." They should teach the criminologist that there are processes in the criminal's mental underworld of which he has no knowledge and which have not been adequately explained. Behavior of this kind is sometimes explained on the assumption that murderers and blackguards are "human beasts." This assumption panders to our narcissism by creating a great gulf between criminals and other men; but the existence precisely in some of the worst kind of malefactors of unconscious impulses of self-punishment and self-destruction kills that legend. On the other hand the recognition of unconscious moral factors in criminals should not tempt us to look upon them as noble creatures.[67]

8. THE "VISITING CARD"

A CHEMICAL examination of the feces which many criminals leave behind has often led to their discovery. This examination has sometimes proved so intructive that a French criminologist, Reiss of Lyons, called the feces the criminal's "carte de visite odorante." It is clear that the grumus merdae becomes connected with many superstitions. Criminals often believe that there will be no immediate pursuit of them if they leave their feces behind on the scene of action. To lengthen the respite they cover the feces with various objects. Popular names for feces, like "Wächter," "Posten" in Germany, "Schuldwachten" in Holland, "sentinelle" in France, "uomini di notte" in Italy,* are evidence of this superstition. Wulffen[68] explains the feces as "a visible sign of the criminal's light-hearted impudence." Sometimes the intention is, no doubt, to mock authority, but that is not the primary motive. Hellwig,[69] who has traced this custom to many countries, explains it more cautiously. He thinks it is based on the idea that something must be left behind if the criminal himself is to escape, the underlying conviction being that every crime must be expiated. By making this sacrifice, the culprit propitiates the gods or even forces them to let him go scot-free. Hellwig evidently adopts the theory of a superstitious motivation. And it does indeed explain the custom up to a point. The character of a voluntary sacrifice, an indemnity so to speak, is really attributed to the custom by many criminals.

* They all mean the same: watchman, sentry, night watchman.

Hellwig's theory, however, cannot be considered psychologically valid, for two reasons. The first is of a general nature, and is the result of psychoanalytic experience. It maintains that the superstitious motives are not ultimate ones but must themselves be examined and explained. The person himself can give only a part of his reasons—the conscious part—but he cannot tell us anything about the more important unconscious motivation for his conduct. Thus we believe that in this case the theory of a superstition needs a deeper psychological explanation. The other consideration is of a more special nature; it becomes clear if we accept provisionally Hellwig's theory of a superstition. If the custom goes back to superstition must not the criminal sometimes be hard put to it to get the material for his sacrifice, since no physical need compels him, only an inner voice? How he is able to produce the fecal material at will, that is the problem.

B. Kraft,[70] who has made the most recent contribution to this subject, rejects decisively the theory of superstition. The criminal's nervousness, he says, produces an increased peristaltic movement of the bowels which obliges him to defecate. This habit—he points out—tends to disappear in a hardened criminal. He therefore concludes that the presence of the feces indicates that a beginner in crime was at work or, at any rate, there at the time. He further supposes that it is this physiological fact which has led to the superstition already referred to.

We owe to Freud[71] the discovery that the child regards feces as a present, a mark of affection to be offered to a beloved person. This infantile meaning does not exclude its use as a means of defiance; the latter is only an application in a negative sense of the primary significance of the act. The *grumus merdae* may mean both, according to Freud: a sneer and a regressive form of restitution. This is a more specific explanation of Kraft's theory of nervousness: the main motive is fear. The fact of the criminal's superstition, the idea of expiation and protection represented by the feces, become comprehensible as an infantile expression of compensation. The part played by defiance and scorn may clearly be seen side by side with the regressive unconscious tendency.

The feces, being part of the person, represent the culprit himself. From the infantile point of view, leaving them behind means leaving one's self behind. On a different cultural level, the same idea is found in the penal code of savage peoples or in early medieval times. By the gift of domestic animals or a fine, one may compensate for murder, manslaughter or robbery.

The demonstrative character of the *grumus merdae* reveals it is an expression of the unconscious impulse to confess. Here the feces express social fear. This agrees with Kraft's theory connecting the presence of feces with criminals who are either young or not yet hardened in crime. Sometimes, if one traces the effect back to unconscious motives, one might infer that the feces were left for the purpose of self-betrayal. Considering how often the examination of the feces provides a clue,[72] we see that the superstitious faith in feces as a means of protection is an optimistic interpretation of an opposite belief. It may rest on the criminal's conviction of having paid his "tribute" to justice or to the injured person in this infantile form. Sometimes self-betrayal shows itself in another way. Gross tells of a dangerous criminal, Demeter Radek, who looted a shop in Cernowitz. Radek, who had just come out of prison, defecated in the burgled shop and cleaned himself with his papers of discharge from that prison.

Perhaps the psychological explanation of the *grumus merdae* goes beyond the special case of defecation and holds good for a whole group of clues. Hellwig[73] mentions a belief, prevalent in the neighborhood of Aleksine, according to which a murderer need only leave some of his clothing on the victim in order to escape capture. The following case illustrates this belief. It occurred about twenty-five years ago. One afternoon, a peasant from Soho Banja began to quarrel with another peasant in a coffee house in Aleksine. Words gave place to blows and the peasant from Soho Banja drew his knife and killed the other. He then pulled off his fur cap, threw it on the corpse and broke through the crowd and escaped. People said he was not caught, because he had thrown his cap on the corpse. According to the popular belief in Bosnia and Herzegovina a murderer is so powerfully

attracted by his victim's blood that he cannot leave him. In order
to be able to do so he has to throw something belonging to him,
a gun, for instance, on the dead man. In the Abruzzi, a murderer
has to throw his weapon in a certain direction. In Sicily, it is believed that if the murderer keeps his dagger[74] it will drive him
inevitably into the hands of the police. The following example,
quoted by Hellwig, shows how a superstition of this kind may
produce a clue. A woman deserted her ten-month-old infant on
a bitter night on the open road. She placed her shoes near the
child, hoping that by this means she would not be found. It was
precisely the shoes which helped to trace her, because the local
shoemaker remembered for whom he had made them. Hellwig
thinks the shoes were left in the belief that without footprints it
would be impossible to know in which direction she had gone.
In another case, the print of a hand covered with blood was discovered on the scene of action, and it was concluded that the
guilty man had either splashed his hand or cut it. When found,
he admitted having cut it purposely in order to leave a print.
Hellwig says that according to popular belief the bloody hand
represented the man himself. All these superstitions, collected
by Hellwig and other authors, testify to a belief in the existence
of a magic bond between the murderer and his victim. The murdered man is supposed to be not quite dead and to be able to
revenge himself on his murderer. To conciliate him or his avenging spirit (originally identical with the murdered bodily ego)
there was only one way, namely, the death of the murderer according to law of talion. Later on, a part of the murderer's person
(his feces, blood, a piece of clothing, etc.) might take the place
of this sacrifice of himself. What was later to become a clue—say
a piece of clothing—was originally a part of the murderer himself,
left behind by him purposely, for magical reasons. A clue of this
kind has a special place in the presentday superstitions of the
criminal. In this connection, the development of the mind has
included two processes—a displacement of the original thing on to
some detail and an extension from the murderer himself to everything he has come into contact with. Ambivalance has changed

into its exact opposite the friendly reconciling, expiatory significance of the object left behind. And in view of this we can see how
it is that the very object which was designed to protect the criminal from pursuit and punishment delivers him up to justice. The
criminal's superstition shows an archaic way of thinking which
subsists along with a technically scientific efficiency in committing
the crime. The history of clues shows how self-punishment may
be replaced by self-betrayal, the need for expiation by the unconscious urge to confess, as expressed by parapraxes (faulty acts).
The expiatory act is replaced by a parapraxis, but the parapraxis
is itself an unconscious expiation. Once upon a time the only
atonement for murder was the murderer's own death. Now the
same implacable law becomes an unconscious one, demands the
murderer's delivery to justice by self-betrayal. And this mental
law knows no pity: *dura lex, sed lex*.

9. THE RETURN TO THE SCENE OF THE CRIME

IF our view is correct, the belief that the murdered man does not
let his murderer go free but wants his life in retribution must
still linger in the minds of people today. Here we should like to
draw attention to one of the phenomena, whose psychological
connection with that belief has not yet been perfectly understood
—the return of the murderer to the scene of the crime.

Of course, not all murderers feel this urge and certainly not all
who feel it give way to it. But for us psychologists it is an important fact that this urge so often makes itself felt with compulsive
strength. What makes the criminal do such a senseless thing? In
some cases, says Wulffen,[75] practical reasons may explain such
a strange act. In one case, for instance, the murderer had forgotten
to search his victim for money and came back to do so. In another case, he had lost his notebook on the scene of the crime;
he had to get it or it would have betrayed him. There may also

be the wish to make changes in the place where the crime was committed. Wulffen quotes a case where the murderer came back and trod down the earth round the corpse so as to simulate an attack by many people. Such obvious reasons need not be the only or the essential ones. May they not serve as a screen for others, more obscure ones, and be used by the latter as a rationalization? Even Wulffen admits that in a number of cases there were no good reasons for such behavior. One murderer said he had come back to see in daylight the place where, in the evening, he had, as it were, been surprised into doing the deed. Wulffen shows a naïve confidence in the criminal's introspective gifts. The murderer of a girl said he had come back because he felt sorry for his victim, and because the beauty of the landscape had moved him. "This criminal was actuated by esthetic feelings," says the guileless Wulffen. Yet he recognises that the murderer himself "sometimes does not know why he comes back," and adds with impressive psychological insight, "They live by instincts and not by principles." In addition to this, he asserts, the place of crime has an involuntary, mysterious attraction for the criminal; the scene attracts him because the deed still occupies his mind. Strange feelings are linked up with this. The criminal sees his deed as an heroic one, glorifies it and finds comfort on the scene of the crime. (This explains the strange feeling of security, so incomprehensible to us, which he feels there and which so often delivers him up to his pursuers.)[76] The murderer thinks his presence in his own atmosphere gives him a certain power over it. Wulffen mentions the return of Raskolnikov in *Crime and Punishment* to the scene of his two murders and his wish to rent the house in which he committed them. That intention, he says, is a very characteristic one even if it is not taken seriously. It at least shows Raskolnikov's wish to live permanently in the house of the murder, an instinctive desire to exert a kind of power over the scene of murder.[77]

If it is correct that the deepest motives of such strange acts are unconscious then the information the criminal himself can give is valid only as a basis of psychological research, not as a psychological explanation itself. The greater and more significant part of the pre-conditions and motives of the crime is obscure. The criminal is equally unconscious of his own mental reactions to the deed. What goes on in him afterwards is to a great extent unknown to his ego. One might maintain that precisely the most serious crimes are a psychological trauma for the doer also, a trauma that has to be mentally digested. To retort that the crime was, after all, planned and prepared, "done" in fact, by the criminal himself, would be to take only the most superficial view of the matter. The deed may, nevertheless, surprise him; he may sometimes see his own act with the eyes of a stranger.

We have to admit our failure to grasp psychologically this strange return of the murderer to the scene of his crime. Paradoxically enough, such an admission is more reassuring than the criminologist's "explanation," which understands the whole question and sees no more riddles in it. The little that we can guess of its hidden sense seems to point to an unconscious intention, alien to the ego, of mastering the deed psychologically. Anybody familiar with psychoanalysis will not be surprised at the idea that an impulse to repeat the deed plays a part in this return; dark impulses urge the murderer towards the scene where he has felt a sinister pleasure.[78] The case mentioned above of the man who murdered a girl and wanted to see the place again in daylight makes it seem probable that this urge represented an unconscious wish to see the girl's body again. The desire to re-experience pleasure is surely one of the hidden motives which lead the criminal back to the place where he committed the crime. The mental mechanism which connects this tendency with the scene of the crime is not yet clear, as little clear as is the question why murderers are more in the thrall of this tendency than other wrongdoers. With this urge to relive a pleasure goes another, not less compelling one—the unconscious need for punishment. That may seem paradoxical, but mental life is full of such paradoxes. If all pleasure desires eternity it certainly desires the eternity of destruction as well. How two similar, yet contrary, tendencies merge in a single action must be further investigated.

This return of the criminal to the scene of the crime has not even been correctly described from a phenomenological point of view. The murderer hardly ever returns soon after the deed. His return is only the reverse side of his flight, and the one is inexplicable without the other. The tendency to return appears late; perhaps it is only the continuation of the first reflex of flight. It is a part of the flight, in which the direction of the flight, not its nature, is altered. It must be looked upon not separately, but in connection with the other mental reactions of a certain criminal type.

Murderers rarely leave their deeds alone. Many criminologists maintain that murders would never be found out but for the criminal's intensive preoccupation with his deed. There are several ways of dealing with the deed. Some criminals try to incriminate someone else; others follow every detail of the investigation; others again write letters to the police, sneering at them or announcing fresh crimes. In many cases, these letters have substantially helped the police, in others the clues have been useless. Probably there is an unconscious intention on the part of the writer to furnish evidence against himself. This strange method of self-betrayal need not exclude the other intention of challenge and defiance. The mass murderer, Kürten, always listened attentively to conversations about the murders, followed the investigations with feverish interest and pestered the investigating police. He described his mental state while doing so as one of apprehensive excitement and expectation; and he also had a distinct feeling of superiority because he knew better and could have told them the whole story in the smallest detail. This peculiar combination of feelings leads us to suppose that the tone of defiance, superiority and scorn is adopted to cover up the hidden sense of insecurity, the secret intention of self-destruction. That hybrid reaction, as it were, represents the criminal's struggle against his unconscious impulse to deliver himself up to justice.

According to the psychoanalytic view, certain mechanisms of projection exist, especially in the most serious crimes. The criminal flees from his own conscience as he would from an external enemy; he projects this internal adversary outwards. Under this pressure, his weakening ego fights in vain and he becomes careless and betrays himself. When the internal forces become unbearable, he flees to the external ones, probably because it is a mental relief to do so—a relief which is in many cases greater than his fear of punishment. In studying the psychogenesis of conscience as Freud has described it, we understand why the external forces are so much less formidable than the mental ones. The Erinyes who pursue Orestes are reincarnations of his murdered mother: from these visible but intangible beings he flees to earthly justice and suffers its punishment because it is more merciful than that terror.

If conscience thus makes cowards of criminals, it also makes daredevils of them, as it grows harsher, more tormenting and more implacable. The strange phenomenon of the return to the scene of the crime shows this. It is like a challenge to fate, an unconscious oracle, an introjected ordeal: "If I succeed in revisiting this place, in committing as it were the deed again, without being arrested; if I can escape, then I am protected by forces stronger than any police." A criminal has sometimes actually got into touch with the police in order to mislead them by false information; and in his conversations with them he has enjoyed his own cleverness and self-control, without an inkling that he has betrayed himself through some detail. His ego fights in vain against the compulsion to confess.[79] The murderer's return to the scene of his crime fits into this scheme of things, for one of its hidden motives is his longing—unknown to his ego—to give himself up to justice.[80]

The royal villain Richard dreads his dream infinitely more than the avenging army:

> "By the Apostle Paul, shadows to-night
> Have struck more terror to the soul of Richard
> Then can the substance of ten thousand soldiers
> Armèd in proof and led by shallow Richmond."

It would be wrong to say that self-hatred drives the criminal to self-betrayal; perhaps it is rather self-pity or love of the object introjected in the ego. What is the judge's severity compared with the torment of the superego? Maybe the law will be milder than self-destruction—a reprieve, a rest for the hunted man. "Somebody pursues me and it is myself," thus a murderer once described his mental state. The most callous criminal fears his superego, the aggression from within which brings about his doom. According to the unwritten law of talion he fears not only death—his victim's fate—but also all the fear and torment of the death which he inflicted on his victim. The police find this type of criminal their best ally against himself. Legal punishment seems like purgatory to him compared with the hell of the unconscious forces of conscience.

It is not surprising that we should find these strong unconscious impulses of self-betrayal precisely in criminals of the most violent type, who show no remorse, no conscious guilt. (Many cases of moral insanity come under this category.) A feeling of guilt would be superfluous in them, because it is replaced by unconscious tendencies to self-destruction.

The secret alliance of the pursuit from without with the superego has its own private language, unknown to the ego, in which these two factors communicate, bridging every gulf. It is precisely those clues, unconsciously produced, which speak so plainly. They are a substitute for the perpetrator himself. In returning to the place of the crime, the criminal has, at last, and in reality, gone where he wanted to go. The clue is changed back into the person— *totus pro parte*. It is quite natural that we should find this happen more often in major crimes than in minor ones like stealing, forgery and swindling. In the former, something in the hidden places of the criminal's soul forces his secret out; his unreconciled conscience wants to speak. Even when he has escaped the police, he is not safe from surprise attacks from within.

We have seen how criminal psychology interprets clues and what use judges make of them. Is this the only possible, the only justifiable way, of looking at them? May it not be pointed out that, in the unconscious production of clues, hidden mental forces are striving for expression which hitherto have not and could not be acknowledged by the law. There is a legend of an Indian judge who acquitted a burglar because, sunk in meditation, he had debated in himself whether the hole by which he gained entry should have the shape of a lyre or a butterfly. Perhaps such judges exist only in legendary India, but one would like to think that every judge possesses a little of the psychological spirit that inspired the verdict.

10. A Case from the Year 1386

A SPECIAL interest seems to have urged us to examine the significance of clues. Was it only because of the pleasure we took in the shrewdness and logic of the criminologist's chain of reasoning? No doubt there was such pleasure; but logic plays only a small part in the investigations of criminal experts. Thus we found ourselves thrown back upon psychology. What psychological factors are decisive in estimating circumstantial evidence? To answer this we have had to consider the role of psychology in general in circumstantial evidence as well as the importance of psychological clues in criminal procedure. In doing so, we have had to consider several fundamental questions, some of a tricky nature. We have not been able to deal with them here with the necessary scientific precision. But we have thought it necessary to enquire whether psychoanalysis could solve the question of the perpetrator and to state our views as to the forensic significance of psychological evidence. As a result, we have gone beyond the old point of view and have recognized that material clues can point to hitherto unknown or unconsidered unconscious tendencies in the perpetrator, to hidden impulses which, though of no importance for the finding of the criminal, are yet of some importance in obtaining a better knowledge of his personality.

It cannot be denied that the results are disappointing. The logical interest in the interpretation of clues has proved narrower than we expected. The psychological one has led us to fields as yet unknown to criminology, and has gone further and deeper than we expected. But it cannot account for our interest in clues. Perhaps we do not know enough about its origin and nature. The literature of crime gives many examples, but they are only examples. The unconscious significance of clues as a means of self-betrayal has opened up a new question. What did clues used to mean? Have they taken the place of other phenomena that in former times used to determine the relation between the law-breaker and society? They are not independent of the development of criminal law. They replace other institutions for the purpose of criminal detection and will probably be replaced in their turn. Here we enter the realm of history. That great teacher and her sister science, comparative ethnology, will be able to show us the genetic side of our problem.

By a happy chance we possess an account of a difficult case of 550 years ago[81] which will make a good beginning to the following chapters.

In the Hundred Years' War, many knights had to leave wife and home for an indefinite period, and put them under the care of a trusted friend. The account tells us of a certain Jean Carouge who went to England from Vienne in 1385. His neighbor and friend Jacques Legris undertook the sacred duty of looking after his wife and his castle. A year later Jean Carouge returned and found his wife, Marie, in the throes of depression. At last she confessed that Jacques Legris had raped her in the presence of his stableman Louvet. Deeply wounded, Jean swore revenge. His wife was innocent, having yielded to force; the stableman had held her down.

The feudal lord, the Duke of Alençon, set up a court consisting of clergy, knights and counselors before whom the two men were to state their case according to knightly usage. Carouge appeared as plaintiff, and threw down his glove as a challenge to Legris. The court wanted Louvet's testimony first, but he could not remember anything. Legris denied everything and threw down his glove like Carouge, declaring that he was ready to prove his in-

nocence by fighting; and after a long sitting the tribunal, in view
of the contradictory statements of the parties concerned, con-
sented to this. Charles VI, who was going to war with England,
postponed the fight till after his return. It took place on December 13th, 1386. The Paris Parliament had everything prepared,
the barriers and stands were erected and Charles VI, Queen Isabel,
the knights and their ladies, and an enormous throng crowded
the lists where Carouge and Legris were to fight for their honor.
Dame Marie had also appeared, dressed in mourning, but the
king forbade her presence. Her husband turned to her and said:
"I endanger my life for you. You alone know whether my cause
is just before God." She answered: "Fight with a stout heart. Your
cause is just." He kissed her, crossed himself and entered the barriers. Both knights swore that they had used no magic. The king
gave the signal to begin. The fight with lances on horseback was
indecisive. In the duel on foot with swords, Legris wounded his
enemy in the hip, but Carouge jumped up and ran his adversary
through with his sword. "Confess that you dishonored my wife,"
he cried, as he knelt on the dying man. But Legris protested his
innocence with his last breath and died. Carouge, the victor, bent
his knee before the king. The guilty man's corpse was strung up
and his possessions given to the victor.

Carouge went to the Holy Land with his page, de Tillières,
who had previously stayed in the castle with Dame Marie. When
she learned later that her husband had died fighting she im-
mured herself in a convent cell where she lived piously for five
more years. It is said that, on his deathbed, de Tillières confessed
to having raped Dame Marie. A monk reported this confession;
the report was shown to the king and he, whom the world had
called insane, wrote these wise lines on it: "What is human justice? What is truth? We are puppets in the hands of a mysterious
fate."

Since these words were written almost six centuries have passed.
The proofs used in court have undergone a radical change. We no
longer believe in the truth-compelling efficacy of a knightly fight,
but those words have lost nothing of their penetrating and melan-

choly truth. In the fourteenth century, mankind was convinced
that God would show the guilty man by letting him lose the fight.
Nowadays men believe that truth is found by logic; they are as
sure of the value of circumstantial evidence as their ancestors
were of the infallibility of the trial by fire. Judges in the fourteenth century also tried to find the truth and did their very best
to solve the question of guilt. It is ridiculous to suppose that the
judges who condemned witches to a terrible death, and those
who burned Jews and Mohammedans in the service of the Holy
Inquisition, were less conscientious and less eager to find the
truth than the judges of our day. Their methods of arriving at the
truth were different from ours, but the evidence they accepted
carried the same conviction for them as, for instance, fingerprints
do for us. Formerly, people used to consult the village god or the
oracle or the flight of birds, and no one can say that their methods
were much less reliable than ours. Torture was used as we now
use cross-examination; special methods were invented, like the
thumbscrew or the wheel. The wish to find out the truth about a
crime has often led to the use of criminal means.

Criminal history is the history of culture. Anyone who investi-
gates the reaction of society to crime will learn surprising things
about the collective mind.[82] Above all, it is astonishing to find that
for many centuries the problem of how to discover the criminal
remained one of little interest. It is not possible for a single individual to go through the enormous material of legal history;
but if he could, he would see nothing but an amorphous mass of
historical facts, a registration of sources, texts, original manu-
scripts, and reports—material that is neither psychologically ordered nor understood.[83] It is left to the student to establish some
line of development, to find something that links together these
disparate elements. It is not our intention to follow the development of legal proof or to study its forms in different primitive
peoples. For the layman, this is not only impossible but unnecessary, because our subject is of a special kind. We have set out to
study only the most recent method of proof—the material evidence—and the older methods used in antiquity and among sav-

age tribes need interest us only in so far as they throw light on the cultural development which led up to the introduction of proof by evidence. We shall try to show the psychological significance of this development by representative examples, which we shall compare with modern criminological methods.

11. THE BEGINNINGS OF CRIMINOLOGY

IT happens frequently in science that some of the initial problems we set ourselves already contain errors which are bound to lead to an incorrect and over-simplified treatment of the subject. I think that the accepted view of primitive criminal detection is a case in point. We are, of course, quite prepared to assume that, on low cultural levels and in prehistoric times, crimes were looked upon in a different way and that what we nowadays call crimes were not then regarded as such. We can easily believe that in primitive times there was no criminology, perhaps not even an elementary method of investigating crime. But as soon as we recognize the existence of such things we assume with the naïveté of the educated European that the principles of criminal justice must have resembled ours.

We assume that the only natural and possible sequence of events was this: crime—investigation—finding the culprit—punishment. In this assumption lies a fundamental simplification. Maybe this order did not exist for a world so different from ours; our premises may be wrong. Certain characteristics of penal law in ancient times and among the half-savage tribes in Australia arouse our suspicions. There is, for instance, a primitive conception that not the individual but the tribe has committed the crime and must suffer for it. The penal consequence of this is the institution of blood-vengeance. Such a primitive conception of murder is alien to us. (There are exceptions like war, pogroms and the suppression by force of arms of minorities.)

Such a view as the one described above would carry our modern conceptions into a time and a state of society where other mental processes reigned. It may sound strange, but in prehistoric times and on different cultural levels a different sequence of events obtained; it began with the punishment, and ended with the solution of the crime. Let us call to mind the primitive conceptions of crime and punishment. Crime means a breach of the all-important laws of taboo, which determine and preserve the organization of the community. He who breaks these unwritten but universally acknowledged laws endangers his whole clan. The necessity of protecting the community, of finding and isolating the culprit, already belongs to a later time. Originally a breach of taboo carried its own punishment; this automatic effect made criminal procedure, in our sense, unnecessary. A man dies suddenly. For the primitive man, there is no doubt that his death is due to some breach of taboo. He died of it as people nowadays are killed by an electric current. A solution of this crime is as unnecessary as it is impossible. To make use of clues, as we understand them today, is unthinkable under such different cultural circumstances; but even other uses of the clue, for magic procedure, for instance, do not occur at this period. The dead man is taboo, the murderer is taboo, everything he touched and that touched him is taboo. Taboo is contagious and therefore an investigation into the deed is impossible. Before this could happen religion had to change decisively, old restrictions had to disappear, powerful beliefs had to be shaken. It is true that the modern priest who brings comfort to the prisoner still makes use, strangely enough, of the words: "Vengeance is mine, saith the Lord." In those times, however, when the Lord acted in accordance with those words, when Jehovah was the terrible and revengeful god of primitive tribes who punished the wicked and paralyzed the hand raised against him— in those times there was no need of a criminal investigation. The god or demon of the clan took good care of his laws and punished their breach mercilessly. The eye of the chief, who after his death gradually became the tribal god, was itself the eye of the law.

This attitude, alien to us, which proceeds from the punishment to the solution of the crime already belongs to a later phase of primitive culture when the belief in taboo had weakened. Taboo still had enormous power and was to retain it for many centuries in spite of all social changes. Crime was still regarded as a breach of the laws of taboo of primitive society. The surest sign of such a breach having been committed was precisely the punishment itself, that is to say, any misfortune or catastrophe which might befall the community or the individual. It was in order to obviate such an event that crime began to be investigated. If there was an institution in that stage of development which was analogous to our present-day institution of punishment, it was the ritual cleansing which followed the solution of the crime.[84] The actual punishment itself was the premise, the *conditio sine qua non* of the solution, not the primary aim of the latter. This reversal of the sequence of events, which seems so paradoxical to us, is not only recognizable in tradition, legend and folklore; it is still operative, though in an altered form, in some Australian tribes.

Once attention is drawn to this reversal of order the examples of it that come to mind are too numerous to be quoted. It was the plague that fell upon Thebes which caused the discovery of Oedipus' old transgressions. And it was the defeat of the Israelites which necessitated an enquiry into the reasons of the Lord's wrath. A famine, an epidemic, have the same criminalistic and religious effect. It is well known that all peoples are a chosen people; so a misfortune is attributed to its tribal god whose former love is turned to wrath because of an unexpiated crime. Myths and fairy tales illustrate these views beyond a doubt. They also seem to prove that the clan god is often nothing but the clan chief promoted to a higher rank. One example must serve for many. The missionary, M. Keysser, has given us excellent reports about the life of the Kais, a half-savage Papuan tribe, in what was formerly German New Guinea.[85] Like most primitive peoples the Kais assume that every death is caused by magic. The guilty magician and his kin are pursued by blood-vengeance. Nearly all wars between villages and tribes are caused by such punitive expeditions. The spirit of the dead man demands revenge and will severely punish his kinsmen if they neglect this sacred duty. Not only will they be unlucky in their hunting, but wild boars will trample down their fields and misfortunes will befall them. The outbreak of an epidemic shows the wrath of the spirit which only the death of the wicked magician or some other person can appease. Even the medieval church argued that disease, poor harvests and defeat in war had their sources in secret sins in Christendom. The individual originally moved along the same lines of thought. Job falls a victim to terrible boils. To him and his environment the thought is natural that his disease is a divine punishment for an unknown or undiscovered crime. His questions center round one theme: "What crime have I committed?" We perceive in this the dawn of a new time, for it is not a question—or not only a question— of some ritual omission or offence, some breach of taboo laws in its original sense. But at this point, where the problem of sin in thought emerges and threatens to drag us into its depths, we must call a halt.

There is no need to go into the slow social and cultural alterations that changed the primitive sequence of punishment (i.e., effect of crime)—solution of crime into the one more familiar to us.[86] We have thought it important to formulate precisely the character of that archaic phase, for only from its premises can the development, ways and methods of early criminal investigation and establishment of proof be understood.

12. THE PRIMITIVE SEARCH FOR MOTIVE

WHEN Ranke was asked by colleagues why he had become an historian he answered: "Out of curiosity." It would not be fair to accuse the learned historians of criminal law of possessing little of this quality or vice. It is, however, not improbable that their curiosity chooses well-trodden paths and avoids the unknown ones. How otherwise is it possible that the origin of evidence should not hitherto have been discovered? That origin lies in magic.

Many wild tribes believe they would live forever if a wicked magician did not cut short their lives. It may be wrong to assert that they do not believe in a natural death, and more correct to say that they assume every death to be violent, and caused by magic.[87] The Abipones, a now extinct Indian tribe in Paraguay, believed that an expulsion of the Spaniards and magicians from America would render them immortal. Even when a man died of wounds or of old age, they believed him to have been bewitched. For instance, in a quarrel between two men about a horse, a third party, who wanted to patch things up, was killed by their spears. We might think he died of wounds, but no Abipone would agree with us. They firmly maintained that their comrade had been killed by magic. Their suspicion fell upon an old woman who was known to be a witch and to whom the dead man had recently refused to give a melon. They assumed she had killed him out of revenge by means of her magic.[88]

The same is true of the warlike Araucanians in Chile. Even when a centenarian dies peacefully, they are sure that an enemy has killed him by magic.[89] When a Bakairi Indian in Brazil was asked to translate the sentence "All men are mortal," he remained silent for a long time. The teacher had to realize that the necessity of death was by no means clear to the savage.[90] We find the same belief among the Indians of Guiana. They believe that every man has a body and a soul, and that a magician can take the soul out of the body and damage other far-distant people by doing so. In carrying out this purpose, the magician is not always visible; he can change into a serpent, a bird or an insect. Thus an Indian who is attacked by a wild animal will assume it to be a magician who has changed into this shape.[91] J. I. Monteiro[92] tells that, during his stay at Ambrizzette among natives of the Congo, he saw three native women go to the river to fetch water. One after the other they filled their vessels. Suddenly the one in the middle was seized by an alligator and devoured. Her family at once accused the other two of having bewitched her. The writer tried to convince them of the absurdity of their accusation, but they answered:

"Why did the alligator kill the middle one and neither of the others?" It was impossible to undeceive them. The two women were forced to drink Casca (the ordeal by poison). Monteiro believes that one of them died of the draught. H. M. Bentley tells of a belief in the same neighborhood that magicians often change themselves into leopards and crocodiles in order to kill their victims.[93] They feel quite sure that a genuine crocodile is harmless. This conviction makes them enter the stream unhesitatingly to attend to their fish traps. When one of them is killed by a crocodile they hold a council to find the guilty magician, kill him and behave as recklessly as before. Nobody in Madagascar believes in a natural death. With the exception of centenarians, everyone is believed to die as the victim of magic. The usual formula of condolence to the relatives is, "Cursed be the magician who killed him."[94] When anyone catches malaria in an infected area it is still thought to be due to a magician who has wished the deadly poison into the victim's body.

These examples, which stand for many hundreds quoted by Frazer, are meant to show the fundamental difference between primitive criminology and ours. No examining magistrate or detective believes nowadays in murder by magic. Is there then such a gulf between our methods of criminal detention and the primitive ones? Yes and no. What is the meaning of the belief in murder by magic? Primitive people mean it is in the literal sense, but the psychological meaning of such a belief is only made clear by supposing the existence of superhuman or at least extraordinary mental powers. Those powers have mainly one aim: to injure a neighbor, to damage his life and possessions. The natives only *seem* to choose their guilty magician haphazardly; they have unconscious motives for their choice. They attribute to the suspect the intention to kill, they assume that the murderer hated his victim. It is true they invest these motives with a special power of becoming immediately translated into reality, as our obsessional neurotics do. To be sure, modern criminology does not start from this assumption; but we have found an element of this

primitive assimilation of intention and deed in the question of
whether a person was *capable* of a given crime. Certainly the
differences must not be overlooked, but neither must the similarities. The natives who believe their magician capable of the deed
kill him outright. Their confidence in their primitive psychological judgment is so strong that it is sufficient proof of guilt in their
eyes. Many judicial errors of our time have no stronger reason
than that a person was thought capable of the crime. So we find
the old magical atmosphere, only slightly brought up to date, in
modern criminology in the form of psychological considerations.
We have recounted the case of the three Congo women and the
crocodile to illustrate the belief in sorcery as the sole cause of
death. It is easy to guess what the underlying psychological assumption was in this case; it was the unconscious realization of
repressed enmity among the three women to which the natives
ascribed the power to kill.

But is the difference between that primitive belief and our modern views really so great? Compare the above-mentioned case with
one taken from our civilized world of to-day.[95] In 1886 a couple
named Druaux settled at Malaernay, where the wife opened a
public house. With them lived her brother Gaston Delacroix.
Their life was not peaceful. The brothers-in-law got on quite well,
but they both quarreled with the woman. She was often drunk
and unfaithful to her husband. For this reason, the couple often
quarreled and the woman sometimes even attacked her husband
physically, as she did her brother, too, who used to take her husband's side and reproach her for her immorality.

On April 6th, 1886, Druaux, returning from work, surprised
his wife with a man. He turned her out of the house and reported
the case to the police. Mme. Druaux, who had no other home,
spent April 7th in the woods and returned at night, begging her
husband to take her back. He agreed on condition that the public
house should be closed. She obeyed. The couple was last seen on
April 9th. As no member of the family appeared on the next day,
a Sunday, the house was entered by neighbors. They found both

men dead. The husband lay dead in bed, the brother fully dressed on the ground floor next to the kitchen door. The wife was in the house and had spent the greater part of Sunday with the dead bodies without calling in help. She seemed to be drunk. The doctor could find no injury or sign of illness on the bodies. The autopsy showed that both men had been poisoned. Suspicion could rest on no one but the woman. She was arrested and charged with the double murder.

She denied the murder, but had to admit to immorality and to having maltreated her husband and brother. What happened on April 8th, 9th and 10th she could only describe as follows: when her husband took her back on April 7th they drank to their reconciliation. They both drank a lot of alcohol, the man so much that he was unable to go to work for the next two days. He complained of headaches on the 8th and 9th, but got up on the 9th at 4 a.m. to have another drink; at 7 a.m. she gave him coffee and then they both went to sleep again. She woke up in the afternoon and discovered that her husband lay dead by her side. She went downstairs to call her brother and found him dead, too. What they had died of she did not know. She had been heard to say that her husband would not live to a great age, that we all had to die and that nobody was irreplaceable. Such remarks seemed very suspicious.

The three experts who were called in agreed that both men had died of the same poison, but there were no traces to show the nature of the poison. No mineral poison had been used. The only possibility was cantharides, an animal poison. A microscopic examination of the intestines produced a small particle, very similar to cantharides. The experts deposed that the two men must have suffered great pain in the stomach and abdomen and considered it "absolutely impossible" that the man could have died next to his wife without her noticing it.

Owing to mitigating circumstances, the woman was sentenced to penal servitude for life though it could not be ascertained where she had got the poison.

In autumn 1887, a young couple called Gautier took the

Druaux's inn. Soon after, Mme. Gautier suffered from giddiness and fainting fits; several times she was found lying on the floor unconscious and quite cold. In May 1888 she collapsed in her kitchen and died. She showed the same symptoms as the two supposed victims of Mme. Druaux.

Other strange happenings took place. Fish which Gautier brought in to the house decomposed in a short time "as if by magic." People who called in for a glass of beer would suddenly drop down unconscious.

After Mme. Gautier's death, a couple called Dubeaux took over the public house. After a short time they, too, were unaccountably overcome by headaches, giddiness, attacks of sickness, etc. One day—this was in the middle of the nineties—Mme. Dubeaux fell down dead, and almost at the same time her husband was found lifeless in the house.

At last it occurred to the authorities that a lime kiln immediately adjoining the inn might be the reason for these mysterious deaths. It was extinguished, and from that day no more cases of illness occurred in the public house.

Experts established the fact conclusively that all the deaths had been the result of poisoning by carbon monoxide which had penetrated from the lime kiln through the wall of the public house.

The widow Druaux was acquitted after having served eight years of her sentence.

Do we not find here the same belief that struck us as so strange in the savages of Africa and Australia? Do we not find in the experts the same disbelief that the two men, whom Mme. Druaux hated, could have been the victims of an accident? Does not the conviction of the savage tribes, which makes them kill the supposed magician immediately, correspond psychologically to the sentence passed by the French tribunal? In the criminal law of savage tribes, too, we have found the effects of unconscious psychology. One might speak of unconscious psychological evidence. In our own preliminary examination of a case the question, "Whom did this murder profit?" is put consciously and valued as evidence. This question is not explicitly put in the primitive world, but it exists unconsciously in the form, "Who had a motive?" and perhaps directs the result of those mystical oracles.

To show the surprising interpretation put upon such evidence by savage tribes, we quote an account given by Malinowski of the legal aspect of sorcery in Melanesia.[96] There also every illness and death is attributed to black magic; and sorcery is recognized as a genuine legal force. This is proved by the way in which reasons are found why a man has been killed by sorcery. It is done by an exact interpretation of certain signs or symptoms in the exhumed body. Between twelve or twenty-four hours after the provisional funeral, the grave is opened at sunset and the corpse cleaned, painted and examined. To the accompaniment of ceremonies, the corpse is washed with coconut milk and certain signs are noted and interpreted. These signs point to habits or character traits of the deceased which have aroused the hatred of some other man, and actuated him to encompass his death through the agency of a magician. If, for instance, scratches on the shoulder are found, similar to the love marks made during cohabitation, they say that the dead man had committed adultery or was too successful with women so that he aroused the wrath of a chief or magician. The same reason for death, or rather for murder, is given if other signs are found; for instance, if the corpse is found with opened legs or covered with lice, because the mutual looking for lice is considered an expression of especial tenderness. Certain symptoms appear before death and are interpreted in a similar fashion. A dying man had smacked his lips (this is done to call a loved person to a secret tryst). When his body was exhumed it was found to be crawling with lice. It was known that he had allowed one of the wives of Numakala, a former chief, to delouse him publicly. Clearly, he had been punished by a higher power. If signs of self-adornment or beautification are found on the corpse, then it is thought to be the personal beauty of the dead Don Juan that has attracted the evil magic. Any red, black or white patches of color on the skin, any patterns similar to those which adorn the houses of nobles, signify that the deceased has decorated his house in a vainglorious manner and has thus aroused his chief's anger. Nor does the chief approve of a subject's laxity in ceremonial, as for instance, not bowing deeply enough before him. Such a man is found crumpled up in his grave. Malinowski has observed and established a whole code of magical interpretation in connection with the examination of the body.

No sensible criminologist will deny that these signs deserve the name of clues. His colleague among the savages does the same as he does when he finds clues on the corpse pointing to the murderer and his motives, and there is no reason why the white-skinned examiner should be the better psychologist of the two. More important than the differences are the similarities: the psychological search for a motive by examining the body. It is also important to note that the Melanesians find the establishment of motive sufficient, as if they thought not the murderer but the murdered man was guilty. This brings us back to the difference we have already mentioned. Primitive interest starts from the fact, or supposed fact, of a punishment and gets from that the stimulus to search for its motive or agency. Other tribes in a different stage of development attribute most deaths to the direct action of evil spirits and only a few to the indirect agency of magicians. The practical, one might say penological, consequences of such a difference are considerable. Death by magicians has to be avenged by their death; death by evil spirits cannot be avenged. The Indians of Guiana illustrate this difference. A missionary tells us[97] that the medicine man is called in to decide whether death is due to a sorcerer or to evil spirits. If it is due to the latter, the corpse is buried and all is over, but if magic was the cause the corpse is examined, and a blue mark, for instance, that is found on it, is judged to be the spot where the magician's invisible poisoned arrow entered. The accused magician is killed. Among those tribes, therefore, a murderer will deem it important to convince the others that his victim was killed by spirits or gods. If he succeeds in convincing the examining magician to that effect he is free, though his crime might have had several witnesses.

13. THE SEARCH FOR THE MURDERER

THE Kai tribes, whom we have mentioned previously, put betel in a dead man's mouth; if his murderer approaches him they believe that he will spit it out or give a similar sign. This explains why the family of a sick man suspects the person who does not visit him or does not come to his funeral when he dies.[98] In certain Melanesian tribes, the sick man is asked to name his murderer. It is believed that a *tabaran* (demon) possesses him and that the answers come from the *tabaran,* though he uses the voice of the dying man. "Who has bewitched you?" they ask; "answer quickly, or you will be burned."[99] In Victoria, Australia, the dying man's legs are carefully watched; their movements show where to look for the murderer.[100] Among the Narrenyerie, in South Australia, a relative sleeps the first night with the dead man, his head on the latter's body; this makes him dream of the magician who killed him. The next day the corpse is put on a kind of bier called a *ngratta* and lifted onto the shoulders of certain chosen people. The dead man's friends then form a circle round it and different names are called out. At last the relative names the person of his dream. The natives believe that at that moment the corpse jerks his bearers forcibly; this proves the name to be correct.[101] Still more direct is the cross-examination of the dead in New England.[102] The relatives meet before the dead man's hut during the night following his death. The priest-magician (*tena agagara*) calls with a loud voice on the spirit of the deceased and asks him who bewitched him. If there is no answer the *tena agagara* names a suspected person. If there is still no result he continues naming people till at last there is a sound in the house itself or in the shell he holds in his hand. This sound is a decisive clue.

The Dieri, in southeast Australia, get their information from the direction in which the corpse sinks away from the heads of his two bearers into the grave. It is in that direction that his murderer will be found.[103] If Australian natives cannot find the guilty man or tribe, they put the dead man into a tree, smooth the earth underneath it and wait till the first drop of blood falls. They then follow the direction indicated by the blood.[104]

In Africa, too, the dead man himself is questioned. In the desert of Guinea, if, in some mysterious way, he causes his bearers to make any movement while he is thus being questioned it is taken as an affirmative answer; if they remain motionless, it means "no."[105]

In Togo, the corpse is given a stick to hold, and is borne twice through the village; he is believed to point with his stick to the guilty man.[106]

All these customs are easily interpreted. Instead of discussing them we prefer to give a few examples from the early Germanic period. The Frisians did not bury the corpse until his death was avenged; the dead man himself took care that his murderer was found. When Hagen approached Siegfried's bier, the hero's wounds began to bleed.[107] As Rudolf His has explained,[108] the ordeal at the bier—which reappears in the above-mentioned Australian customs—had as its original purpose the detection of the murderer from among a number of people. In Freiburg, in Uechtland, this proof was used in relatively recent times in cases of drowning; the corpse was touched with the judge's staff and adjured in the name of the Holy Trinity to name his murderer, if any. Later still, it is not the dead man who names his murderer, but God Himself—one might say the dead man in his deified and sublimated shape. In the scene of the trial beside the bier, the dead man is present in two forms: in his earthly shape, dumb and cold —a corpse, but one whose spirit has not quite fled; and as a god, divine, but possessed of human attributes. This doubling of what was originally one person shows itself also in the transformation of the ordeal of the bier; it becomes the judgment of God. Instead of the corpse indicating the murderer, God does so by a visible miracle at the bier. This ordeal survived in its theological and criminological form until the seventeenth century. The Faculty of Law at Marburg considered it decisive as late as 1608.[109] In Shakespeare, when the terrible Richard appears at the bier, Anne exclaims:[110]

> "O! gentlemen; see, see! dead Henry's wounds
> Open their congeal'd mouths and bleed afresh.
> Blush, blush, thou lump of foul deformity,
> For 'tis thy presence that exhales this blood
> From cold and empty veins, where no blood dwells."

Shakespeare's plays also show how near the Elizabethans still were to the belief that the dead man named his murderer:

> "My father's spirit in arms! all is not well;
> I doubt some foul play . . ."

exclaims Hamlet when he is told of the ghost. (Act I, Scene 2.)

Certain facts incline us to regard this belief as a development of a still more primitive attitude, namely, that the dead man himself avenges his death, and pursues and kills his murderer.[111] In the wealth of material from which we have quoted, he already has to play a more modest part. We can only make a passing allusion to that earlier attitude, traces of which are still discernible in early Germanic penal law,[112] since our concern is to elucidate the methods employed for finding the culprit. The dead man who appears before the court or the priest-magician is originally as much *corpus delicti* as plaintiff. The blood that flows from him, the movements he makes, the tremor that passes over his features, the jerk he gives his bearers—all are clues in the most exact criminological sense. The native of central Australia, who is our own contemporary, and the German of the pre-Christian era meet in the belief that the dead man is not quite dead, but capable and desirous of naming his murderer. In prehistoric times it was certainly believed that the victim himself exacted that vengeance for his death which in later times was carried out by his relatives as a sacred duty. The Erinys is originally the murdered mother who, as a ghost, pursues Orestes.

What about our belief in the silence of the dead? Consciously we are fully convinced of this truth, but unconsciously the belief in the dead man's power to name his murderer still persists. Modern criminological methods still show traces of this belief, though in an entirely changed form. Those hidden fears that led our ancestors to institute the ordeal at the bier, are they not still extant when we lead the suspect up to the corpse and to the scene of the misdeed? To examine the dead may throw light upon the murderer. The savage learned something from the direction in which the blood flowed: nowadays we get information from the kind of blood, how it flows, whether there is a flow or not, etc. The evidence from blood is the predecessor of our modern clue. What we now make scientific use of was then meant to work by magic. The hidden connection between the two problems, apparently divided by a large gap, is unmistakable. Let us compare the scene at Siegfried's bier where, at Hagen's approach, the body begins to bleed, with the following description by Gross of a modern criminal investigation.[113]

The naked body of a peasant girl was fished out of the river. It was summer, and therefore it was assumed that she had been drowned while bathing. An autopsy revealed, however, that she was four months pregnant, and public opinion veered round and affirmed that she had drowned herself for this reason. But there were two dark-red parallel stripes all along her back. This proved that she must have been dragged over some object with two protuberances of equal height. The reactions to these stripes showed that she must have passed over this object while still alive. The stripes were measured and photographed and the river-bank was investigated in the direction from which the corpse had come. In the river bed, the root of a tree was found and on it a piece of clothing. Meanwhile, the identity of the poor girl had been established. Her mother was brought along and recognized the clothes as her daughter's. The girl had therefore not entered the water naked; the rushing water and the tree roots had torn her clothes off. But she had worn no shoes. After following the course of the river for some time the investigators passed the dead girl's house without having found the obstacle that had produced the stripes on her body. In the meantime the mother told them that her daughter had had a lover who was employed by a tanner. The tannery was a little higher up, so they walked upstream to it. Just below was a weir across which went a large rake, with crossbeams protruding several inches above the main beam, which was about a foot under water. Measurements showed that the space between the crossbeams was exactly the same as that between the strips on the victim's back. There was therefore no doubt that she had got into the water above the rake, though not far from it, because the reactions had shown that she was alive when the scratches were inflicted. Near the rake was the tannery where the girl's lover lived, the man was the father of the baby she expected. It was discovered that he had asked her to come to his house two days before, and that since then she had not been seen alive. There was hardly room for doubt that he had pushed her into the water.

The blood from Siegfried's body and the dark-red stripes on the girl's back are both clues for the examiner. And yet how different from our interpretation is that of the men of old gathered round the hero's body! The bloody scratches on the girl's body also point to the miscreant and suggest certain conclusions, and yet how different is the effect of those signs. The whole development of mankind—some people would say the whole progress of civilization—from magical thought to a belief in mechanistic causality is mirrored in this difference.

14. THE CRANES OF IBYCUS AND THE FLIES OF MR. BREESE

IN Schiller's poem the dying Ibycus charges the passing cranes to avenge him and the murderer betrays himself when he sees them flying over the theatre. What we live through in this poem is a psychological process. The appearance of the cranes is only a releasing factor in what follows; the essential thing is the unconscious compulsion on the part of the murderer to confess.[114]

One is tempted to reconstruct the original form of the legend[115] by taking into consideration the methods employed by ancient and primitive peoples for discovering the culprit.

In their view, as we have seen, the simplest way was to question the murdered man. But let us suppose that the victim cannot or will not answer. One of the ways of finding the miscreant then is the animal oracle. J. Dawson tells us about certain Australian tribes who bury the corpse and smooth the earth round the grave; the first ant that runs over it shows them the direction in which to look for the murderer.[116] The ant takes the place of the murdered man in answering the question. The Watschandis[117] in Australia clear the ground of stones round the grave and smooth it carefully. Every morning they look to see whether a living creature has passed by. Sooner or later they are bound to discover traces of some animal or other, and the direction indicated by them shows where the tribe is situated to which the murderous magician belongs.[118] The Wanyanwesi in Africa are convinced that all deaths are due to poisoning. To discover the murderer, the *bafüme* (priest-magician) cuts up a chicken and reads the murderer's name from the intestines.[119] This belief is also found among other peoples.

But who is that ant or that scarab which crawls over the grave and betrays the murderer? It is easy to guess. We need only remember the belief, widespread among ancient and savage peoples, in the soul-animal.[120] Later on the soul is represented as a bird; Odin's ravens accompany and represent him. The cranes of Ibycus have perhaps taken the place of the vultures which have eaten of the corpse, but they are originally the dead man himself in multiple form.[121] Their flight, not the murderer's exclamation, was the original clue; they indicated the direction, like the ant in Australia. No doubt this clue is as reliable for primitive peoples as an essential, objective clue is for us.[122]

These ordeal animals, as we shall call them, are probably animals that have come into contact with the dead man; they have perhaps eaten from his corpse.[123] This may include animals who have been near the dead, the idea of contact being extended as it is in the primitive belief in taboo. Ordeal animals, therefore, fulfil a magic function. The fact of their having originally been supposed to be the dead man himself in animal shape is quite consistent with the fact that in some cases they appear as ghosts or supernatural beings.

The primitive belief that an ant crawling over the victim's grave indicates the murderer must seem fantastic to the scientifically minded man of today. Naturally, such superstitious beliefs are alien to our modern criminology. The whole "pre-logical" thinking of primitive peoples is so fundamentally different from the strictly logical methods of our criminologists that it is almost sacrilege to name the two in one breath. To recognize the whole distance that divides them—a distance that represents a mighty piece of cultural development—we need only contrast with these instances of magical procedure, based on primitive beliefs, the logical processes of inference involved in a modern criminal case. Why not gain some satisfaction from the progress we have made in this field?[124] The following excellent example from American criminal history will serve the purpose:

On the morning of June 1st, 1925, a well-known millionaire, Mr. Ellington Breese, was found murdered in his home in Philadelphia. There was no doubt that he had been killed by poison gas manufactured in his bedroom. Breese's sevant, a Negro, had found his master dead in bed at eight o'clock in the morning. On the mantelpiece stood a quart bottle and beside it lay the stopper. The bottle was of the shape used in laboratories. The experts declared that a certain fluid had been poured on another one and poison gas manufactured that way. The gas must have spread rapidly in the room. Neither the glass container nor any other object showed fingerprints. Every living creature in the room had been killed by the poison, although the windows (two sash windows with curtains) were open about ten inches at the bottom. The bird was dead in his cage; a number of flies and midges lay dead on the window-sill.

Two young men, both well-versed in chemistry and familiar with the habits of the dead man, were at once suspected. One of them was Walter Breese, the nephew and only surviving relative of the deceased. The other was Breese's private secretary, Adam Boardman. Both protested their innocence; both could prove an alibi. The police ascertained that neither were in debt or had expensive habits. The only ground for suspicion in each case was a strong motive for the deed. Breese's will divided his fortune between charitable institutions and the two young men. Their combined share amounted to about half a million dollars. They both knew the terms of the will. The medical examination, undertaken two hours after the body had been found, established that the victim had been dead at least four, possibly ten, hours. To judge from the position of the body, death must have come unexpectedly.

It was thought that it would be possible to tell which of the two young men was the murderer if the hour when the gas was generated could be determined. Everything turned on this. For the private secretary admitted having been with Breese till shortly after midnight. The housekeeper, whose room adjoined Breese's room, deposed that the secretary had left the house about twelve o'clock. Boardman had discussed an urgent matter with Breese; he could prove its urgency before the court. He said he had returned once more to fetch his case. Then he had turned out the light in Breese's bedroom and pulled up the windows, leaving an aperture of about ten inches, all according to Mr. Breese's wishes. After that he had gone home to his flat which he shared with two other young men. His alibi for the rest of the night was quite reliable.

The nephew, Walter Breese, had been away and had returned from Washington unexpectedly about one in the morning. The housekeeper had heard him arriving and had talked with him in the corridor on the second floor. She had asked him if he wanted anything. He had answered that he was not hungry and was going to bed at once. He asked after his uncle and learned that he had had a business conference with his secretary until midnight. Then he went up to his room on the third floor. The housekeeper said she had not gone to sleep until four o'clock because of her rheumatism. She was bound to hear any steps going to the dead man's door. The detectives arrived at the following conclusion: if Breese had died before midnight, his secretary was the murderer: if he had died after that hour, his nephew was guilty.

Walter Breese had done the deed. The inference as to the time of the murder and from this to the murderer rested upon one single observation. The dead flies and midges were all found on the window-sill and not scattered about the room. Since the poison gas must have killed such small creatures instantly, they must have been near the window when the gas reached them. This meant that it was already dawn, because, in a dark room, light coming in by the window attracts insects. If it had still been night-time when the gas was generated, the flies and other insects would not have been on the window-sill.[125]

So Walter Breese was cross-examined again. At last he broke down and confessed. At break of day he had crept down to the second floor. Losses at the gaming table had driven him to the crime. He was executed in 1926.

Nobody would attempt seriously to equate the shrewd conclusions of the Philadelphia police with the superstitions of the Australian medicine man. Nevertheless, the two are connected by a path—not a straight one, but one with many curves and bends, rather like the line of development pursued by human institutions. The cold, logical inferences of the detective, which are carried on in the abstract and lead to such certain results, and the superstition of primitives, who set up causal connections that baffle our logic, have nothing in common. And yet—the ant running over a grave and flies in the room of the dead Mr. Breese —do they not fulfil the same function, namely, that of assisting in the discovery of the murderer? The American police started from a single observation, like the Australian magician—and yet a whole world seems to lie between them.

How do the priest-magician and his people arrive at the view that the ant indicates the direction in which to look for the murderer? It is so mysterious that in order to understand it we have to presuppose something still more mysterious—namely, that in the belief of these tribes the ant represents the dead man, indeed, *is* the dead man. This belief has deep underlying mental reasons, some of which we can guess.

How about that detective, whom we shall call Inspector Smith, whose chain of inductive reasoning solved the case of Mr. Breese? Well, he is, of course, officially, a Methodist or a Presbyterian and, among his intimate friends, an agnostic. Such senseless or grotesque opinions as those of the Australian magician are far from his mind. His method is not based on magic but on logic. In the case of Breese, for instance, the decisive factor was the exact time of death, not a mysterious belief. After examining the rooms, the inspector's gaze rested once again on the flies on the window-sill. Of course, he had seen them before when he made his first meticulous examination; they belonged to the scene and had been noted in his report as having succumbed to the poison as quickly as the dead man in his bed. What he noticed the second time was different. "How strange that they should be on the windowsill, the whole lot of them!" And from this not at all unusual perception there took place—so the layman would say—that precise and purely logical process of inference which led to its inevitable conclusion.

I do not think, however, that this view represents more than the uppermost layer of the psychical processes involved. It is for the most part a question of unconscious trains of thought that are not apparent in the logical deductions but rather hide behind them. The sight of the dead flies on the sill has led the inspector's thoughts back to how the deed happened, that is to say to the murdered man himself. By one of those unconscious identifications which take place on a level inaccessible to the ego, the dead man and the flies were equated, were, so to speak, connected by the same feeling. But this is fantastic, you will say; it means that the sober American detective is almost on the same level as the Australian magician who likens the ant on the grave to the dead man. But such a likening, especially under the influence of an affect whose extent need not be known to the ego, does occur. It reflects a regression into an ideational world hidden from consciousness, as we may assume it to exist in savages and children.

The thin veneer of culture, whose durability we greatly overrate, is stripped off for a few seconds and the individual has returned, unconsciously and for the time being, to a very early and primitive level of thinking. Probably this mental process is nearest to the one described by Freud in the psychogenesis of wit. In our example, a pre-conscious impression ("Strange that all the flies should be collected on the window-sill") sinks into unconsciousness for a fraction of a second and there undergoes a modification that leads to a surprising conclusion. This conclusion is seized upon by consciousness; the process itself remained unconscious and can be discovered only in retrospect. The essential underlying factor in this process of modification is the identification of the flies with the dead man, an equation based on the fact that both were killed in the same place, at the same time and from the same cause. At that moment, the barrier between man and animal, which is so important for our world, was removed in the mind of Inspector Smith, no doubt a very enlightened man, without his being aware of any such process. The train of thought that started from the observation of the dead flies on the sill and ended with the conclusion "they and Mr. Breese were killed in the morning" must be compared to a short circuit. The details of the mental process concerned are not accessible to analysis, but certain things become suggestive when compared to similar and known processes. I think, for instance, that we may assume that affective factors were involved in the perception of the flies. Moreover, the body of Mr. Breese was invested with a considerable amount of unconscious affect. This unconscious, unresolved affect accompanied the period of thought which followed and which itself proceeded only partly on a conscious level. The fact of the flies being on the sill must have been connected with a pre-conscious impression of their wanting to regain the light and freedom—to fly away. It was only afterwards, in order to justify this affective connection of ideas in the light of reason, that the inspector arrived at the conclusion: dawn must have been breaking.

It may sound unbelievable, but the logical process does not precede perception; on the contrary, it follows it. The result which our detective arrived at, with its admirable logical precision, is not, or only to a very small extent, the outcome of keen and sustained conscious thinking, but the working out of an unconscious association by the means supplied by consciousness. The most important function of logic, then, is to organize this intuitive perception coming from the unconscious, to give it the form of a logical operation and to examine its reliability. We suspect that the importance of this secondary character of logical processes goes far beyond our present subject and has not as yet been sufficiently recognized.

How did the specific impression of the flies lead to the conviction that the murder must have been committed at dawn and not during the night? The observer's mental processes go back from that impression to the unconscious affective cathexis of the dead man and in virtue of that association the affective cathexis is partly resolved. The fly, struggling towards life and light, and the unhappy old man, whose struggle for life began simultaneously, have been equated. Once more it is only afterwards that logical thought will seize upon this unconscious association and give it the form of a strict inference that can be presented to the critical intellect. Out of the raw material of such unconscious impressions emerges the fact of the time of the murder—a fact which is understood by consciousness and given its due value for the solution of the crime. It is possible that the conclusion: "If Breese was murdered at dawn his nephew must be the murderer" was based on unconscious impressions in the same way and only later received its logical superstructure, and appeared as a strict process of reasoning from cause to effect. Logical processes cannot deny their origin altogether; in the case of Mr. Breese and the flies they still retain a connection based on the time element—a connection which, psychologically speaking, of course, is a secondary and artificial one. What appears so surprisingly as the last link in the chain of logical inference had already been in existence in the unconscious. The surprise consisted in meeting with and recognizing something that was already known but repressed. In our case this repressed thing was the affective psychological equation of man and animal.

I am afraid that we have strayed rather far from our subject—the nature of clues. But the ants of the Australian magician and the flies in Mr. Breese's room are both clues in the criminological sense. Both constitute "circumstantial evidence," as our American inspector would call it; both point to the unknown murderer. I hope I have illustrated the deep psychological connection which still exists between modern criminology, so proud of its technical and scientific character, and the superstitions of certain Australian tribes on the lowest cultural level. All the progress we have made in criminology has not enabled us entirely to overcome our ancestors' animistic thinking. The old methods of thought have had to appear in a rationalized form and adopt the disguise of logic, like a kind of camouflage. However, we are not out to discuss those disguises but to show that the clue of modern criminology has its origin in the most primitive superstitions which we thought we had long ago overcome.

Naturally, the criminology of our time does not acknowledge oracle animals or animal oracles. The ant is no longer looked upon as the messenger of the dead or of the gods and as the betrayer of the murderer. One single chord of the ancient symphony of magic belief which once resounded through the universe still echoes in our sober time; we retain one trace of the old animal oracle, although so changed as to be hardly recognizable. It is no longer an oracle, but a rational form of help, methodically applied. I mean the police dog.[126] He is put on the track of the murderer,[127] follows his scent and eventually discovers him, sometimes many days afterwards. In the place of primitive magical practices we have put the training of animals in the service of criminal detection.

15. "Exoriare Aliquis Nostris Ex Ossibus Ultor"

WE have seen that, as primitive beliefs developed, the dead man gave up his function as the pursuer and avenger and was content merely to point out the wicked magician who had killed him. The process was like a cross-examination; the survivors asked the question and the dead man answered. The replies were given through his body, his blood or some imaginary movement.

Much more numerous, however, are the accounts of half-civilized peoples concerning another method—though one still connected with the dead man—of tracking down the miscreant. In these, the dead man, or rather some part of him, speaks and accuses the murderer. In *Grimm's Fairy Tales* we find the Hessian story of the singing bone. A jealous elder brother pushes his younger brother off a bridge into the water and buries him under the bridge. Many years after a herdsman drives his sheep over the same bridge. He sees there a white bone, picks it up and carves out of it a mouthpiece for his horn. When he puts it to his mouth the bone itself starts to sing:

> "O, my dear little shepherd boy,
> Out of my bone you've made a toy.
> My brother gave me a treacherous blow
> And buried my corpse in the sand below."

They dig under the bridge and find the boy's skeleton. The murderer is punished by drowning.[128] We hazard the guess that the phrase "spilled blood cries to Heaven" must once have had a literal sense. The theme of this Hessian fairy tale is found among many African tribes. The story of the murdered man whose arm comes up out of the grave is closely akin to it. An avenger does in fact grow out of the bone of the murdered man, as Virgil's lines predict. The same type of fairy tale is found in many countries.[129] In a Sicilian tale, a bagpipe is made out of the dead man's skin and bones, and gives the murderer away. In north African fairy tales, a pomegranate tree or a vine grows on the grave, and the fruit changes into the dead man's head.[130] There is a legend[131] about a dog belonging to a Viennese nobleman that unearthed some bones on a hunting expedition. They were given to a craftsman to carve handles for hunting knives, but as soon as he touched them they began to bleed. That terrified him so much that he confessed to having killed a comrade long ago in the woods and buried his corpse there.

We see that the bones of the dead man take over the rôle of accuser which was formerly played by his body. The bones "speak" and their words give the clue. In certain African and Australian tribes, this same belief is the basis of the criminological practice of the bone oracle.[132] A Kaffir consults the witch-doctor to find out the name of the witch who killed his child. The witch doctor takes some bones out of his bag and throws them like dice. He then asks the bones the name of the tribe to which the guilty witch or magician belong and the name of its chief. Each question is answered by a fresh throw of the bones; the witch doctor goes on asking until he has guessed the kraal and the hut of the offender.

The following is another example from west Africa.[133] In cases of disease or death, the Ganguellas call in a soothsayer to learn who has caused the misfortune. They move round in a circle and he stands in the middle. His outfit consists of a calabash filled with beads and dried maize and a basket filled with stones, human bones, sticks, bird and fish bones, etc. He invokes the spirits by wildly swinging the calabash. Then he upsets the basket and decides according to the spilled objects whether evil spirits or magicians are responsible. In the latter case he calls out the name of a certain person. The same is true in the Brisbane district in Australia; here, too, the bones of the dead man can tell the name of the murderer.[134] In Moreton Bay and the surrounding country, the question is answered by the skin of the murdered man.[135]

These methods are very different from those used in our civilization. And yet we are sometimes reminded of them when we hear of the way in which murderers of our own times are discovered. In the neighborhood of Hanover, the river washed up a human head and then a second one. A few weeks later a third was found. The river was dragged and a heap of bones was discovered out of which twenty-six complete skeletons could be made, all those of young men. It was evident that a mass murderer had been at work here. He was eventually found. It was the terrible George Haarmann, who, while acting as an agent of the criminal police, had killed countless people.

The savages think the bones of a dead man are gifted with

mysterious powers and talk a special language known only to the magician. In the Haarmann case, the bones also played a decisive part, though no longer a magical one. It is no longer the medicine man but his successor, the medical man, who does the investigating; and it is in the dissecting room that the bones tell tales about the murderer or, rather, about his victims. Medical reports and the deductions based on them became important for the work of the criminologist. One sees the contrast of magical as against scientific observation, and of divination as against deduction.

This difference of point of view is even more apparent if one compares the magical observation of bones with the mechanistic-causal one, when the latter is carried out not by scientific men but simply by experts. We find some examples in the field of magic. If the Watschandis in western Australia cannot find the miscreant in any other way, they take a handful of dust, throw it into the air and watch the direction in which it comes down. They then run in that direction to avenge the death of their friend or relative.[136] Levy-Bruhl, who quotes this custom, comments on the incompleteness of the report. It is not dust and fire as such, he thinks, that answer the question. This particular dust and fire have some connection with the dead man. It is he who answers the question by these means.[137] The custom of the Dyaks in Borneo belongs to the same category. They carefully watch the smoke of the fire in which the dead man is burned; if it does not burn steadily, but is diverted by wind or other causes they assume that the *anzu* (spirit) is not yet satisfied and there will be another death.[138] No doubt the dead man himself is accusing his murderer as he goes up in flames, and rendering a service to criminology in this ethereal form. The punishment is always death. The same holds good in the tribes of Victoria (Australia). Here also the smoke tells in which direction the guilty man can be found.[139] The dead man's sons or relatives start off in the direction indicated on an expedition of revenge and kill with their spears the first man they came across, quite convinced that he is the murderer.

Contrast these primitive conceptions with a modern example of observations of clues. Feuerbach tells of a young priest who had

killed several girls whom he had made pregnant. He cut up the
bodies carefully and burned them in the courtyard of his vicarage,
hoping to wipe out every trace. One day the little house opposite
the vicarage was bought by a butcher. His expert eye noticed that
the smoke coming out of the chimney opposite was of a peculiar
color, only produced by the burning of flesh and bones. This
observation brought to light the connection between the missing
girls and the priest's house.

16. The Technique of Magic and of Criminology

We have followed the development of the primitive solution of
crime up to a certain point. We have seen that at first the dead
man was himself the pursuer; then that he became the informant;
and later on that he delegated that office to others—to his relatives,
or to the priest-magician, or to animals, plants, etc., into which
he or a part of himself had been transformed. But the agent is
still the dead man himself, and only later do we find the view that
the elephant which tramples down the suspect, or the worm which
creeps in the direction of the enemy tribe are only acting on his
behalf. According to the original view—and it has its own consistent logic, though it is "pre-logical"—the dead man can lie in his
grave and yet be the worm creeping over the grave, a supposition
by no means more absurd than the Christian doctrine of tran-
substantiation. *"Hic et ubique,"* exclaims Hamlet, who hears
everywhere his father's call for vengeance. The dead man is indeed
here and everywhere. He is in the magician who names the murderer, in the bones that show the unknown murderer, in the
branch growing from the grave and in the bird which starts its
flight from there.

Repeated comparison of magical methods of detection with
modern methods produce a strong impression of certain similarities between them. The differences are too obvious to be

emphasized. For us it is more important to find in what layers of the mind the belief in clues originates and what the hidden connections are between those primal beliefs and the exact scientific premises of modern criminology.

If we start from the fairy tale, we find that it reflects the legal point of view of its time just as truly as other traditions do. In a Saxon fairy tale from Transylvania, a murder is betrayed by a flute made from a reed which has grown on the victim's grave.[140] In Hans Andersen's story of the *Rose Elf*, a murderer is killed by the jasmine flowers that grow on the grave of his victim. In the night the spirit of the flowering tree flies to the murderer's bed and kills him with its poisoned darts. This is a specific form of the revenge by flowers, a well-known fairy tale motif. The plant here takes over the will and force of the dead man. These motifs show the effect of the magic of transference. The nearness in space has produced a firm magical connection; a kind of infectious effect emanates from the plant growing on the victim's grave. The common belief on which the power of sympathetic magic is based is the belief that a sympathetic bond persists between a person and everything that has been a part of his body or has been closely connected with him. In some cases a plant has constituted a clue in modern criminology, too. Here, again, contiguity in space has been the decisive factor, but the use made of it is no longer magical, but mechanistic and rational. Contrast this revenge or betrayal by flowers, which so often occurs in fairy tales, with a modern case.[141]

On August 15th, 1910, a thirteen-year-old girl was missed in a little village near Arnhem in Holland. After a prolonged search the child's corpse was found in an oak wood. The girl had been raped and then strangled with a ribbon. There was no trace of the perpetrator. The spot showed nothing but dry oak leaves. Police dogs were employed, but with no result. Two suspected workmen, A. and R., were brought before the examining magistrate. The latter had been seen near the scene of the murder. Both were medically examined. When R's foreskin was drawn back a small dark substance was found which was removed with some cotton wool. The expert found it to be a piece of dried oak leaf, like the leaves that lay on the ground where the murder was done. This discovery was significant, because of the place on R's body where it was found. From the nature of the crime, this place was easily accessible for the oak leaf. The discovery made such an overwhelming impression on R., as he himself admitted, that he confessed to the crime.

Even when we recognize the enormous gulf between the betrayal by a plant in fairy tales and this example, the parallel is surprising. The expert's report may well have seemed to the prisoner like a piece of magic; hence the deep impression it made on him. There is no doubt that the expert's report has taken the place of the witch doctor's oracle, and that exact scientific observation has inherited the position of divination.

These examples would be classed by Frazer as contagious magic, because they accept connection in space, contiguity, as an effective principle. The principles of imitative or homeopathic magic are equally important for the development of criminology. Their importance is obvious when we remember that they are the direct ancestors of modern criminalistic methods. If one wants to injure an enemy, one must get hold of a part of him, his hair, nails, excrement, etc., and do that part an injury. The same thing that is done to this part will happen to the person—so magic avers. To injure an enemy, one makes an image of him out of clay or wood, and pierces it with a sharp nail. The Peruvian Indians used to make an image out of a mixture of fat and corn and burn it at some place which the hated person had to pass. They called this "the burning of the soul." The modern parallel might be the putting of a "wanted" person's photograph in papers, the *portrait parlé*. We learn that magical procedures can be performed on a person's footprints in sand. The natives of south-east Australia, for instance, believe that they can paralyze a man by putting sharp pieces of flint, glass or coal in his footprints. A. Howitt[142] says in his report on the Kurnai tribe of Victoria: "When I found a Tatungolung very lame, I asked him the reason. He said an enemy had put a bottle in his foot. I had a look at the foot and found that he suffered from rheumatism. But he maintained an enemy had seen his footprint and put a piece of glass into it."

Modern criminalistic technique no longer uses magical means, but physical and mechanical ones, to make bodily imprints serve for the finding and punishment of the unknown culprit. The magical use of fingerprints becomes dactyloscopy, the inimical treatment of the enemy's excrement, a chemical examination of the *grumus merdae*.

Among certain tribes in New South Wales, it is forbidden to put a young man's tooth in a bag for fear of exposing him to great danger. And the Basutos of Africa are afraid that an enemy may do them grave injury if he gets possession of a tooth that once belonged to one of them and subjects it to magical practices. These superstitions remind one of the many examples of criminal detection in which the imprint of a tooth in an apple or in a piece of bread has led to the finding of the culprit. We remember the successful examinations of such men as Jerserich and Papp who have contributed so much to the discovery of unknown criminals by their methods of minutely examining hair, nails, stains of blood and semen. A magician in the Marquesa Islands also takes the hair, nails or sputum of a man he wishes to injure, wraps them in a leaf and puts them into a bag; this is buried with certain ceremonies and the victim dies a slow death. A Maori magician who wants to bewitch a person gets hold of a piece of his hair or a fragment of his clothing. He chants curses over the object and buries it. While it decomposes, its owner is supposed to die a slow death. The modern criminological parallel to this is found in numerous cases. About ten years ago, a car was found on a high road near Berlin. It had run against a wire rope stretched across the road which had cut off the chauffeur's head. In the wire of the rope a microscopically small particle of wool was found. A minute examination showed that it must have belonged to a green sweater. The police looked for a man with a green sweater. They found such a one, and a comparison of the wool proved the two materials to be the same. The guilt of the suspect was eventually established.

We know what is the guiding principle of magic, thanks to Freud's investigations;[143] it is the belief in the "omnipotence of thoughts." Every example of a magical act which we have given in these pages shows this principle in full operation. And we shall demonstrate its continued existence in the later form of the clue. If we trace out the long path leading from magic, which has been called the technique of animism,[144] to modern criminology, which represents one of the techniques of our scientific age, we are struck by the tenacity and longevity of old beliefs.

We shall now go on to deal with the second characteristic that is common to magical procedure and the modern use of the clue—the phenomenon of "displacement on to details." The special importance attributed to small details in modern criminology has played the main part in the solution of crimes during the last few centuries. Magical procedures of primitive peoples show the same trait; the psychical accent shifts to small objects, far removed from the original magical ones. We have already given some examples which have shown this compulsion to displace on to details in connection with the investigation of murder.

These characteristics of belief in the omnipotence of thoughts and displacement on to details—both of which are observable in magic in an undisguised form and in criminology in a disguised and distorted form—are best understood if they are compared with neurotic symptoms. We must not of course expect to find an exact parallel. It is a question of similarities based on fundamental psychological premises. Let me compare the two aforementioned mechanisms with the symptoms of a certain patient who suffered from obsessional thoughts. This patient, a woman, wanted to buy a frame for her father's photograph. But she could not do so since the first frame she saw was of black wood, and this reminded her of a coffin. She could not buy this frame because if she did so her father would die. Eventually she could not buy any frame at all. This symptom corresponds exactly with a primitive belief in the magical effect of a given action and is on a par with the magical avoidances and precautions which we find in primitive peoples. Another exmple taken from the same case, shows the fear of the omnipotence of one's own thoughts still more clearly, as well as the displacement on to a small detail, such as we find in the magical acts of priest-magicians. The patient wanted to buy her little nephew a toy. She saw a beautiful little kangaroo figure with a baby looking out of its pouch, and was about to buy it when a terrible thought occurred to her. The kangaroo reminded her of the little boy's mother, her elder sister, who was going to have another baby. The toy with the baby kangaroo had suggested to her the possibility of an abortion. She struggled against this thought by forbidding herself to buy the toy. As in magic,[145] she presupposed the connection between the ideas to exist also between the objects themselves. The displacement on to a detail is also well illustrated in this example. The neurotic symptom tries to ban the unconscious wish that the sister should have an abortion. It shows a strong resistance against that unconsciously pleasurable idea.

Criminological detection most nearly resembles those magical procedures which exercise a hostile spell over a far-off person, and hold him fast or inhibit or injure him. Here criminal and criminologist are alike, because the latter uses means which in another connection we should call criminal. We shall understand this likeness better if we remind ourselves that both methods originally served magical purposes. The primitives have a public magic for the common weal, apart from private magic—which later on becomes secret and forbidden. The criminologist and the expert who are engaged in the solution of crimes are the successors of those priest-magicians who work in the service of official magic.

17. Oracle and Ordeal

We have, nowadays, become suspicious of those supposedly sound methods of reconstructing a hidden or mysterious deed. For many centuries nobody doubted the reliability of the strangest means of finding out the truth. The oracle, the judgment of God, the oath decided what had happened. The question put in an ordeal was answered unequivocally by its result. God's word was "Yes" or "No." Only later did it become more explicit; but it also became darker and more uncertain.

Our investigation has shown that the judgment of God was not a very primitive form of finding out the truth, although it probably existed in all peoples during a prolonged period of their development.[146] Originally it was not God who was questioned, but the dead. The dead—who were not quite dead—were asked the name of the unknown murderer and answered the question in their own way. This was, so to speak, the beginning of their divinatory powers, for later on they were asked all sorts of questions about private and tribal enterprises, war, hunting, etc. There is no hint of the origin of this art in the institution of the later religious oracle like that of Delphi or Dodona. In it the being who is questioned is no longer a dead chief but Phœbus Apollo, a god; but this god is himself perhaps only a successor of a forgotten chief of the Danaides. In the successive phases of primitive criminal justice, in which judgment is at first given by the dead man himself, and then by parts of his body, or by objects which have been in contact with him or in some way associated with him, we see that there is a common factor. The decisive clues are signs on the dead man's body or else stand in close connection with it. It is the dead man's body which, among Australian tribes, tells his relatives the name of the murderous magician, or which, in west Africa, pushes his pallbearers in the direction of the unknown murderer's house.

But this aspect of the ordeal stands in contrast to a much larger and more widely spread one in which the clues appear on the body of the suspect. Comparative folklore and cultural history give us a much richer material in connection with this second aspect. Let us choose some examples of the trials of strength and skill in Africa which a suspected person has to undergo and which no longer show any connection with the dead man. In Badagry the suspect is decorated with a large wooden three-cornered cap. If it trembles on his head he is condemned; if it does not he is acquitted.[147] Very similar to this is the oracle of carrying water among the Bafiotes. The suspect has to lift up a vessel brimful of water and imitate every movement of the priest-magician's dance. The priest discovers the culprit according to the direction in which the water is spilled.[148] The ordeal of pricking the suspect's tongue or ear lobe with a pin, or pouring certain fluids into his eye; the different poison trials, the trials by fire, hot oil, hot and cold water, etc., all belong to this category. All these ordeals have one thing in common; the clues are looked for in the body of the suspected person; this constitutes a striking contrast to the clues of the first group.

You will remember that our modern word "clue" refers to both kinds of signs and to many other kinds as well. In a murder case, the wound on the dead man's body is a clue as well as, for instance, the handkerchief left behind by the murderer. So far, in attempting to trace the idea of the clue from magic beginnings, we started from the signs found on the dead man's body. Now that this second kind of clue has emerged, we are led to ask ourselves which of the two is the primary one? How did these two groups develop historically and psychologically? What is their interrelation? And how and why are other clues observed that do not belong to this scheme? Let us contrast these two groups sharply and examine the origin of the second one. Any example will serve as long as it corresponds to the ordeals or oracles already described, and is directed to the detection of murder. Our example shall be the ordeal by poison, the effect of poison on the body of the suspect. The essential characteristic of this test is the effect of some food or drink on the suspected person which is to prove his guilt or innocence. This food or drink need not be poison, but it is always a special substance producing a magical effect. To limit our interest to ordeals by actual poison would be to miss their full significance. As Curt Wiedemann observes, "While all other kinds of ordeals occur in the Middle Ages, no ordeals by poison can be traced."[149] We must not forget that, in the Middle Ages, Christianity replaced the ordeal by poison by the Holy Communion. What is characteristic of the ordeal by poison is the expectation of a distinct effect on the suspect's body. The guilty man falls ill or dies, while the innocent shows no ill effects or else brings the poison up. According to medieval belief, the sinful man will die if he takes Holy Communion, while the pure may receive the Host with a quiet conscience. It is the same ordeal, but it has taken on a different form.[150] I should, therefore, suggest our using the more general term "oral trial" or "oral ordeal" instead of the narrower one, "ordeal by poison."

18. The Oral Ordeal

There follow a few African examples from our rich ethnological material. In Atakpame, poison is made from the bark of the *iroko* tree which is sacred to the fetish and may be touched by fetish people only. The poison is given to the suspect to drink with the words: "You have killed." He answers: "You kill by your accusation." If he vomits he is considered innocent. Otherwise he dies and is buried after his heart has been cut out.[151] The Beronga in southeast Africa add to the poison the fat of a man who has died of leprosy as well as a powder made from his bones. If the accused shows certain symptoms he is held guilty. Compiegne[152] describes how, in Jombe, the fetish priest makes a furrow about ten steps in front of the suspect to whom he hands the poison. He has to swallow it in one draught and advance at a given sign. If he falls in a fit before reaching the furrow his guilt is proved. His death agonies are shortened by the furious throng which tear him to pieces. But if he succeeds in passing the furrow he is considered innocent. Most African tribes believe in the innocence of the man who brings up the poison, and in the guilt of him who retains it or on whom it acts as a purgative. In Papabella, an infusion of Casca rind is used for the ordeal. Anyone who does not bring it up is hacked to pieces by the natives or roasted over a slow fire. According to Johnston,[153] everybody who is held responsible for a death undergoes this ordeal. The Masai drink a mixture of blood and milk.[154] In ancient Greece bull's blood[155] was drunk as an ordeal. The Israelites took the dust of the golden calf mixed with water, a kind of collective ordeal. Similarly, in India, a suspect had to drink water in which the images of the "terrible gods" had been soaked. While drinking he turned to the gods and said: "I have not done this deed."[156] In Madagascar a strong poison, *tanghin,* was used for the ordeal.[157] The accused had to eat some rice, then the accuser put his hand on the other man's head and began the adjuration of the poison: "Listen, listen carefully! Manamango! You are only a simple seed, quite round. Without eyes you see clearly, without ears you hear and without a mouth you talk. Through you God shows his wishes." It is hard to estimate the number of the victims of tanghin; according to what people say one person in five dies from its effects. In the last century about a tenth of the inhabitants of Madagascar underwent this ordeal; this means from forty to fifty thousand deaths in one generation through the ordeal, or fifteen hundred to two thousand deaths per year. A French official tells us of the Neyaux on the Ivory Coast where similar ordeals decrease the population, since each death causes four or five others. When a chief died, fifteen people followed him by ordeal. The French Government had the greatest difficulty in suppressing the ordeal, since the inhabitants were absolutely convinced of its justice, and, if innocent, willingly subjected themselves to it.[158] The same deep belief prevails among the natives of Calabar; this makes them appeal voluntarily to the ordeal to prove their innocence. According to a missionary, the Rev. Hugh Goldie,[159] a small tribe, the Uwet, in the hills of Calabar has become almost extinct through the consistent use of the ordeal by poison. On one occasion the whole tribe drank the poison to prove themselves innocent.

What is the significance of the oral ordeal? What does the belief mean—if there is any meaning in it—that he who retains the poison or magic substance is guilty while he who brings it up is innocent? So far there has been no satisfactory explanation; yet the psychoanalytic technique of interpretation refuses to think a custom absurd merely because it may seem so at the first glance. It looks for a hidden sense, a psychological connection that has been lost to consciousness. If we apply those principles of interpretation here the result is amazing. Originally, and to this day unconsciously, the poison or other substance which is taken must stand in a connection with the crime which it attempts to solve. It is not difficult to guess this relation. In a murder case the magic substance comes from the murdered person, is perhaps a part of his body or blood, or replaces these. If this view is correct the first explanation of the latent sense of the oral ordeal emerges. It is, whatever else it may be besides, a repetition of the crime (practised on a substitute) for the purpose of detection. Let us accept this suggestion provisionally, grotesque and improbable though it may seem. The suspect is made to take a piece of the murdered man's body. This means that if the suspect is guilty the flesh or blood of the murdered man will take vengeance on him by causing his illness or death; but if he is innocent he will vomit up what he has swallowed as something with which he has nothing to do. What is the special relation between the nature of the crime and the eating of a piece of the dead man? Our understanding of the unconscious principles of the mind carries us to a conclusion which alone will satisfy the archaic law of talion. If the suspect succumbs to the ordeal of eating a piece of the dead person his crime must have consisted in eating that person. This result seems less strange when we remember that for primitive man killing and eating was the same thing—that the murderer actually ate his victim. Our conclusion is, therefore, that the oral ordeal referred originally to cannibalism.

This origin of the oral ordeal has become lost to consciousness with the increasing secular repression of cannibalistic tendencies, but its effect points to its primary motive even in its later stages of development. We recognise the psychologic connection behind the magical one, since the deed which has to be expiated is repeated on a substitutive material in the later development of the ordeal. It is from this point that we can carry our hypothesis back into an earlier prehistoric time. We can see that the oral ordeal as met with nowadays in half-savage peoples is a later and weakened development of an original, much cruder trial. Originally the suspect had really to eat a piece of the murdered man's body or to drink some of his blood. Does not this remind us of the Christian Eucharist? Does not the mediæval use of the Holy Communion as an ordeal signify a return to an earlier form? In the belief that he who eats of the Lord's body in a sinful state shall die, the cannibalistic nature of Holy Communion is clearly recognizable.

An objector might reply that the oral ordeal is by no means restricted to murder, and that in those other cases the supposed operation of the law of talion could not hold good. Let us choose an example from southwest China, from the Lolo tribe[160] where, according to Colborne Baber, the oral ordeal is in frequent use. If anything valuable is stolen and the thief cannot be discovered the medicine man collects the people together and gives each one a handful of rice to eat. An interval of solemn chewing follows. The chewed mass is spat out. The presence of a bloodstain in it infallibly proclaims the thief. It is said that the gums of the guilty man bleed, and that he then confesses to the theft. Here, as in numerous other cases, there is no corpse and the ordeal stands in no visible connection to the nature of the misdeed. But our inferences refer to the origin of the custom and we cannot tell what changes it has undergone through the psychological mechanisms of displacement and generalization. The rarer the crime of cannibalism became, as a result of repression, the easier would it be to displace the oral ordeal on to the detection of other offences. Cultural changes helped this process of displacement. The oral ordeal appears in cases of other serious crimes besides murder or manslaughter; the original eating of a piece of the corpse and drinking its blood are replaced by other substances, which later on are only hinted at symbolically. But the figure of the murdered man still lurks in the background. The Bukongo in giving the casca bark to the suspect believe "that he will bring up the devil and spew him out."[161] Most African tribes regard the tree from whose bark the substance used in the oral ordeal is prepared as a fetish tree. In Angolo the taking of poison is called *nuam kissi,* the swallowing of the fetish. The primary meaning of the oral ordeal is almost symbolically expressed in what happens in Loango when a serious theft is committed. A banana is placed in the mouth of the fetish who is supposed to assist in the discovery of the criminal. The suspect has to extract this with his mouth and eat it. If he is guilty his body will swell and he will die. Does not this correspond to the óriginal picture of the guilty man eating a piece of the fetish, the sacred thing?[162] And the fetish undoubtedly stands for the dead chief.

Our investigation, which, it is true, has dealt only with a representative example of this second group of clues, has led to a surprising result. The difference between the clues observed on the dead man's body and the clues observed on the suspected man's body is not of any fundamental significance. An analysis of the oral ordeal has shown that its essence lies in the incorporation of a part of the murdered man by the supposed culprit. The oral ordeal may be regarded as the most significant example of a proof made upon the body of the suspect. Its most important element is still the effect of the mystical, magic substance. The effect of that substance on the suspect's body showed us the way to an analytic interpretation. The substance gives every indication of something alive and active, though it may be only a piece of dead flesh or its substitute. We suggest that the presence of this element as the earliest and most essential factor can be ascertained in most ordeals, whether they consist of hot water, fire or hot oil. It is not for us to trace in very single group of ordeals this latent connection which has become unconscious.[163] An expert in the comparative history of law should, with the help of the analytic method, be able to bring us nearer to a solution of this interesting problem.[164] We have come to regard the interpretation of magic clues originating in the dead man's body as an early form of criminal detection. The culprit is discovered through contact with the dead man's body or with a part of it; it is immaterial whether this contact takes place by means of the ordeal at the bier, or the bone oracle or the ordeal by poison. The ordeal furnishes the clue. We have supposed that the clues appeared at first on the dead man's body and then transferred themselves to the body of the suspect. This happens in a way that can best be compared to the process of infection. We should venture to differentiate the special kinds of infection according to the development of the different groups of ordeals. But our interest in the problem is, for the present, exhausted, since we have realized that, even in the disguised form of the oral ordeal, the dead man is alive enough to bring his murderer to justice.

Venturing farther into prehistoric times, we assume the existence of a period when the taboo of the dead was even more effective. The ordeal at the bier is undoubtedly connected with a taboo of this kind. In touching the man who is dead but whose soul has not yet fled, the murderer experiences the mysterious effect of that taboo. The solution of crime and its punishment, the production of evidence and the execution of justice are here still the same thing. The ordeal discovers the guilty man and expiates his guilt. Both happen in a magic way.

19. No Expiation Without Repeating the Deed

The analytic investigation of the ordeal by poison led us to the prehistoric original ordeal showing a single form of the proof which later became so differentiated. We found that the oral ordeal consisted in the suspect having to commit his cannibalistic crime again in an indirect way and on a substitutive object. But how can it be that the perpetrator is made to commit his crime over again as an expiation of it? Does this not make a thesis of a paradox, elevate what is contradictory to a scientific hypothesis? On the other hand, it cannot be denied that all the elements which we have discerned in the oral ordeal constituted a repetition of the deed. Has, then, our interpretation gone astray?

We must keep in mind that the main part of the ordeal lies in the production of evidence and not in the execution or punishment. The ordeal is meant to show whether the suspect is guilty by making him commit the crime again on a substitute. This is without doubt the original character of the ordeal. But is cannot be denied that it is at the same time a penal procedure: it ends with punishment. But we doubt whether punishment is the primary aim, the essence of the ordeal. Once again a symptom exhibited by obsessional neurotics offers itself for comparison. It is what Freud has called the unconscious tendency to annul or undo the act. The term is justified; but the presence of a tendency to expiation or penance is so marked that it would deserve to be included in the nomenclature. This tendency shows itself in small unobtrusive actions or movements that are seemingly absurd or ridiculous. The patient has to walk round a certain object in a certain way, or stretch out his right hand and touch something or gaze at his reflection in a mirror, and so on. He has a compulsion to do these things and would feel anxiety, or at least great uneasiness, if he failed to do them. Analysis leads to the conclusion that these actions are meant to undo or expiate former acts or movements, to paralyze their effect.

Through our technique it becomes possible to recognize the latent significance of such behavior and the nature of the acts the patient wishes to undo. Here is an example: a patient, a young woman, had to see about a hundred times in one day whether the water tap was turned off and did not drip. She could not explain her symptom, but it became clear when it was put into relation with her sexual life. That act, so often repeated, replaced symbolically another precaution that should prevent her becoming pregnant before marriage. The mechanism of displacement had so radically distorted the meaning of her action that it remained unknown to her consciousness. At the beginning of treatment the symptom strengthened, as is usual, before it became finally explained and disappeared. At the same time as it became intensified it changed its character. It had appeared as a precautionary or defensive symptom; the tap had to be closed, no drop must flow out. But now the patient's need for conviction became so intensified that she kept opening the tightly shut tap again and again to make quite sure it was closed. The suppressed impulse had come more and more strongly to the fore in the defence mechanism until it pushed the latter aside and remained victor in the substitute displacement. The character of annulling an act is first seen clearly in the displacement; the symptom appears as a reaction to the sexual act. The defensive symptom already contains what is being defended against, and becomes more and more apparent as a mixture and compromise between the impulses of warding off and the impulses that are being warded off—only, in the end, to give satisfaction to the forbidden set of impulses. This development of obsessive symptoms has a special, typical character; the symptoms begin with a strong defence against the instinct, and end, while apparently increasing this defence, with a victory of the instinct itself, with the repetition of the deed, in a changed form.

The development of the ordeal seems to find its psychological parallel in the genesis and change undergone by those symptoms of obsessional neurosis. Originally, to be sure, the ordeal was more in the nature of expiation than punishment; it probably developed out of the cleansing and expiation ceremonies which primitive tribes use after a taboo has been violated. It started as an expiation for the crime; but the tendencies that were operative in the crime must have come more and more to expression until the ordeal became a distorted repetition of the crime done on a substitute. Here a correction of our former hypothesis must be made in the sense that the oral ordeal cannot have been a very primitive phenomenon. Precisely this return of the repressed in the midst of the repressing forces proves that it must have been a later development. For the primary impulses emerge in a very distorted and generalized form. From this point the penal institutions can develop no further. Other institutions will henceforward carry on the old conflict between the defence against and the breaking through of forbidden instincts.

The oral ordeal as a repetition of the crime commanded by the community reminds us in many respects of an element in primitive religion—the solemn killing and eating of the totem animal.

In spite of the important differences between the two, the totem feast has the character of a collective ordeal. Its collectiveness is one of the differences; it is true that there are cases where whole tribes or villages subject themselves to an ordeal. Again, in the totem meal, all commit the crime once more; but the community sanctions it and so the crime becomes a duty. Like war, it is a crime ordered by society, and it probably awakened the same feelings in our ancestors as the order by the state for mass murder does in us. By participating in the killing and eating of the flesh and blood of the totem animal, all have repeated the old deed and satisfied the instincts which come to expression in the act. This satisfaction sanctioned by the community differs essentially, nevertheless, from the original one. It unites the participants with the totem and among themselves, and guarantees future abstinence. This collective ordeal, if the name is permissible, already exhibits all the features of compromise as we have come to know them in the oral ordeal, but it is without a doubt a sacred repetition of an otherwise forbidden deed. This characteristic still appears in the Christian Eucharist.

We have traced the ordeal by poison from the Middle Ages back to its prehistoric days, to the totem meal; we shall now follow its later development until it gives way to other institutions. An essential part of its latent significance, namely the repetition of the deed for its detection and expiation, is still recognizable in the latest and most varied developments of the ordeal, though that repetition may no longer have the same dramatic and plastic expression. The progressive distortion of the original meaning will take on more abstract forms.

A survival of the ordeal in modern penology is the oath. The oath substitutes the word for the original action and only reminds us dimly of the latter by a movement of the hand. And that earlier dramatic repetition of the crime has now to be enacted in the spoken word only, and receives a modest expression suited to our present-day culture. Examinations, production of evidence, explanations of the accused, reports of the experts, pleading of the counsel, all these are fragments which make up the whole—the repetition of the crime through the word. Culture has partly changed the function of this repetition; it has become a means of producing evidence and is now more complicated, difficult and time robbing, so that it is distributed among many people. But the main part is still played by the accused. He is as it were the hero of the tragedy and he must undo his crime. This, paradoxically expressed, can only be done by repeating it, by showing how it came about that he did it. The psychological effect of confession is better understood when we realize that it is a repetition of the crime in its palest form, in words. With this repetition a kind of undoing of the deed, in a magical sense, has been achieved. But this endeavor to undo by word and gesture, may be insufficient unless there is a strong affective reaction. Yet it remains an endeavor to master the deed mentally. Such an effect may seem strange. Perhaps it becomes clearer by a description of what happens when such a repetition, in the magical sense, does *not* follow. As this repetition consists in the partial coming to consciousness of the genesis and the significance of the crime, repentance or expiation is impossible without it. A thorough consciousness of guilt and an effective tendency to expiation is possible only when the instinctual satisfaction in the crime has become conscious in its whole depth. A condition of its becoming conscious is the recollection and its translation into words, as well as the affective reliving of the whole. Without a repetition of the instinctual satisfaction experienced the deed is lost to consciousness like hieroglyphics in the earth of Egypt. In analytical practice we observe that the fantasied repetition of what the patient feels as criminal and sinful is a pre-condition of the mental upheaval that leads to the overcoming of pathogenic experiences. Here the inner reliving of the deed combines with the "cathexis" of verbal images to bring about therapeutic success.

Without such a reliving of the deed and the gratification contained in it a consciousness of guilt is impossible, and this consciousness is a necessary condition of expiation. Without it, the word "expiation" or "punishment" loses its sense or descends to the level of a purely formal or mechanical legal term. It would be as though an untrained animal were to be punished for its natural behavior; the animal must first be aware of what its behavior implies before the punishment can have any sense—if, indeed, it ever does have sense.

The word "deed" must not mislead the psychologist. The culprit has committed the deed; but it would often be better to say that the crime happened through him. It is only possible for him to take cognizance of the participation of his ego in the crime if he remembers it affectively, that is to say, if he re-enacts the deed on a representational substitute. The problem is to lead the criminal to a recognition of his guilt in the psychological sense ("Do you recognize that you are guilty?") and not in the legal sense ("Do you admit being guilty?").

We regard modern criminal procedure as the most recent development of the ordeal. It contains—for a new purpose, to be sure, in order to find out the truth—a reconstruction of the crime, just as the ordeal does. But while the ordeal carried out the repetition of the deed on a concrete substitute, modern criminal procedure attempts to achieve it, in the form of language and logical inference, on an ideational one; and in this procedure circumstantial evidence is perhaps the most important element of such a reconstruction.

As a kind of a postscript to the history of the ordeal it may be mentioned that when the public expresses its pleasure of displeasure in court, the judge admonishes it sternly, usually adding: "You are not in the theatre." This is to emphasize the serious character of legal procedure. But not every judge knows how near to each other originally were the two institutions he separates so strictly. We have said that the ordeal was a representation of the deed, an expiation in dramatic form, an annulment by repeating it in a plastic displacement. But the content of ancient tragedy is nothing else than the reproduction of a serious crime, the rebellion against the gods, its solution and expiation. This is true, not only of the oldest Greek drama, but also of *Oedipus Rex* and of the Passion plays of the Middle Ages.

In the ordeal and its modern substitute the individual expiates

his crime. In the theatre the mass identifies itself with its individual representative, as Aristotle puts it, "in terror and pity" and
so deals with the emotion psychologically.

20. OATH AND TORTURE

IT is a naïve conception of history to suppose that when one institution succeeds another, the first one disappears entirely to
make room for the second, while this in its turn grows slowly old-
fashioned and at last becomes obsolete and gives place to a new
one. This is only broadly speaking true. The new institution is
very often only the old one in a modified form; and even the old
one survives in its original form side by side with the new one
and emerges, even though it seems to be submerged, again and
again under a new name. Sometimes it has stood aside in favor of
its descendant only for a time, and takes up its course again later
in the same or in a different direction, or else prolongs it in
another of its derivative forms. Like a human being, a social institution has often several heirs.

One of the descendants of the ordeal—the oath—still survives,
though not vigorously. It is a late differentiation of the ordeal.
At first the spoken word played no part in it. The oath on the
sword, on the pelt of an animal, etc., are originally by no means
symbolic acts, but magical actions. They are real ordeals. The perjurer was expected to perish by the sword or be devoured by the
wild animal upon which he swore. In ancient times and among
half-civilized peoples at the present day,[165] the swearer of the
oath called down a curse upon himself, but this is already a late
and differentiated form of an initially magical procedure. The
accompanying gesture or supporting action that is performed in
reciting the oath is a survival of what was once the only important
thing in the ordeal. The primal oath and the cleansing oath still
bear witness to its nature. The adjuration preceded the oath and

lives on in it. In the ordeal, the revered dead of the tribe were to designate and punish the culprit. In the oath, the gods were originally expected to punish the perjurer. The oath in legal procedure, though it may have become an abstract, empty symbol, nothing but a legal ceremony, is yet a degenerated relic of magic in law. Its survival shows how tenacious and long-lived social institutions can be.

Historical and ethnological material shows that, in a slightly more advanced stage of the ordeal, the accused will often take poison in order to prove his innocence. The oath isolates this aspect of the ordeal—the protestation of innocence—and only hints at the rest of it. In the ordeals of primitive tribes the protestation appears either not at all or is a mere detail. The main thing is the ordeal itself. Examples seem to show that the protestation of innocence or adjuration is a later appearance. The development from the ordeal to the oath is the result of two mental mechanisms. A piece of the original procedure became separated and gained a more prominent position while the rest lost more and more of its significance and was at last forgotten. They are the same mechanisms, isolation and displacement of psychological accent, the effect of which we study in the neuroses.

Another descendant of the ordeal is torture. The ordeals of half-civilized peoples often involve severe bodily pain. The ordeal seems sometimes to be a partial punishment; the full punishment follows when the guilty man is found. When we read in medieval reports of a thief who has to undergo the ordeal by fire and that "the red-hot iron burned his hand; so the bishop had him hanged,"[166] we ask ourselves whether the burning was not sufficient punishment. Indeed, investigation shows that ordeal and punishment were often one and the same thing. He who perished in the ordeal by poison had his punishment. We may suppose the tendency towards cruelty in the ordeal to have become strengthened, for here, too, as in the more recent oath, a part of the process of the ordeal, i.e., its purpose, became isolated and went through a special development which later on led to its having an entirely independent existence. In addition, a new motivation and a transformation of purpose appear in the development of the oath and the ordeal just as they do in neurotic symptoms. The ordeal was a conjuration but the oath loses its character as ordeal more and more. Its aim becomes a different one. From a magical adjuration to the gods it becomes a solemn confirmation of a statement—at first the statement only of one's own innocence in the cleansing oath. Only in the belief that higher powers will mete out terrible punishment to the perjurer do we still find a trace of the original nature of the oath. The decrease of religious faith has replaced the fear of superhuman powers by that of the punishing state.

Hans Fehr has shown how superficial the usual interpretation of medieval torture is. I consider him right in his opinion that there is still a strong connection between the judgment of God and torture, that torture is, so to speak, the heir of the ordeal. The original aim of torture was, according to Fehr, a magical one. The devil who possessed the miscreant must be expelled. Only very late did the other motive—that of obtaining a confession—become predominant. The preparations and the ceremonial preceding torture of which we read in medieval documents show that its origin was the ancient ordeal.

Evidence obtained from witnesses is also by no means so recent a feature as modern compendiums of the history of law would have us believe. It would be truer to say that such evidence was recognized only later on in its material significance. This institution, too, had its magical predecessors; it is recognizable in the institution of the *Eideshelfer* ("co-jurors") in early Germanic criminal procedure. Those respectable friends and neighbors of the accused were not meant to support the objective truth by their oath, but to draw the wrath of the gods upon themselves if their friend was guilty. It was only under the influence of great cultural changes that this magical custom was transformed into rational statements of fact by witnesses under oath. The statement itself had appeared earlier in penal law, but its magical character had to recede before it could become important for the establishing of the actual facts of the case.

Christianity at first rejected these institutions—which is an other proof of their magical and pagan origin. The ordeal was at first damned by the Church, then assimilated and changed. The same applies to torture which was only much later used *ad majorem Dei gloriam*. The oath was originally a magical means of finding out the guilt or innocence of the accused. It belonged to inquisitional procedure like torture, which is a modified ordeal. Later on both oath and torture became a means of procuring evidence and of assessing its value. The change was at first slow, then became more and more rapid as the belief in the effectiveness and significance of those means decreased. It is as if, in proportion as their function of discovering the crime disappeared, they tried to become more important as a means of procuring evidence. At last examination and cross-examination took their place.[167] We have already met with this inverse ratio between belief and official significance in the development of the ordeal. Here we come across it again. And we shall rediscover it once more in the field of circumstantial evidence.[168]

21. From Magical to Scientific Circumstantial Evidence

We have expressed our mistrust of the traditional interpretations made by the history of law, which postulates an ordered sequence of ordeal, oath, torture and the modern adducing of evidence, especially circumstantial evidence. We have said that such an interpretation was only broadly speaking true. A deeper investigation will show how superficial it is. Circumstantial evidence has always been known; it is only the nature of the clue and its interpretation which have differed. Historians of law cannot see, it is true, any connection between a bone oracle and the evidence of a chemical analysis,[169] but to us the inherent, psychological connection is abundantly clear.

The development from one to the other could be demonstrated

in the case of murder. The ordeal at the bier was founded on the animistic conviction that the dead man would accuse his murderer. The wounds starting to bleed afresh were clues like those in our modern court procedure. Later the custom was changed. If the suspected person could not be brought before the bier, the corpse was carefully examined, and if death by murder was diagnosed the clothes worn by the dead man were carefully preserved before he was buried, in order to take the place of the corpse as soon as the culprit was seized. Here we come within sight of modern circumstantial evidence, though we still have the animistic interpretation, as the clothes were believed to retain the magical powers attributed to the corpse. In our modern procedure also, the clothes of the victim are shown to the suspect, though not as magical objects. The transition is best seen in the institution of the *Scheingehen* as once used, among other places, in Bamberg. A man could be executed, according to Grimm,[170] if he confessed (*Gichtiger Mund*), if he was caught red-handed (*handhafte Tat*) or by visible proof (*Blickender Schein*). The murdered man's hand was severed, usually by the plaintiff, and placed on the table while the court was sitting. The accused, dressed only in a loincloth, had to advance, kneel down and put his hand three times on the *Schein* (i.e., the hand), lift it up and protest his innocence. If he was guilty, the dead hand gave some kind of sign (e.g., blood would appear on it). If there was no sign, he was acquitted. Schroder and other historians interpret this *Blickender Schein* as an inspection by the court in our modern sense. But the dead hand is not like our modern proofs. We have here a real ordeal, as the signs on the hand and the whole ceremonial clearly show. The part possesses the same power as the whole. The belief that the hand will give a sign is a product of a later phase of animism. But when the hand becomes a means of adducing evidence in modern court procedure, then we have left the medieval world behind and stand on the threshold of a new era. It is no longer the magical power of the object, but its value as a material clue that is decisive.

It is for the historian of law to follow up in detail the ideas here outlined. He should show us how the old ordeal slowly made room for inquistional procedure and yet continued to live on in the new method in a disguised form, how the psychological accent shifted on to the understanding of the facts, and how, when the ordeal was forbidden in 1215, a new form of ordeal, that of questioning under torture, inherited all the evidential value of its predecessor.

The ordeal might be described as primitive circumstantial evidence of a magical kind. Owing to social and cultural changes the belief in the magical powers of this evidence weakened. The *Constitutio Criminalis Carolina,* the criminal code promulgated by Charles V in 1532, already acknowledges circumstantial evidence, but views it differently. It lays down that such evidence shall never be the basis of condemnation, because no clue can give absolute certainty. But if suspicion against him was strong enough the accused might be questioned under pain and tortured. Condemnation was possible only after confession or on the declaration of two or three "reliable and good" witnesses—so-called classical witnesses (C.C.C. Art. 22 and 67). In most cases to obtain such a confession torture was used.

When feeling revolted against this questioning under torture a reaction set in. Torture was restricted and later abolished altogether, though the voice of authority predicted the end of morality and all social order as a consequence. There was a return to circumstantial evidence, although it was regarded with suspicion, as the strict rules imposed upon the courts show. The authorities differentiate between the clues, give a list of those that alone carry weight and declare that condemnation is only possible on the basis of a certain number of clues belonging to different groups. The statute of Joseph II of 1788 and the Austrian Penal Code of 1803 quite rightly use the expression "proof by a concurrence of circumstances" when referring to circumstantial evidence.

It was an elaborate and formal system: what did not fit into it did not as it were exist. Here we are in scholastic times where not the content of the clues, but their grouping and dialectic nature were decisive. This precision was meant as a protection for the accused, but was in reality the climax of the inquisitional process, since all the officers of the law vied with one another in finding such clues as would serve to condemn the accused. With a conscientiousness that can only be compared to that found in obsessional neuroses, the clues were examined minutely to ascertain whether they conformed to the rules laid down. Strangely enough the material proved plastic and obedient; it did conform to the rules. Torture had disappeared, but the new psychological examination became a kind of psychological torture. It must have been this carrying of the rules of evidence to extremes, on the lines of a neurotic system, with its contrasts of conscious and unconscious intentions and its tendency to isolation, that led to a new reform.

The new penal code of the nineteenth century, with its features of publicity, directness and oral pleading, and with its marked character of an accusation, shows the breaking through of old tendencies. This renewal involved a change in the procedure relating to proof. The catalogue of evidential clues was enlarged, and even the adducing of evidence of a crime was considered only as "illuminating judicial reflection." The condition that the evidential matter had to belong to different groups was given up. In the last phase of this development, all rules for bringing proof were dispensed with. The judge no longer decided according to formal, external criteria but according to his own free conviction. His judgment was based on the impressions he had gathered from the case as it was conducted before him.[171] He might regard as evidence anything that seemed to him to have a bearing on the crime and the accused. He had to draw his own conclusions about the evidential value of specific clues. Indirect or circumstantial evidence was now equal to direct proof, and could serve as a basis for the infliction of the severest sentences.

The use of circumstantial evidence has been more and more enlarged. And indeed a conclusion reached on the basis of circumstantial evidence may be as convincing as one founded on direct statements of witnesses. It is well known that there are many objections to circumstantial evidence; but judges and counsels for the prosecution, criminologists and teachers of penal law assure us that it is better than its reputation. Yet the long record of judicial errors founded on circumstantial evidence carries its own warning.

Attacks on circumstantial evidence have often been directed against conclusions drawn from witnesses' statements which so often doomed the accused. Psychology has shown that an erroneous statement is the rule and not the exception. The newest phase in the establishment of proof is characterized by the high value set upon material clues. They cannot lie, nor give a wrong or distorted evidence, nor contradict each other; they are excellent witnesses that cannot be bribed. The odium that used to attach to indirect evidence has disappeared with the increased importance of material clues. A well-known criminologist says:[172] "Though wrong conclusions based on such evidence are not entirely impossible, if experienced experts are employed the possibility is smaller than with any other kind of proof, except perhaps a direct confession." This conviction, which has become general, was summed up by a judge who declared that there could be no doubt that the future belonged to circumstantial evidence. This was soothing and inspired confidence; it was a paraphrase of the prophecy, *Quidquid latet apparebit; nil inultum remanebit.* Yet doubt will raise its head in spite of such prophecies.

22. THE LATENT CHARACTER OF CLUES

SINCE the comparative study of law can tell us little of what we want to know, we have ventured to embark on researches of our own into those fields of interests. Badly prepared and undertaken with insufficient means, our investigations are bound to exhibit the faults of the layman. But they arrived at a result which in spite of, or because of, its strangeness seems to deserve re-examination. They seem to show that the origin of the clue was magical; that the prehistoric clue resembled the clues of modern criminology and that it, too, could be used to solve a crime. It is true that it was differently valued and interpreted. But the connection between the magical clue and the modern one is recognizable in spite of the difference in their cultural level.

An early form of the magical clue was the signs on the body of a murdered person, which were interpreted by primitive man in a certain way. From here the idea of the clue shifted to the suspect, to signs on his body, his weapons and other belongings, and furthermore to the time and place of the crime—in short, to everything that could be associated with him. We do not know how such a displacement came about, but the fact remains, and we have to resort to an hypothesis to explain it. One explanation is based on the strong consistent belief in the power and effect of the taboo in primitive cultures. Crime was originally a breaking of taboo; and the criminal was detected by the effect of the broken taboo. There is no absolute proof of the correctness of the theory here outlined, but there are many facts that render it probable. I will give one example that shows plainly not only the origin of the later clue and the line of development from magical inter-pretation to our modern scientific one, but also supports our view that the displacement undergone by the magical signs or clues follows the same paths as the laws of taboo.

The Kai, in what was formerly German New Guinea, among whom the missionary Charles Keyser lived for a long time,[173] re-tire quickly after a successful expedition and spend the night at home or at least in the shelter of a friendly village. The reason for this haste is their terrible fear of being caught during the night by the ghosts of the enemies whom they have killed. Like blood-hounds, these powerful ghosts follow their tracks in the dark; they want to catch their murderers and by touching their blood-stained weapons regain the life they have lost. Only then can they find peace and rest. For this reason the victors do not bring back their weapons to their native village, but hide them provisionally in the bush. There they are left for several days until, it is assumed, the disappointed ghosts have returned to their mutilated corpses and burned-down huts. The first night after the warriors return is always the most dangerous time. All the villagers are on the watch against the ghosts; but when this first night is over, their terror slowly passes till at length they are afraid of their enemies alone.

The belief in the magical attraction of spilled blood arouses this terrible fear in the victors, causing them to flee in haste and to hide their murderous weapons. A suggestion, supported by other ethnological material, offers itself. The hiding of the weapons may also be due to a general fear of the contagion inherent in the bloodstained spear or axe, a fear that the weapon may turn against the victor in the sense of talion. In any case it is a measure of safety dictated by the belief in taboo. I think we are right in calling such a weapon a magical object, a forerunner of the clue. The ancient dread of the murdered enemies' ghosts, who find their way with the help of the bloodstained weapon, is in modern times replaced by the fear of the police who make use of the instrument of murder as a clue, and still has its unconscious effect just as in the case of the victorious Australian warrior. He, as well as the modern murderer, will hide his weapon, though the conscious reason is a different one. The motive has only changed its shape, not its essence. Clues become rational indications instead of magical objects; their importance shifts from the psychological sphere to material reality. Long ago they were examined by the magician; now they are interpreted by the chemist.

The magical character of the original clue presupposes an animistic view of the world. The clues which we regard as inorganic and material were for the primitive man not only alive, but imbued with a personal will. They betrayed the murderer because they wanted him to be punished. When the unknown murderer approached, blood flowed because it wanted to proclaim him. A scrap of paper left in the place of crime is nothing but a scrap of paper; though we may say it "tells a story" this is only a poetic mode of expression. When we measure the footprint of the escaped criminal, take a plaster cast of his teeth, retain the lines of his hand for comparison with other hands or have a thread of his suit chemically examined, we do so because all this helps to catch and punish him. We treat these clues as part of him. But for the fetish priest in the primitive world such a clue really *is* a piece of the culprit and he treats it accordingly. He will drive a nail into the footprint to arrest the unknown criminal, burn a hair he has found or murmur curses over a tooth.

What we wish to stress here is not only this difference in the interpretation of clues, but the survival of animistic ideas within our rational and scientific principles. That is to say, modern man still unconsciously believes that those inorganic objects which he calls clues are endowed with life and with magical powers. His purely rational view, which values clues only according to the laws of science and logic, is opposed by a secret trend of thought which sees in them objects with an existence of their own and having a hidden power. Often both tendencies lead to the same goal by different paths, the rational, modern tendency following in the traces of its magical predecessor. Applied science has had many triumphs in the field of empirical circumstantial evidence. But it not infrequently happens that judges and jury, counsel for the prosecution and experts, all too sure of their logic and reason, are guided by invisible powers that have already decided the question of guilt or innocence. The infallibility of judicial decisions is still endangered by an unconscious animistic belief which resists rational interpretation. In many cases the judge might avoid coming to an erroneous conclusion if he could banish magic from his path.

23. CIRCUMSTANTIAL EVIDENCE AND JUDICIAL ERRORS

THE famous case of a young baker who was hanged, although innocent, a few centuries ago, led the Venetian Senate to adopt the following practice. Every time there was a trial which might result in sentence of death, an ambassador of the Senate appeared in court and exclaimed solemnly, "Remember the poor baker."

If such an institution had survived into our own times, the

official in question would have to recite a whole catalogue of judicial errors. Even so, the catalogue would not represent the real number of terrible miscarriages of justice, since so many have remained, and will always remain, unknown. One might object that in former times the methods of investigation were poorer and, therefore, there were more judicial errors and that such errors should be rare events with our improved modern methods. But the rich material collected by Sello, Alsberg, Hellwig, Rittler and others shows how many judicial errors result precisely from circumstantial evidence, on which our penal code is based.[174]

Nobody can gainsay us if, as psychologists, we examine the material before us as data for a pathology of judicial judgments, so long as we confine ourselves to the field of psychology. We could, out of many examples, select now one characteristic, now another, and show how each contributed to the commission of a judicial error. I should prefer, however, to illustrate by a representative example the part played by psychological factors in the genesis of such errors. I realize the objections to such a procedure and propose to deal with the most outstanding ones at once. It is true that a single case cannot show all the psychological possibilities; it has to leave out of account many important ones. But I only want to consider those psychological factors that are especially important in the psychogenesis of errors of justice. And any of the more important psychological aspects of the problem which this one case cannot demonstrate, I shall attempt to indicate by a brief reference to other examples of misleading circumstantial evidence. I cannot, of course, hope to exhaust the rich material before us in this way, but I can draw the attention of other workers to its richness.[175] The minute description I propose to give of this one example is justified by my intention to illustrate through it the important mental happenings with which we are concerned.

The most suitable example is, I think, a murder case that occurred forty years ago. The case was very carefully conducted at the time and the evidence was entirely of a circumstantial character. It is cited as a representative instance of a judicial error based on circumstantial evidence in the collections of Sello and

Hellwig and has been carefully studied by teachers of criminal law, judges, and counsels for the prosecution. After studying the case, no unbiased person will doubt how frail are the foundations of human justice.

On the morning of October 28th, 1886, the body of a domestic servant, Juliane Sandbauer, was found near the little market town of Finkbrunnen in southern Austria.[176] It was lying in a barn which belonged to a certain Andreas Ulrich. The head was terribly injured; the skull was quite battered in. The whole village was convinced that a tanner, Gregor Adamsberger, was the murderer. Juliane Sandbauer had been in his service several years. He had not been married long and had two young children, but he had started at once to make love to the girl who was eight years his junior, and in the course of four years they had had four children. Though she left his service she came to see him practically every day. Both had a bad reputation; she was said to be unsteady, he brutal, revengeful and hotheaded.[177] Talk went round that they pilfered fields at night. There had been violent scenes between them because the woman kept asking her former lover for money. The Sunday before the murder a witness, Hans Berger, had seen Juliane leaving Gregor's house and had heard her exclaim, shaking her fist at the house, "I'll report you to the police." The circumstances to which this referred were well-known. On September 30th, 1879, one of Gregor's outhouses had been burnt down, and he had received 3,000 florins from the insurance company. In 1882, Juliane told several people that she had set fire to the outhouse at the instigation of her employer, who wanted the money. One evening in 1881 she had called out to Gregor in the marketplace, where everyone could hear her: "You made me set fire to that outhouse; I have stolen more than 200 gulden for you." Later she said she was drunk when she told such stories, and had only done so to get her own back on Gregor who ill-treated her. It was known that he used to beat her; he had been seen driving her out of his house with a stick. Another neighbor deposed that Juliane had often threatened to report Gregor for arson. Only the week before the murder she had said that if she did not get money from

Gregor for herself and her children she would go to the police. Gregor himself used to threaten to "kill that devilish woman."

Gregor had to admit that Juliane had spent the last hours before her death in his house. His mother-in-law, a woman respected in the village, had not much good to say of him. She told the court that on the evening of October 27th Gregor's two children had rushed into her room and said their mother had sent them away because their father was quarrelling violently with Juliane. She seemed almost to have heard the quarrel, for she continued: "Soon after, I heard a sudden scream in Gregor's house. I thought it was Juliane's voice. Then all was quiet." Nobody had seen Juliane alive after that. Next morning her body was found.

When Gregor was confronted with these facts, he protested his innocence in the strongest terms. He admitted that Juliane had been to see him on the evening in question, but she had not stayed long. She said she was going to her lover, the son of Anton Kunz, the baker, and he had not seen her since then. The first examination ended here; he had no more to say.

Nevertheless, some days later, he added a few details before the examining magistrate. He said that Juliane had often told him that she was in the habit of meeting young Franz Kunz in his parents' garden house. On these occasions he had given her food and drink, and that evening she had promised to meet him secretly in the garden house. He, Gregor, had lent her an old coat as she had said she was cold. Indeed, an old coat, later identified as Gregor's, had been found on the corpse. But why had he not mentioned this before? Why had he waited till the coat was recognized as his? If this looked suspicious, what about his story of Franz Kunz? Franz was a weakly adolescent of sixteen, who was known in the village as a modest and virtuous youth. A love affair between him and an ugly woman twice his age, who stood in bad repute, was most unlikely, and the more so because nobody in the little town had any inkling of it. Gregor's story, to which he stuck obstinately as stupid liars will, was obviously untrue; that was proved by what Franz Kunz's mother said in respect to the fatal evening. Her son, who was apprenticed to the father's business, had, she declared, retired at 6 p.m. that evening and gone upstairs with her and his brothers and sisters. He had gone to bed at once and had only got up at midnight to go down to the bakery. Franz himself, in the quietest and most convincing way, denied having any connection with Juliane. He said that the story of the meeting at night was "of course" invented. He also mentioned the well-known fact that Juliane expected another child by Gregor. He finished by saying: "I should like to say that everybody knows how cruelly Gregor treated the woman. I know myself that she came crying to our house with injuries to her head, saying that they were inflicted by him."

Later on, Gregor tried to strengthen the suspicion against Franz, but what he said was shown to be quite untrue and made his own case worse. He said that Juliane had told him she had sent a letter to Franz on October 27th by her thirteen-year-old son, asking him to keep money handy for her. This letter the boy had given inadvertently to the errand boy, Valentin Pirgauer, and Franz had scolded her soundly for being so careless. Juliane's son declared the story to be untrue, and Valentin Pirgauer said it was a pure fabrication, adding: "I don't believe a word of this love story, because Franz is too young and inexperienced, and such a story would not be likely to remain a secret in a little village like Finkbrunnen." This strengthened the official view that Gregor had invented the story to save his own skin by incriminating Franz Kunz.

Gregor's subsequent behavior made this seem even more probable. Seeing that his story had not had the desired effect he tried to incriminate another neighbor who had, so he said, lived in enmity with Juliane. A search of the man's house produced nothing.

The whole village voiced the conviction that Gregor was the murderer.[178] When the dead woman was found on October 28th, she was lying on her back with her face turned sideways. The barn was in a field near the hamlet. The body had twelve injuries, mostly on the head, some of them very serious. The inquest proved another important fact. Juliane was in the seventh month of pregnancy. Franz Kunz had mentioned this. Was this not the true motive of the crime? The doctors declared the injuries had been inflicted with a sharp axe and the murder had been deliberately planned.

The owner of the barn, Ulrich, made a strange statement. When he found the dead woman her clothes were pulled up round her body, and he and the man who joined him had therefore concluded that she had been murdered during or just after sexual intercourse. They pulled down her skirts for the sake of propriety, so that when the body was examined by the police it was no longer in its original condition.

Counsel for the prosecution moved that the corpse should be exhumed, as several points in the post mortem report were not quite clear. This was done; the corpse was re-examined and a second report made, stating that Ulrich's suspicion did not correspond with the facts. The experts further declared that the murder could not have been committed in the place where the corpse was found. There was only a little blood on the ground and the clothes had very few bloodstains in spite of the terrible injuries inflicted on the body. They also said that the blade of an axe found in Gregor's house fitted exactly into one of the victim's head wounds. A wound in the shoulder of a crescent shape had obviously been inflicted with a knife with a curved blade, such as tanners use to cut soles. Since it was improbable that the murderer had carried the corpse alone to the place where it was found, the assumption was that Juliane had been murdered in Gregor's house and that he and his wife had carried her to the barn where she was found. Now Gregor's wicked story appeared in a new light. He had arranged the girl's clothes in such a way that the suspicion he threw upon Kunz would appear more likely.

Gregor's wife must have helped him. She must have hated her rival. Her behavior on the day after the murder had been suspicious. A neighbor made the following deposition: "I went to the Adamsbergers when I heard of the murder and asked Mrs. Adamsberger, 'Where is Julie? She has been found killed.' 'Killed,' Mrs. Adamsberger repeated, without showing any emotion. Then Adamsberger, who must have heard my words through the open door, came in and I saw that his face, which was very red, changed to a remarkable pallor. 'How is that possible?' he said. 'Last night she was still here. I lent her a coat and she went through the cutting which leads into the field to fetch milk.' I know that Juliane was very timid and never went out alone at night. I then left their house, and I learned that Maria Adamsberger followed me very soon after down to the brook, where she was said to have washed something in a great hurry."

This witness, a peasant woman, who, according to the record, spoke such correct official language, added that Gregor always ill-treated Juliane when she was pregnant by him. At such times she used to come to the witness, show her her injuries and complain that Gregor meant to kill her. Two other women deposed that Mrs. Adamsberger had indeed secretly hurried down to the brook. What was more likely than that she had washed the bloodstained clothes, as she had to reckon with a search in her house?

The motive was clear. Gregor wanted to get rid of his inconvenient mistress, and the increased responsibility of another child. She also shared the secret of his arson and was always greedy for money. He was accused of murder and convicted. Such a conviction should have entailed death. But there were formal difficulties in the law which limited the punishment to imprisonment for life.[179]

At first Gregor lodged an appeal but he changed his mind and began his prison life on July 30th, 1887. And so a serious crime seemed to have found its expiation. No official connected with the case appears to have had the slightest doubt about Gregor's guilt, and he seemed to admit it himself, since he did not appeal against the verdict. In such a case where all the evidence, material and psychological, testified to the man's guilt a confession was unnecessary.

Two years after Gregor had begun to serve his sentence a decisive change in the situation occurred. Since the spring of 1889, a baker in Seefeld called Georg Halter had had an assistant with whom he was highly satisfied. He was cheerful and had a good character, avoided the company of women and spent his leisure hours in doing fretsaw work and playing on the zither. This assistant was Franz Kunz who Gregor had, for such obvious motives, accused of murdering Juliane. On January 20th, 1890, Franz Kunz handed two letters to his master's son, saying: "Deliver these letters at their addresses. I have been an unhappy creature for the last four years." He then locked himself in his room; and when the door was broken in he was found with his arteries cut open. The doctor was able to stop the bleeding. The two letters, one directed to the law court at Marburg and the other to his own parents, gave his reason for suicide. They contained a detailed confession of his murder of Juliane. He had been unable to bear the reproaches of his conscience any longer. Later he repeated this confession before the court. He said he had been seduced by Juliane when she came to buy pastries and found herself alone with him. Since then they had often met secretly in his parent's garden house, but nobody in the village had an inkling of their relations as they kept them very quiet. After some time Juliane told him she was with child by him, and began to frighten him with threats and blackmail. He had to steal food, liquor and money from his parents and give them to her. She threatened to put the baby on his parents' doorstep. Two days before the murder she had again asked him for eight gulden which he was unable to give her. His life had become such a burden to him that he had decided to rid himself of her at all costs.

He described exactly how he had proceeded. When Juliane asked him for money in the afternoon of October 27th, he arranged to meet her late that evening in the garden. At six o'clock he went to bed in the same room as his brother Victor. About seven he tiptoed downstairs into the garden. The woman was waiting and he asked her to come with him into the field because he felt safer there. He took with him secretly the short wood axe which he had hidden near the garden house on the previous day. When they reached Ulrich's barn Juliane lay down and, without being asked to do so, lifted her skirts to have sexual intercourse.

"Without a word I knelt between her legs. She begged me to hurry, but with my right hand I felt for her head, holding the axe in my left, for I am left-handed. Then I brought the axe down on her head with all my strength." He went on to tell how he had hurried home, sawed the axe to bits and thrown them into the privy. And there, in fact, the rusty weapon was found.

The case was tried again and Gregor Adamsberger was acquitted. Franz Kunz, being under twenty years of age when he committed the murder, was sentenced to seven years' penal servitude.

Jurists and criminologists have had no difficulty in severely criticizing the conduct of the trial from the point of view of acceptance of evidence. These criticisms may be found in the book by Nemanitsch which has already been mentioned, and in various discussions of the case by Sello, Hellwig, Professor H. Gross[180] and Professor Stooss.[181] There is no need to repeat their remarks in detail, but we will quote some important points. Nemanitsch says that the conclusions arrived at could not have been due to chance or accident alone, and yet on the other hand nobody was to blame. The error of justice committed was sorely attributable to the suggestive power of the *vox populi*. He holds that this error was a tragic fate and inevitable. Stooss too blames public opinion for this miscarriage of justice, but blames the experts and judges for being swayed by it. Hans Gross comes to the same conclusion. He blames the superficiality of the preliminary examination, the responsibility for which he attributes to public opinion, calling it "that prostitute which everyone can buy," though it has so often been acclaimed as *Vox Dei*.[182] He makes use of this occasion to point out the many dangers with which the deposition of witnesses are fraught, as compared to the advantages of indirect evidence. He sees the future of penal law governed by "realities," those "objective and incorruptible factors which are incapable of misleading us and which may be attained by the teaching of criminology and increased and improved by research to an unlimited extent." Carl Stooss, unlike Gross, does not see in this case an argument for basing all evidence on circumstantial evidence;[183]

but he thinks that there is no reason for supposing that such evidence is not useful. The case merely shows the need for observing the greatest caution in its use. If the functionaries of the law had impartially considered the question whether it was proved that Gregor Adamsberger had murdered Juliane they would have had to arrive at a negative answer in view of all the known facts. For even if the facts point to a certain person as the perpetrator of the deed, the answer must be negative, unless those facts are of such a nature as to put the event beyond a doubt. If the judge were to follow any other principle he would be convicting "on suspicion." He would condemn a person because "he *might* be guilty, not because he *must* be guilty and could not be innocent." Hellwig, himself a judge, also holds that the judge was to blame. In his opinion, if great caution had been exercised a false conviction must and would have been avoided. Public opinion, he thinks, had exerted undue influence, with the result that experts and judges carried out their examination without the necessary care. Gregor Adamsberger would never have been found guilty if the examining magistrate and counsel for the prosecution had regarded the case objectively, uninfluenced by public opinion. The case merely shows how important it is to be very critical in the evaluation of evidence.

24. A Note on the Psychopathology of Judgments

We make no secret of the fact that in our view the explanations which the representative criminologists and jurists have been able to give us about the genesis of judicial errors are of a very superficial character. They have given us no deep insight into the problem. Conceptions such as "the power of the *vox populi*, lack of moral courage or of due caution" cannot compensate us for the absence of psychological understanding. It was easy to point to some of the factors that contributed towards the judgment, but this did not explain the psychological motives or mechanisms, the premises or hidden aims of these judicial errors. Nothing else could be expected, since these experts in law are laymen in psychology. They give us promises instead of explanations. It is like presenting a bill of fare instead of a dinner to a hungry man.

The very point of departure of their psychological enquiries is ill-chosen. For them it is a matter of course to regard the processes of evaluating proofs and forming a judgment in court as an isolated thing. Such an artificial isolation blocks the way to a psychological understanding of those processes. The easiest method of approach is to compare them with similar processes that have been better understood. But where are we to find them and by what means are we to explain them?

Psychoanalysis shows us a whole class of mental phenomena which are analogous to judicial errors in their psychological structure. But, it will be asked, what similarities can exist between the characteristics of the establishment of circumstantial evidence and the foundation of a neurotic system? Yet I think that a comparison between the two would be worth making.

What strikes us most in the Gregor case? What were the chief factors which led to the judicial error? Every single clue seemed to point to Gregor as the murderer, and the general agreement of the witnesses' statements did not seem to admit of any other possibility.[184] The powerful logic of facts was against him, and where there was a gap it was easy for the experts to fill it in by their superior knowledge and intellect. Everything pointed in one direction and everybody took that direction. It was clear to the wise man and to the fool how the terrible deed had come about. Gregor's guilt fulfilled all the conditions of logic and psychology and provided the one possible explanation of all the known data.

And yet it was all false. It turned out that the chain of events which seemed the only possible one had been artificially constructed. The contribution made by the intellect had been deceptive and distorted; the psychological view was suddenly seen to be dubious, the arguments and proofs employed uncertain, the logic expended, built on sand. But of what does such an ambiguous mental situation remind us psychoanalysts? We have met with such data before which seem to prove unequivocally a certain connection of things while they were in fact hiding a deeper and more important one.

Let us recall all the clues of this case and compare them with a seemingly far removed group of phenomena, namely, with the conscious explanation of the genesis and character of a psychoneurosis. Here is an example. A young builder in a largish provincial town suddenly became the victim of deep depression. He had been a serious and conscientious man who took pleasure in his work; but he now refused to go to his office, stayed in bed in blank despair, cried for hours, ate very little and that with disgust, saw no friends and declared his life had come to an end. When I was called in to see him I found him desolate. He assured me that nothing and nobody could help him, that all was lost and his existence ruined. What had happened to him? He lived a comfortable bachelor life with his mother and was one of the most esteemed representatives of his profession. His work left him time for recreation and entertainment, which were not difficult to find since he had many interests, especially artistic ones. His reputation was in the ascendant, his health excellent. He was thirty-five and attractive, though rather effeminate in his appearance. His friends had always regarded him as a mentally stable person. The reasons he gave for his depression made it seem comprehensible and also accounted for its depths; for he was serious-minded, very ambitious and cared for his own reputation and that of his firm of which he was the head.

This is what he told me: a few weeks ago he had finished a large block of flats for one of his best clients, on which he had spent much long and careful work. The building was to be given over in the near future to the tenants who were impatiently awaiting the event, for the scarcity of dwellings soon after the war was considerable. The man who had acually built the house and supervised the building operations was satisfied with his work. Characteristically enough, my interlocutor did not make it clear when and under what circumstances the doubts he began to feel about the safety of the building first assailed him. Did they occur spontaneously or in consequence of a remark made by a member of the commission appointed to examine the building? He was inclined to think that it was after the main structure of the house was finished and the walls, ceilings and roof had been examined, that a doubt first crossed his mind as to whether it was not endangered by underground water. He described to me with great emotion the precautions he had taken before starting to build, the care with which he had examined the site. He always returned to the conviction that the time was not far distant when the water would undermine the foundations of the building and cause it to collapse. His description showed his expert knowledge and made clear, even to my untrained mind, the dangers that threatened the inhabitants. A horrible catastrophe, which would be entirely his fault, might destroy everybody. The thought of this possibility haunted him. At his urgent request, a special commission of experts had once again examined the building and the sites. He showed me their report. I lacked the technical knowledge to understand fully the details of it, but certain passages seemed to admit the possibility of danger through water, while other passages seemed to exclude such a possibility at any rate for a very long time. The intelligent patient succeeded, however, in convincing me that the latter conclusions did in reality admit, though in a veiled form, the existence of a danger.

To the non-analytical observer there might have been nothing incongruous between the misfortune that had befallen the patient and the extent of his affect. When an ambitious young builder, after months of toil, finds that his work has endangered many lives, and consequently that his own ruin is assured, is it not natural that he should become the victim of a deep depression? The intensity of his depression seemed the more justified the more one learned about his fears and their causes. His own account of the state of affairs was orderly, logical, clear and consistent. And, as to the expert's report, even a layman reading it for a second or third time could find in it some justification of his fears. All the data fitted in with the patient's statement, the reliability of which could be proved.

Nevertheless, all the logic of his train of thought was only an apparent one—all the mental connections were purely artificial. Quite different, unconscious reasons were at the bottom of his depression. It was obvious to a careful observer that there were some discrepancies in his behavior, though his grief and depression were easily understandable. Some of his interpretations of certain sentences in the experts' report were forced; much of his argument gave the impression of sophistry. Although logical enough, it was somehow unconvincing. His story, though in general consistent, contained one or two slight inconsistencies. Everything in it was straightforward and yet some of the details did not seem quite natural.

In giving vent to his despair about his impending ruin, the young man mentioned in parenthesis that he had no house of his own, but lived with his mother. This remark was quite incidental and, made in reference to his profession, might have been meant humorously; yet it made an impression on me. Hints given at long intervals and pieced together like a mosaic yielded a strange reconstruction of the mental processes that had determined his depression. The main points were as follows: not long ago he had entered into sexual relations with a married woman. These relations were fraught with many difficulties, not the least of them being the question as to where the lovers should meet, since he shared his mother's flat. In the little town, where gossip was rife, the possibilities of a secret meeting were few. The question became acute at the time when he was building the important house. Just as he was considering whether he could take a flat of his own without arousing suspicion, a quite different kind of trouble overtook him. His old mother had developed symptoms which necessitated the advice of an expert gynecologist. The latter suggested that she might have cancer of the womb, and advised another, more thorough examination. The son was naturally very anxious about his mother. All this I learnt much later in a way quite unconnected with the alleged reason for his depression. But it would have been a strange thing if his concern about his mother had played no part in the genesis of his depression. My reconstruction of the situation, which did not go far outside the ascertained facts, suggested a close association between the two. It is true that it was not concern about his mother's life, as such, which was the direct cause of his depression. But certain hints, recurring again and again, led me to the following conclusion: during that time of anxiety about his mother, the thought of the woman he loved came to him one evening and with it the difficulty of their meeting. The two sets of thoughts met for one moment and suddenly another one presented itself, which he rejected with horror. This "terrible" thought, as he often called it later, was, "If my mother dies, the flat will be mine and I can receive my mistress undisturbed." In its primary form it was without doubt a wish. His psychological reaction to this wish, his horror of it, the increased sorrow for his mother and the reactively increased affection for her—these constitute the hidden causes of his illness.

Where are the connections between those unconscious thoughts and the ones put forward by the patient as the reasons for his depression? There is no doubt that he was worried about the building. On the other hand, analysis proved that he had thoughts and wishes referring to his mother's illness and death that he rejected with horror. The real train of thought which caused his depression was unconscious. Since it was unknown to the ego, an artificial one had to be constructed. The construction of a substitute train of thought, designed to explain those unknown urges which shook his ego to its depth, gave rise to a system whose peculiar qualities we know so well in psychoanalysis. This case is a good example of the construction of a neurotic system. We know what strong motives urged him to wish for his mother's death and what mental powers fought this wish and repressed it. The secret thought said: "Perhaps the cancer will kill my mother." The redirection of this latent mental material to a different aim was effected by making it have reference to the newly finished building. We can observe, moreover, the psychological connections that existed between the repressed material and the material which was accessible to consciousness. It was the wish for a flat that led to the quickly suppressed death-wishes. There were small flats in the building, enough and to spare. We are now in a position to compare the neurotic system and the hidden thoughts that underlay it. The form of the material that is capable of being conscious is determined—as we know—by secondary elaboration which rearranges the mental material, connects the separate elements in it and creates a meaning where the original, true meaning is no longer accessible to the ego. This new, artificial meaning, as it appeared to my patient's consciousness after secondary elaboration, was as follows: "The house I am building does not rest on firm foundations, the incessant action of the water underground will undermine it till it falls. This catastrophe will destroy my whole career." Broadly speaking, the corresponding repressed mental material was this: "My mother is dangerously ill. The sudden destructive action of the cancer is making alarming progress; that is why I am in such despair."

It is easy to see the points common to these two lines of thought. The medical examination corresponds with the examination made by the building commission; his mother's diseased body is equated with the endangered building; the subterranean force of the water stands for the hidden power of the disease, one catastrophe symbolizes the other. Naturally, the substitution cannot be complete. The secondary elaboration cannot rearrange all the elements and provide new details for all the missing ones. Sometimes, behind all its logical consistency and strictness of thought, one can discern the old unconscious instinct, like a poor undergarment under a gorgeous, but inadequate cloak. This is how those small gaps occur, those minute inconsistencies, those cracks in the system, which only acute observation can descry. They are analogous to the errors and inadequacies which a critical survey of the summing up of the Adamsberger case has exposed.

By examining piece by piece the circumstantial evidence in this murder case one can fit each element into two series. The data is comprehensible when one starts with the assumption that Gregor is the murderer; and it is also comprehensible and correct when one views it in the light of what actually did occur.[185] The whole material is reasonable and incontrovertible on the assumption that Gregor was the culprit. The same is true of the young builder's depression when looked upon as a reaction to the insecurity of his building. Yet anyone trying to see in this the true, or rather effective, connection would be mistaken.

What happens in the conscious and unconscious mind of the individual may be likened to what happens in the minds of the judges, experts and other functionaries of the law. The builder's deep depression needed an explanation, and his consciousness, unable to grasp the repressed factors, took hold of the first psychological material that offered. So an intelligent connection came about where before there had been mental chaos. It was the only way of forcing a strange event into the connection of known happenings. The explanation arrived at not only represents a synthesis achieved by an ego-function; it serves to keep the unconscious connections at bay. Its success shows that the more deeply laid chain of causes was not meant to be recognized. In the murder case the officials were confronted by the question "Who has committed this murder?" Their investigations pointed indubitably to Gregor Adamsberger; each clue seemed to support the next one. Any other culprit seemed out of the question. To deny Gregor's guilt would be to be confronted with a riddle, and riddles are unpopular. Gregor Adamsberger was not guilty, but he might have been guilty.

That mental function to which we attributed the construction of a system can be observed in the symptoms of the psychoses even better than in the neuroses. In paranoia, for instance, the whole disease is governed by a system, and what impresses us as delusion is for the most part mental material which has been "edited" by secondary elaboration. The paranoic ingenuity of combination succeeds in distorting the whole world in the sense of that system, and achieving a reconstruction of a kind which is truly imposing in its logic and consistency. Everybody can observe the results of secondary elaboration in the product nearest akin to delusion, the dream. A dream which on waking sometimes seems so chaotic and

disconnected can at other times make a very reasonable and co-
herent impression. But what appears so orderly and logical covers
up and substitutes the real connections underlying the latent
dream-thoughts. In some parts of the dream one element fits in
with the other and it all makes sense; but this smooth and reasonable surface deceives and is meant to deceive; it is an expression
of dream-distortion, a result of later reinterpretation. What seems
order is already a reordering, what fits so exactly and naturally has
been inserted later, what appears to be all of a piece has been laboriously pieced together.

Here is an example of this kind of dream-'façade' brought about
by secondary elaboration: a woman related a dream, one part of
which depicted an artistic production, a dance. She said, "Then
the audience clapped for the dancer. Somebody said, 'That is not
in time (in Takt); it is very modern.' " This part of the manifest
dream-content fitted the other one perfectly; everything was well-
ordered and seemed to grow out of the situation. It is because of
such clear and logically consistent dream-parts that the manifest
dream-content is still mistaken for the latent dream-thoughts. The
temptation to do so is particularly great when the dream-material
is of recent origin, as it was in the present case. It looks, then, as if
the dream was nothing but a slightly changed recollection of the
previous day. For the dreamer had, in fact, seen a display given
by a school for rhythmical dancing on the day before her dream.
When the dream went on to say that she had heard an exotic
melody played, and the thought had crossed her mind, "this is
very modern," it seemed obvious that the manifest content of
the dream was expressing the meaning of the dream. Indeed, who
can deny that much modern music gives the impression of not being "in time"? Part of the dreamer's associations leads us to take
the direction our conscious mind would like us to take, but only a
part. Another part does not fit into this scheme of things. One
can still see the proper connection when the dreamer went on to
say that her thoughts had been occupied with the problems arising
from the differences in outlook between different generations.
This seemed at first to confirm our impression that perhaps

thoughts about the difference between the music of the new and
the old generation were finding expression in her dream, and that
such thoughts had been suggested by the composition she had
heard. Such an apparently natural connection of ideas would,
however, hardly be in keeping with the following associations, and
could only be maintained in a very artificial way. For the dreamer
then told me how her thoughts about the generations had arisen.
She had been invited to speak at a women's club, and had chosen
as her topic the difficulties and differences of view that existed between the older and younger generation, especially between
mothers and daughters. That led her on to think, as she had often
done of late, about the conflicts she had had as a young girl with
her own mother. She had submitted to all the moral conventions
of her time, and when she married rather late in life she was still
a virgin; but she had to fight a hard battle against her strong
sensual feelings. Thinking of the present generation she could not
help having a bitter feeling against her own mother. No girl
nowadays worried much about remaining a virgin; it was not
important that the hymen should be intact on the wedding night.
The husband did not even expect it; it was no longer "modern."
She could now herself interpret the dream fragment as "This is
not intact (*intakt*); it is modern"; and, by a reversal which makes
the sense clearer, "It is modern—that is, not intact." Thus we
see that the thought did not refer to the music, but to sexual morality, and to the question of virginity which she had wanted to
discuss in her speech. The surface of the dream which seemed
so clear was a secondary elaboration; its logic was artificial and
deceptive. The harmless chain of thoughts replaced another,
hidden one. The dream-"façade" covered, rather than helped to
discover, the real kernel of the dream. Just as we were deceived
by the conjuring tricks of conscious thoughts, so may the functionaries of the law be deceived by a logical surface in questions of
guilt or innocence. The compulsion radiating from the synthetic
function of the ego is so strong that it makes us sometimes overlook an important discrepancy and even sometimes unconsciously
falsify the truth of the material presented to us. It can often effect

its purpose by merely making a slight change—a slight displacement or distortion—in an unnoticeable and seemingly unimportant detail before introducing it into the manufactured context. The sentence *"Das ist nicht in Takt"* which seemed to correspond so well with the thoughts about dancing and music, was meant to prepare us for a very natural, almost obvious association. We accepted it and referred the remark at once to the music, and that made us regard the content as logical and all of a piece.

Innumerable examples from criminology illustrate this point. I will quote one example, which shows how the mental factors concerned can deceive us even when we are wide awake and keenly observant of the external world. Katherine Fellner, who had come from Trieste to Vienna, had been found shot in the Lainz deer park. The Vienna police displayed a feverish activity in solving the case. A curious coincidence enabled them to identify the victim; and, this done, they went into the details of her previous life. She had been a waitress, had become a rich kept woman, and had later married a Hungarian of ill-repute, from whom however she soon separated. Although there had been no connection between the two for a long time, the Vienna police force, which is renowned for its psychological shrewdness, considered that the man was bound to have noticed the disappearance of his wife, and that his silence was the result of a bad conscience. Besides, near the park in question some people had seen a "sinister-looking man with a long mustache" who, they said, must have been a Southerner. With the help of a little imagination this description might easily refer to Andreas Fellner. In addition to all this there was a decisive fact. Fellner, who had lived for some time in Italy, had been on his way to Vienna the night before the murder. His name was registered at the frontier at Maribor on July 17th, 1928; he had crossed the Italian frontier that day, travelling in the direction of Vienna. The long pent-up energy of the Vienna police now broke forth. The divorced husband of the murdered woman was found and arrested at Abbazia in the summer of 1928. Investigation had revealed that he had often been convicted before. Could anything more be necessary to prove his guilt?

But it happened that the arrested man could prove that he had been involved in a auto accident on July 17th, 1928, in the Istrian village of Oderzo where he was treated by a doctor. He could not possibly have crossed the frontier on that day. The investigating officials must have made a mistake, owing, probably, to the Hungarian custom of the wife using the first and second name of her husband, adding only a short suffix to distinguish her identity from her husband's. In the register of names at the frontier was written "Fellner Andreasne" meaning "the wife of Andreas Fellner." And indeed Mrs. Fellner, the future victim, had crossed the frontier that night. So the whole construction of the Vienna police fell to pieces.

The comparison of the unconscious misunderstanding of the phrase "*nicht in Takt*" with this wrong construction made by the detectives is psychologically instructive in more ways than one. Here as there it was a question of overlooking a detail, but in the Fellner case a wrong interpretation might have led to a tragedy. In both cases we find the same psychological agency reinterpreting a certain fact in a more or less forced way so as to make it fit into a presupposed context. In both cases this rearrangement happens unconsciously. A number of such reinterpretations, put into relation to each other, leads to a system which screens the true state of affairs in the neurosis.

Yet another lesson can be learned from such a comparison of secondary elaboration in dreams and in criminology. In our work of interpreting dreams, we have learned to mistrust especially those parts of the dream which are most logical, consistent and clear. Criminologists and examining magistrates would do well to do likewise when they meet a chain of events which seems simple and easily comprehensible. Criminals sometimes quite deliberately play up to that natural preference for the simple and make the facts appear in the way that they would appear according to secondary elaboration. They can depend upon it that even the best criminologists will have a strong desire to suppress doubts and take an obvious possibility for a reality. Sometimes only the most unlikely possibility remains if the obvious is not accepted.

But it is precisely in crime that the unlikely so often happens.

Judges and jury, experts and counsels for the prosecution, are tempted to fill up the gaps in their material in the sense here indicated. They succumb to the psychological compulsion to understand clearly how things happened and to furnish a "reasonable" explanation; but it is their business not to provide a "reasonable" explanation, but the correct one.

25. The Psychological Acumen of a Criminologist
(Intermezzo Capriccioso)

This overestimation of comprehensibility, of logical sequence, and the reasonable character of a chain of thoughts has delayed the progress of science as well as that of justice. It is not true that people do not want to learn the truth. The greatest obstacle to the attainment of new knowledge is rather the firm conviction that the truth is already known. In such a belief the scientist and criminologist enjoy sensations of a most pleasurable kind.

By accident I found an example the other day which illustrates very clearly the phenomenon I have described. The example is all the more apt in that it shows a scientist at work who was at the same time a criminologist and who had made use of his medical and psychological knowledge in criminology. Here again it is the process of secondary elaboration that obstructs the way to the truth. The example is taken from a paper entitled: "Zum Mechanismus des Versprechens" ("Contribution to the mechanism of slips of the tongue") by the well-known physician and criminologist Dr. P. Näcke, published in the Archiv für Kriminalanthropologie und Kriminalistik, 1908. The author refers to Freud's Psychopathology of Everyday Life, and to the theory put forward there as to the psychogenesis of slips of the tongue. "In reviewing the book," says Näcke severely, "I remarked that Freud's explanation was certainly not the only one, and that he exaggerated everywhere and always. A pretty example is given in the publication *Leipziger Abendzeitung,* of April 12th, 1908, showing a similar slip to the one I mentioned about myself. A Protestant priest held an examination of his confirmation candidates. The children were all, of course, in a state of greater or less excitement. He began to quote the words of Christ: 'Watch and pray that ye enter not into temptation,' and asked a little girl to continue. She said quickly, 'The spirit indeed is willing, but the flesh is dear.' (*Denn der Geist ist willig, aber das Fleisch ist teuer.*) Here there is no question of a split-off affect, for the word *willig* called forth at first the rhyme *billig* (cheap) and then by contrast the association *teuer* (dear)." This is Näcke's explanation of the psychological process. This "pretty" example, he thinks, shows "how anxiety, emotion, and expectation, as well as certain psychotic states make one miss one's aim and call forth obvious and banal associations of sound. The apperception is weakened, as Wundt would put it, and now association proceeds without direction, therefore without aim, though always natural and according to mental laws. It is not impossible, indeed it is very probable, that the child had heard complaints about the price of meat so that in this way, too, the word 'meat' was associated with the word 'dear.' "

Does not this explanation sound probable? It is very attractive at first; but when we look at it more closely it seems an artificial, *ad hoc* construction. Näcke supposes that the phrase *Der Geist ist willig* had awakened the rhyme *billig* and then as a contrast the thought "*Fleisch ist teuer*" ("meat is dear"). It sounds consistent and logical and contains a certain amount of truth; but it is not complete and stays on the surface of psychology. The state of anxiety and excitement in which the girls were are given as the cause of the mistake. But of what kind was that anxiety and excitement?

This instruction, which the girls receive at puberty, is full of admonitions with regard to chastity. When the priest quotes the words of Christ "Watch and pray lest ye fall into temptation" every girl present, as well as every adult, knows that temptation means sexual temptation. In the next sentence, the contrast be-tween flesh and spirit is suggested, and "flesh" was understood by the girl, unconsciously or pre-consciously, in the adult sense. She connected it with sensual pleasure. The warning against tempta-tion had led her thoughts in that direction—if they had not al-ready gone there. After the words "The spirit is willing" comes "but the flesh is weak." But now suppressed thoughts came to the surface. The word "temptation" in connection with the coarse, sensual interpretation of the word "flesh" recalled to her mind those women who live for sensual pleasure and—in the little Leipzig girl's imagination—are well paid into the bargain. The association is not far to seek: "The flesh is weak"— that means that one easily falls a victim to sexual temptation. The line of thought culminating in the slip of the tongue is clear. Flesh—sensual pleasure—one is paid for it—the flesh is dear. The change from "the flesh is weak" to "the flesh is dear" is not without reason.

It seems as if the girl has not received sufficient moral strength from her religious instruction—as if she were not as yet so pure in heart as she should be. The sentence in question hit upon a weak spot—the resistance to forbidden lust. But the disturbing thought continues, "And you will get a lot of money, too." The girl had not been talking about the retail price of meat as Näcke thinks, but rather about the price of prostitution in "little Paris." More than that, the words show her surprise that pleasure is paid for into the bargain. She will understand later why the protest against the watchful spirit is strengthened by the temptation of money. But her slip shows that even now she is concerned with other matters than Christian doctrine.

Probably the chain of association really proceeded via the word *billig* and made use of the rhyme (*willig—billig*) as Näcke sup-poses. Nor is it improbable that the girl had heard complaints about the high price of meat. But it is certain that she had many obscured thoughts about prostitution and about the connection between sexuality and pleasure, and that at this juncture they interfered with her intended sentence. Anyone who doubts that girls have such thoughts, even while being prepared for confirmation, does not know the power of the evil one against holy doctrine.[186] Even a criminal psychologist and medical expert can be unwary. "Not even if he has them by the collar will these folk ever scent the devil."

The genesis of the slip and the nature of the suppressed thought recalls a saying of Nietzsche. It was he who coined the malicious phrase about women, "The flesh is willing but the spirit is weak."

Näcke's theory is a proof of the effect of secondary elaboration; indeed, it is a model of it in scientific work. It shows how a criminologist may judge a psychological fact, and explains why he so judges it. What made Näcke at once accept the nearest explanation to hand and view the facts of the case from this standpoint only? Everything at once appeared reasonable and comprehensible, but, like the birds which pecked at the painted fruit of Apelles, he had allowed himself to be deceived by appearances.

26. Material and Psychological Reality

It is not my intention to make a psychoanalytical investigation into judicial errors, the sources of which are many. I will show only a few of those factors which work unconsciously and affect conscious and rational thinking.

If we return to the case of Gregor Adamsberger, it is not to discuss the question of clue and counter-clue, but to enquire into what made the judge and jury arrive at their decision besides rational considerations. What made them overestimate the value of the evidence against the accused and underestimate or even overlook the contrary possibilities?

Let us focus our attention first on the victim of the miscarriage of justice, Gregor Adamsberger. Was it only a mischievous accident that made him the object of that judicial error? Is any kind of person liable to such a fate? This question does not concern the judge, the counsel for the presecution or the jury. It does not concern the functionaries of the law today, but nobody can tell whether it will not do so tomorrow. And even today this point of view cannot be ignominiously dismissed if we can show that it is important for the finding of the truth and that a hitherto unknown or unrecognized psychological factor can upset investigations designed to discover the truth.

It would, of course, be ridiculous to try to find in the personality of the victim an explanation for every judicial error based on circumstantial evidence. In a great number of such errors, the personality of the victim plays no part at all; they arise out of a combination of external circumstances and chance events and have nothing whatever to do with the psychology of the accused. But among those avoidable errors there are certain cases which, on closer investigation, encourage the psychologist to point out in the behavior of the accused certain psychological factors that play an essential part in bringing about his judicial conviction.

All the witnesses agreed that Gregor Adamsberger was a brutal and fierce-tempered man who had often ill-treated his former mistress and had sometimes even threatened to kill her. These threats were without doubt of great importance as psychological evidence. It is true they were only the expression of his hatred against a mistress who had become inconvenient, but they assumed importance in the establishment of his judicial conviction.

Behind the conscious evaluation of the man's hatred lies an unknown realm—the unconscious realization of the intensity and direction of that hatred. At first sight this seems grotesque, because his hatred was not unconscious; it had been amply displayed. It cannot be said that his threats and insults were not taken seriously and that blows among people of that class need not imply violent hatred. But, if we admit that he cordially hated his former mistress, was this conscious hatred strong enough to bring about a murder? We do not know. All we know is that Gregor did *not* commit the murder. What I wish to emphasize here is that it was the echoes of this hatred in the man's unconscious, and its intensity there, that influenced the court and led to the mistaken verdict.

But is it not absurd to suppose that Gregor's hatred against Juliane, though intense enough to make him contemplate murder, should be the decisive factor in his conviction? How could the judge and jury have taken cognizance of what happened in Gregor's unconscious mind? The answer is, that their unconscious minds recognized the unconscious, or only partly conscious, processes in the accused by certain signs and reacted to those signs as if they were manifestations of his guilt.[187] It is as if the judge and jury regarded secret thoughts, wishes and impulses as real deeds. They react to the expression of the prisoner's hatred by equating psychical and material reality. I maintain quite seriously that the mistaking of unconsciously perceived psychical actual reality constitutes an important etiological factor in judicial errors. The precise nature of the communication between the two unconscious minds, a phenomenon most readily comparable to the instinctive knowledge possessed by animals, remains as inexplicable as before.

It is not possible in these pages to exhibit this new factor in the genesis of judicial errors in a series of examples; but one instance may be quoted to illustrate certain features that have not been stressed before. I refer to the Steiner case which occurred in Vienna in 1878.[188] A prostitute, Katherina Steiner, was accused of having murdered her neighbor, Katherine Balogh, who was found strangled at nine o'clock on the morning of April 3rd, 1878. The other people in the house said that as late as 7 a.m. a young man had been in Balogh's room and had taken breakfast with her. The deed must therefore have been done between seven and nine in the morning. Katherina Steiner consistently denied her guilt, although the provisional examination had yielded some suspicious facts. The indictment is a representative example of the convincing proof of circumstantial evidence. The dead woman had been very beautiful; she and Steiner had often quarrelled because the latter was jealous of her. Several witnesses had heard her threaten the victim with death. The accused was known to have a violent temper; she had also frequently been convicted of theft. When the murder was discovered her behavior was peculiar, and since then she had been afraid of being alone. This was interpreted as an expression of a bad conscience. Her nervousness, her nightmares, several remarks made by her to her prison companions, were similarly interpreted. Contradictions in her story were easily discerned. In court she behaved, according to her counsel, in "such a bold and unseemly way as to forfeit everyone's sympathy. She dressed in her be-ribboned best and flirted with the audience; her bold looks and her provocative conduct contrasted sharply with the gravity of the accusation. At the same time she showed such an ungovernable temper that she had to be put in the dark cell for three days." She was found guilty of murder and condemned to death. Her counsel, Dr. Neuda, said that the solicitor-general and the judges of both courts,[189] after serious study of the case, communicated to him their unshakable conviction that nobody but Steiner could have killed Balogh.

But such convictions are no guarantee against judicial error. The death sentence was commuted to penal servitude for seven years. After four years the murderer came forward. It was the young man who had breakfasted with Balogh on April 3rd, 1878, and then strangled her.

Here, without a doubt, the judges perceived the unconscious wishes of Steiner, mistook them for a clue, and used them as a basis for their verdict. Here, too, it was a question of conscious feelings of hatred being continued in the unconscious and there leading to death-wishes; for there had been scenes between the two women, and Steiner had frequently uttered threats. But if the officials mistook psychical for material reality, it was the accused who first made the mistake. She hated Balogh because of her beauty; for years she had wished, consciously or unconsciously, for her death, and now her rival was really dead. Of course, Steiner knew that she had not killed Balogh. She denied the murder at once; but the fact remained that she had *wanted* to kill her. In this coincidence of wish and reality lies the solution of one of the most important questions presented to us by many instances of circumstantial evidence. This coincidence does not merely supply the material for an essential reason which led the judges to their decision; it makes understandable much in Steiner's behavior

which would otherwise remain incomprehensible, since she did
not commit the deed. Her behavior when the murder was discovered becomes psychologically clear. It could not help being peculiar because it was the expression of the terror felt by human
beings when suddenly and without effort on their part, one of
their most insistent but forbidden wishes comes true. This behavior was interpreted as a sign of guilt and, judging by psychological reality only, it *was* a sign of guilt. The unexpected coincidence of psychological and material reality, which struck Steiner
like a shaft of lightning, also explains her fear of being alone
after the murder; she was afraid of the murdered woman's revenge. Her fear was interpreted as the expression of a bad conscience. So it was, but it referred to the murder wishes, not to the
actual murder. The court acted, however, as if the person who
wanted to commit the murder was of more importance than the
real murderer.

Instead of quoting any more examples, I want to stress the fact
that manifestations of terror, dismay and guilt which have often
been regarded as psychological evidence as to fact may be the
result of a surprising coincidence of this kind between a material
reality, such as an accomplished crime, and an endopsychically
perceived strong impulse leading to a certain wish. Again, facial
expressions and signs are often interpreted by judges and juries
as evidence of guilt, where such an interpretation is only true in
a psychological sense and not in a factual one. For instance, an
accused person is frightened because a murder has been committed at a certain time, and this fear is considered suspicious.
But his terror is psychologically quite understandable if he has
remembered that at that very time he was thinking with great
animosity of the murdered man. There have been numerous
other cases in which coincidental circumstances of this kind have
confronted the accused with similar psychological effects, and
have been interpreted as circumstantial evidence against him.

In other cases of judicial error based on circumstantial evidence
it is not the intensity of an unconscious impulse that influences
the judge; it is certain repressed trends, inaccessible to conscious-

ness, that play a part in his judgment. The example of "ritual murder" is a classical one. The Jews have an excessive fear of blood; and it is as if people had guessed their repressed sadistic and cannibalistic tendencies—severely taboo—even in prehistoric times—and had based on them a suspicion that lacked any real basis. It is precisely the contrast between the repressed impulses and the conscious psychological situation that is decisive here. Obviously the exaggerated patriotism of Captain Dreyfus, and his somewhat snobbish endeavor to cut a figure in a clique of Gentile and nationalistic officers, had nothing to do with any tendency to betray his country. As a Jewish officer he must unconsciously have resented the haughty "Aryan" chauvinism of his fellow officers, but this would certainly not have driven him to any action against the General Staff. The very fact of his isolation, his patience and his conscious indifference to the coldness shown towards him must have annoyed them. The unconscious perception of his superiors made use, in all likelihood, of those crosscurrents of anger, rebelliousness and resentment. His condemnation was certainly in part brought about by this latent, unconscious perception of his repressed affects against his environment.

We have already discussed the case of the Druaux couple, in which there was no crime at all and yet a suspected person was found guilty of murder. The psychologist would have no doubt that here the judicial error was based on the unconscious perception of the impulses in the accused woman. Such cases, where there has been no crime at all and yet a false conviction is made, are especially instructive examples of how judges and juries and all the functionaries of the law often unconsciously mistake psychological reality for material reality in this way. Can it be that experienced, worldly-wise and practical men are sometimes taken in by this delusion even in our own day and not only in medieval times, when everybody believed in witches? There is no guarantee that judicial errors cannot and do not happen now, perhaps at this very moment. Yet if there is no guarantee, there are certain precautions that can be taken, but only if we know what are the dangers we must guard against. As far as I know, this source of psychological error that I have been pointing out has not yet been recognized. Perhaps these lines may contribute to an avoidance of judicial error by enabling us to take into account the unconscious factors concerned.

Have we done justice to our topic—the neglect of unconscious processes in the finding of judicial truth? Not unless we have made it abundantly clear how little reason there is for our judges to look down on their primitive predecessors, the magicians and Shamans. We have discovered the hidden road leading from their primitive and superstitious conceptions to a highly developed criminal procedure. *Justitia est fundamentum regnorum.* But what sort of a state can be built upon magic? And yet, in the majority of cases the same motives determine the judgment of the modern judge and that of the magician in the Australian bush. Consider again the case of Madame Druaux. The husband and brother were found dead in suspicious circumstances; the woman was half-conscious. The men had been poisoned. There had been a violent quarrel just before, and nobody doubted that the woman had poisoned them. The judges found her guilty. The most primitive Negroes in Australia believe that every death is, without exception, caused by magic. Sir George Grey says of the tribes in western Australia that the natives do not admit of death from natural causes. They believe they would live for ever if it were not for the magician's murderous and malicious intent. When a native dies from natural causes—an accident for instance—the natives find out with the help of certain ceremonies in what direction the magician responsible for his death lives.[190] Frazer gives an enormous number of examples showing how universal is this belief among savages.[191] Are these modern French judges, who condemned Madame Druaux for the murder of her husband, really so very different from the Australian magicians who investigate a death? Both perceive the unconscious tendency of aggression and make it the decisive factor in their judgment. If we compare the judgment in the case of Gregor Adamsberger with the decision of a magician in a murder case, the comparison would not redound so greatly to the credit of modern criminology.

Let us consider the methods of African tribes. According to Nachtigal,[192] the guilty magician is distinguished from the other men present by the movements of a bundle of hay or grass. This is placed on the head of a wise man and makes him sway to and fro, finally driving him in the direction of the guilty man. What is to prevent us from comparing the swaying of the wise man with the consideration of Judge Z. in the Adamsberger case? The former has probably just as good reasons for his decisions as the latter. The mistaking of psychological reality for material reality connects the judges in London, Paris and Berlin with their black, unlettered colleagues in spite of the difference in their cultural level.

This point of view can best be called the unconscious recognition of the omnipotence of thoughts. Explorers and missionaries tell us how deeply rooted is this belief among savage and half-savage peoples; they also say it has valid psychological reasons. Pechuel-Loesche, in his report about the Loango expedition,[193] says there are persons who believe themselves to be witches in the worst sense of the word. That is comprehensible, for if bad intentions are in themselves sufficient to kill and do damage, such intentions must be equated with deeds. When we read that, to the mind of the Negro, evil thoughts produce effects and that they cause a bad conscience and lead to self-accusations, or at least to conduct that rouses suspicion in others and encourages them to make accusations, especially when the manifold personal relations of the person concerned are known, we are reminded of the psychogenesis of many a judgment built on circumstantial evidence. It is the same unconscious recognition of the omnipotence of thoughts that is responsible for many of the judicial errors of our times.

An old German proverb says, "One is not hanged for a thought." But psychoanalytic investigation of the etiology of judicial error shows that many people have in fact been hanged for a thought; and so, like many another good old German saying, the proverb proves untrue.

27. THE FUTURE OF CRIMINAL JUSTICE

WE have dealt with the error into which those who are responsible for detecting crime and verifying evidence sometimes fall; of mistaking psychological reality for material reality in that they unconsciously treat thoughts as deeds. They would certainly reject with horror the idea that they do so. Perhaps this error is made possible by the very fact that the thoughts which they unconsciously equate with deeds by no means deserve the disrespect, not to say contempt, with which they are regarded in consciousness.

We have tried to show here the importance of unconscious thoughts in criminal justice, and how they may even decide between life and death. Here emerge new problems of criminal justice—problems that were unknown, indeed unimaginable, to the generation that preceded us.

We can best reach an understanding of these problems by considering the following points. Certain indications have warned us against an overestimation of the power of human wishes—an overestimation which is often even to be seen in the psychogenesis of judicial conviction. These indications give us an intimation of the other side of the problem. The reason of this unconscious overestimation is that in our exaggerated zeal for the rational we have underestimated the psychological effect of unconscious thoughts, indeed, have sometimes not even recognized it. Those thoughts have, as it were, taken their revenge by blotting out the line of demarcation between thought and deed, between criminal act and forbidden wish, even when a judicial decision between guilt and innocence is in question.

In view of this fateful step across the line of demarcation, we are confronted with the question of whether the commission of a criminal act is in our own case so unimaginable, so remote from possibility as we assert. If we all unconsciously habor such evil wishes, if their domain is so extensive that judges sometimes arrive at false conclusions on the strength of them, is there really such a world of difference between the wish and the deed? Is punishment really the proper reaction to a breaking through of the boundary line between the two? Must not deeper research lead us to question this attitude?

It is no valid objection to say that such considerations have little practical value and no prospects for the future. Metternich, the Prime Minister of the old Austria, said about that state: "Our enemies cannot destroy us because they do not know what to put in our place." The same dilemma is present in the problem of punishment; but such an optimism has its limitations. We cannot look into the future, but we see from the past that penology has had to undergo radical changes. The change in human outlook will also have its effect on the problem of guilt and punishment. The history of penology shows that century-old legal institutions disappear, as it were, overnight. In their wildest dreams our ancestors would not have guessed that there would ever be such an institution as being bound over. The penal law of ancient times knew only the conceptions of absolute guilt or innocence; the individuality of the culprit did not come into question. The fact of the deed was decisive. The doer was responsible even if he had not willed the deed or had only been an unintentional instrument of it. There is a considerable difference between this point of view and that in which not only the deed, but also subjective guilt and malicious intent of the doer, is a deciding factor. We read with amazement about the criminal institutions that have been superseded. We surmise—indeed we may be certain—that future generations will regard our methods with the same pity that we extend to those of the past.

The great changes that are bound to take place in penology will be the result of the new insights we shall have gained from the modern science of psychological processes, which shows that the concepts of guilt and innocence are inadequate.[194] If the man who has only wished to murder is completely innnocent while he who has accidentally occasioned it has to suffer the extreme penalty, then the idea of justice becomes quite grotesque.

We cannot imagine today the disappearance of conceptions such as guilt and punishment. The enormous importance attached by criminal justice to the deed as such derives from a cultural phase which is approaching its end. A great writer has shown by an example of circumstantial evidence how inadequate the conception of the deed may be, how problematic our penal law still is. The more profound meaning of *The Brothers Karamazov* is intelligible only to those who are able to recognize the worthlessness of the so-called objective method of arriving at facts. It is comparatively unimportant which of the three brothers has committed the deed. It is much more important psychologically which of them has wished it; and all three have wished it. That being so, it is a short step to the assumption that we can all be guilty.

This mistrust of justice goes further than even reformers imagine, and has far deeper reasons than Alexander and Staub assume in their book. It is not merely a question, as these authors rather shortsightedly assume, of a classification of criminals, of differences in the degree of participation on the part of the ego, etc. Other questions will have to be discussed. What seems Utopian today may be a commonplace tomorrow; and our present cultural level may appear barbarous to future generations. The deed as such will then be estimated very differently and psychology will play a very different part.[195]

But perhaps we are too optimistic; perhaps the future is more distant than we think. Perhaps what applies to changes in the point of view of the individual applies to the more general question of penology as well. On the stage we sometimes see choruses of brave warriors singing valiantly "We march, we march" without moving from their places. We are occasionally tempted to think that this is meant to symbolize the rate at which the reform of criminal justice is advancing.

28. The "Omnipotence of Thoughts" in Criminal Cases

THE psychological considerations that we have put forward may
also explain many things in the behavior of accused persons.
When a man has a secret feeling of guilt, it is understandable that
he should suffer from a kind of intellectual blindness that finds
expression in contradictions and stupid excuses, in complete contrast to his normal level of intelligence. A perfect instance of this
is the Halsmann case. Halsmann was wrongly accused of parricide, but in his defence he contradicted the facts as well as previous
statements of his own. According to some observers, his defence
was "so clumsily invented that it seemed to invite accusation." In
such cases it often seems as if the most intelligent people had been
forsaken by reason and logic and could only follow their own
secret affects. They obstinately adhere to contradictions which
they would easily detect in other people. One of the experts in the
Halsmann case said, in his report on the prisoner's behavior:[196]
"Above all he attracted unfavorable notice by his obstinacy and
his crafty argumentativeness. He hampered the defence by refusing to be guided by it and, taking a hand in it himself, emphasized
in a long-winded and redundant manner things which seemed to
him important. But he often fought tenaciously for points that
were unimportant or had already been dealt with." The same expert said that Halsmann's "aggressive behavior, compared with
the gravity of the charge, could not fail to make a bad impression."
Such strange conduct is sometimes seen in innocent people; they
appear to want to provoke the antipathy of the court by their
argumentativeness and arrogance. No doubt this is partly due
to their feeling that they have been falsely accused; but it is often
the result of their hidden guilty thoughts as well. No citizen is
in duty bound to please the officers of the court, but on the other
hand there is no duty to the contrary. The behavior here described

usually has the unconsciously desired effect, and often forges a secret link in the chain of evidence for the prosecution. It is frequently understood by the judge and prosecuting counsel as a sign of defiance and guilt. There is no doubt that in many cases this reaction, dictated by unconscious guilt, has seriously damaged the interest of the accused. As we have seen, the counsel who defended Katherina Steiner stated that she "behaved in such a bold and unseemly way to forfeit everyone's sympathy. Dressed in her be-ribboned best she flirted with the audience; her bold looks and her provocative conduct contrasted sharply with the gravity of the accusation. At the same time she showed such an ungovernable temper that she had to be put in the dark cell for three days." Again, observers assure us that Dreyfus, with his Jewish appearance, his short sight, clumsy gestures and wooden behavior, was very little like an officer. Anatole France, who was in the van of his defenders, remarked how unattractive was the personality of this wrongly accused man; and even his own counsel Derange was impelled to mention this point in his summing-up before the Court Martial at Rennes.[197]

The fact that Dreyfus changed his attitude after the trial does not invalidate our contention. Here we are concerned with a conflict of psychological forces whose intensity we cannot measure. He felt unconscious guilt about his revolutionary feelings against his fellow officers and the army; but when the worst dishonor befell him, this little man stood up to the fate that was meant to crush him. The testimony of those who witnessed his degradation in the court of the Military College, on January 5th, 1895, is unanimous. "I am innocent," he exclaimed, lifting his fettered hands above his head. Every time he tried to speak the drums sounded, and when his stripes had been torn off and his sword broken, the defile of the traitor before the troops began. The crowd pressed against the railings, shouting "À mort, à mort." Dreyfus pushed the stripes away with his foot and joined his escort of soldiers without waiting for the order. He almost marched in front of them; he seemed to have got taller, his bearing was erect, his step steady, his head high. One of the officers, incensed at such haughtiness in a traitor, exclaimed loudly: "The scoundrel walks like an officer at the head of his company." It is not unlikely psychologically that Dreyfus did walk like that for the first time.

Other traits, otherwise inexplicable, become clear in this connection. Through the effect of unconscious guilt, many people are prevented from fighting for their rights.[198] The old saying of law, *Volenti non fit injuria,* is not quite true, even apart from the many wilful and stupid acts of various officials. The unconscious of an accused man may wish for the very thing he consciously strives against with all his might.

So we revert once more to the problem of the mental reaction of judges, counsel and jury to the unconscious wish of the accused. If our supposition, borne out by research in other subjects, is correct, those functionaries have not quite lost their faith in omnipotence. These secret tendencies are apt to break through in the most unexpected quarter, namely, in the realm of logic, and particularly in the matter of circumstantial evidence. It is, of course, a highly sublimated way of satisfying instincts of cruelty and power. In forming logical conclusions or exposing contradictions or in cross-examining the accused, the wish for omnipotence appears disguised as "compelling logic." Such unconscious tendencies have their best opportunity of finding an unimpeachable expression in the building up of an unbreakable chain of circumstantial evidence. The "will to power" appears as the will to truth. It has been rightly pointed out that passing judgment is not an abstract logical operation, but an act of will, a deed.[199] The metaphors and images we use in connection with circumstantial evidence indicate obviously this sadistic basis. We say that the "net" of circumstantial evidence "closes ever more tightly" round the accused; we read of the "inexorable" logic of the prosecution, of the "spatial-temporal encircling" of the culprit.[200] The relationship between certain techniques of examination and torture is unmistakable. Hans Gross, the most eminent criminologist of the last decade, involuntarily identifies examination with *tortura spiritualis* when he writes:[201] "The essential quality in an examining magistrate is one that can only be described as 'sharpness.'

There is nothing sadder and more useless than a slow, half-hearted and sleepy magistrate; such qualities would be more tolerable in a cavalry officer than in an examining magistrate, and anyone without this indispensable 'sharpness' would do well to take up another branch of jurisprudence. . . ." It is not merely the simile which breathes the spirit of *Justitia militans*.

This belief in omnipotence is seen most clearly as the mental representative of narcissistic and cruel impulses when, in constructing a chain of circumstantial evidence, it tries to force reality to suit its ends after having started from false premises. I have already shown how a construction may be built up out of small suspicions. At first these suspicions are subjected to searching criticism, then they are treated in an ever bolder and more reckless manner until the logic applied to them is the same as in a system of delusion. The cooperation of conscious and unconscious impulses is not recognized by the judges, since the derivatives of the unconscious processes take on the disguise of conscious factors. Judges and juries are usually proud of the fact that obscure feelings have no power over them and that in the weighing and establishment of evidence they listen solely to the "language of facts." The magistrate has often no inkling that he is adjusting all the facts to his theory and that in his mind he is, like a god, reshaping reality according to his will. Witnesses are unconsciously pushed in a certain direction, the evidence of the accused is proved to be contradictory and untrue, every word of his is interpreted according to the desired system, every fact adapted to it. In the Adamsberger case, we have seen the tremendous power of error, the tenacity of prejudice, the undeviating march of false logic and the hopeless incapacity of so-called common sense. All these traits are psychologically explicable only on the supposition that violent passions are operative behind this search for clues, which we call evidence. That sadistic wave of feeling, which finds expression in a spiritualized form in the inexorable processes of logic, becomes more clearly visible towards the end of the proceedings. The chain of evidence is, so to speak, a provisional substitute for the prisoner's chains. The zeal of the judge and prosecution in-

creases, contradiction makes them stick more firmly to their point
the more impossible that point becomes. Filling up gaps in circumstantial evidence becomes unconsciously an achievement and
assumes the importance of a sporting event. Behind the prosecution's narcissistic pride in its shrewdness the impulse of cruelty
is discernible. The hounds follow the scent of circumstantial evidence and the hunt goes on to the kill—the judgment. As the
trial proceeds, the ambition of the judge and prosecutor increases,
and they try to make the circumstantial evidence unassailable.
The striving for omnipotence in the judge is only satisfied when
the world has become the expression of his will and his conception. He has proved that what he thought was right, that his
beliefs agree with reality. Proof has been established. *Quod in-
deciis demonstrandum erat.*[202]

If such impulses are operative, the frequency of judicial error
is not surprising. In fact it is strange that there are no more of
them.[203]

The victory of logic over the contradictions of reality is a victory of the omnipotence of thoughts, too. Any mystery is unsatis-
factory to the intellect; its existence injures our self-sufficiency
and creates an element of psychological tension. It is a great
temptation to remedy this by mentally filling up the necessary
lacunæ. Behind this aim, instinct seeks to find gratification, the
cruelty of man secretly craves to be satisfied.[204] No doubt the conviction of the judge and jury is in itself one of the most important
pieces of evidence in the question of guilt or innocence. There
is an unconscious urge to find confirmation of one's own opinion.
In a world that delights in making us feel our helplessness, such
a confirmation serves to enhance our feeling of self-importance.[205]

A sure sign of the strength of such an impulse is to be seen in
the distinct reluctance felt by judges to reopen a case. I cannot,
naturally, enter into the juristic aspect of this question, and even
in regard to the psychological aspect I must limit myself to one
remark.[206] The reopening of a case obviously inflicts an injury
on the narcissistic pride of a judge. Hirschberg rightly says[207] that
"to expect a judge to admit that his own sentence on the prisoner

may have been wrong, especially if it was a crushingly severe one
and was inflicted many years ago, must meet with violent opposition even, or perhaps, especially, in the case of a judge of the
highest standing." Unconscious guilt plays its part here as well
as narcissistic injury. Only thus can it be explained, as a witty
writer[208] rather exaggeratedly describes it, that "the authorities
of the law prefer judicial murder to anything that may compromise them."

29. Repression in the Adducing of Evidence

The case of Gregor Adamsberger, the tanner, has been more instructive than we thought, since, viewed analytically, it can enlighten us about more than one of the dangers connected with
circumstantial evidence. In this case there were a number of
clues against the accused whose evidential value was dependent
on time, opportunity and motive. We know that their importance
was increased by a hidden circumstance, i.e., the perception of
an unconscious tendency in Gregor to kill Juliane. No one who
has followed the case can fail to ask, "But did not Adamsberger
himself say that on the evening of the murder Juliane told him
that she was going to her lover, the son of the baker, Kunz?"
Gregor also deposed later that Juliane told him of frequent meet-
ings with Kunz in his parents' garden house. On that evening, too,
she was to meet him secretly. These were definite and unequivocal
pieces of information. What use was made of them? The judge,
the counsel for the prosecution and the jury could not possibly
say later on that they had never been told them. It would be
truer to say that they had taken no notice of them. They might
say, to be sure, that Adamsberger's story sounded incredible. What
a suspected person says is usually discredited and this time it
seemed particularly fantastic. In view of young Kunz's youth and
good reputation and of the fact that no one knew of his relations

with the woman, who incidentally was more than twice his age, Gregor's suspicions would have been disbelieved even if the young baker had not had a good alibi. Kunz's own quiet denial made those strange sexual relations still more unlikely. When Gregor was found to have told a lie, his suspicions about Juliane and Kunz were "proved" to be entirely untrue. He had talked about a letter which Juliane's son had given Kunz in which she asked him for money; and he had added that Kunz had scolded her for her carelessness. Obviously it was all invented.

What Gregor had said about Kunz was clear and definite. It is true it did not accord with other facts and nobody thought Kunz capable of such a deed. Every rational consideration spoke in favor of Kunz and against Gregor; and yet in the innermost soul of judge and jury there must have been a strong prejudice in favor of Kunz. I think that we can apprehend what it was if we are able to realize the secret meaning of those apparently rational arguments, if we will listen to what they want to say, not to what they actually do say. We may think it incredible that the shy, six-teen-year-old boy should have had sexual relations with a woman of bad repute and twice his age. He might have been her son. It seems to me that it is from this point that the unconscious motives sprang for refusing to credit Adamsberger's statements. Does it not sound like the denial of an accusation of incest? And another circumstance, too, strengthened this unconscious, affective idea of incest. Juliane's son, who, according to Gregor, had acted as an intermediary, was thirteen years old and her lover sixteen. The power of repression that showed itself here by ignoring a well-founded suspicion will also have the same effect in other cases, perhaps by overlooking important clues, separating certain con-nections, etc. Such an ignoring of suspicions is often combined with the construction of a very different picture of how the thing happened—a procedure which we have called a "system." A set of ideas of this kind, which is comparable to delusions, is made to seem still more convincing through the effect of the mechanisms of repression. The existing clues become more weighty because those pointing in another direction are ignored. The omission of clues pointing in the opposite direction can sometimes lead to calamitous results.[209]

The criminal history of the last few decades exhibits a large number of cases in which certain possibilities which turned out later to be facts have been ignored by judge, jury and prosecution simply because there were other more likely possibilities. This cannot be explained by negligence or carelessness, nor can the intellectual qualities or the personal integrity of the functionaries concerned be doubted. Something irresistible, because hidden and intangible, must have prevented them from seeing a certain fact; at a certain point repression must have diverted their thoughts. Nietzsche hints at this barrier of repression when he says: "Even the most courageous man has rarely the courage to recognize what he knows." It is nonsense to brand all the judges, witnesses and experts in the Dreyfus case as idiots, scoundrels and fanatics, as is sometimes done. Some of them must have revolted against seeing in a French officer, one of themselves, a traitor; for that meant the deterioration of the army, of national honor, of the glory of the army. If such a thing were possible there was the possibility that similar impulses lived in them, too. It was simpler to assume that the stranger, the Jew, had committed the fell deed. Clearly one aim of repression is to save pain, because the discovery of the real culprit in these cases is apt to injure the narcissism of the individual and the masses.

The unconscious factors traceable in the psychopathology of judicial error may follow two courses. They may cause the deed to be ascribed to an innocent person (innocent in the material sense), or, on the other hand, they may prevent the real culprit from being found. In regard to circumstantial evidence, that is, they may smother the seemingly guilty man with weighty clues or else overlook existing clues against the real author of the deed. An unconscious attraction to the one course is assisted by the work of defensive repression belonging to the other. A larger proportion of the false judgments arrived at in such cases is due to the combination of these two unconscious tendencies, which are supported by sound, rational arguments and a strong chain of circumstantial evidence.

I cannot in this place give specific examples to show how the psychological components interact. I must be content to illustrate the effectiveness of unconscious factors in a single typical instance. The lessons that can be learned by exploring the depths of the mind may not be pleasant for judges and juries who pride themselves on their shrewdness; but let us hope that they will quickly get over such a narcissistic injury and realize that even their intellect may sometimes be dimmed by the irruption of unconscious impulses. How stupid is the man who thinks he is always clever!

30. Unexplained Murder Is Uncanny

In the present inquiry, now nearing its end, I have chosen cases of murder and manslaughter as my examples, and this for several reasons. For one thing, murder is the most serious of crimes. It is regarded in that light by primitive peoples, too. Even in low cultures murder is considered different from other crimes, not in degree, but in essence. The decisive part that clues play in murder cases is well known. It is precisely in such examples, therefore, that the essence and evolution of circumstantial evidence can best be illustrated.

I want, furthermore, to stress the point that unexplained murder has for most people some uncanny quality that other unexplained crimes, as, for instance, robbery, do not possess. The special feeling connected with the deed is one of pronounced psychological uncertainty, as if we ourselves and those dear to us were exposed to unknown dangers. This feeling is mixed with others, equally vague. A murder, the author of which is undiscovered and of whom there is no trace, has for our modern times something unreal about it. It contradicts our methods of thought and the rational view we take of the world and of life. Whence comes this feeling of uncanniness? Such a deed seems to confirm a belief in magic which we thought we had overcome. A murder without a murderer, a deed without a trace—these seem to revive an old belief which once lived in all of us, namely, the belief in the possibility of murder by thought. The fantasy expressed in the phrase *tuer son mandarin* seems to become a reality. A murder has been committed by the power of thought alone. No weapon is found, no tool, no sign of human activity. The victim has been killed at a distance, it would seem; for nothing, or next to nothing, points to a human agency. In such a situation, our primitive belief in the omnipotence of thought emerges out of the darkness whither the power of reason has long since banished it. It is easy to explain the satisfaction we feel when a mysterious murder case is unravelled. The part played by the punishment of the crime and the social guarantee connected with it must, of course, be recognized. But besides that there is the psychological effect of being once more able to recognize that our belief in the omnipotence of thoughts was a delusion, that there is no magic, no murder by thought in our sober world. Everything can be explained in a natural way, nothing is supernatural. In the light of these considerations the place belonging to clues is easy to find. Clues are tangible signs which prove—or seem to prove—that no crime can be committed by thought only and that we live in a world regulated by mechanical laws. The dead man was not killed by a ghostly hand but by a murderer of flesh and blood. The question "Who did the deed?" is answered by the clue, which assures us that it was not done by an evil magician. Like the glove in Kleist's *Prinz von Homburg* a great many clues point to the improbability, but nevertheless to the certainty, of some human agency. The solution of the question of how the deed was done no longer leaves room for the unconscious suggestion that it was done by magic. The proof that a shot came from a certain revolver makes a great difference to our secret belief in omnipotence. We recognize the criminal as a creature of flesh and blood if we know how he got there, how he committed the crime and how he managed to get away. All the uncanny elements disappear. He did

not fly through the air; he came in by the window. The absence
of any clues was no proof that magicians committed the crime,
but only that clever culprits had wiped out their traces. Now we
understand the secret meaning of clues and what constitutes their
psychological value over and above their significance in the eyes
of the law.

We observe the change undergone by the clue across the centuries and through the different levels of culture. In ancient times
they were a sign to primitive man that magicians had been at
work. No one might go near those signs; they were only sought
out for the sake of safety and one's own protection against the
magician.[210] Among the questions so important to modern criminologists, one was certainly missing: "How was the crime committed?" For that was already known: by magic.

Here we have reached the source of the clue. Originally clues
showed that a magician had done the deed; today they serve to
convince us that no magician was concerned. Once the silent witness to the belief in ghosts, they are now signs of the mechanistic-
technical belief (or superstition) of our day. In the development
of their function in society is mirrored an important phase of
history, extending far beyond the realms of criminology and jurisprudence. This phase is defined by the origin of clues and by the
stage, presumably the last, which they have now reached. In the
beginnings of criminology, the clue confirms the belief in the
omnipotence of thoughts, only to help in the end toward its destruction. We must, however, remember that it is precisely a
highly sublimated form of this belief that finds expression in the
logical and factual circumstantial evidence of today.

Is it really only the weakening of primitive conceptions and the
theoretical conviction of the existence of a rational and mechanical world that gives us reassurance? Does not murder make a
deeper impression, bear features of a terror that cannot be explained merely by the sacredness of blood? Analytical investigation not only shows that in all of us there still lives on some of
this belief in omnipotence, but also that we have often wished
another man's death. The elucidation of a murder brings the

comforting certainty, "Not you, somebody else is the murderer."
This completes our previous explanation in the sense that there
is an unconscious fear that our thoughts may compass another
man's death.[211] On the basis of such unconscious conceptions
many people might feel responsible for the death of their relations and friends.

Psychological analysis of the obsessional neuroses, which seem
so enlightening on the subject of criminology, shows that he who
unconsciously feels responsible for such a sin in thought is burdened with expectations of impending disaster. Such expectations,
which are so difficult to relieve, are, as analysis has shown, the
reaction to those strong, inimical and cruel wishes that the patient
harbors. He is constantly awaiting the punishment which he feels
he deserves for his evil thoughts. Some of the same dark fears must
exist in us, too—of the feelings that we are threatened by severe
punishment for our hostile and bloodthirsty desires; and we seem
to be able to overcome them when we read of a murder that has
been satisfactorily cleared up.

Now at last we see more clearly the origin of the interest in the
question "Who was the murderer?" and "How was the deed
done?" The affective interest attached to the fantasy of secret killing by the power of thought has become displaced on to our
curiosity as to who the unknown murderer is. Through the effect
of repression, the origin of our curiosity remains unconscious,
but its nature shows its derivation from the unfathomed depths of
the instinct to destroy and to get power over things. Moreover, the
old aggression still lives on in this curiosity itself. The supposed
omnipotence of thought not only commits the deed but finds out
the murderer, just as in the belief of savages one magician uses
his secret powers to kill and another (or even the same one) to
detect the culprit.

Society gets rid of the criminal as wild tribes do of a member
who has broken an important taboo. What they fear specially is
the contagion of the taboo. Freud has discovered in this fear the
unconscious fear of temptation common to every member of the
tribe. It is based on the strongly suppressed impulses of the in-

dividual who wants to commit the same antisocial deed. The horror of the crime, the desire for expiation, the urgent need to find the culprit, all these bear witness to a defence against his own repressed impulses. In the judge, the other legal functionaries, the public and all of us, the same unconscious tendencies that led to the murder are operative. It is as if these impulses, stimulated by a murder case, felt a temptation to break through. The counter-tendency, strengthened by reaction, finds an outlet in the wish to find and punish the murderer. Though economic and social reasons may play their part, it is in all probability the reaction of our own hidden impulses that accounts for the haste with which such cases, from the preliminary facts to the final stage of judgment, are dealt with.[212]

31. "THE CANARY MURDER CASE"

THE essential character of circumstantial evidence and the psychological sources of judicial errors based on it could be illustrated by an analysis of the Dostoevski novel *The Brothers Karamazov* better than by quoting actual criminal cases. Though Dostoevski's story is not "real" it is truer to life than life itself.[213] But if I had taken it as my example instead of the case of Gregor Adamsberger the objection might have been made that it was all invented and that things like that do not happen in reality.[214] There are judges who seriously maintain that judicial errors belong exclusively to the realm of fiction.

But now that I have proved my theory by material examples taken from real life, I will quote one from literature. Our theory should hold good generally, and so I will choose a story of good average merit rather than one of outstanding worth. It is Van Dine's *Canary Murder Case*.

The story is this: Margaret Odell was found dead in her flat in 71st Street, New York, about eleven o'clock in the evening. She

had belonged to the demimonde of Broadway, and had been one
of those cocottes who exert such a mysterious influence over men.
At first the murder looked like a robbery, in which the girl had
been strangled. Every clue the police followed proved that nobody
could have killed Margaret Odell, but the corpse, lying doubled
up on the wide silk sofa, gave the lie to this absurd conclusion.
The flat had only one entrance, the windows were barred. The
servant and the telephone operator in the building declared unanimously that Miss Odell had gone out to dinner on the fateful
evening with one of her men friends. She had returned with the
same man at about 11 p.m. The telephone operator knew and
described him. The man had remained with Miss Odell for about
half an hour. Nobody else had called, otherwise the operator must
have seen him because everyone had to pass the telephone box.
It looked as though the man who had taken her out to dinner was
her murderer. After every possibility had been examined, only
this one remained. But the telephone operator, a quiet, reliable
man, related to the examining chief of police an occurrence that
excluded this possibility. "It was just this, Sir. When the gentleman left about half-past eleven he asked me to phone for a taxi.
While we were waiting in my office for a taxi, we heard Miss
Odell shout for help. The gentleman rushed to her door and I
followed. He knocked, but there was no answer. He knocked
again and asked what was the matter. This time Miss Odell
answered and said everything was all right, he had better go
home and not worry. The gentleman came back with me to the
telephone switchboard. He said Miss Odell must have fallen
asleep and had a nightmare. We talked a few minutes longer and
then the taxi came. He said good-night and went. I heard the
taxi drive off."

Careful inquiry showed that the visitor had left Miss Odell's
flat five minutes before the telephone man heard her cry out.
He had just got the connection when the cry was heard. Of course,
the criminologist, who conducted the examination, went into
every detail of the incident. "Did the man stand near the switchboard?" "Yes, Sir, he leaned one of his arms on it." "How many

times did Miss Odell cry out?" "She screamed twice and then she called 'Help, help.' " "What did the man say when he knocked the second time?" "As far as I can remember, he said 'Open the door, Margaret! What is the matter?' " "Can you remember exactly what she answered?" "As far as I can remember, she said 'There is nothing wrong, everything is all right. Please go home and don't worry.' These may not be the exact words, but that is what it came to." "You could hear all this through the door?" "Yes, sir, the doors are not very thick."

The visitor went to the police himself and his story was in full accord with the one told by the operator. His name was Spotswood. He came of a good family and was a respectable member of society. He was married and very much afraid that his connection with the girl might leak out and damage him socially. He said he was worried when he heard her cry for help, but when she said everything was all right he thought she must have gone to sleep and had a bad dream. He had gone straight to his club and played poker till the early morning. His alibi was watertight. If he had been the murderer he could not have been in the club when the murder was committed. While he was in the house where Miss Odell lived she was alive, for a dead person does not cry out for help or talk to her murderer. Spotswood had neither the time nor the opportunity for murder; the facts were undeniable. They excluded his guilt as thoroughly as if he had been at the North Pole. Other people who were suspected also produced a faultless alibi. Here we have the uncanny situation of a murder without a murderer.

At this juncture, Philo Vance, the rich dilettante and amateur detective, who is assisting the police in this case, conducts a fresh search of the flat. He goes over the furniture again, examines— half-interested, half bored—the piano, rugs, dressing table and wastebasket, and then strolls over to the phonograph cabinet. He wants to sample the musical taste of the famous cocotte. "Cheap, bad music, no doubt," he says to his friend. He lifts the lid of the phonograph; there is a record on. "Look at that! The *Andante* of the Symphony in C minor, by Beethoven," he says, "the most beautiful *Andante* that was ever written." He puts the needle on and lets the record run, but the only sound is a slight scratch. The needle has nearly reached the end of the silent record when suddenly the flat is filled with terrible screams, followed by two shouts for help. After a short pause the same voice says: "There is nothing wrong. Everything is all right. Please go home and don't worry." The needle has got to the end.

And so the murder was explained. Spotswood had had a record prepared with his own voice speaking in a falsetto. He had taken the label from another record and stuck it on his own. He had given this record to the girl, together with some others, on the evening of the murder. After the theatre he had murdered her. He had put the record on before he left, after covering the phonograph with a rug to make it look as if it was very rarely used. Then he asked the telephone operator to order him a taxi. While he was waiting the needle got to the place where it released the screams. He then calculated the pause with the help of his wristwatch, and put his question at the right moment. The plan, carefully rehearsed in the laboratory, succeeded. The murderer had arranged the screams at the end of the record so that he had sufficient time to go and order the taxi.

This example is psychologically instructive because our interest is directed to the solution of both questions, "Who was the culprit?" and "How was the deed committed?" Judging by appearances, no living man had murdered Miss Odell. It really seemed as if she had been killed by that uncanny power, the omnipotence of thoughts. This impression is intensified by the evidence of the telephone operator. When the amateur detective finds out that Spotswood is the murderer—and he does this in a very interesting way which I have not told here—the tension is diminished but has by no means disappeared. For how did he commit the deed? We know that Spotswood is a rich business man; yet there is a secret about him. He has killed Miss Odell for obvious reasons; so much we understand. But still there is something supernatural about it. The girl talked to him, was alive when he left her. Though we know from the clues that Miss Odell was strangled in a very material way, the relics of belief in black magic are still alive in us, and suggest that she was bewitched, killed by magic.[215] This doubt comes out in the displacement on to a detail, in the fact that the girl who at that time was presumably dead, talked with the man who was perhaps her murderer. This detail reminds us of the animistic belief that the dead person is not completely dead and can raise his voice and speak.[216] An echo of this belief is awakened when Vance (and we with him) suddenly hear—weeks after Miss Odell is buried—her shrill voice calling for help. We now understand that Vance is conducting a kind of modern ordeal because he re-enacts, without knowing it, a piece of what has happened. And just when the uncanny reaches its highest pitch through the re-emergence of animistic conceptions, comes the explanation, which is a perfectly natural one. After experiencing a real fright for a second we understand how the deed was done. The record shows us. Here is no miracle, at best only a technical one to which we have become accustomed so quickly. Nevertheless, for the space of a second we had returned to the level of a superstitious Australian Negro and believed that the dead could speak, that a murdered woman could accuse her murderer. Then we realize that the voice did not come from a grave, but from a phonograph. Mystery has given place to a knowledge of mechanics. The murder is solved.

Here the double aspect of the clue is visible. What looked like something supernatural and magical, transcending all the laws of nature, is now precisely the thing that convinces us that no magic forces were concerned, that no supernatural power shapes our fate. The clue, once the messenger of the uncanny, now saves us from it.

We thought the interest in the questions "Who was the murderer?" and "How did he do the deed?" was far removed from psychology. Now we recognize that these questions are psychological questions. The investigation of criminal problems has led us by devious paths to psychological problems and has perhaps found the answer to some of them.

32. FINAL NOTE

OVER the mighty portal of the Dresden Law Courts we read the legend, "Truth will come to light." Such a legend satisfies our sense of justice, which does not allow a deed and its doer to remain unpunished, or an innocent man to suffer in his stead.

When we think of the number of examples of judicial errors that have caused many an innocent man to languish for years in prison, we are bound to remark that it is not a matter of indifference whether the truth comes out in 1920 or in 1933. The memory of the Jakubowski case will make us still more skeptical about that legend. For it is not a matter of indifference whether the light of day to which the truth at last comes will still be shining down upon the innocently condemned man or not.

PART TWO

The Compulsion to Confess

Translated from the German
by Norbert Rie

Foreword

THE FOLLOWING lectures were designed for a course at the Teaching Institute of the Vienna Psychoanalytic Association. The analytical orientation of the audience allowed me consistently to maintain one point of view, as I could assume a knowledge and appreciation of the other aspects of the problems we were studying, aspects which I have not discussed here in detail. This deliberate plan, used to keep the material within limits, should certainly not tend to underrate the significance and importance of other factors I have omitted which have already been recognized by psychoanalysis. In trying to make clear the part played by the superego in every neurosis, my emphasis is meant only to underline the enrichment of our thinking by stressing this new point of view.

The lecturer's manner and style which have been faithfully retained in the following pages may justify the lightening of tone here and there, the expansive style elsewhere, as well as some minor repetitions.

I am especially indebted to Dr. Ann Angel and Dr. Karl Abraham for a number of fruitful suggestions.

Vienna, February 1925.

I

Introduction

LADIES AND GENTLEMEN: I understand that you are well acquainted with the essential results of new research in psychoanalysis. I should not presume to ask for your attention for many hours, were I to lay those results before you once again. On the other hand, I cannot promise that I am about to offer completely new material. Rather, my talks will connect everywhere with what is known to you, and much of what the following lectures contain will be old material brought together and described from new points of view. You will see the facts already known to you from another angle.

In several places, and particularly in those which seem to me the most important, as in the hypothesis of the unconscious compulsion to confess and its psychological consequences, there results a new understanding of the body of facts, an understanding that, to my knowledge, has not yet been set forth and described in analytical literature. This understanding fits well with our earlier views concerning unconscious happenings. It nowhere contradicts them, and it supplements them in a certain way. If it should be acknowledged as scientifically significant and fruitful from a practical point of view, then this contribution will find its place within the frame of our analytical views, and it will be considered as a supplement to them in the psychoanalysis of the future.

The new angles, a scrutiny of which I should like to recommend to you, result from the continuation of the analytical research of recent years. The *repressed* has been so far, and will always be, the main objective of analytical examination, but Freud has always included in the scope of our research the analysis of the ego, and hence of those emotional factors in which repression originates and which maintain it. Everything that I have to tell you now will start from the results of those recent contributions of Freud and will attempt to continue them in a certain direction.

It may perhaps be advisable to explain briefly the wording of the title of these lectures. I shall try here to show the origin and the aims, the effects and forms of the expression of a significant, unconscious tendency. It is this *compulsion to confess,* which has not yet been appreciated adequately in analysis, and to which I am inclined to ascribe universal significance, presupposing certain cultural conditions. For reasons you will understand later, I have called this tendency the "compulsion to confess," without meaning to stake out the extent of its influence by this nomenclature. I should now say for clarification that, in this phrase, the *confession* is to be given prominence as practically and socially the most significant and, from an evolutionary point of view, the youngest function of this tendency. Its compulsive character can be deduced from its nature, which overcomes all inner and outer resistances, and from its direct derivation from the drives. That this tendency belongs to the system of the unconscious has been ascertained by clinical experiences in analysis. (The forms in which the need for punishment appears and its psychic effects will be dealt with here only as far as they are connected with the compulsion to confess.)

The assumption of a compulsive, unconscious tendency to confess, or more generally speaking, to communicate or depict endopsychically perceived happenings, has been occurring to me for several years because of certain experiences in my analytic practice. Moreover, it also appears to me to be irrefutable as a scientific postulate because of the theoretical points of view of psychoanalysis.

I shall start out from those experiences. And I shall choose at random an example from the analytical material of the day, one of those usual examples that has no outstanding features; the account of which can be heard in manifold variations originating from the sessions of any analyst. Patient A. starts his analytical session with the account of a small observation. He says that when entering my apartment, he noticed that my hat, which usually hung on a certain hook on the wall in the foyer, was not in its place, but on a distant hook. Usually he put his hat next to mine. He felt it might perhaps seem ridiculous but, when he missed my hat on the hook today, he could not ward off the suspicion that I had changed its place intentionally.

After a short pause he continues. Perhaps I do not want his hat to touch mine. Here the topic ends.

Then, apparently without transition, there follow reminiscences from early school days, among them an obscure, uncertain one of scenes of mutual masturbation, in which A. and an older boy rubbed their genitals together. From still earlier times a memory emerges now that he had pressed himself tenderly against his father and so rubbed his penis on his father's elbow. His father, he says, brushed him off angrily. Still less certain and more confused, seem to be impressions from farther back, in his home overseas, of all kinds of teasing and of games that he says he played as a quite small boy with a monkey. Then follow lively feelings and memories concerning the experiences which he had with his military superiors during the war. His behavior had expressed itself then as wavering between embittered defiance and humble submission toward those authorities. I will not give you more exact descriptions of details such as the manner of speech, the facial expressions, the hesitations and the changes of voice of the patient. I should still not be able to convey to you the impressions which are, for the observer, a better proof of certain conclusions than are logical deliberations.

His remarks at the start of the session were rooted in the patient's neurosis transferred to the analyst. They show hurt and bitterness over an imagined rejection of a homosexual attachment. We can ascribe symptomatic value to the excitement released in the patient by the observation of the changed place of my hat. We shall certainly evaluate and treat it in his analysis as a symptom. From the subject of the hat as a stimulus, ideas now lead backward to reminiscences of former homosexual actions and rejections, the type of which subsequently contributed to the development of the patient's relations to older men. Associations followed each other spontaneously. The analyst listened passively during the session.

Bringing the situation into sharper focus, we find that it contains three noteworthy psychological contradictions. The patient has communicated what came to his mind—the observation of the changed place of the hat. Does he wish to signify something? Yes, certainly. He wants, of course, to communicate the result of his observation. But what did he really express? You know from subsequent associations that what he thus expressed was much more, and quite different. You know it concerned impressions and reminiscences strongly suffused with emotion.

Assume for a moment that the case were less favorable than it actually turned out to be. A. would have communicated only that observation concerning the hat, and then would have changed to completely different, distant subjects, whose connection with the preceding ones could not be proved. Would he still actually have said the same thing? Yes, we should be forced to come to the same conclusion even though subsequent associations seemed to show no connection whatsoever with the subject. We saw the patient's emotional attitude toward the analyst change during the preceding period. We were able to observe the manifest signs of his feelings, realizing that this attitude of his had its forerunners in A.'s life. We would then reach the same opinion, even though we would not know the sexually symbolical meaning of the hat in the patient's unconscious processes. Hence, the first noteworthy fact is that the patient communicated something without knowing what he had actually said in his words.

The second enigmatic fact is closely connected to the first. It reveals itself immediately if you proceed as analytical technique requires in this case. You tell the patient what he unknowingly divulged to you, that he is under the impression that he has been homosexually frustrated, an impression which elicits in him feelings of hurt and bitterness. You would expect him to receive this announcement with astonishment, but expect him also to recall the whole sequence of his associations, and to recognize that his words really had this hidden meaning. Yet you will notice that the patient by no means accedes to this view. He will, although all psychological logic speaks for its acceptance, resolutely deny that he has given expression to such thoughts and feelings. You will be left then only with the assumption that, although he has said something, he does not know what he has said, and that he has said exactly what he did not wish to say.

Was the expression of the feelings evoked by the changed place of the hat really pointed at the analyst? One might think that to be the case, but it isn't quite so. The analyst's person acquires only a borrowed significance from the effects of transference. Those strong feelings relate to the father or to another person significant in the patient's development. It is to the other person that the patient really wants to complain, whom he wants to accuse, to whom he wants to show tenderness and anger. The analyst here actually plays the part of the "lightning conductor," as one patient put it. I'll make a comparison to illustrate this role. I know a gentleman who boasts that he gives his opinions of his acquaintances and friends, even if these opinions imply unpleasant truths, that he says these unpleasant things to their faces, calmly and without special consideration of narcissistic sensitivity. One of his malicious friends, however, characterized him by saying that he "tells everyone the truth as it applies to somebody else." The behavior of our patient is similar. He tells one person what is intended for another.

The third noteworthy fact, therefore, consists in the patient's telling something to a person for whom it is not intended. I imagine you have not found it difficult to divest these three facts, whose underground interconnection you recognize, of their enigmatic character. The differences between conscious and unconscious knowledge and purpose, as well as the effects of transference, furnish the explanation.

The second of the facts pointed out by us is a good place of departure for our research. The patient says something he does not wish to say. You know, of course, how that occurs. Analysis has accustomed you to acknowledge a difference between man's conscious purpose and what his unconscious emotional powers compel him to do. This difference became especially clear to you in the theory of resistance. You have come to understand that those powers, which once exiled disagreeable or proscribed ideas and tendencies to the realm of the unconscious, oppose their return with the same intensity that was used in banishing them to the netherworld. The force of repression manifests itself now as resistance. The sentence of expulsion is valid also as a ban against the return to that land from which the forbidden impulse or thought was ejected. In psychoanalysis, the problem presents itself to you somewhat as follows. The patient is consciously ready to say everything which the basic rule of analysis obliges him to say, but the resistances due to repression prevent him from doing so. You know that the strongest resistances of this kind are of an unconscious nature. The analyst applies himself to uncovering these resistances, to overcoming their effects and to reopening for the repressed an entrance into the realm of conscious perception. He acts, therefore, like a lawyer who reintroduces a suit that was once decided, and who wants now to show the court that the condemned did not deserve the particular punishment, that of deportation, meted out against him.

You were right in your studies of analysis to direct your most intensive attention to the processes of repression and resistance. These emotional processes are, according to Freud, the pillars of analytical theory. It cannot require a great effort to change the angle of consideration and to occupy yourself more closely with those psychic powers which aim to make an access to the conscious possible for the repressed. In doing so, it will be best for you to start from the following consideration: surely some emotional effort was required to repress certain ideas and impulses. The very term "repression" implies that. Also a certain amount of repression is required to keep them in that state, and it is exactly the same amount which we come to feel as resistance in analysis.

I said earlier that the strongest resistances were of an unconscious nature, but I beg of you not to misunderstand this statement. Resistances against the return into conscious thinking do not originate in the unconscious instinctual impulses. It is, therefore, neither possible nor permissible to speak of a resistance of the unconscious—a phrase you often hear, even from psychoanalysts. The repressed thoughts and tendencies have, mind you, the strongest inclination to return by themselves, to be voiced and to be realized.

To resume our comparison with the exiled or deported delinquent, he is homesick and makes every effort to achieve his return to his forbidden homeland. Every comparison limps, I know, but —to continue with ours—the lawyer, in our case, the analyst, supports those efforts, assuming, of course, that the goal will be achieved in a legal way and that the applicant will, in the future, behave in accord with the law of the land. Analysis has characterized this psychic situation by stating that the repressed ideas push against the censorship of the preconscious and that they succeed sometimes in returning. I think that, particularly in the realm of research into the emotional processes which we call the return of the repressed, analysis still owes us many an explanation. It is here also that it will be able to give us important psychological revelations.

What we know best about those processes Freud has shown us. We have learned to understand from him that repressed ideas have by no means remained ineffective, but that, subterraneously, they unfold an intensive activity. They send distorted representatives into the conscious, able not only to exist there, but also to thrive and to produce substitute formations and symptoms.

Again to continue our comparison: it is, therefore, as if the condemned person had changed the cut of his hair and beard in the foreign country, as if he had changed his clothes and were now returning with a false passport to the forbidden country. But Freud acquainted us with still another dynamic process. Exactly from the center of the repressing force, out of the highest intensity of the repressive expenditure, repressed traits of thought and feeling sometimes enter into the conscious without distortion. One can't fail to realize the differences between these two processes. In one, that alert guardian of the preconscious which we call censorship is outwitted, while, in the other, he is overpowered. The exile in our comparison uses in one case a special kind of vigilance against the stern guardian who is on the lookout for one person only, a person he knows from certain characteristics, and therefore the exile is able to slip through in a disguise. In the other case, the exile follows an overpowering urge that draws him to his homeland. Disdainfully he rejects all art of disguise and attempts an act of despair. In his true guise, he overcomes the surprised guardian after bitter opposition. You might call the first case deception, the second a breakthrough.

Going back to our original example, we argued that the patient told us something he did not intend to say. But through analytical psychology you have become accustomed to maintaining a point of view which proves itself by understanding neurotic illnesses in general as well as in their individual expressions. It traces the end result of the disturbance back to its essential motives. The apparent consequence of the illness is, according to Freud, actually the cause, the motive for falling ill. This conclusion, drawn from the effect, concerning psychic motives is justified in the entire realm of unconscious emotional life. Apply it to our case. Unconsciously the patient intended to say something that consciously he did not intend to say. He meant unconsciously to say just what would be especially embarrassing to him consciously, were he to express it.

We have therefore arrived at the assumption of an unconscious tendency which brings to expression repressed material without the conscious will of the person. This unconscious trend has nothing to do with the conscious intent to follow the basic analytical rule. It may make use of this intention, may sail under its flag, but it is separated from it by the deep-reaching, essential contrast of conscious and unconscious processes.

To continue our comparison again: our exile may, in his applications to the authorities for return to the homeland, state various reasons, stress professional motives, emphasize family interests, but he will conceal from the authorities the strongest motive that draws him to the homeland, for instance, the hope of winning a beloved girl there. Although the emotional processes which especially interest us in analysis are withheld from conscious thoughts, they are not deprived of all ability to express themselves. As these processes are of themselves unconscious, it is understandable that their tendency toward expression also remains unconscious.

Yet let us reflect. The very possibility of analysis, after all, rests on the existence of just such an effective urge of those rejected impulses toward expression and their ability to assert themselves to some extent. Only through that ability of the repressed unconscious to express itself somewhere, in a distorted and displaced form, in substitute and reactive formations, have we reached a position where it is possible to recognize and interpret its signs. We have, therefore, indeed, to thank for the existence of psychoanalysis as a research method, as well as a therapeutic procedure, only the effect of the urge of the repressed material toward expression and the possibility of its representation, even though distorted. This fact alone, perhaps not yet adequately advanced, justifies our expectation that within the unconscious processes a special significance is to be attributed to the tendency toward expression. But it also raises the hope in us that the analytical exploration of that urge toward expression, and its special properties, may bring a harvest for analytical practice and theory.

In order to go forward we start again from concrete examples. Up to now, we have always referred to what was to some extent known to you. The tendency of repressed ideas toward expression has seemed obvious to you ever since you have been occupying yourself with psychoanalysis. The incompletely suppressed material retained a possibility, however limited, of revealing itself. The following case of a slip of the pen will quickly show you that the tendency toward expression sometimes seems to pursue more specific intentions than we could have expected. I am indebted for the example to the report of a patient, who had separated from his wife after profound differences of character between the two had come to the fore in painful ways. From the time of separation dates a letter from the lady in which she writes literally, "If I return I am afraid it will *me* the same again." Clearly this is a slip of the pen. It should, of course, say, ". . . it will *be* the same again." What the writer means to express is this: "Even if I return to you we cannot be happy together. I am afraid it will be the same as before." But what the slip expresses is something entirely different. It really says, "Even if I return, I could not change anyway," or "I cannot possibly change my character. I am afraid I will be the same as before." The slip amounts to an unconscious confession. It expresses the conviction, "My unfortunate character is to a large extent the cause of our differences, of the impossibility of marital life together." However, this is an opinion to which the woman was never willing to accede. We have here, therefore, an expression of unconscious thoughts, an expression which is of the nature of a confession or of unconscious admission.

I should like to reinforce this impression on you, so I add, therefore, an example of a slip of the tongue which greatly amused a small group of people last summer. At a resort hotel where we were stopping, a young man met a charming girl. He had a spirited conversation with her at a party until late at night. As he talked to her, he was strongly attracted to the young lady. At the breakfast table the next morning she appeared earlier than he expected. Pleasantly surprised, the young man greeted her with these words: "Good morning! I thought of you still in bed."* He meant to say, of course, "I thought you were still in bed." He became quite embarrassed because of this "silly" slip. For us there can be no doubt that this slip of the tongue is tantamount to a confession which might be put into these words: "How I longed for you still in bed." It is, therefore, the confession of his tender and sensual wishes that forced itself past his lips, into the middle of a conventional sentence. Their expression would have been impossible otherwise for reasons of propriety. It is clear that here the suppressed, as in a *Putsch,* put itself impetuously in the place of the suppressing powers, and, almost undistorted, made the breakthrough.

Compare with this slip of the tongue another one which Freud

* "Guten Morgen, Fräulein, ich habe Sie noch in den Federn vermisst"— the word "vermisst" taking the place of "vermutet" (missed and thought, respectively).

mentions in *Psychopathology of Everyday Life*. A man approaches a lady in the street with these words: "If you will permit it, I should like to inscort you."** In this example, different from the first, not only a wish but also an apprehension created an expression. How do the two examples differ from each other? In the first, an unconcealed wish enters as a disturbing factor into the conscious intention of speaking; in the second, it is a wish with a bad conscience, as it were. Both represent self-betrayal, but the young man in our first example made his slip from a full heart, naïvely, one might say. The second one showed in his slip the apprehension that his offer to escort the lady might insult her. So he admitted unconsciously that his intention was not quite honorable. Freud adds to this example, "By the way, the young man probably was not very successful with the lady." We may assume not only that the young man suspected he would be rejected before he spoke out —his slip points, indeed, to some doubts in his mind—but also that it was his unconscious intention to deny himself success.

The first gentleman, however, who had betrayed his sexual desire so openly in his slip, was apparently not at all harmed in the eyes of the young lady. She blushed for a moment, but continued the conversation in a friendly and unselfconscious way, as if she had not heard the slip or had not paid attention to it. It is possible that she unconsciously understood the confession that came through in the slip as a kind of involuntary compliment. Freud points out that the second gentleman, by his parapraxis in addressing the lady, anticipates in a way the conventional reply: "What do you think I am? How can you insult me so?" The lady would thus react to the slip as if she had understood and interpreted it, as if she had actually made into reality the man's uneasy anticipation.

I said that the young girl of the resort incident continued the conversation after the slip as if it had not happened, as if the gentleman had said the correct thing. However, that is not quite so. Besides her blushing, there was a small matter that allows us

** "Wenn Sie gestatten, mein Fräulein. möchte ich Sie gerne begleit-digen" —the word "beleidigen" (insult) combining with "begleiten" (escort).

to note that she, too, clearly observed the slip, and unconsciously understood its significance very well. This was what she said right after the slip. It sounded quite banal—apparently an answer to the young man's words of greeting. But I should say that under the surface there is a connection with the slip and that her reply made sense and even had a special point. She said, "I slept very well." This seems to be an answer to the man's assumption that she would sleep longer and get up later. On closer examination, one notices that her sentence is scarcely a reply to what the man intended to say. Had he really said, "I thought you were still in bed," we would perhaps expect the reply, "I am accustomed to getting up early in the summer," or, "The sun woke me. I am planning an outing . . ." or something of the sort. But, "I slept very well" does not indeed seem to be exactly the reply we'd expect. It merely *seems* to be appropriate. But it surely must seem to you to be forced.

However, the young lady's reply is quite appropriate if we recognize it is unconsciously influenced by the preceding slip of the man. He had indicated that his sleep had been disturbed in the morning by thoughts of the girl, that his impatience to see her had driven him out of bed so early. If the lady, after he expressed his surprise at seeing her so early, assured him that she slept very well, this can only be a demonstrative rejection of the tenderness unconsciously implied in his slip. It can only mean something like this: "Thoughts of you haven't disturbed me for one minute. On the contrary, I slept very well. Do not, by any means, imagine that the longing to see you made me come here so early."

But if you consider the sexual wishes unconsciously betrayed in the man's slip, then the deeper reasons of that unconscious defense will become clear to you also. What sounds so forced when considered as spoken, consciously has meaning and significance for the unconscious of both persons. It is as if between the two there existed a kind of secret understanding. The man's words and and the girl's reply are unconsciously attuned like two fine musical instruments.

In comparing these last slips with other instinctual manifestations, we have come across significant differences which might cause us at times to ascribe special effects to the general urge of the unconscious to express itself, effects not attained in the form of instinctual eruption, as we know it. In certain cases the urge of the unconscious to express itself will assume the character of a trend, the goal of which is confession. We have not overlooked the fact that there were important differences between the two examples. The psychic mechanisms are different in the two cases and it seems as if this difference corresponded to a difference in the reactions of the external world. The lady who had been addressed with the suggestion of being "inscorted" would perhaps, as we said, reply in an offended or angry vein. The girl whom the young man had thought of "still in bed," replies with a rebuff, but in a roguish or teasing vein.

You may perhaps argue that there are different persons and situations before us and that this fact alone causes different reactions. You are certainly right but I venture to assume that not the differences in persons and circumstances, but the emotional difference inherent in the two slips of the tongue is decisive. Both slips are expressions of incompletely suppressed instinctual impulses, but the kind of expression varies. One is, in a way, a hidden confession, the other an open confession of these instinctual impulses. You may now wonder why the hidden confession meets a sharper rejection than does the far less ambiguous one. That may be connected with more general questions which we will perhaps discuss later. For the present we shall underscore a similarity. Both expressions represent confessions and have a certain effect upon the external world, differing apparently from the effect of other instinctual expressions. Meanwhile, you have certainly remembered other examples of slips of the tongue or of the pen which you would characterize as confessions. You can perhaps tell of having forgotten a plan whereby you confessed unconsciously your repugnance against its execution, of one of those little symptomatic actions, the nature of which is easily discernible as that of confession. Tugging at the tuft of a cushion, playing with a wedding ring and similar inconspicuous actions often become for the analyst unconscious confessions.

At this point, questions arise: "How does it happen that expressions of instinctual impulses can assume this new character —that of confession? Why and under what conditions does it occur? How does the effect on others of a confession differ from the effect of other kinds of expressions of the same instinctual impulses? Is it perhaps the external world which has a determining influence upon the transformation of an instinctual expression into a confession?" These questions, which concern only the most superficial relations of the two emotional phenomena, will certainly be followed by others of greater importance.

Let us, for the present, keep in mind that we have found, as we believe, that the general urge of unconscious material to express itself sometimes assumes the character of a tendency to confess. We cannot yet tell when this occurs, what its psychic meaning is and whether or not this emotional process should be considered one of general importance. But can we yet maintain that the analytical examination of these examples of self-betrayal in slips permits us to speak of an emotional tendency to confess? It has been ascertained only that those instances of parapraxis represent a confession in effect. But is it not perhaps rash, on so narrow and unstable a basis, to draw conclusions as to motives from this effect? It is not our intention to conceal those uncertainties from ourselves. In any case the question seems to us to warrant careful psychological examination.

Today we intended to occupy ourselves only generally with the information as to where our exploring trip would take us. Next time we'll start out on our expedition without further preparation.

II

The Unconscious Compulsion to Confess

LADIES AND GENTLEMEN: In the study of development of instinctual expressions, it is best to begin with their initial situations. The hungry suckling experiences, in hallucination before he is fed, as Freud assumed, gratification of his need for nourishment. As stimulus mounts, he tends to shove off his displeasure by screaming, crying and thrashing about. These expedients do decrease the tension of frustration, when memory later shows that it was followed by the gratification of the need. Soon the motor action which originally served to achieve release becomes a means of expression to notify the external world of certain needs and to demand gratification. The original function is, of course, preserved, and it will never in the future completely lose its meaning. Furthermore, remember that this urge for expression is not new and is an independent emotional tendency. It is the emergence of this very quality of instinctual impulses that we call their urging, their driving character, and it is just this nature of the instinctual impulses, the imperative desire for gratification, from which we derive the compulsory character of the urge for expression.

We have thus determined the primary function of the urge for expression which must be recognized as the most significant, other than the discharge. It serves to announce the instinctual needs. The child first follows this urge for expression entirely naïvely and without inhibitions. Under the influence, however, of his parents and educators in the external world, he learns to use conventional signs in place of the natural ones, as well as to tone down and restrict them.

The suppression of primary drives as required by education also modifies the expression of these instinctual impulses. The suppression of an instinctual impulse creates the indispensable condition in which its expression may assume the character of a confession. In the communication of the instinctual need, the limiting or inhibiting forces of the external world bring their influence to bear and contribute in determining the character and form of the expression.

We now begin to comprehend the difference between a primitive urge for expression and representation on the one hand, and the tendency on the other to confess which I'll describe here. If instinctual impulses striving for expression are spurned or condemned by the external world, the still feeble ego can manage only to express them in the form of confession. The concept of the urge for expression is, therefore, the more general, more comprehensive one. The tendency to confess is the narrower and more specific one. Hence, the inclination to confess is a modified urge for the expression of the drives. They have been altered under the effects of the reception by the external world of certain instinctual manifestations, and have started serving new purposes.

The suppression of an instinctual impulse is by no means identical with its repression. However, we concern ourselves here with the changes to which the urge for expression is subject when a drive is repressed. Repression, as you know, does not condemn suppressed ideas and tendencies to utter ineffectiveness and silence. In the processes of the return of the repressed, the unconscious outgrowths of the repressed to some extent are allowed to express themselves. Those descendants, finally admitted into consciousness, still show traces of the repressing forces, as escaped convicts show signs of prison life. Substitute formations and symptoms will not only bear the features of the suppressed instinctual impulses, but also the imprint of the repressing factors. This effect can be explained because they also have their origin in unconscious drives. In this way, the repressing powers themselves become objects of unconscious expression, and, under the influence of the repressive forces, the expression of instinctual impulses representing the striving for gratification also becomes the manifestation of the reaction rejecting those wishes.

While the urge for expression was originally instrumental in the discharge and communication of the great drives of man, it has changed its function gradually. The forms of expression are still there, of course, representations of the instinctual needs, but in their shape and in the way in which they emerge they testify now to the effectiveness of the factors that caused the repression. They may, therefore, be called, in this sense, unconscious confessions. The example of that slip "inscort" (*begleit-digen*) shows you clearly the influence of opposing impulses, and it approaches the neurotic symptom in its structure and emotional genesis. Characteristic of this symptom is that it satisfies not only the demands of sexual and ego tendencies, but also betrays both as the powers engendering it. Like our slip of the tongue, it combines opposing impulses in one compromising expression. The symptom not only represents the force of forbidden wishes, but also the power of the forbidding agencies, not only the force of the temptation, but also the intensity of its defense. Yes, in some neuroses, as in the obsessional neurosis, the symptoms will show much more clearly the character of a reaction-formation than that of the gratification given the patient in his substitution by displacement. The fact of the disturbance itself, the nature of the suffering, also becomes the sign of those profound effects, however, in those forms of neurosis in which the influences of the powers of repression are not so clearly discernible as in obsessional neurosis. The symptom, thus following the urge for expression of the repressing forces as well as of the repressed tendency, takes on the character of the confession, because we call a statement about impulses or drives which are felt or recognized as forbidden, a *confession*.

Insofar as the symptom establishes and maintains itself essentially as a substitute formation and substitute gratification of unconscious impulses, we can speak of it as having the character of an unconscious confession. I'd like to add that the designation "unconscious" justifies itself also after further deliberations. As I have said, we were concerned with a statement about instinctual impulses which are felt to be forbidden. From Freud's new theses about the genesis of the superego we have learned that not only impulses become unconscious through the process of repression, but also that the most significant part of those ego agencies which forced repression becomes unconscious. The character of confession we ascribe to the neurotic symptoms is therefore determined by the quality of the unconscious which the repressed shares with the repressing powers from whose simultaneous effects it resulted. Still a third factor enters in: the symptom is rated as suffering without being recognized by the patient as a confession. The emotional forces, through whose dynamics the symptom derives its existence, as well as some of its essential intentions, remain unconscious. The confession is therefore characterized as unconscious because its origin, its substance, and its confessional character remain unconscious.

If you add the fact that the patient makes his confession without knowing to whom (as in the situation of analytic transference), we are back again to stating those noteworthy psychological facts which we characterized in the first lecture. I could describe them now in a new manner. The patient admits something, confesses something, that is not known to him. He confesses something and does not know either what he has said in doing so, or to whom he has said it. I could even add two more noteworthy facts. The patient confesses something and does not know that what he says *is* a confession and he does not know what drove him to make this confession. I think the enigmatic character of these facts speaks loudly enough for the existence and effectiveness of unconscious trends.

The character of compulsion which I attribute to the tendency to confess cannot be derived from the force of the driving impulses alone. In the transformation from a primitive urge for expression into the compulsion to confess, two factors can be recognized that determine its compulsive character. The first is a resistance against free instinctual expression, a restraint that came from without and eventually remained within. It is reflected in the character of unconscious confession. The second factor results from, or is at least felt through, the reactive reinforcement which the intensity of the drive experiences through repression. This will find its expression in the difference between an uninhibited expression and the unconscious confession, and therefore the designation as compulsion to confess seems to me to be a quite legitimate one.

It seems to me we have reached the point where we understand psychologically the transition from a tendency for free-floating expression to the compulsion to confess. It first occurred under the sign of the social application of the expressions of drives. Although originally only processes serving the motor discharge, they became the representation and communication of our needs to the external world as a kind of invitation to accomplish gratification. The kind of reception those expressions are given by the external world becomes decisive for their further development and formation. The refusal or rejection of these expressions by denial, for instance, will make them represent also the factors that inhibit gratification. The repetition of this process in the repression stage presupposes a primitive identification with the people with whom the inhibition originated, an identification which will perpetuate itself later on in the institution of the superego.

Under the influences of the external world which have become decisive for the still feeble and undeveloped ego, the original expression modifies its intentions. A different reaction on the part of the external world corresponds to this change. The neurotic symptom is subject to similar transformations. All of you know how the symptom has changed its original meaning and intention, and in psychoanalysis you have become acquainted with the historical stratification of its various meanings and aims. But analysis is only a piece of artificial life and the confessional character of the symptom comes forth clearly enough outside the analysis. You may argue that a confession which the other person does not understand as such is no confession. But the matter is not that simple. The fact that, until a few decades ago, we were not able to unravel hieroglyphics would not mislead us to assume that they were only senseless play. We had no doubt about hieroglyphics being a means of communication. Now another secret code in ciphers, not understandable to us, clamors to be understood, and conceals itself only from those who have no key to it.

The external world reacts to neurotic symptoms as it does to the slips of the tongue quoted by us as examples, as if it understood them and comprehended their meaning. This is, however, understanding of a special kind. But if this is the success of the symptoms, it must also be one of their motives. The patient must wish unconsciously that his symptoms be understood in this way. An obsessive patient under my observation suffered especially from the painfulness of his compulsive looks at others which he could not control and which expressed his unconscious hatred, contempt or scorn for people particularly close to him whom he consciously held in high esteem. It was noteworthy that he continued these glances, which were so painful to him, making them even more clearly aggressive if those who were targets for them did not change their friendly behavior toward him. He continued this behavior until the person singled out became unfriendly or cool toward him. Generalizing in this case, we can say that the longer a neurotic illness lasts, the more clearly the symptoms reveal their meaning to the external world, as though obtruding into it, no matter what desperate efforts at concealment the patient may make. "Man's self-betrayal oozes from all his pores," Freud said. We now want to emphasize, as an additional fact, that this self-betrayal is actually an unconscious confession.

So far I have pointed out the significance of the symptom's character of confession before the external world. We now face the difficult task of understanding its meaning and its function within the emotional life of the individual. We'll be most successful if I again utilize the experience gained in psychoanalysis. It is, after all, analysis which gives us the best opportunity to reconstruct the sequence of emotional processes. In the intermediate realm between fantasy and life presented by analysis, the analyst personifies unconsciously for the patient his father or another person important in the emotional life of the child. The patient complains to him of his troubles, shows where his unconscious intentions had aimed and what obstacles life had put in the way of their realization. In this analytical renewal and reliving, it is as if the old shadows of the underworld were drinking blood once more, were once again assuming vivacious significance and becoming a part of daily life. Along with the old memories, the old affects awake too, now mostly directed at the analyst who is the phantom of the patient's transference. Words now must regressively replace actions. As he expresses in words, countenance, movements, his tender or inimical, respectful or contemptuous feelings, the patient has accomplished with a lesser expenditure of energy what he had earlier been driven to do. In this substitution by displacement on to words, etc., the young man who directs his resistances against the analyst really repeats the actions planned against his father. These manifestations themselves are the extraordinary mitigated and modified substitutes for actions.

The narrative or description of his feelings of resistance is thus not merely an account of actions displaced onto the analyst, but their diluted repetitions transposed into words. The old emotions expressing themselves in this manner have lived on in him indestructibly since childhood. They have found here for the first time their appropriate expression in words and emotional eruptions. We call the re-experiencing and reliving of the condemned actions expressed in the words of the narrative their confession or admission. We realize that the patient does not know what he communicates or what his communication means. This is, therefore, an unconscious confession. We know also that in the realm of the psychology of neuroses we must drop the difference between material and psychic reality. It goes without saying that here I use the one word "action" to signify unconsciously imagined or desired action. We may say that confession is a repetition of action or of certain behavior substituted by displacement and with different emotional material, as words must substitute for action.

If confession is characterized in this way as a displaced, weakened repetition of an act, we may not understand what it is that constitutes the liberating, releasing and resolving effect of analytical therapy, how such a repetition in confession could have a therapeutic effect. This question, of course, touches on the most important and controversial problems of analytical therapy, the discussion of which cannot concern us here. The problems of active therapy and its necessary limits would have to enter the discussion and we would have to concern ourselves with the question of whether and to what extent the repetition of the act in transference should be helped by the analyst, whether and to what extent it is of advantage for the analysis to push its limits toward material reality. These questions are at times insidious.

Today, however, I'll avoid the temptation to concern us with these problems and only emphasize several points of view, in addition to those pointed out by other analysts, which seem to me to be especially worthy of consideration. The first is that the resistances emerging in the transference to the analyst, for instance in which the patient re-enacts hostile feelings aimed at his father, as well as resistance against homosexual tendencies, seem, indeed, to give to those impulses some gratification they had not enjoyed before. However, this gratification is of a special kind, an extraordinarily limited satisfaction, restricted to imaginary life, relegated to smallest quantities. That, however, does not destroy its emotional reality. Therefore, I'd say that a measure of relief seems to come from the partial gratification brought about by confession of the act, since this confession is a weakened repetition of the act in a changed form. It is as if a small gratification of his drives were actually indispensable to man, and as if a renunciation of their gratification could be achieved only after indulging in them to a certain extent. The French have a saying: *Réculez pour sauter mieux* (run back in order to leap farther). It is not, however, the stepping back that is more important, but rather the jump. There are perhaps quantitative factors of unpleasant tension not yet fully understood by research, factors that make a material satisfaction necessary in some form or other. Only in this way is it possible to make a renunciation of the whole satisfaction. It is as though an impatient creditor has to be paid at least a small part of the debt, to show him, as it were, the debtor's willingness to pay so that he will be more patient with the delay. I'll return to this problem later.

The other factor of therapy which is implied in this confessional character is more difficult to recognize and to comprehend psychologically. Like the first, it is clearly of an instinctual kind and lends itself to preliminary interpretation: i.e., there is a partial overcoming of some obscure anxiety involved. We surmise what this anxiety signifies. It has the character of the social anxiety which we call a feeling of guilt. I believe we are able to describe correctly what happens in saying that latent anxiety is regressively transformed into a bit of pleasure by the admission. With it, a repression is lifted.

I remind you of the special techniques of the joke as described by Freud. A similar removal of a repression takes place through them in favor of an otherwise rejected representative of an impulse. We cannot tell what kind of pleasure this is, but drawing a conclusion from the subject matter of the affect of anxiety, we should arrive at certain assumptions about it. Can it be the pleasure that is connected with the partial gratification of suppressed impulses? Surely that pleasure is, to a certain extent, contained in this gratification, even though the latter is extremely small. At least as significant a share of that pleasure must, however, be of a masochistic kind, because the anxiety that inhibited the expression of a forbidden impulse concerned punishment.

Something of a need for punishment finds its partial gratification in the compulsion to confess. The feeling of guilt reacting to the forbidden wishes finds a partial satisfaction in confession. We may, therefore, contend that a part of the therapy of confession in psychoanalysis is based on the fact that in it impulses and thoughts as well as the need for punishment find a certain quantitatively limited gratification which is qualitatively different from a material satisfaction, from their "real" fulfillment.

I realize how inadequate this description is to the actual situation and I therefore wish to anticipate your problems. You will correctly say that the need for punishment is not being actually satisfied, as no punishment follows the sulky or defiant, hostile or contemptuous manifestation of the patient's resistance in the transference-situation. Besides the endeavor to transform the repetition into memory, no other reaction whatsoever occurs on the part of the analyst. You are entirely right—so much so, that I also hasten to show you the weak spot in my other contention concerning the partial gratification of the suppressed representative of the drives. These needs are not really being satisfied either since the patient does not give vent to his hostility toward the analyst's authority. Not even the slightest aggression occurs. Nor does a young woman in transference-love fall on the analyst's neck. But, as I said, it is a partial gratification achieved only by expressing, by putting into words or signs, emotions otherwise difficult to express. Yet you can still assert, with some justification, that the suppressed impulses experience some, though a greatly restricted, gratification. Please consider that the frequent repetition of these expressions of strong feelings is a possible substitute for a certain amount of gratification. Freud called thinking "acting in small quantities." Uttering or voicing these thoughts or impulses comes even closer to doing or acting "in small quantities."

We do not yet understand, of course, how the unconscious need for punishment also receives its due in analysis, or, more specifically, in confession in analysis. Consideration of the fact that the patient frankly bares his weaknesses anchored in his drives, that he admits actions and feelings he does not find compatible with his moral and esthic views, could afford us a first approach to such a contention. But we feel how little that means since it concerns only a conscious confession.

We take a step forward when we learn in psychoanalysis that the need for punishment shifts from punishment to confession. Compare the situation with that of a little boy who seems to fear punishment for some secret misdeed. In most cases, on closer observation you can make the surprising discovery that least of all does he fear the punishment itself. Rather, he shows feeling of anxiety because of what his parents may be thinking as they learn of his little misdeed and because he must confess it to them. He has transformed the fear of punishment into the fear of confession. The confession itself, as that which precedes the punishment, has now become in the highest degree terrifying. The child himself says in many cases that it is not punishment he fears, but the scene in which he will tell his parents what he did.

You have certainly heard of the tragic cases of the suicide of pupils in which fear of confession obviously played its part in the sad end, while fear of punishment, which in many cases would not have occurred, did not have a significant role. The student who is not afraid of the examination but finds the preceding tension unbearable, the soldier, who longs for the battle that will perhaps bring death because he cannot bear the anxious hours that precede it, will have come to your mind as examples of similar situations in which a displacement of fear can be established. Here we see that the need for punishment, like any other strong drive, produces tensions that are displaceable. The intensity of these displaced impulses can be lessened only by partial gratification.

If we were to compare these psychological facts with analytical studies of sexual development, we could find similar mechanisms there. I remind you of the normal and the pathological role of fore-pleasure. The dangers of fore-pleasure in sex are especially obvious when the activities which only prepare for pleasure and pave the way to orgasm, take the place of the normal sexual goal, when fore-pleasure becomes end-pleasure. As a confession usually leads up to punishment and implies a loss of love by the parents, it can, as a preliminary stage or as a substitute, become ultimate punishment itself and satisfy the need for punishment. In the normal process, the wrongdoer would feel a certain tension before confession. At the prospect of punishment this tension would experience an extraordinary increase. We guess, at this point, that there is perhaps a more general significance to the psychic mechanisms of the displacement of anxiety, but we can follow these in this lecture only in their relations to punishment and confession.

I suggest we acknowledge the existence of the displacement of anxiety by using a new phraseology analogous to the Freudian nomenclature for the pleasure-mechanisms. I think we should call the first stage of anxiety "fore-anxiety," which is in the same relation to end-anxiety as fore-pleasure to end-pleasure. The

close psychological connection of pleasure and anxiety makes it appear likely that the exploration of the relations between fore-
anxiety and end-anxiety should lead to an important enrichment
of the ego-psychology. To suffer the anxiety of confession and the
act of confession, which itself is felt to be painful, is, thererfore,
that partial gratification of the need for punishment which we
claim for the confession. We know that what means unpleasure
for one psychic system can have the character of pleasure for another. Therefore I'll by no means deny that there is pleasure in
the unpleasurable overcoming of anxiety in the confession.

If we return to an earlier assertion we can make an important
correction. I said that suppressed impulses receive a partial gratification in their verbal expression. However, this very act of expressing is part of the fore-pleasure of their gratification. I will, therefore, say that the partial gratification brought by the confession
to the repressed impulses or drives, and to the need for punishment, is rooted in the partial granting of fore-pleasure, and that
along with this the overcoming of fore-anxiety is implied. As a
preliminary, but by no means adequate result of our efforts to
understand the problem, we have, up to now, only realized that
the confession grants a partial gratification to the repressed wishes
and impulses by the fulfillment of fore-pleasure and by the overcoming of fore-anxiety. By its character of compromise it is thus
well able to replace the neurotic symptom. The symptom, on its
part, has established itself as the substitute for the gratification
of repressed tendencies and of the need for punishment. Actually,
we often see symptoms disappear in analysis when needs of this
kind, at odds with each other, have found a completely adequate
expression in confession. The confession, as an essential part of
psychoanalysis, thus refers to two great centers of feelings and
ideas, centers which are wrested from the unconscious. The patient admits his forbidden impulses and the wishes they have
stirred up in him. He simultaneously admits the need for punishment that has reacted to the pressure of these drives and wishes.
We so come to appreciate one of the most important tasks of the
analyst by understanding that he leads the patient to understand

first what he has unconsciously confessed and also its psychological significance.

This statement reminds us of the third of the factors contributing to the determination of the therapeutic value of the analytic confession. This is the transfer of unconscious material into verbal presentations and verbal perceptions. This transformation has a definite significance for the pleasure-depreciation of the repressed impulses as well as for the unconscious need for punishment. We have learned from Freud that verbal presentations are necessary to make consciousness possible. It is only the confession that enables us to recognize preconsciously what the repressed feelings and ideas once meant and what they still mean for us, thanks to the indestructibility and timelessness peculiar to the unconscious processes. By the confession we become acquainted with ourselves. It offers the best possibility for self-understanding and self-acceptance.

Why should a transformation into verbal presentation like this acquire significance for repressed drives and impulses? Mainly because it appears likely to discontinue the process of repression and thus to prepare the possibility for a better kind of adjustment to reality.

This discontinuation of repression is quite clearly shown by the fact that in the confession not only the suppressed impulses, but also the agencies driving toward repression achieve appropriate expression. In this sense, confession is conscience speaking up. The accuser lays on the table his bill of accusation. Keep in mind that what we conceive as conscience proper is mute. The criminals of Paris call it "la muette." In the confession it starts talking. What was mute finds voice in it. Here we come across the double emotional function of the compulsion to confess. It shows the act and the impulses leading up to it. It shows the distance between the ego, overpowered by the wishes and impulses of the id, and the superego. The understanding of the act (you remember that we speak here always of imagined, unconscious acts) in its deep meaning for the individual, unrecognized until now, and the compromise of the ego with the demands of the superego indicate that the person who is making his admission is beginning to get acquainted with himself.

Schopenhauer, in a passage in his essay "About the Basis of Morals," is not quite correct when he calls conscience "nothing but acquaintance with oneself originating in one's own way of action and becoming ever more intimate." Conscience is, in its most essential features, itself unconscious. Only the emergence of conscience into consciousness brings about such "acquaintance" in Schopenhauer's sense. I should point out a contrast at this point: the imagined criminal deed which we can conceive as substitute action for patricide or for incest, occurred in the unconscious. Its repetition by means of its transfer into verbal presentations produced by psychoanalysis occurred in the preconscious. It is, therefore, this difference that now causes the patient to become better acquainted with himself, to understand himself. He begins to give a more tolerant understanding to the contrast between ego-ideal and actual ego, superego and ego. To become acquainted with oneself means also to understand preconsciously that the limits of our emotional life are drawn upward and downward much farther than we thought. This means, conventionally speaking, that we are unconsciously much more wicked, but also much better than we thought we were.

Conscience has in the confession reacquired the ability to speak. Let me please use a comparison to illustrate how psychoanalysis works in this direction. A criminal case, the file of which has been buried in some corner of the archives, is reopened and comes before the court of appeals. The third therapeutic factor thus consists in the retroactive annulment of repression, as the repressed thoughts become preconscious through their connection with their corresponding verbal presentation. In schizophrenia the therapeutic character of the verbal presentation results from the clarification of the emotional processes. In this case the introduction of verbal presentation forms the first attempt at restoration to health, as Freud has shown convincingly. He demonstrated how these efforts at first aim at regaining the lost objects and how, with this intention, they choose the way to the object by verbalization, and in doing so content themselves eventually with words in place of things. We suspect that the unconscious confession, too, represents such an attempt at a reconquest of the object, and that this is one of its essential intentions.

Several other experiences from clinical analysis will perhaps allow us to understand still more thoroughly the basis of emotional relief through the compulsion to confess. One of the most revealing experiences of this kind is the recognition of the significance and latent meaning of *acting-out* in analysis. We know that acting-out serves the compulsion to repeat. Analytical experience shows us that acting-out appears during treatment under conditions of resistance. It is clear that in this repetition the patient yields to the urge of his unconscious drives.

It may perhaps first appear strange to you that I should assure you that the impulse to replace reproduction in narration by acting-out appears especially when the events to be reproduced are under the pressure of a particularly strong feeling of guilt. As you know, the need for punishment drives toward the repetition of forbidden acts. A feeling of guilt accompanying certain memories and emotions is certainly not the only condition for acting-out, but is perhaps the most important, and in practice the most significant one or so it seems to me. Under conditions of an intense need for punishment the patient then puts the acting-out (which is so much closer to the repetition of the act) at the time of remembering, instead of reproducing the memory in words. Acting-out as a process experienced in psychoanalysis finds its place within the more general emotional sequence that drives the patient, oppressed by feelings of guilt, toward forbidden acts followed up by a considerable psychic relief.

If, however, reproduction through narration is a confession that repeats the act in the verbal and attenuated form and with different material, then acting-out, too, can be called a confession. It serves the same purpose—to show something, to admit it. We know what it wishes to show—exactly the same as what the patient might act out. Hence, it is a demonstration. "Look here, how jealous, malicious, spiteful and petty I was" (or: still am). Such a demonstration certainly is meant to express suppressed drives or impulses. In addition, it displays the patient's need for punishment. In this sense, one may compare it to the behavior of children who show off how "naughty" they are. There is no doubt that this seemingly unnatural behavior, such as the patient's acting-out, still follows the pleasure-principle, as it aims at the gratification of strong emotional needs. Often enough, a child becomes naughty because he feels guilty and unconsciously wants to be punished.

In addition to the tendencies pointed out earlier, another one now becomes apparent. Parading one's own weaknesses remains incomprehensible unless one keeps in mind the fact that it is, after all, not the repetition of the act, however strongly one may be driven toward it, but still only its communication. If the hidden meaning of this most peculiar confession were to be translated into the language of consciousness, we would need to provide an introductory and a concluding sentence as supplementary. We would need to say in advance that the subsequent acting-out concerns a confession, a *demonstratio ad oculos:* "Look here, how spiteful, how malicious and vengeful, etc., I was!" This confession is often not an end in itself. It has the meaning of an appeal to the parents or their substitutes, which is what makes necessary the addition of a concluding sentence: "Please consider those weaknesses! Just because this is how I am, you must forgive me! Punish me, but love me again!" Thus the confession becomes an eloquent plea for absolution. Without the introductory and concluding sentences added by us, without such an alignment with the large emotional continuity, the patient's peculiar behavior cannot be understood.

The acted-out confession serves not only to represent one's own concealed impulses and secret wishes. It not only serves the need for punishment, the unconscious urge to achieve the loss of love. To the same extent it also serves the wooing for love, the urge to receive renewed love through the very punishment itself or even the form of punishment. In some cases, especially as in the neuroses in which masochism stands out, the need for punishment will even be the predominant meaning of the acting-out. An obsessional neurotic, who was under my treatment and whose perverted gratification consisted in being beaten on the behind, exhibited conspicuously in his acting-out a tendency which could be described only in those words. He raised his rump demonstratively into the air to receive blows. The concluding sentence to be added by us in cases like this would take this form: "Punish me, go on, beat me!" To receive blows meant unconsciously the same as to be loved, hence, the gratification of masochistic and homosexual desires. You will remember that such acting-out for the sake of a gratification of the need for punishment is not the only emotional phenomenon in which the need for punishment and some erotic tendencies are welded together into a whole.

In psychoanalysis there exist, of course, various transitions from the reproduction in telling to the acting-out. There are, indeed, even various kinds of acting-out. In some cases, as for instance when an attack of hysterics always repeats itself in the analytic session at a particular spot in the sequence of associations, the character of wish-fulfillment in the symptom's appearance certainly becomes very clear to the analyst, but the double function of the symptom proves that those other factors, too, are in the picture. In line with the special character of the neurotic illness, the factor of an emotional break-through will stand out in the patient's behavior in analysis, at other times, it will be the factor of confession. Both factors in varying intensity are constantly present in acting-out. As I emphasized earlier, one can observe in many cases that precisely as the need for punishment increases the acting-out appears especially lively. I'll call your attention to only one more interesting complication, one which you can observe in cases where a borrowed feeling of guilt appears. In these cases, the acting-out frequently becomes the representation of the behavior of those people who really should have the feeling of guilt. It so acquires the character of the represented confession of a third person who was of significance for the patient's illness. This person had been absorbed or was taken into the ego by introjection.

Having shown that the acting-out in psychoanalysis also has unconsciously the character of confession, we still must keep in mind how widely it differs from the unconscious confessions that we otherwise see in analytic treatment. Unlike the spoken confession, it is a displayed or represented *Pater peccavi*. But the idea itself, not having been put into words, remains repressed in the unconscious. To make thought or wishes conscious, however, is our goal and, therefore, we must endeavor to accomplish the transposition into verbal presentations. We know now why we keep changing back the acting-out into reproduction, into remembering and narrating. We cannot do without verbal presentations in the transfer of unconscious processes into preconscious ones. Certainly the same motives cause the Church to demand that confession be made verbally, that it be *vocalis,* as the ecclesiastical term goes. Acting-out occurs with other psychic material than that of memories, which are closer to the system of perception. Acting-out occurs almost entirely on the unconscious level.

I don't care to go into a discussion of the technical problems of psychoanalysis here, but our deliberations make it clear that acting-out alone can never be enough for the fulfillment of the tasks demanded of analysis. Acting-out is much closer to the eruption of urges and to gratification of the need for punishment than either remembrance or confession. Strong encouragement of acting-out carries the danger that the transference in psychoanalysis no longer remains a "realm between illness and life," as Freud called it, but that it has transformed itself into a slice of morbid life. Analysis would then see the borders between it and material reality vanish completely, and it would not steer clear of repetition-compulsion at any one point. But analysis should be a "safety island" in street traffic, as it were, close enough to the maze and danger of life, but still removed from it. The active technique recently recommended to us in psychoanalysis would, in its exaggerations, favor the retransformation of the compulsion to confess into the elementary urge for expression. It would lead to new conflicts between the pressure of drives and the need for punishment in the repetition of the original experiences. Acting-out, if elevated to be the dominating element of psychoanalysis, ruptures the frame of the treatment and transforms the provisional device of analytical experience into a final phase which is nowhere essentially different from the experiences "outside." That technique gives the suppressed impulses and wishes, as well as the need for punishment, full gratification, while we wish to avoid just that in psychoanalysis, which should, according to Freud, be accomplished in abstinence.

We said earlier that acting-out is not an emotional end in itself. Rather, it serves the expression of impulses and of the need for punishment. But the patient is not conscious of and cannot comprehend this fact without the analyst's explanation. It is the duty of the analyst to add in one form or another those introductory and concluding sentences we mentioned earlier. In doing this he will make the unconscious meaning of the acting-out conscious also to the patient. This means that the analyst reopens to him the way from acting-out to remembering which we expect. In this sense, acting-out, too, is an unconscious confession in the form of representation or display, its interpretation is an essential part of analysis. In it, the suppressed urges and wishes certainly receive partial gratification, but that gratification never exceeds a certain very limited measure and remains in the frame of the transference relation that does not have to give up its exceptional position. We must reject the inorganic, artificial provocation to act out that an overacting therapy would like to push into the center of analytical treatment. Also the acting-out should evolve in analysis under the banner of the compulsion to confess. The analyst will consider it a special kind of return of the repressed and will endeavor to transform the memories, acted out, into memories expressed in telling them.

At this point we must give our attention to the relations between the process of repression and the compulsion to confess, relations which urgently require elucidation.

III

About the Return of the Repressed

LADIES AND GENTLEMEN: Repression is a process that consists in sending away and keeping away certain urges, impulses, and thoughts from the conscious mind. The repressed exerts a continuous pressure against the censorship that guards the gate to the preconscious. You know, furthermore, that it is not repression that creates those symptoms and substitute formations with which we concern ourselves in analysis, but that the symptoms, anxieties and inhibitions are indications of the return of the repressed.

The compulsion to confess may be considered one of the strongest forces leading to the return of the repressed. Its goal, the unconscious confession, represents a special form of a return of the repressed material. Both repression and compulsion to confess are unconscious processes. We may compare them to boatmen who carry the same emotional material from one bank to the other. But while one ferryman, the repression, takes care of the crossing from the preconscious realm to the unconscious, the other, the compulsion to confess, carries the same cargo back again from the unconscious area to that of the preconscious.

This comparison may lead us even further. The task of each boatman is determined. One is to deliver his cargo at the opposite bank and to keep it there. The other should transport it back and release it again. But that does not say at all that they must succeed in their tasks. We see that, in neuroses, repression fails thoroughly, and what was banned threatens to return. But we see also that the confession (in its unconscious character as attributed to it by us) does not quite accomplish its intention. We have only to add that the boatmen receive their orders from the same person. Repression

212

starts from the ego and confession returns to the ego. The consignor does not have to be identical with the person whose orders he transmits. Perhaps he only substitutes for another personality who remains in the dark and whose interests partly coincide with those of the consignor. You will guess that I mean the superego which represents the *sine qua non* for the repression as well as for the compulsion to confess. In order to complete the picture, one must add that crossing and return basically serve the same intention: to avoid unpleasure. This comparison should illustrate, to some extent, the functions of repression and of the compulsion to confess. It can, of course, apply also to all processes of the return of the repressed.

I think I know where your objection to my comparison will start: "Isn't it nonsense to expect that the sending off as well as the return of the same material should have the same motives?" No, that is by no means so absurd as it seems to be on first sight. Observe, if you will, that the two crossings are separated in time. In between, considerations about the fate of the cargo, new experiences, a prospect for better ways of using the cargo, can necessitate a change of the order while the purpose still remains the same, as for instance, to make a profit. Consider that changed inner conditions, for example, an increase in the cargo, may necessitate a counterorder.

Still another factor appears that does not find representation in our comparison (admitted an inadequate one), namely, the economic factor. It renders the situation less transparent or rather shows its complexity. The repression fails and the unpleasure that should be avoided is increased. Wouldn't it be better, then, to accept some of the initially present quantity of unpleasure in order to escape more of it? Besides the pushing tendency of the drives, certainly there are other determining factors, too, in the return of the repressed. Secondary factors may have been added to those already present in the first phase of repression. Displacements among the various quantities, a slackening of the censorship, for instance, in sleep, favor the return of the repressed.

The confession, which we labelled as a special kind of return of the repressed, is characterized also by the special way in which it takes place. It presupposes a change in the play of emotional forces, a change that aims at giving now a pleasurable tone to that which otherwise causes unpleasure. This change is, hence, the same as the modification of the conditions of pleasure-unpleasure production that has been proved by Freud in the evolution of pointed jokes. The result, too, is the same. The repression of an otherwise rejected instinctual representative is removed.

A joke with an aggressive or sexual tendency is close to the confession also in that it unconsciously implies a confession of otherwise repressed, or at least suppressed, impulses. We now observe that at this point we have crossed the border between conscious and preconscious confession, and we have come back to the comparison of repression and compulsion to confess. Repression is something that can happen to an impulse under certain conditions. It forms a pre-stage of condemnation. To use Freudian language, it is something intermediate between flight and condemnation. Comparison with the confession shows that it, too, is an intermediate between flight and condemnation, but standing much closer to condemnation than does repression which may be likened to the real reaction of flight. I'll try to make my meaning clear by a comparison. Let us assume that a man is standing before Tiffany's jewelry store and thinks he would like to break the window and to steal a diamond. He dismisses this fleeting impulse after he has thought of the commandment not to steal or of the consequences of the crime and continues his walk along Fifth Avenue. Compare this process with what we call a condemnation. Then contrast this result with the vicissitudes of a repression of the same impulse. Our comparison would come closest to that process when you imagine that the man, terrified at the emergence of his thoughts, would run away from the jewelry store as if he were hunted by the Furies.

Consideration of this comparison seems to invite us to concern ourselves more closely with the relations between the compulsion to confess and the emotional institutions that become the determining factors for the process of repression. I'd like to say in advance, as in all our previous discussions, that we understand confession to be a preconscious expression of the unconscious compulsion, that confession joins the other descendants of the unconscious instinctual urges that combine opposing qualities in themselves. It belongs, for instance, as do fantasies, qualitatively to the system of the preconscious, but actually to the unconscious.

If we are to understand the significance of confession in the dynamic setup, we should turn again to the transformation of the urge for an expression of the drives into the compulsion to confess. The urge for expression came from the ego which must communicate its needs to the external world. The reception of this communication by the external world became decisive for its further fate and led to the repression of certain impulses. In that external world, those played a special role. They were later drawn into the ego by identification, and led an independent existence there as the superego. Under the influence of the superego, the elementary urge for expression, connected with the eternally demanding power of the drives, transformed itself under certain conditions into the compulsion to confess. All it can do then is to communicate to the external world those urges in the form of the confession that the superego demands. But the inner perception of needs, too, must assume this form if the attitude of the superego demands it. We must, therefore, point out here that the degree of strictness or the extent of tolerance of the superego decides whether an impulse appears to the ego as a statement or as a confession.

But we indeed know that those very qualities of the superego decide what is to be the fate of an impulse. The strictness of the superego in one person lets an impulse or thought drop into repression, while in another person, the greater tolerance of the superego permits it to remain conscious. We can therefore say of the compulsion to confess (as of the repression) that it works individually. The character of mobility, which Freud attributed to the repression, is peculiar also to the confession. The emotional expenditure required by confession can be renewed, reduced or spared.

The ego, as the representative of the external world, receives news of the processes in the id from the impulses. This news the ego may accept or reject, as a man may treat his morning mail. The confession is just such a piece of news, and it has been presented to the ego by the superego, hence, by a representative of the first ego-identification. It is the messenger, not the message, that causes the ego to accept the message. This, however, presupposes that the superego itself agrees to the transmittal of the message, that it was willing to perform this service. We know at what price, at least in the case of confession that simultaneously gratifies the need for punishment.

The psychic relations become clearer if we use the example of neurosis for comparison. According to Freud, neurosis is the result of a conflict between the ego and the id. Or it can be better explained by saying that, in neurosis, the ego, while serving the superego and reality, came into conflict with the id. Now it is clear that the compulsion to confess endeavors to mediate between the hostile parties, the ego and the id. This, however, is possible only if to some extent it satisfies the demands of both parties. Only on that basis can there be talk of mediation at all. Does that remind you of certain situations in contemporary politics?

Confession is, therefore, an attempt at reconciliation that the superego undertakes in order to settle the quarrel between the ego and the id, perhaps as when a father mediates in a conflict between two hostile brothers. That the ego happens to come into conflict with the id, while taking the part of the superego, does not contradict this assertion. Here, too, the historic and the economic factors should be noted. The changes caused by them in the meantime have become decisive for the interference of the superego. The goal is clear—peace is to be restored in the family—in our case, the oneness of the personality. The father is often exceedingly well suited for this peacemaking. He knows he is held in esteem by both brothers and he knows their weaknesses better than they do themselves.

Confession is one of the instances in which the superego knew more of the unconscious id than did the ego. The processes in the id, as in obsessional neurosis and in melancholia, were unknown to the ego, but not to the superego. Therefore here, too, the superego behaves as the representative of the internal world, the id. As you know, the success of this mediating activity is by no means guaranteed in all cases. The ego can, as in obsessional neurosis, struggle against the acceptance of the unwelcome news, presented by the superego. Or it can accept merely that part of the message which the superego emphasizes, but reject the real content. This is the case in those obsessional neuroses which are oppressed by a feeling of guilt, the content of which they don't know. In these cases it looks as if the ego had acknowledged a part of the internal message, but had made it the cause of new bitter quarrels. The ego can also accept the message in fragments, or misinterpret it, as is shown by clinical observation, particularly of obsessional neuroses. In disturbances of a hysterical type, the ego fends off the messenger as well as the message. Here the feeling of guilt remains as unconscious as the material to which it relates. Other cases, such as melancholia and narcissistic psychoneuroses, are the outcomes of conflicts between superego and ego. The confession that the ego accepts all too readily is actually an accusation against the object that had been taken into the ego by incorporation. The cases of obsessional neurosis, in which a borrowed feeling of guilt, in Freud's sense, can be found, show the same use of the confession.

I must not neglect to point out that all analysts also know about a special kind of momentary but not accepted confession. Frequently, the repressed body of facts shows itself to the ego, like a sudden thought at any given moment, and is recognized, but this lucidity is forthwith submerged again. The ego has received the message, but it withdraws attention from it. It has heard the message, but it doesn't believe it. It is as if the ego had perceived the unwelcome message that reached its address, but quickly got rid of it.

Another possibility may interest us here, too. The ideational content of an instinctual representative can have become conscious to the ego, while its portion of affect has remained repressed. In this case, it looks as if the ego had taken notice of the content of the message, but only as of something trivial, or insignificant, something not interesting. Hence, here, too, a withdrawal of psychic energy has occurred which relates only to the share of emotions. Likewise, it happens frequently that the ego displaces that charge of affect onto an unessential detail of the message and turns overly great attention toward it, as we can observe in the mechanisms of displacement in obsessional neuroses.

We have shown how important a part it is that the superego plays in the compulsion to confess. It transmits the message to the ego and the message may, only because of this messenger, often count on being accepted. Proof of this interpretation is easily given. In cases in which the superego refuses to do this service, the message is not given. By that, I mean if the superego is too strict, and doesn't wish to transmit the message, the confession cannot take place. However, the silence of the superego will show itself in the unconscious feeling of guilt. This concerns all those severe cases of neurosis in which it is the very depth of the need for punishment that puts such serious obstacles in the way of recovery in their analysis. Although the superego knows, then, of the processes in the id, they remain unknown to the ego.

Hence, we have to differentiate carefully between two cases. If the superego is sufficiently tolerant, an offspring of the unconscious will be in a position to represent itself to the ego as instinctual expression. Under an excessive strictness of the superego, it won't even be allowed to appear before the ego as a confession of drives. The importance of the superego for the processes of confession shows itself in still another instance. One of the essential motives for the confession originates in the superego. It is not only a transmitter of the news but also one of its originators. The message brought by the superego also concerns the messenger himself.

In all these cases, it can be seen that the id communicates with the superego. In the conflict between superego and ego, too, as it appears in the narcissistic psychoneuroses, the confession will maintain its special significance. There, too, it originates in the superego which seized upon the conscious. However, it is used not for reconciliation, but for an accusation to which the ego submits. Then the superego treats the ego cruelly by continually presenting to it the confession as an ideal demand with which it cannot comply. It is like a hard creditor who continually shows the debtor his unpaid bill. The painful reproaches of conscience in many forms of obsessional neurosis are of this kind. Here, too, the super-ego has combined with the id, but now gratification of the need for punishment has become the only, or at least the most prominent, instinctual aim. The unending self-torture of the obsessional neuroses and the attempts at suicide of melancholics give testimony to this strong trend. The ego wishes here to reconcile the superego through submission, through sufferings, but doesn't succeed any better than it can successfully defend itself against the demands of the id. Mania offers the only example showing that the ego has overpowered the superego and strewn confession to the four winds. The rebellion that the ego sometimes achieves in those cases of obsessional neurosis against the superego that has grown overly powerful is nearly always an attempt at a *Putsch* that miscarries, because the ego then falls under the mastery of the scarcely less destructive demands of the id.

It frequently happens that both forms of the conflict occur together, one conflict superimposing itself upon the other. Then the analyst often finds himself facing an unexpected result of his endeavor. He has reason to believe that his patient is recovering, but then he discovers that the conflict is continuing on another plane. The confession was then, too, an attempt at reconciliation, on the part of the id with the ego, which was made by the intermediary superego; but the success was only short-lived. The confession could not quite fulfill its mission because the need for punishment was too great to be consumed in it. It is clear that the analyst, whose attention was captured by the noisy quarrels of the ego and the id, did not notice that there existed a primeval conflict between the ego and the earliest objects on the part of the id, which now continues in a conflict between the ego and the superego.

We have not considered so far another use to which the ego can put the confession, and we must now make up for it. The ego can accept the confession and apply it to the purpose that it should serve—that is, the reconciliation with the id. This is the normal outcome. In that case, the confession also serves the recovery of the self-regard threatened by the clash between the demands of the ego and the id, the reconstitution of the narcissistic ego-strength. The ego feels as one again. We would go wrong in assuming that self-recognition of the proscribed impulses must unconditionally lead to a depreciation or lessening of the secondary narcissism. On the contrary, with those very capabilities of achieving this self-recognition, it can restore the damaged narcissism. It can happen that the very confession becomes the means used by the ego to recommend itself to the id as love-object. It is as if the ego were saying, "Now, I know of your wishes. You can love me, too." Freud showed us that this is, indeed, the way in which the transposition of object-libido into narcissistic libido sometimes takes place, and that this is actually the general way of sublimation.

Many cases of conflict between the superego and ego create the impression that the ego does not use the confession so unequivocally in one way. Now it becomes clear that the superego presents the ego with a confession which the latter receives with humility at first. Yes, the ego even makes these accusations its own, transforming them into self-accusations, merely to please the superego. In this case, the ego forces itself upon the superego as a love-object, and uses the confession to win love. We recall having discussed in the last lecture this psychic function of the confession in the processes of transference occurring in analysis. The ego first renounces all its rights and uses the confession to woo for love, like a child who expects, after chastisement, yes, by means of the chastisement itself, to wipe out the loss of love on his father's or mother's part.

In some cases, the ego actually acquires, at the cost of unheard-of sacrifices, the affection of the enraged superego, but, in return, it has to suffer this tyrant's eternal tortures. In this category falls the religious belief in being "chosen," the view that God chastises those whom he loves. Suffering as a test of staying power, humble understanding of all pains as a touchstone in the Jewish and Christian religions, can be considered an example of this attitude of the ego. Here suffering itself comes to achieve its termination. "Only he who suffers his calamity frees himself of it," says Laotse.

Indeed, more than that, suffering, persecution become an instinctual aim because they alone satisfy the superego and the id. Jesus preaches, "Blessed are the meek: for they shall inherit the earth." Punishment itself has become the sign of being loved as in the masochistic perversion. This peculiar way out is perhaps one of the few by which the ego, having grown humble, attains its goal —to be loved again by the id. As you know, not even this goal is ever fully assured, and new punishments are needed to preserve the love of the superego. It is important to consider that, meanwhile, the ego is being assaulted by the id's instinctual demands of other kinds, which it must ward off. The temptations of the hermits in the Thebais and the tortures to which they submit for penance, the privations that they impose upon themselves in ever increasing measure, may be considered a religious example of that wooing for love which the ego renews time and again toward the superego, after having warded off the instinctual demands. Obsessional neurosis supplies the modern pathological analogy in its symptomatology.

Another way out, to accept the confession and to put the superego back into its place by pointing to suffering already sustained, fails, almost as a rule, in obsessional neurosis. The superego always has in readiness, in those cases, a fresh abundance of confessions, and the need for punishment has become insatiable. In melancholia, the confession replaces an accusation against the formerly beloved person who has been introjected into the ego. Hence, it is the rejection of the love-demands of a person embodied in the ego by introjection. Here the superego uses the confession for an attack against the ego which has been altered by introjection of the object.

We said that the abstention or the involvement of the superego decides whether the message received by the ego about the processes in the id assumes the form of an instinctual expression or of a confession of forbidden impulses. If the superego was the cause of the repression, it later becomes also the basis for the compulsion to confess, which has the same relation to repression as the positive process to the negative in photography. Confession is, therefore, the more or less successful attempt at making repressed impulses preconscious again. Thus, the process which has not yet withdrawn from the sphere of the unconscious is directly the opposite to that in repression.

There remains now only a short discussion of the relation between the compulsion to confess and the external world. This is made easier for us through our knowledge of the fact that the ego functions as the attorney of the external world within the psychic institutions. Thus the compulsion to confess, in its relation to the external world, will essentially pursue those intentions which determine its behavior toward the ego. It advises the external world of what endopsychic perception has observed under certain conditions. It announces to the external world, through special signs, the otherwise concealed intentions of the instinctual impulses and, at the same time, those of the superego. It serves the need for punishment as well as the repressed instinctual impulses, and the external world reacts according to its own attitude and according to the larger or smaller share that the two great instinctual trends find in the confession with hostility or with tenderness, with rejection or with acceptance.

While observing the accomplishment of these two intentions, we find a third one—namely the urge to reconquer the lost love of the external world through the very confession. In tracing down the relations between the compulsion to confess and the external world, we can appreciate still another interesting fact. In the unconscious confession, the superego, but not the ego, has taken notice of the processes in the id. However, the external world which doesn't receive the confession consciously either, understands its latent meaning unconsciously. The confession to the external world came about, therefore, without the assistance of the ego. One person's unconscious can interpret and understand the confession as the unconscious expression of another person.

For the child at the decisive age, the external world has, as we saw, caused the transformation of forbidden tendencies toward expression into the compulsion to confess. More correctly, the most important representatives of the external world, the parents and

THE COMPULSION TO CONFESS   223

their later representatives, have brought about this change. This brings us again to the psychogenesis of the compulsion to confess. Now we feel confident enough to supplement and correct its previous description with the insights acquired to date.

Governed by his most vital needs, the child first felt himself driven to express his hostile or tender, jealous, sexual and crudely egotistic impulses to his parents who were his first confidants. The repression of certain drives and impulses leads to a serious estrangement from the parents. The cause of this change of attitude toward the parents lies, as you know, in the feelings and excitations that originate in the Oedipus complex. The estrangement from the parents is really a consequence of the partial estrangement in the ego. That is introduced through the repression, by which an esential part of the ego is separated from the whole and now faces the remainder of the ego as a stranger. Hence, the Oedipus complex, and the feeling of guilt resulting from it, is the cause of the inhibition of the child's urge for expression and for its latter transformation into the compulsion to confess.

The child, who earlier came naïvely to his parents with all his instinctual expressions, is now inhibited in his communication by the increasing power of repression. This inhibition of expression, however, is the sign of a deep change in the love-relation to his parents, because when and where we love entirely we are also ready to communicate all our instinctual impulses to the other person. You know that substitute formations, unconscious confessions, take the place of instinctual expressions left unsaid.

The purpose of analysis is to clear again the road that was blocked up, under certain circumstances, and again bring to consciousness those old emotions which caused the blocking. The unconscious confessions which the patients furnish us in their symptoms give us the most important leads for that work. The disturbance in the relationship with the father shown by the inhibition of the urge for expression is overcome, and the overly great moral anxiety is removed. I should dare to say in so many words, "You will have attained the essential goal of your analytical endeavors with your patient when you succeed in restoring peace between the ego and the superego, which has become more tolerant in analysis." It has already been pointed out what great importance the transposition into verbal presentations has for this process.

The strongest resistances to this work must be sought in the nature of condemned impulses to be expressed, and in the transference relationship. The confession of proscribed wish-impulses is, after all, to be made to the very person whom those impulses concern. Freud has already said that this necessity results in situations that appear in reality as scarcely capable of being coped with. But the approach to the situation of childhood in which the solution of the problem was not achieved is necessary. It is exactly the representative of the father to whom the confession of the impulses directed against him has to be made in order to overcome the unconscious feeling of guilt. The increase of difficulty in this analytical situation must be met because of the aim of analysis. The urge for expression inhibited toward the parents finds its repetition in analysis in the compulsion to confess that is inhibited by feelings of guilt and by the need for punishment. The compulsion to confess, functioning toward the analyst, has the significance, therefore, of a resuscitation of the old impulses of love as well as of the need for punishment. The technique of analysis furnishes us the means of overcoming the resistances opposing the compulsion to confess.

As the goal of analysis, a process inhibited in childhood, especially by repression, should now be made to run its course again in the situation of transference. Those strong, proscribed feelings and impulses of the Oedipus complex, as well as the need for punishment and the feeling of guilt that, at the time, were the reactions to those proscribed feelings and impulses, should be shown to the father. An affectively stressed communication of this kind is what we call a confession. You know that the other task, the reproduction of the psychic processes that, at the time, caused the prevention of the confession, also is accomplished in the analytical process.

Certain experiences in analysis that we shall perhaps discuss, suggest tracing the conflict between the tendencies of the compulsion to confess and the feeling of guilt and the need for punishment still farther back into childhood. In that early period there is, of course, no question of conflict between ego and superego because the superego has not yet established itself. There are instead, conflicts between the ego and its earliest love- and hate-objects, hence pre-stages of those much later processes. We come, thereby, into a period of childhood in which the ego was still weak and undeveloped and repression of a psychic process was still out of the question.

The important bodily processes of that period particularly considered in child training—elimination and retention of the stool—become significant as the prototypes for instinctual expression and suppression. You know from the study of anal erotism how feelings of love and dislike or of yielding and defiance already express themselves in the tendencies that appear in the regulation of those needs.

A reference to the proverb that calls speech silver, silence golden, may help in building the bridge to the behavior of the patient in the analysis of the adult. The fight between giving away and keeping back still dominates the analysis. The mastery of the highly sublimated tasks of psychoanalysis is in this way, as with invisible threads, connected with one of the first tasks put to the child. The aim in child training was to induce the child to give away the material of the bowels as completely as possible at a certain time, and it coincided with the earliest education toward love. The analyst wants nothing else but to aid the compulsion to confess to come through. You know that child training finds itself facing still another task, that of limiting the child's functions of excretion to a definite time and occasion. Overly great or, rather, unregulated liberality in the way of gratification of the need doesn't seem to the educator to be right. He suppresses this untoward loquacity of the bodily function. Analysis continues the after-education in this direction also.

The regressive character of analysis and the frequent failure of that first task of child education explains why analysis first puts the main emphasis upon uninhibited expression. To help the compulsion to confess to victory must be its main concern. Later normal behavior will result automatically between the tendencies to give away and to keep back, of compulsion to confess and repression. The path that was obliterated and reopened doesn't have to be used constantly. It is only important that it be passable when need be.

LADIES AND GENTLEMEN: Psychoanalysis still is based upon the analysis of the dream and the psychology of the processes of the dream will remain the touchstone of any theory concerning the happenings in the unconscious. What about the compulsion to confess as it operates in the dream? In the dream, a fragment of the unconscious, that otherwise could not have done so, has come up in consciousness. This is, as you know, made possible by a diminished alertness of the censorship and the dream-work that subjects the thoughts to disguise and distortion. The preconscious thoughts and wishes that became the inciter of the dream have found connection with others, that, to quote Nietzsche, had been "thinking beneath the day." The decreased alertness of the censorship makes it possible for the dream to regress to the infantile tendencies toward expression and so to take on the character of wish-fulfillment. Within the sphere of childhood to which the dream leads back, there exists neither the compulsion to confess nor its psychological presupposition, the repression.

From the return into the early infantile period, as well as from the fact that the latent dream-content belongs to the unconscious, follows the conclusion that the dream, in accord with its very essence, can be only the representation of a wish-fulfillment. The dream-distortion, which is related to the phenomena of psychic censorship, points to the influences of emotional factors which we find again in the compulsion to confess. These forces determine the dream-work, with all the forms of which Freud has acquainted us. It is the form of the dream which makes the interpretation necessary and it depends upon those factors. Their effectiveness proves that the repressed wishes represented in the dream are rejected by the ego and can reach consciousness only under the special conditions of the state of sleep and in the dream-distortion.

If, therefore, only the latent dream-content is considered, that part in which the real essence of the dream consists, the dream is to be determined as the representation of a wish-fulfillment. But if that particular form of representation in itself also should be considered, that is, if the participation of the dream-work also is to be taken account of, it may be understood as the confession of an unconscious wish. Accordingly, it is clear that this latter point of view reveals nothing about the deepest driving force of the dream itself, and that its definition concerns only the higher psychic stratum of dream-formation. It is, thus, precisely the psychology of the dream-processes, in which the compulsion to confess plays only a secondary part, that becomes a proof of its existence and effectiveness. In analytical translation: the hidden dream-content always represents a wish-fulfillment, but the form of the dream points to the confession of those wishes. In other words, the character of a confession that the dream has when it confronts us as a whole is caused by the transposition which the latent dream-thoughts experience in the dream-work. It concerns only this psychic stratum of the opposing energy.

The very fact that a dream-distortion of this kind was necessary implies that the compulsion to confess played its part in the formation of the dream. The strongest proof of the secondary nature of the influence of the compulsion to confess which determines merely the façade of the dream, lies in those dreams of children in which wishes of the previous day find their undistorted expression. Here the primary wish-character of the dream becomes quite clear. The compulsion to confess leaves the latent dream-content untouched and its role can be recognized only in the dream-work. These are the punishment dreams about which Freud reported in his lecture before the Hague Congress. In them, the emotional reactions to repressed tendencies become themselves the driving force of the dream. But even here, where the confession is in the latent dream-content, the wish character of the dream remains intact. The dream-content is then the representation of the wish-fulfillment of those tendencies toward self-punishment which, still turn out to be libidinal ones.

It can easily be seen in what respects the compulsion to confess remains significant in the dream processes. The dream presents itself to the awakened ego as an unconscious and unrecognized confession, and equally so to the external world in the event that it is communicated to it. Talking in the dream can undoubtedly appear as self-betrayal, and as a special form of expression of the unconscious compulsion to confess. Hence, the wish character of the dream concerns only the share of the id in our psychic life.

Under the special conditions of the dream we return to visual representation, and, with it, to childhood's primary tendency toward expression. According to Freud, thinking in pictures, as it prevails in the dream, is closer to the unconscious processes than thinking in verbal presentations. This difference makes understandable, too, why the hidden dream-content cannot be a confession even though sometimes a suppressed confession may be used in the dream as psychic material of the preconscious, as Freud showed it in the analysis of a dream. We have seen that the fact of dream-work and of dream-distortion itself represents an unconscious confession because it shows that the unconscious wishes that are the basis of the dream dare not appear undistorted on the psychic surface.

I referred earlier to the child dreams which allow those not familiar with analytical theory clearly to recognize the dream's character of wish-fulfillment. The tendency toward an expression of the impulses, suppressed during the day, dominates in these child dreams. I would have misgivings at making the primary urge for expression in its elementary nature responsible also for those dreams of adults which let consciously proscribed wishes like incest appear quite undistorted on the surface as fulfilled. While we cited dream-work earlier as evidence of the effectiveness of the compulsion to confess, here, too, we won't fail to see its influence. It reveals itself in the unhidden undistorted form of the dream's wish-fulfillment. As in the discussion of acting-out, we should not ignore the increased intensity of instinctual pressure. The fact, in itself, of the undistorted return of the repressed in these dreams is proof of the earlier high expenditure involved in repression. Only where the psychic pressure has become overly great can the dream show wishes in so undistorted a form as fulfilled. As in acting out in analysis, that special kind of reaction points back to the action.

The confession shows itself here in the very omission of any dream-distortion just as it shows itself in other dreams in the presence of dream-work. This is no contradiction, as the degree of defence decides the kind of dream-formation. The unconscious confession consists in this especially undistorted form of the dream and points to the intensive emotional work during waking hours that has been expended to overpower the instinctual pressure.

What has been said of dreams of this kind is, furthermore, also valid to a high degree for other unconscious processes. In considering a symptom, an idea or a sequence of thoughts as to content, we would often have to pass the judgment that it is an instinctual expression, but the very form in which it appears, as well as the high expenditure involved in repression, the removal of which made it possible, mark it as confession. This is often the case, particularly, where instinctual expression stands manifestly in the foreground of the content, appearing quite undistorted at the psychic surface.

Purposely I have not described to you a dream analysis because its detailed discussion would take too much time. Allow me, however, in conclusion to give you one single example. It shows clearly that the undistorted return of a repressed instinctual impulse in the dream evolves from the highest intensity of the expenditure involved in repression during the day, and that this very form of the dream represents a confession of those repressed wishes. The example may incidentally be considered perhaps the loveliest story of a miracle which medieval legend has to report. Gauthier de Coincy tells the story of that unhappy deacon of Laon, who suffered inordinately under the observance of his vow of chastity. The young monk fought with all his might against the lewd sexual fantasies that persecuted him everywhere. One day, while he was again fighting these temptations desperately, he fell asleep, overcome by tears. The Holy Virgin appeared before him in his dream, brought her bosom near his lips and let him drink from her breasts. The chronicler reports that the divine potion cured the young priest forever from his tortures. He could spend his pious life calmly and remote from reality after this love dream.

About the Dimension in Depth of Neurossi

LADIES AND GENTLEMEN: The assumption that in analysis we are concerned only with experiences of which the patient was once conscious and which were then repressed would be quite erroneous. Actually, it can be said that, in general, we do not really know, at the time of the experience itself, what our experience is. And, strange as it may sound, we know least about the most important experiences of our lives. Many people's lives are lived without acute awareness of their experiences. Most of us need a long interval of time to realize that this or that event has taken place in our lives. Often we don't know for a long time what an event means for us emotionally. People are like deep wells (to use a beautiful image from Nietzsche) that take a long time to recognize what fell into their depths.

Analysis shows people not only what they have experienced in the remote past, but also what they are currently experiencing. Of course, it can do so only by reaching back to past experience from which the present takes on in its deepest resonance. Analysis extraordinarily shortens the interval between experience and the understanding of it, but it can't make the interval disappear. In fact, analysis itself has to suffer it to a certain extent. Often we hear from former patients that it was only long afterward that they recognized what analysis meant for them psychically. Freud rightly calls the father's death the most incisive event in a man's life. Every analyst can frequently find that the patient accepts that loss only many years after the actual death of his father, although he consciously knows very well that his father has been dead for a long time. Compare this delayed burial in analysis, as it were, to an incident reported by the excavators of Tutankhamen's tomb. When they opened the burial chamber, Lord Carnarvon and Howard Carter found among the treasures a small, exceedingly well-preserved figure. It still could be thoroughly inspected and there was still time to photograph it. Suddenly it collapsed without a sound, changed into dust. For over three thousand years the small statuette had remained intact and only the light and the touch of fresh air streaming into the subterranean chamber had caused it to collapse.

Frequently the analyst finds himself in a position to observe that people don't really know what is happening to them nor what they are doing. I analyzed a man shortly after he had learned of his wife's adultery. He seemed extremely calm, talked in a composed manner, almost cheerfully, of the event and behaved altogether as if nothing had happened. Only analysis allowed him to understand why, soon afterwards, he had caused his children "by oversight" to be in extreme danger, as if their death could make the divorce from his wife easier for him. Only much later did he understand what it meant that, when swimming, he had incautiously stayed too long under water and struck his head hard against a post. Only in analysis could he find out what extremely deep feelings of pain, hatred and despair were active in him at the time of the discovery. None of that was known to him and only by a long detour could he recognize the reactions which the event had caused. It is by no means a rare exception that experiences remain unconscious for a long time in their emotional significance.

Perhaps the strangest and the most astonishing fact in analysis is that people often suffer without knowing it.

From an exploration of the symptomatology of neuroses, I came to the conviction that patients enjoy some gratification in the symptoms unknowingly, that the symptoms warrant them unconscious pleasure-gain. Those of you who have acquired some experience in clinical analysis will be in a position to confirm the statement that many patients do not know what causes their suffering and how deep it is. I should like to say emphatically that it isn't that the patients cannot express themselves, cannot tell of their suffering, but that unconscious suffering like unconscious pleasure really exists. You may easily make an objection to this statement: the patients complain and lament enough, you say, they show their neurotic misery with sufficient, sometimes one would even say, exaggerated affect. But even the neurotics who do that do not necessarily know how deeply and from what they suffer.

All neurotics do not by any means recognize and acknowledge their affliction. On the contrary, the majority even tend to belittle their illness, to ascribe to it the character of a slight disturbance, to limit its range to a single, sometimes small, realm of life. It would be incorrect to say that the neurotics dissimulate their illness, as that would mean conscious concealment. However, the patients do not know that this or that activity, these feelings and impulses are to be charged to the account of neurosis. One of the first accomplishments of analysis consists (strange as it may sound) in convincing the patient that the illness deserves to be taken seriously and that it really signifies suffering. It is only in the course of analysis that the illness acquires, as it were, courage, shows its real extent and its deeply penetrating influence upon the patient's life.

In some cases the analyst actually comes to wonder how the patient could have borne so much suffering in the past without having taken energetic measures toward its limitation. Sometimes he would be inclined to think that any, even the most desperate, way out would have been taken by other "normal" persons in order to escape from such unbearable suffering. We shall soon see how rash an assumption of that kind would be that doesn't take the psychological circumstances into sufficient consideration.

In many cases, however, it is certain that the patients knew as little of the suffering that the neurosis meant for them, as of the sources of pleasure that they found in their symptoms. One may be tempted to assume that this suffering didn't really exist for them because they were not conscious of it, but this conclusion would be as erroneous as are all assertions that exclude all psychic effects but the conscious ones. Analysis allows us to recognize beyond any doubt that, even though the suffering as well as the pleasure was unconscious, it has influenced the life and fate of the patient deeply, at times decisively. The same is true of sensations and feelings that can be unconscious, too, even though, according to Freud, their counterpart in the excitatory process is the same. Even physical pain, which may best be compared with emotional suffering, can remain unconscious. Analysis has determined the psychic processes that develop into pathological mourning and melancholia as a special case of such unconscious suffering. But also in cases where the patient knows the neurosis has brought him suffering, it is beyond doubt he does not know to what depth and because of what causes he has been suffering so much. The fact that the illness unconsciously also brought pleasure-gains does not exclude suffering from it. It is not a case of either/or, but of the one and the other. The suffering was there in spite of that fact and we may be certain the greater the degree of hidden gratification brought by the illness, the greater was the depth of the suffering.

The impressions of analysis, then, converge into the opinion that unconscious suffering itself was a gain from illness, even one of the foremost and most treasured ones. One could often be tempted to think that the latent substitute gratification in the symptoms of which the suffering was only a payment, as it were, was considerably overpaid. One would think it wasn't worth it to undergo so much suffering for so little pleasure. "The game is not worth the candle," as the expression goes. Yet the relation between both quantities should somehow be right. Price and ware, stake and profit should correspond approximately to each other.

Suffering as gain from illness can be derived only from the unconscious need for punishment, having clearly the character of punishment. Freud has pointed out the great part that the unconscious feeling of guilt plays as resistance against trends to recovery. Confrontation of this emotional factor with the compulsion to confess results in the following situation: in cases of neurosis in which an over great need for punishment is active that need will turn out to be the agent that most successfully opposes the compulsion to confess, and limits its efficacy.

On first sight this seems strange. Should the compulsion to confess, which owes its existence to a significant extent to the need for punishment, be prevented from achieving its end because of the increased intensity of the need for punishment? This is, however, true. The need for punishment functions like the driving force that propels a machine with a certain power, which, if it increases above a certain measure, destroys the machine. The compulsion to confess can certainly experience annihilation or limitation of its efficacy from other sides also. We know, for instance, that under conditions of sleep it transforms itself regressively into the urge for an expression of the instinctual impulses. A reduction of any other kind or the radical removal of the expenditure involved in repression will certainly lead to the same result. The most important obstacle to its unfolding, however, is the over great intensity of the need for punishment.

We have seen that confession itself means a bit of self-punishment and is thus used for the partial gratification of the need for punishment. But for an over great need for punishment, this punishment is not sufficient as a relief. It insists on continued suffering. There are actually cases of obsessional neurosis and anxiety hysteria where the need for punishment allows emotional relief through analysis only to a certain extent or not at all. The compulsion to confess can, of course, not be completely eliminated even in those cases, but it will limit efficacy to the unconscious confession of the need for punishment. In these cases conscience is mute. It can't make itself heard.

Here we have one of the few cases where the analyst has to take the initiative and tell the patient that it is his need for punishment that prevents him, for instance, from observing the basic analytical rule to say everything that occurs to him. It then becomes the analyst's task to endeavor to transform the patient's unconscious masochism into a conscious feeling of guilt. On the way to this goal it becomes necessary for the need for punishment to content itself with that mildest form of confession as self-punishment.

The temptation suggests itself in analysis, especially to the beginner, to free the patient through special efforts and as quickly as possible from the feeling of guilt that depresses him so much. But he will soon find that the patient obstructs these endeavors with a mute resistance that can increase and become the most embittered obstinacy. We get the impression that the patient clings unconsciously with all his might to his need for punishment and that he defends it, as if it were a treasured possession, against all efforts to wrest it from him, that he seems even less willing to renounce it than he would his justified or unjustified demands for a gratification of his drives.

We have no difficulty in explaining this astonishing contradiction. The need for punishment is, after all, itself an outgrowth of the strongest instinctual impulses and it strives for adequate gratification like any other instinctual impulse. It will, therefore, be necessary to note that the need for punishment in neurosis finds at least as much hidden gratification as other emotional impulses.

Reducing the need for punishment, difficult as it is, is in many cases the most essential part of the analysis. In some cases, it is only this reduction which makes it possible to carry through the analysis. In those forms of neurosis, the need for punishment is like a heavy bar put across the path of analysis, that must first be removed laboriously before the complex tasks inside the house can be taken care of. It is as if the superego had subdued the ego so greatly that the main task is, first of all, to transform its tyranny into a milder kind of reign before the accomplishment of other reforms can be taken up.

I think it would not be too daring to describe resistance in analysis as the force of the need for punishment opposed to recovery. One could venture to handle the analysis as far as the superego is concerned on the basis of the compulsion to confess, as long as one keeps in mind that, in doing so, no moral principles have been acknowledged, but a psychic process has been described.

LADIES AND GENTLEMEN: At the end of ancient Indian stage plays a loud call was sounded, "May all who live remain free from pains!" This wish holds good also at the inception of psychoanalysis, as of every medical or educational activity. But the recognition of the "biological and psychological necessity of suffering," as Freud called it, is perhaps the start of the mastery over suffering. First one has to submit to this necessity for a while before trying to overcome the suffering. The need for punishment is, to a certain degree, one of the psychological necessities and does not yield to any violent measure. It has the power to convert good into bad. An obsessional patient under my observation reacted to every friendly response and advance of his relatives and friends with a hostile or ugly act. In his case, analysis showed with special clarity that he couldn't brook such friendliness. He had to react to it in this peculiar way even though he suffered much from his ingratitude and impoliteness. He had to deprive himself of friendliness and make himself disliked. His behavior was equivalent to a confession. "I don't deserve this friendliness. I shall show you how bad and ungrateful I am."

This strange kind of reaction, as you know, is by no means rare. Children who unconsciously feel guilty sometimes behave in this way toward adults who show them love. It is as if all the sincerity of which they are capable were contained just in the ungrateful, hostile act that is simply an expression of the pre-existent feeling of guilt. Perhaps you remember that precious story by Anatole France in which the hoary Archbishop Charlot tells his abbé a fictitious, canonically interesting case as if it had just happened and Abbé Lantaigne discovers by chance that his Eminence had once again made a fool of him. His eyes raised to heaven, the abbé exclaims, "That man will never tell the truth except on the steps of the altar when he takes into his hands the holy Host and speaks the words, '*Domine, non sum dignus.*'" Similarly, the obsessional patients of the kind I have just described will reveal their deepest selves when they show the feelings of their inferiority and betray their need for punishment.

The importance of the need for punishment, the suffering as gain from illness and the fact pointed out by Freud that the behavior of the superego determines the severity of a neurotic illness create new problems and cause several uncertainties in analytical technique. There is no reason to conceal these difficulties that also appear in other branches of therapeutic or educational activity. Analysis is not a finished system and it declares that the dogma of infallibility, which takes so prominent a place in religious beliefs and perhaps has to do so, is in contradiction to the character of a science.

The reduction of the need for punishment is one of these difficult therapeutic problems. The analyst's attitude toward this emotional power is, one would think, dictated by the principles of analysis itself. He has to uncover gradually the repressed causes of that need for punishment, to transform unconscious feelings of guilt into conscious ones. But this is an extraordinarily slow process and would, in severe cases, take years. How is one to cope with the patient's need for punishment in the meantime, how can his suffering be alleviated? The answer to this question gives little comfort—almost nothing can be done about it. It seems as if the patient must be allowed a certain measure of gratification of his urges, even of the need for punishment.

An active therapy in the way of prohibition or command does more to damage than to help. Prohibition of a certain instinctual gratification makes the patient strive for the forbidden just because of his need for punishment. It produces furthermore a new feeling of guilt. Something morally harmful has perhaps been avoided. But the moral of this is: new harm has resulted. Even when undertaking something spontaneously against his obsessional prohibitions, the patient is often overpowered by a feeling of guilt. Often it can be observed how neurotics are driven to the forbidden act by the need for punishment.

But to promote the gratification of the need for punishment is equally wrong, as it permits the patient the enjoyment of his masochistic impulses, namely revelry in self-torment or in torture by others engineered by him. The course of analysis shows the therapist that the patient is also in this respect the stage manager behind the wings.

You know where religion stands on this need for punishment. It preaches "not to kick against the pricks," "not to resist evil."

Until the unconscious causes of the feeling of guilt are uncovered, even analysis can do little more than perhaps protect the patient from the crudest self-inflictions, and it can furnish him only minor means to resist evil. As is the case in so many actual conflicts, it must console the patient by holding out hopes for the time after the conclusion of the analysis. It acts, therefore, somewhat like the French Encyclopedists who could defend themselves against coercion by Church and State only by resolving to obey unconditionally the absurd laws while they were in effect, but not to tire in fighting against them. During the period in which the reduction of the need for punishment has not yet been accomplished, the patients can, in very severe cases, take no other attitude than that of submitting to suffering, to the command of compulsion or to anxiety while not desisting from protests against them.

Two important considerations, however, limit the value of that decision in great measure. The patient cannot be told when he will be wrested from his suffering. You will point to the technical principle of setting a time limit in analysis, but I may perhaps admit to you that to me it seems to be of very limited therapeutic value. To set a time limit is really in complete contradiction of the essence of psychoanalysis as an organic process. The Gordian knot was cut in two by a stroke of the sword, but only dialectics can contend that this was a solution. In analysis, violent measures are very rarely called for. Under certain conditions, the setting of a time limit may be granted as an expedient in an emergency, as sometimes a beginner is successfully made to swim by being thrown into the water. But this is certainly not the best way of teaching swimming.

In setting a time limit it is necessary to note that this is not useful at all as an aid in overcoming a resistance. If this is to be done at all, it may be done only in the state of positive transference, and, if possible, with the patient's consent. The ideal case of termination of analysis is, of course, that of a "gentlemen's agreement" between the patient and his analyst.

You will say that conditions for setting a time limit exist because analysis has become the patient's compulsion, that in it he settles down comfortably, as it were. But certainly it would be better to awaken in him the resolution to make a friendly and voluntary separation, rather than to evict him. There is another factor to be considered. A fixation of this kind on the analyst is the expression not only of a love impulse but also of an attitude of defiance, of a defiant love. But, it is much more the expression of a still powerful need for punishment. The lack of independence, the patient's need for love is, of course, what stands out. But I think in this case, as well as in general, such an insatiable need for being loved is itself the sign of an unconscious sense of guilt. The feeling of guilt affects the ego like a narcissistic impairment and the patient strives to regain his self-confidence by being loved. Only he who feels guilty is so exaggerated in his love demands. Love is expected to help appease the feeling of guilt. This is not a contradiction of my earlier assertion that the need for punishment frequently causes direct rejection of the show of love. It might, of course, be possible for this need to react in two different ways, and thus it is in fact. The two forms of reaction correspond to the effect of economic factors in the dynamics of the psyche. With very strong need for punishment, the tendency to reject love, even to make oneself disliked, will prevail. With less need for punishment, tempered by analysis, the exaggerated need for love will betray itself as the expression of moral masochism. I believe that even in children it can be observed that an especially increased need for love points back to a feeling of guilt. Here too, the feeling of guilt engenders a loss of primary narcissism for which the child wants to compensate with the security of being loved. Otherwise put: an extreme need for being loved often appears when a person feels guilty, as if being loved means the same as being forgiven.

The way in which analysis should be concluded frequently becomes a problem, especially in cases of severe neurosis, and this problem must be solved individually in every case. Perhaps fractural analysis, the gradual reduction of the analytical sessions, offers better emotional possibilities, but this way out is not always indicated either. All these questions are related to the problems of active therapy. The comparison of analysis with a surgical operation explains many relations, but should not be misunderstood. In other relations, analysis can be likened to a conservative therapy. In a case of poisoning, it will certainly be the physician's aim to eliminate the source of the poisoning. But if that cannot be done successfully, he will endeavor to support the antitoxin forces of the organism in the fight against the intruding poison, to weaken the effects of the toxins, to stimulate the formation of leucocytes, etc.

A second factor that makes it difficult for the patient to assume an attitude toward his illness is a change caused by analysis itself. Yet this change is often difficult to avoid. We have pointed out that patients often learn only in analysis what suffering they have endured and still are enduring. It is noteworthy that the further analysis progresses, the more impatient neurotics grow toward their suffering that they had previously endured, often with heroic patience. It is as if now that they can more consciously recognize their suffering, they try to show that impatience to be freed from it which they had not consciously experienced.

The inner connection of this phenomenon with transference is entirely obvious. The presence of a person who is seen unconsciously as the representative of a parent and the expectation of help from him make a patient more intolerant, like a child who expresses his pains more strongly when his parents are near. No less clearly can it be seen that patients grow increasingly intolerant toward their own need for punishment as the gain from illness is threatened with depreciation through analysis.

Another difficulty is caused by the lack of transparency in the dimension in depth of neurosis. Sometimes cases of clamorous and especially dangerous appearing symptoms are not at all so stubborn, and pose by far fewer difficulties than the analyst sees in other cases that present themselves as inconspicuous and create the impression that the patient's personality has remained largely intact.

There is no neurosis without a participation of the superego. Even if we characterize neuroses as the result of the conflict between ego and id, we have to emphasize the fact that our concern is the ego that sides with the superego. If we ponder this statement we find that for us analysts it is really a banality because it only means that there is no neurosis without Oedipus complex, the superego having been characterized by Freud as the heir of the Oedipus complex. We do not possess any means, any yardstick with which to measure the strength of the superego. We don't know when it will be willing to rest satisfied. But the behavior of the superego is the decisive factor in determining our prognosis. Only the understanding of the character and the effects of the superego gives the most convincing insight into the dimension in depth of neurosis. Beyond that, it can be said that it affords us the comprehension of many developments in people's lives and that it makes us recognize in the unconscious need for punishment originating in the superego, one of the mightiest, fateful powers' in human life.

Frequently we observe in later phases of analysis that neurosis permits freer expression than had scarcely come forth earlier. It seems as if not only the repressed sexual and hostile feelings, but also the need for punishment, had acquired more courage for expression. This, too, points out that the intensity of the need for punishment opposes the compulsion to confess. Had we not recognized this dimension in depth of the neurosis, the impression could often have arisen that two forms of neurosis existed in the same person, one superimposed upon the other. As I mentioned before, we would then face the apparent result that the conflict between the demands of the drives and ego-tendencies had been overcome, but the deeper layer of the neurosis, which comprises the conflict between ego and superego, had been left.

Actually, there is, of course, just the one neurosis, the depth of which has not been plumbed. The superego is only the heir of the Oedipus complex and it was the lastingness of the instinctual impulses rooted in the Oedipus complex that had remained unnoticed. This underestimating of the dimension in depth of a neurosis becomes significant for the patient, too, because it is important that he acquires the conviction of the profound effect of the feelings that originated in the Oedipus complex.

I should like to attempt to illustrate by one single case what part this factor plays in analytical treatment. A patient who suffered from insomnia, impotence, manifold scruples and inhibitions in work had severed relations with his father many years previously. The father had made higher and higher monetary demands of his son who earned his living abroad with great difficulty. The father had gambled the money away time and again in unsuccessful speculation in stocks. Finally, the son, who had imposed severe restrictions on himself for his father's sake, abruptly severed all relations with his father, leaving his "sentimental" appeals unanswered. Soon afterwards the father died in a spa in Italy without having seen the patient again and without having been reconciled with him. In a farewell letter to the mother, his father had with obvious intent not mentioned the patient.

The analysis slowly led back to the earliest experiences of childhood and the details of the Oedipus complex without substantial improvement in the patient's symptoms. Even after a year in analysis, he spoke only with scorn and irony of his late father whom he had bitterly criticized at the beginning. But this scorn was too demonstrative to be accepted as unartificial. My effort to convince the patient that his symptoms were in underground connection with an unconscious feeling of guilt concerning his father were apparently unsuccessful. As an extreme rationalist and skeptic who often enough made fun of himself also, he was not willing to acknowledge the effectiveness of feelings of that kind, and at first he had only scorn for them.

On one occasion, however, he started the analytical session with the story of a peculiar event that had taken place the night before. He had been to the theater in the evening where he had seen Nestroy's comedy "He Wants to Have Fun." In the play appear two humorously drawn robbers who break into a shop through a subterranean passage, and are filled with terrible fear. This scene, especially the remark shouted by one cowardly burglar at the other, "It seems to me you even tremble!" amused my patient very much.

When he returned home he read the newspaper before falling

asleep and thought, while he was reading, of the decline of the Italian currency, as he feared he might suffer financial losses because of it. His last conscious thought before he fell asleep concerned the devastating earthquake in Yokohama, of which he had just read. During the night he was suddenly awakened by the vehement vibration in the room caused by a passing truck. Later recognizable reasons made a certainty of the assumption that he had made the causal connection between the vibration of the room and the passing truck a few minutes afterwards but that he had first lived through an instant of panic. Then he jumped out of bed and called to the bed in parody fashion those words of the Nestroy play: "It seems to me you even tremble!"

The associations following this report pointed in the following direction: the last conscious thought before falling asleep—the quake of Yokohama; preceding that thought, the decline of the lira, the eruption of the volcano in Japan, the eruption of Etna in Italy, the father's tomb in Italy. Now we have only to insert a few links in order to make the associative connection. In the instant of the vibration of the room, an obscure reminiscence emerged of what had been read the evening before, which was left to the unconscious to be digested; then it caused repressed thoughts to become preconscious for an instant. The sensation produced by the vibration of the bed recalled a quake in Italy and the father's death in that country. It awakened, perhaps by the detour of the decline of the lira, memory-traces of the quarrel with the father over money, and of the death-wishes of the son.

Allow me now to continue under topics: the father's tomb in Italy, the movement of the earth, the rising of the father from the grave to punish him. The words, "It seems to me you even tremble!" that had amused him before in the theater performance and now concerned the bed, were certainly directed originally at himself and corresponded, in the patient's manner of poking fun at himself, to an attempt at liberation from that obscure momentary ·fear. The identification with the cowardly burglar who betrayed his fear by trembling while in the subterranean passage testifies to this intense emotion. Hence, the quotation of those words corresponds to a warding off of all the feelings which the re-emerging animistic belief of his childhood had awakened in him. Skepticism had finally regained the upper hand in him. The thought of the decline of the lira, on the one hand, makes for the unconscious connection with Italy, on the other hand, with the money that had been the last cause for the break with his father. It should not be overlooked that the words used in parody fashion, "It seems to me you even tremble!" finally bring recognition of his anxiety with a moral origin, denied in the analysis time and again.

The relations in emotional processes of that night with the patient's symptoms become clear as soon as we connect the vibration of the bed with childhood memories, in which an obscure anxiety appeared that still could be traced in the psychogenesis of his insomnia. The fear of the robber as he penetrated into the subterranean passage points to castration-anxiety in a condensation of ideas of his father's grave and of the female genital.

Castration-anxiety was the strongest unconscious cause of the patient's impotence. In this psychic element, the defensive impulses that concerned the fulfillment of the Oedipus complex are, as it were, brought together closely. The secondary significance of this underworld, as the realm of psychoanalysis, becomes easily recognizable. Even the fact that the two robbers had resembled each other fits into an unconscious connection which was known to us. A person with the qualities of self-irony and of self-critical alertness, like the patient, is called by the French psychologists "observateur de soi-même," a self-observer. A little earlier, he had had a dream in which two identical clowns appeared, one imitating and parodying the other's gestures.

At this point, the way in which the superego took over the heritage of the Oedipus complex becomes clear, as we find the expression of childhood death-wishes against father and of the incest-wish directed to mother (symbolized by the penetration into the bowels of the earth) again operating behind the scene.

The impotence disappeared for the first time after this emotional material had been worked through in psychoanalysis. So did the insomnia. This therapeutic success was, of course, partly lost by new resistances, but part of it was saved and his own experience never again allowed the patient to doubt the depth and effectiveness of his feelings of guilt, to which he had hitherto kept his eyes shut in scorn. The patient left analysis a cured man.

Insight into the dimensions in depth of neurosis can be gained from another angle: the indestructibility of the tendencies striving for love. We should not forget that the need for punishment has taken the place of sexual needs and that it gratifies erotogenic and feminine masochism, according to Freud, as well as moral masochism. The origin of the need for punishment in infantile object cathexis is also decisive for the fact that moral masochism still strives toward hidden sexual aims. The psychic energy which appears in the need for punishment and in the capacity for suffering would in some cases suffice to achieve great social successes, if it were applied in positive and constructive action.

The inadequacy and the secondary character of Adler's theory of neurosis built upon the striving for power is shown clearly also by the fact that even the most significant gain from illness, the gratification of the need for punishment, cannot deny its descent from the sexual area and that it remains still unconsciously directed at the attainment of love aims. We do not deny, of course, that the aims of power, too, play a part in neurosis, but they stay far behind sexual aims. In many cases, a tendency toward vengeance can actually be proved, the intention to represent the illness as the guilt of family or environment. But, even here, the sexual impulses in the background remain more efficacious than the more obvious tendencies toward vengeance and defiance. The love impulses that escaped into the form of regression become still apparent. In many cases in which those hostile intentions become very clear, the unconscious endeavor can still be recognized. The aim is to attain through sympathy the increased love of the same relatives upon whom the patients have put the entire blame for the illness. In analysis, the striving for power often turns out to be the very way, though inadequate, chosen by neurotics for the achievement of their love aims. They are not easily dissuaded from the pursuit of that way. The theory of the male protest as the basic principle of neurosis is refuted by the proof of the effects of the unconscious need for punishment.

The neurosis that is essentially built upon a conflict between instinctual demands and the need for punishment shows that the ego, giving in to one factor, must serve the other factor, too, to a certain extent. The ego behaves like the funny soldier in a comedy of Nestroy's who calls out, "Please, Captain, I have caught two enemies but they hold *me*."

In many cases, it can be shown that the greatest instinctual gratification in neurosis corresponds to the greatest gratification of the need for punishment. Take as an example a rather usual case of sexual gratification. Experience shows that the boy in this case changes from the manual to other practices of masturbation. Usually the manual action is eliminated more and more, rhythmic motions on the bed sheet or pillow replacing the earlier method of friction of the genital. In puberty a connection is frequently made, during masturbation on the pillow underneath, with the fantasy that it represents the body of a love object.

We recognize, then, in analysis, an approximation of the situation that produced, besides the physical stimuli coming from the inner organism, the child's sexual excitation, that is, the fantasied situation of incest. The role of the pillow in fantasy as a substitute for the female body can, of course, be quite conscious. In fact, it is sometimes deliberately imagined thus and equipped with imagined properties, but the incestuous fantasy behind it is still removed from consciousness. However, we see here the approximation to the original incestuous fantasy that returns in distortion. But another point of view appears to be no less significant. The hands have gradually become taboo. Their occupation with the boy's own genitals seems forbidden. Their action has been marked by an unconscious feeling of guilt.

I could observe this connection very well in one of the symptoms in a case of obsessional neurosis. The patient, a young girl, frequently had the peculiar feeling that her hands were not hers, that they were not part of her own body. They seemed entirely strange and detached from her. This sensation occurred often in the middle of various activities like letter writing, sewing, etc., and it prevented her from doing certain jobs. Hence, a case of partial depersonalization. In analysis it became clear that the patient, in describing her sensation, had done so correctly. Her feeling really replaced the astonishment suffused with emotion over the fact that those hands that could write and sew now were the same that had been able to perform actions so embarrassing to the patient in retrospect, as was masturbation. Incidentally, many cases of manual awkwardness seem to me to be of a similar kind. It is as if the need for punishment had been detrimental to the hands that could perform actions so definitely forbidden, and had affected their functional efficiency in other activities as well. You will remember that Freud has already shown the same dynamic processes in psychogenic visual disturbances.

But I'll return to the situation I have already described. In the form of masturbation, the approximation to the proscribed situation coincides to a certain degree with the infliction of punishment, as we might have expected according to analytical assumptions. The elimination of the hands, consciously considered the means for easier production of the desired libidinal fantasy, becomes the sign of self-punishment, the unconscious representation of castration. Where the symptom affords the repressed impulses the greatest measure of gratification, there, also, the need for punishment receives the greatest satisfaction.

This functional relation between the extent of instinctual gratification and the fulfillment of the need for punishment may generally be considered valid in neurosis. It corresponds to the analogous relation between expenditure involved in repression and intensity of temptation. It sheds a new light also on the protective measure toward the substitute gratifications in obsessional neurosis.

Take another example from the symptomatology of this kind of neurosis. A patient, a young widow, protects herself from leaving the house, which means exposing herself unconsciously to sexual temptations, by locking the door and putting the key away. Later she has to take the key to another room. The following stages that reflect the processes of displacement are these: the key is tied to something, for instance, to the door. The knots in the string that hold the key increase in number and complexity. The key later on goes into a box which is locked and tied down, etc. Thus, when the door has to be opened for a visitor or the letter carrier, a somewhat difficult situation results. Finally, the old cook is ordered to hold the key and keep it safe from her mistress, whose unconscious wish is to go out and to be picked up by a man.

One might say that the described development really accomplished the prison sentence. In these processes, not only does the displacement of substitute gratification and protective measures become clear, but also the degree of the need for punishment that corresponds to the intensity of temptation, and is likewise displaced. Also the actual gratification of a forbidden impulse can, at the same time, satisfy the need for punishment. We can observe this in cases of masturbation that unconsciously also have the character of self-castration. Therefore, it will be advisable to discern carefully three phases: the need for punishment which sometimes initiates the instinctual gratification; the need for punishment during the gratification proper in the form of self-punishment; and, finally, the need for punishment recurring secondarily upon the gratification of condemned urges.

Another point of view that is connected with this one seems to be important. As Freud has shown, repression engenders the uninhibited unfolding of the instinctual representative in fantasy, and results in the actual damming up because of refused gratification. The resulting forms of expression are of an extreme nature and frighten the neurotic by feigning an extraordinary and dangerous overwhelming force of the repressed impulse. We should like to add that this semblance is produced also by the need for punishment that seems to intensify the force of the drive. To this reactive effect of their need for punishment, people, who are otherwise strongly inhibited in instinctual gratification, often give in and commit actions that we would never have expected of them. Criminology ought to make this consideration its own and explain why particularly decent and law-abiding men and women so often commit surprising crimes. In analysis we have often heard the expression of astonishment from patients as to how they ever could have done this or that, something not even in line with their conscious intentions and contrary to their character. The individual instinctual force of repressed tendencies is not an adequate explanation. In most cases, we have to assume that the power of a drive leads to actions whose accomplishment would never have been effected by the energy of the repressd instinctual representative alone.

The wisdom of all peoples proclaims that the forbidden incites to transgression. But it does not say that the greatest stimulus originating in the forbidden consists in the unconsciously foreseen gratification of the need for punishment. That gives, for instance, the explanation of the Biblical tale of original sin. The pious proclaim suffering to be the consequence of sin as the punishment for sinful deeds. But if punishment is the effect of those actions, it must also have been one of their most essential motives.

Something similar can be said about the psychology of neurotic disturbances. Here, too, gratification of the need for punishment must be one of the secret motives of the neurosis. Hence the illness is unconsciously made equivalent to punishment. It may be stated with assurance that the answer to the question about the nature and the unconscious reasons for this self-punishment furnishes, in most cases, the key to the neurosis. Also, in the statement of the point of view mentioned earlier, religion intuitively preceded psychoanalysis. Earlier we pointed out that instinctual reinforcement itself can be traced back to the reactive influence of the need for punishment. Religion asserts that original sin also has the character of punishment, and one of the greatest psychologists of Christianity, St. Augustine, declares that covetousness, concupiscence became a punishment as a consequence of sin. The facts concerning this matter as described here by theology, can in psychological language, be only these. The pre-existent feeling of guilt can often engender an increase in the intensity of temptation. The stimulus of the forbidden consists largely in its being the goal of the instinctual impulses reactively reinforced by the need for punishment. In some cases, it may even seem that removal of the emotional pressure of the feeling of guilt by the forbidden action is more significant than the gratification resulting from it.

I'd like to return to the problems of the compulsion to confess that are so intimately connected with those of the need for punishment. The relations between these two psychic phenomena seem clearer now. They can be summarized in a few sentences. The compulsion to confess is the unconscious tendency toward expression of repressed instinctual impulses that is modified by the influence of the need for punishment. Its result, the confession, unconsciously represents a punishment and satisfies a part of the need for punishment. If the need for punishment is too great, a confession cannot be arrived at, only a substitute of the original action in which the need for punishment had its beginning.

This is not the place for us to concern ourselves with a description of the changes in analytical technique that have developed during the past three years since Freud's last investigations. They are mainly determined by a consideration of the role of the superego in neurosis. As it seems to me, an ideal requirement of analytical technique must be that it comprehends the significance of the symptom in two ways. The treatment should make recognizable to what extent the symptom suffices for the instinctual gratification as well as for the need for punishment. The theory of the compulsion to confess for which I speak here, and which attempts to show the participation of the superego in every neurosis, is expected to be of use in this modified technique also.

I have told you too little as yet about the extent of the compulsion to confess in the dimension of width. Therefore, I am adding the following. The universal yearning for transference, which we meet not in analysis alone, but which has found its most conspicuous form in it, can be allied with the compulsion to confess. It is as if we were constantly waiting to entrust to somebody our secret wishes and our emotional reactions to them. We know now that this somebody is a substitute for the father or mother, to whom we first told everything. But the compulsion to confess extends far beyond the realm of the instinctual impulses. Through the underground connections among our thoughts, judgments, plans and ideas on the one hand, and the repressed impulses on the other, it becomes understandable that the compulsion to confess extends to these psychic performances also. At some time we must betray them unconsciously, however much our conscious will may remonstrate. It is not difficult to find the unconscious confession even where it assumes more concealed forms. Analysis proves that even the lie, even the *pseudologia phantastica,* still represents some involuntary truth, signifies an unconscious confession. Also gossip, the transmission of malicious remarks or rumors to a third person, is an unconscious confession of hidden hostility on the part of the intermediary. An old Viennese proverb says that carrying back means wishing to offend.

Allow me to mention a few more neurotic symptoms in which the compulsion to confess makes an especially conspicuous appearance, so conspicuous that it becomes obvious even to the non-analyst. There is, for instance, stuttering, which clearly enough represents the confession of the tendencies that impede and interfere with speech. One of my patients always stuttered when he had to pronounce a word beginning with f. Analysis showed that the stuttering came from unconsciously remembering the word "fuck" which, as a child, he had heard once somewhere and kept from his parents as a secret. The stuttering dated from that time and had the unconscious meaning of a confession. Other testimony to the compulsion to confess immediately recognizable to everyone presents erythrophobia, which commits compulsory self-betrayal by blushing. Dr. Abraham reminds me that erythrophobia is often accompanied by extravagant activity of fantasy or by pseudologia. The patient has obeyed partly the compulsion to lie (his lie making him appear as something different from what he is) and partly the compulsion to confess this pretence. We know that, even in this transformation by lying, the compulsion to confess still finds its hidden expression. You see that in erythrophobia also, as in stuttering, the interference between compulsion to confess and the forces opposing it becomes manifest in the symptom.

That division into the representation of the aims of the repressed instinctual impulses and manifestations of the secret aims of the need for punishment becomes obvious in the dichronous actions of obsessional neurosis. There, the instinctual breakthrough and the subsequent action of penitence separate from each other. The progress of the neurosis leads to the result that the repressed instinctual impulses eventually dominate the clinical picture that earlier had seen the reaction-formations in the foreground. In hysteria often the opposite impression is gained. Here, first the repressed impulses become clear to the analytical observer and only later the opposite factors in their effectiveness.

Now I have only to mention a variation of the unconscious confession, which will become important to the practicing analyst and which may be called confession in defence. The patient's choice of words, never one of chance, turns out to be a significant hint in self-betrayal of this kind. For instance, I explained to a patient that he had unconsciously wanted to stab his brother to death, when he told me about a quarrel with him at the table, after which he had handled the fruit knife carelessly. Outraged, he rejected this interpretation, adding that hostility against the brother is also one of those catch phrases of analysis. He used the German word "Stichwort" for "catch phrase." Literally, "Stichwort" means "stab word." With this expression, seemingly used by chance, he not only supplied the confirmation of my statement, but he also made an involuntary confession. I called another patient's attention to the fact that an important feature of a dream that we were analyzing, pointed to his Aunt Clara, who had played a great role in his childhood. He supposed that this was not probable at all, while it was clear that etc. Here the German word "klar" (equals "clear") functions as a confirmation of my conjecture concerning Aunt Clara. Every analyst knows that little symptomatic actions, playing with a pencil, an unusual motion of the hand, can in the same way become unconscious confessions.

Our short survey has shown that repressed impulses are generally subjected to the urge for expression, while the need for punishment makes itself felt through the compulsion to confess.

V

The Compulsion to Confess, in Criminology

LADIES AND GENTLEMEN: In the compulsion to confess, as it has developed from the urge for expression under the influence of the external world and the superego, we have recognized a remarkable psychic power. Its effects in the life of men and women merit our full attention. It would be a rewarding task to trace the expressions of this tendency in their variations caused by factors of various kinds, and to pursue their significance in all fields of individual and social life. This task goes, however, far beyond the scope of these lectures. Since I am not in a position to delve so deeply, I'll limit myself to calling your attention in the following lectures to the special role played by the compulsion to confess in the development and psychic construction of our most important social institutions.

In doing this, I'll find the opportunity to point to some problems resulting from the introduction of our new points of view in their respective fields. Their solution must, of course, be left to the representatives of the respective special branches of learning. On the other hand, I shall allow myself to call attention to the fact that the very theory which we developed can well contribute in a decisive way to the answers to those questions of other sciences.

The combination of several external and internal factors implied in the material itself causes me first to include criminology and criminal jurisprudence in the scope of these considerations. The close inner connection between need for punishment as an

254

emotional phenomenon and punishment as a social institution, between the unconscious confession as a psychological concept, and confession as a legal concept, makes this special position of criminology appear to be justified.

Consider now that there must be a meaning to the fact that the German word *gestehen* (to confess), according to Grimm, has its derivation in the phrase *sich dem Gerichte stellen* which means to surrender to the court. Obviously this means to confess to the deed, to admit one's guilt, and it is by itself the expression of the victorious need for punishment. When I chose the expression "compulsion to confess" (*Geständniszwang* in German) for the psychological facts that in psychoanalysis have increasingly attracted my attention and that I have described to you in these lectures, I did not know that this name was a legal technical term. The phrase "compulsion to confess" designated the means of coercion in German medieval criminal procedure with which the accused was to be made to confess. This fact, with which I became acquainted later when reading several works of criminology, appeared to me as confirmation of my views. It was bound to be true that what presents itself now as an inner emotional compulsion is the transformed acquisition of former external coercion, as we could observe in the psychogenesis of the processes of repression.

The compulsion to confess of former generations with psychic pressure, the effect of which we are observing in confession today, is also part of that development which transfers the accent from external to internal processes.

It is easy to predict that the psychological insights of psychoanalysis are destined in the near future to transform criminology and criminal jurisprudence in an incisive manner. They will attain this effect not only by allowing old problems to appear in a new light, but also through the emergence of new problems caused by them, problems to the solution of which psychoanalysis will contribute to a large extent.

Attempts at applying psychoanalysis in the solution of criminological questions have to date been one-sided. They were not undertaken with the understanding and special knowledge that will in the future give results of a significance as yet not thought of. However, certain methodical suggestions made by analysis have already shown important new points of view in the field of interpretation of facts, a field equally important for judges, prosecutors and criminal psychologists. As you know, this concerns the application of methods of finding the guilt or the innocence of a person by identifying signs which can lay claim to objective validity. The future shaping of these diagnostic methods of association will decide to what extent they should and can be used in courtroom practice.

Criminology will, I am sure, make use of analytical points of view and methods to a much larger extent than it has in the past. These uses concern not only the theory of instinct, the dynamics of emotional life and the effects of unconscious feelings, but also the forms of expression of the hidden compulsion to confess that appears, for instance, in people's slips of tongue and of pen.

Also, in the criminological field, applied psychology must give its attention to the tendencies leading to the compulsion to confess. Consideration of those unconscious impulses, resulting in self-betrayal, will give significant results in the interpretation of the facts of a case.

All of you remember the characteristic slip of the pen of the killer and poisoner H. mentioned by Freud in his *Introductory Lectures on Psychoanalysis*. That murderer H. had complained about the ineffectiveness of several consignments to the management of the institute that sent him deadly cultures, supposedly for bacteriological investigations. Instead of the words, "in my experiments with mice and guinea pigs," H. wrote, "in my experiments with people." In German, all three words—*Mäuse* (mice), *Meerschweinchen* (guinea pigs) and *Menschen* (people)—start with the letter M. At this time, we'll ignore the question discussed by Freud concerning the practical application of a slip of the pen of this kind. Let us only point out that a confession is implied, regardless of whether it concerns fantasies or facts. It seems important that the subterranean power of the need for punishment disturbed the writer's intention and forced the slip of the pen. The unconsciously desired effect of this compulsion to confess can, it seems to me, be expressed as follows: "Listen, the bacteriological cultures were too little effective in my experiments with people. Herewith, I indict myself. I confess that I undertook such criminal experiments." It cannot be without significance that the murderer directed his complaint containing the slip of the pen to the very management of the institution. Of course, the management alone was answerable in a complaint of this kind, but was it not that same management whose responsibility was strict supervision to make certain that the dangerous bacteria were not put to wrong or dangerous use? Can it be an accident that this involuntary confession was directed at the very authority that had the duty to see that the cultures were used for scientific purposes only? Didn't that slip of the pen as well as the unconscious wish to confess contain a warning directed to the management?

If more were known about the emotional processes in that criminal, in other words, if criminology would make analytical points of view its own and not consider merely the bare facts of conscious will, a psychologically significant hypothesis could be arrived at. This would have consequence also in penal law. We would not deny significance to the circumstance that it was precisely the complaint about the ineffectiveness of the cultures in which the slip of the pen found its place. The actual emotional process was perhaps that the criminal took the ineffectiveness of the cultures unconsciously as a bad portent for his plan, for a warning which seemed to shed doubt on the result of his undertaking. Did it not seem as if the very ineffectiveness of the cultures indicated that something opposed the completion of his plan? Did it not seem as if in this "malice of the object," like a portent, an obstacle had arisen against his action? His slip of the pen assumes, however, a further meaning. The suppression of this anxious doubt, behind which we see the powers of the conscience of the ambitious criminal at work, had not entirely succeeded and his slip of the pen consequently became the unconscious admission of failure as well as a confession. The cynicism implied in the fact of the complaint could be explained by an effort to overcome those dark feelings emerging from his conscience.

Perhaps the criminal unconsciously expected his letter to bring a decision as to whether he should continue those disastrous "experiments." Perhaps that confession by a slip of pen was unconsciously meant to ask the question of fate. The self-betrayal implied the unconscious hope of being prevented from committing his crime at the last moment. The slip of the pen shows, therefore, the underground fight, that was thought unconscious to the criminal, between the tendencies which drove him toward the crime and the deeper powers of conscience. It is understandable that he unconsciously left the decision to the authorities, to the parental substitute, namely, the management of the bacteriological institute.

You see, the observation of a case of this kind produces a number of interesting problems from the analytical point of view. Let us start from that slip of the pen, to which nobody will deny the character of a confession, and say that cases of seemingly unintended self-betrayal cannot be isolated, but that they regularly repeat themselves, obeying the iron laws of the unconscious compulsion to confess.

How else but through a compulsion prevailing against all conscious intentions would you explain the innumerable cases where a criminal plan executed with extraordinary intelligence and ingenuity, taking into account all possibilities, is frustrated by a minor detail of which the criminal had "not thought" although he had carefully considered much less important circumstances? Afterwards it is frequently of interest to observe how just such a weak piece of circumstantial evidence develops into the decisive proof, as a pyramid develops from a grain of sand. Do you not think that strong unconscious tendencies toward self-betrayal have set in just at that weak spot with their effectiveness? Could not the compulsion to confess hide behind all these instances of "oversight" and "carelessness"?

Certainly you have read recently in the papers the report about a little story that occurred in our city. A young man had an affair with a married woman with whom he used to spend nights while her husband was away. Was it by chance that he used the absent husband's bathrobe and put a letter written to him by the lady into a pocket where he carelessly forgot it? The reverse case, that of a husband leaving in one of his garments a letter or other tell-tale object received in an illegitimate affair, is so frequent that wise wives can do without a direct confession of the escapade. You surely followed not long ago the story of the murder of a boy, committed by two young people, sons of very wealthy fathers in Chicago. Do you believe that it was a mere accident that one of the murderers forgot his glasses at the location of the crime, after their plan, thought over a thousand times and prepared with all possible refinements, had been executed? The behavior of the young people in court, seemingly demanding the death penalty with demonstrative insolence and strongly marked defiance, can only confirm our interpretation that that slip was an unconscious act of self-betrayal. I believe that methodical consideration of the compulsion to confess ·as an emotional phenomenon opens up new prospects for criminology.

By the way, there is in the field of criminology a peculiar fact in the foreground of discussion, a phenomenon which cannot be understood without the assumption of an unconscious compulsion to confess. It is by its form and effect the most persuasive testimony to the existence of that compulsion. I refer to the conscious confession. Confession in this form is, of course, only the substratum for its psychological analysis which should consider the acknowledgment of guilt merely as an outgrowth of the unconscious trend that became admissible into consciousness. Only analytical pursuit back to its unconscious causes supplies deepest insight.

Now you will perhaps say there is nothing special about a criminal confessing to his deed. But with this judgment you place yourself in direct contradiction with the opinion of our most prominent criminologists. An expert as important as Hans Gross states in his *Encyclopedia of Criminology* approximately in these words that confession "is a unique psychological phenomenon, difficult to explain, inasmuch as it always works to the detriment

of the one who made it." Of course, this does not concern confessions made because of jealousy, of vengeance, or in order to gain
time. Criminologists enumerate a whole series of other effective
motives, but they say almost unanimously that a considerable
number of the confessions cannot be explained in this way, and
they remain more or less incomprehensible. They have in mind
confessions made voluntarily by criminals obeying an inner pressure and these confessions, made because of motives of conscience,
appear puzzling to criminologists. However, they make exceptions
of people who have inclinations toward hysteria or are deeply
religious.

If this is indeed so, consideration of another psychological fact
would cause some confusion. It remains incomprehensible then
why the judges in criminal courts and criminologists direct all
their efforts at eliciting confessions from criminals. Logically, they
ought to say to themselves, "None of the special motives like
vindictiveness, jealousy etc., is under consideration. The criminal
certainly will not obey any uncertain and mysterious pressure of
conscience which causes him damage." I freely admit that we don't
understand the effects of this pressure. A phenomenon occurring
as extraordinarily often as a confession under the pressure of conscience doesn't necessarily lose its mysteriousness because of its
frequent occurrence. But those who work toward obtaining a
confession ought to make it clear to themselves, so that we too
should consider, what its nature is and according to what laws it
occurs. Gross says in another work, *Criminological Psychology,*
that he really cannot think of any analogy in man's psychic nature
where anyone would do something with open eyes exclusively to
his own detriment and without any perceptible advantage, as is
the case with this kind of confession. Well, to us psychologists, it
would certainly be a greatly disquieting phenomenon were the
confession really to stand thus without any analogy in human
emotional life.

But is this really the case? Anybody possessing analytical knowledge has recognized the fact that the world is full of actions
performed by people exclusively to their detriment and without

perceptible advantage, although their eyes were open. Think for instance of the abundance of masochistic acts! We should therefore by no means be discouraged by the mysteriousness of confession. It cannot be impossible to fit the confession into the framework of psychic processes known to us and to recognize its meaning. This sphinx, too, will have to surrender her riddle. Its solution, like that other one, will be: man. Analysis, as the psychology in depth of human processes, has shown that there exist, indeed, numerous analogies to the phenomenon of confession. It has proved the existence of a compulsion to confess that obeys the laws of psychic dynamics, and it has clarified the nature and effects of that unconscious need for punishment in which confession originates. The alleged incomprehensibility of the confession is caused by the fact that criminal psychology does not yet know the psychogenesis of conscience, of the superego and of the moral factors which operate unconsciously.

The practical consequences resulting from the psychological insights produced by analysis can be seen from the fact that a confession will serve as proof for the criminologist only if the motive has been made completely clear. Gross points out that it is not sufficient to prove that a confession has been made, "but we must find the confession to be comprehensible as we consider all available factors." Without understanding the course of certain ego-agencies, the unconscious need for punishment and the compulsion to confess, certain confessions will, of course, be difficult to comprehend. The criminal himself can say nothing as to the nature of the unconscious processes, the result of which is the confession. This means that he can say nothing that would suffice for their explanation.

Only from the points of view of such a compulsion do the false confessions and self-incriminations until now only interpreted as originating in "morbid inclinations" find their explanation. The same emotional claim to the deed and the unconscious feeling of guilt based on endopsychic perception of suppressed tendencies can make those processes leading to false self-incrimination understandable to us. Object introjection in melancholia and identification with another once beloved person, which has been proved by Freud in the borrowed feeling of guilt, will certainly explain a number of cases of false confessions.

I'd even go farther in psychological assumptions than the criminologists and judges in criminal courts. I'd dare to say that many of the confessions, in which adequate motives like vindictiveness, boasting, jealousy etc. can be recognized easily, find their deepest motivation only in the need for punishment. In cases of "defiant confession" in which the criminal even boasts of his deed, those tendencies originating in the need for punishment do not, by any means, have to be absent. Before we proceed to apply experiences gained in analysis to some obscure points of criminal psychology, I must state that the following remarks concern only those criminals who are at all capable of a feeling of guilt.

Furthermore, we shall have to take into account the differences between the psychology of the criminal and that of the neurotic. To them, correspond, of course, the differences between the psychological situation of the procedure in court and that in analysis. Freud has formulated those differences clearly in his article "Psychoanalysis and the Ascertaining Truth in Legal Proceedings." The neurotic maintains his secret from his own consciousness, the criminal his only from the judge. The neurotic patient is genuinely ignorant, though not in every sense. The criminal only simulates ignorance. In psychoanalysis the patient helps with his conscious effort against his resistance, expecting an advantage— namely the cure. The criminal, on the other hand, does not work with you because he would be working against his whole interest. Freud, of course, knew better than we do that he intentionally formulated those differences so strongly because he could not, in a short lecture, concern himself with finer similarities and differences. Actually those differences are correct only in the broadest sense, as shown by several delimitations and indications even in Freud's articles.

This discussion will be limited to the one difference between the neurotic patient directing his efforts at overcoming his resistance in cooperation with you in the hope of a cure, while the criminal is not cooperating with the judge, lest he act against his strongest conscious interests. We know that the neurotic, though desirous of the cure, fears the surrender of his gains because of his illness. We know, too, that his unconscious resistance is directed against getting well. The powerful factor of the secret need for punishment, therefore, does not come into its own in this differentiation. Indeed, it can be shown that the criminal often actually cooperates unconsciously with the judge, that he really "works against his whole ego." Our new understanding of the psychological nature of the confession has practical usefulness also in that the investigating judge, in his procedure, may count on it that, in spite of all conscious efforts to keep his secret and evade punishment, an unconscious opposition will act in the criminal to betray the very thing he strives to conceal with great emotional expenditure. It may be ascribed largely to this factor perhaps that the criminal entangles himself in contradictions, allows himself to be carried away into rash statements about small matters that later become significant, and betrays himself in seeming quite trivial points during the investigative and the criminal procedure.

Freud asserts that the neurotic is genuinely ignorant of his secret "although not in every sense," but that the criminal simulates his ignorance. We should also like to add here "although not in every sense." Certainly the criminal knows about his deed. He knows that he prepared and executed it and he tries to conceal that from the judge. But it can not be mere simulation if he maintains he knows nothing about it. Even here we have to grant him credence to some extent. We have to realize that the statement that he knows nothing about it has the character of a wish. He really does not want to know anything about it, anymore than the neurotic wants to know about his suppressed instinctual impulses.

But another point of view appears to be more important—he knows very well that he executed the deed, but he does not consciously know why he did it and what it means psychically.

Here the criminologists will, of course, refuse to believe us. They will point out that the very nature of the deed furnishes information: here is a murder for lust, this is a theft of money

and this is an assault because of jealousy. It is the perpetrator himself who names the motives of his deed if he makes a confession.
The criminologists will also definitely oppose the second part
of this assertion: what, this intelligent man who exhibited so
much ingenuity in the execution of his crime should not know
what a murder is, an act of rape, a theft? Shall we not be reproached for complicating this question which we should rather
simplify as much as possible? But this does not make the question
simpler.

The conscious motives may, of course, be given, and we do not
deny that they had a part in the deed. But are they sufficient or do
we have to look further for other more deeply hidden ones? Who
would care to say seriously that Rasholnikov in Dostoevski's magnificent work killed the woman usurer merely to get hold of
money? Certainly, the perpetrator knows what a murder or a theft
means, but does he also know what it means psychically, what it
means to him? You remember that in an earlier lecture we discussed the fact that we do not know what we experience and
especially what we experience in the most decisive events of our
life. Reforms of the investigative and criminal procedure will
have to set in also at this point.

The inadequacy of the inquiry into the psychological clarification of the deed, of the usual questions concerning the closer
circumstances and motives of the crime and the previous history
of its perpetrator, became clear long ago to every good observer.
Even in the ideal case, the criminal, if he were willing to answer
all questions truthfully, could not say that which is psychologically
essential and decisive, because the motives of the deed and the
determining emotional processes preceding it are largely unconscious. The peculiar psychic tension preceding the deed, the suffering from obscure impulses and countercurrents, the driving
feeling of guilt before the deed or the motives of an action of a
criminal nature—these are emotional phenomena for which
criminal psychology cannot have the right understanding until
it has made the results of psychoanalytical research its own. But
the deed itself often happens unconsciously. The criminal feels

strong emotions, but perhaps those are not the ones that are really the deepest, that lead to his decision. The perpetrator knows of his deed but he does not know in what underground connection it stands with the emotional processes since his early childhood, and what unconscious meaning it conceals. The deed originated in the id-tendencies. The ego has perhaps not yet taken notice of the crime.

You recall now our earlier explanation of the psychological nature of confession. You will be tempted to say the deed is partially repeated in the very confession, only now, as it were, the active psychic overcoming of that traumatic event, the deed, sets in. Even purely linguistically, that seems to be a contradiction. We always say the criminal commits the deed. To be sure, his act seems to us to be the strongest expression of activity. But perhaps we delude ourselves in this, no less than in many naïve statements that we make about our psychic life. The very large share of the id in the execution of the deed, though not excluding the practical material activity, restricts substantially the emotional activity of the ego. To apply Freud's beautiful allegory—the rider has relinquished himself to the bolting horse. Does he know where it is running to and why it takes just this path? Perhaps we should say more correctly that the act occurred through him. Did he do it? Was it not rather done to him by id, by something in him?

Only in the confession does the ego begin to take notice of the deed, but it would by no means be correct to state that the confession suffices to convince the ego. Indeed, for the perpetrator also, the crime is a traumatic event that has flooded the psychic apparatus. To overcome it psychically requires time and effort. It sounds perhaps paradoxical, but it is none the less correct, that sometimes it takes the criminal years before he knows what he has done and what his deed means.

Analysis gives us an indirect confirmation of this assertion. The difference between neurotic and criminal has, of course, great weight and it would be wrong to belittle it as some psychologists do. But you would be equally wrong in basing that difference only upon the difference between the actually executed and the imagined deed. In the psychic life of the neurotic, the imagined or desired act has the same effect as the executed act. We see every day that a neurotic patient is oppressed by an unconscious feeling of guilt that is built only upon strong repressed impulses. He is slowly made able, through analysis only, to recognize this feeling of guilt as operating, and also to find its connection with those suppressed impulses. But an obsessional neurotic who would be unable to hurt a fly can be oppressed by a guilt feeling that would be appropriate for a mass murder.

Confession thus marks the beginning of the widening of consciousness that the understanding of the psychic significance of the deed implies for the criminal. We assert that many a criminal really has nothing to say about his crime. Of course, he conceals a secret, but he conceals it also from himself. His conscience is still mute or it cannot yet make itself heard clearly enough. A case came to my knowledge in which a murderer remained silent and sulky, then collapsed psychically later under the overpowering impression of Dostoevski's *Crime and Punishment*. Only then was he consciously accessible to the deep feelings of remorse.

It is clear that in this case, as well as in others often discussed, we are concerned with the difference between intellectual and emotional recognition or knowledge. Of course, the criminal knew very well that he had committed a murder and what this act meant socially, but he knew it only intellectually.

Allow me to place under a common heading the dynamic processes that lie between a committed crime and its confession and call it work of confession. This name would be in analogy to analytical expressions like dream-work or work of mourning. This effort will predominantly consist in the entry into his preconscious of that which drove the criminal to his deed, and in a certain recognition of what it means and why he had to perform it. The time of the work of confession is taken up with the conflict between his endeavor to conceal the crime from himself and the opposite tendency to admit it to himself and to think clearly about it. We may, indeed, compare the dynamic process of this kind of violent pushing away of an unpleasant series of facts from consciousness with a kind of instantaneous repression, a "thinking away from it" as a patient once called it.

The same tension also dominates the relations of the criminal toward the external world, to society. Some criminals report later about the conflict between these two trends. There is the endeavor to deflect any suspicion from himself, to efface all traces of the crime, and an impulse growing more and more intense suddenly to cry out his secret in the street before all people, or in milder cases, to confide it at least to one person, to free himself from the terrible burden. The work of confession is thus that emotional process in which the social and psychological significance of the crime becomes preconscious and in which all powers that resist the compulsion to confess are conquered.

It can definitely be seen that the very work of confession betrays itself while it goes on in unconscious substitute actions, in partial confessions. All those words and small actions that we called unconscious confessions will be considered similar to descendants of repressed material in analysis. Indeed, the criminal reacts to these unconscious partial confessions with anxiety, as if he had betrayed himself through them. The essence of the processes of the work of confession can be described as the overcoming of fore-anxiety, an expression that will sound familiar to you. Its external goal is to pave the way to confession itself, regardless of whether it is in the form of speaking out toward one person or of admission before the state authority.

It is not out of place to compare the work of confession to the dynamic performance accomplished by the patient in psychoanalysis. The psychic processes in the patient during analysis could be called a more special case of the work of confession. In those outgrowths of the repressed that occupy us in analysis, we recognize anew unconscious partial confessions.

There is no contradiction in our saying that the criminal reacts with anxiety to the small signs that we recognize as unconscious self-betrayal, and that he still feels them as emotional relief. As you have heard, one of the more general findings of analysis shows that one thing can mean unpleasure for one psychic system, pleasure for another.

The whole emotional expenditure in confession in many cases weighs only little compared with the work of confession, that painful performance in which something has to be overcome and as little as the punishment weighs compared with the suffering that originates in the superego. No earthly judge will attain the strictness of the superego in many persons. Describing the work of confession in the expressions of ego-factors, it can be conceived of as the effort that succeeds in having the super-ego allow the ego the benefit of confession. The masochistic pleasure of suffering and of torture through the super-ego, during the period in which the work of confession takes place, can easily be recognized afterwards. The work of confession itself affords a partial gratification of that masochistic need for punishment. Only in this way—through the preceding suffering—does it become understandable that the criminal, with little anxiety, awaits the real punishment after the confession.

This partial gratification of the need for punishment in some cases explains also the fact that the confession takes place without special expression of affect, even without obvious signs of remorse. The very work of confession means remorse, to some extent, and it is unconsciously replete with all the tortures of conscience. In these cases the fore-anxiety was so intense that compared with it the end-anxiety is no longer emotionally intensive.

> "Of all terrors of conscience speak to me,
> But do not speak to me of my father!"

exclaims Don Carlos in Schiller's drama. But the very thought of the father comprises all the terrors of conscience.

As you know, the early unconscious identification with the father was itself most instrumental in causing the conscience to constitute itself. Hence, the antithesis in that exclamation of the prince actually likens one to the other. One cannot speak of all the terrors of conscience without speaking of the father at the same time. The work of confession consists in the criminal's living through all the terrors of conscience in the unconscious thought of the father, before he goes to the father-representative and tells of his deed. Confession marks the transition of pre-insights from the inner work of confession to consciousness by means of verbal presentations and verbal perception. It is the counterpart to the deed. It brings also as to quantity, approximately the same emotional relief of tension as the deed. The extraordinary psychic work that occurred in the depths before the deed is still almost entirely unexplored by criminal psychology. Its analysis represents one of the most important desiderata of scientific criminology. As far as intensity is concerned, it can actually be compared only to the work of confession, to the effort leading to the confession. It has to be considered equal in significance for the individual's emotional life. Both these psychic performances are in a certain quantitative relation to each other, but the discussion would lead us too far from our topic.

May I be permitted to add a small supplement to what has been said earlier? The work of confession adduces the fury of the superego directed toward the ego, which we usually call pangs of conscience (in German "Gewissensbisse" means bites of conscience). The expression "bites of conscience," which appears in many tongues, is a metaphor, the origin and meaning of which is by no means clear.

Psychoanalytic exploration of a case of obsessional neurosis offered me an excellent opportunity to gain some insight into the obscure meaning of this metaphor. The patient's father had died during the analysis. Besides the doubts that usually appear after an event of this kind as to whether anything important had been neglected during the father's illness, for instance whether the patient had been sufficiently ready to help and loving toward his father etc., there appeared fearful dreams and painful ideas. There was, for instance, the recurring thought that a ghost or a skeleton would enter the patient's bedroom during the night. In addition to that and other fantasies, a particularly absurd idea combined with great anxiety presented itself. First it disclosed itself in a rather uncertain way. The patient reported that now

when he sat in his father's room reading or smoking he was sometimes pursued by the image of a horse. The complete wording of
his obsessive thought, as it was later clarified through analysis,
and as it found its expression in dreams, was this: the horse of his
father's hearse comes into the room and is about to bite him. He
added later on that the horse was a pony.

We shall not go here into the actual connections of this idea
and into its connection with a submerged childhood phobia of
horses but shall only mention that the obsessional idea soon vanished, after self-reproaches and their causes rooted in the Oedipus
complex had been made conscious.

In using other results of Freud's explorations that are known to
you, the resolution of the obsessional idea seems to me to confirm the assumption that in the "bites of conscience" the primeval
fear of being devoured or castrated appears again. Later this primeval fear transforms itself into social fear with its more variegated significance. The metaphor "bites of conscience," as analysis
of this case shows regressively, betrays thus its origin and its
latent significance of an archaic fear of cannibalistic punishment.
It also throws light upon the primary nature of conscience. Freud's
great hypothesis of the origin of religion and ethics is here confirmed because it implies those assumptions, as the fear of being
eaten by the father or father-totem is the core of moral anxiety,
of the ego's later fear of the superego.

I should like to take this opportunity to present to you in this
example, the difference between the anxiety of the child and its
later use by the superego. Examples of this kind convey to us
certain assumptions about the development of childhood anxiety
into moral anxiety. This transformation was made possible only
by the establishment of the superego in the ego. In the dark
dream of those weeks after his father's death, there also appeared
time and again a gloomy, sinister-looking figure who seemed to
threaten the patient. The figure showed enigmatic features. Its
identification with the dead father suggested itself but we had to
drop this interpretation because those characteristic, peculiar features were not explained in this way. After many efforts we had to

recognize in the mysterious figure—Napoleon. The patient and I were equally surprised at this result. The great Corsican had never particularly interested the patient consciously. The answer to the question as to how Napoleon entered into the dream did not quite seem to be given by making connection with a residue of the day, a conversation about Nelson.

The connection was made through an early childhood memory that emerged the following day in another association. The British patient had spent a significant part of his childhood, until he reached the age of two years and nine months, on an island near St. Helena. The population there had preserved the memory of Napoleon's stay on St. Helena in their tradition and the patient remembered how often his old Negro nurse had threatened him, "Poni will catch you if you aren't a good child." A later inquiry must have afforded him the knowledge that this feared "Poni" was identical with the great adversary of the British. You will remember the image of the pony that often occurred to the patient and immediately recognize the word-bridge he unconsciously built here.

The old childhood fright had thus been used here to deepen the anxiety of conscience with which the memory of an unusually gentle and kind father stood in conscious energetic contradiction. It is of some importance to keep in mind that moral anxiety is, to a great extent, independent of the real character of the person whom it once concerned. Sometimes, indeed, it seems as if the superego were the stricter, the weaker and the more loving its archetype had been in reality. This can be explained by the fact that the anxiety took the place of an old object-love and that it ultimately betrayed itself as a repressed demand for love.

The opinion, already developed by us, that an oversized need for punishment works against the compulsion to confess, also sheds new light on other problems. The question of the stubborn or mute criminal will have to be restudied by criminology under these analytical aspects. In many cases the intensity of an unconscious need for punishment will certainly have a deep influence upon the criminal's behavior, besides the motives so often mentioned by psychologists, such as defiance and obstinacy, fear of punishment, wrong estimate of the consequences of confession.

Allow me to make up here for part of what I failed to say in earlier lectures. Silence itself is a bit of negative confession and we unconsciously appraise it as such. A most intelligent patient once said in analysis that her silence really meant that she was dead. This is also the meaning of silence, as Freud showed, in the representation of death in dream and myth. We use the phrase "to treat with deadly silence," ascribing thus to silence the power to kill. One of the most impressive novels by Arthur Schnitzler, in which the work of confession and eventually the eruption of the compulsion to confess find their artistic representation, is entitled "The Dead Are Silent." How closely fiction approaches life in it was shown to me by the fantasy of a patient who had a love affair with a married woman. In his daydreams, he often imagined his death in an accident to the carriage on an outing with the lady. In his fantasies, his own death became not only the expiation, but also the confession of his relations with the woman because the secret affair would be divulged to the deceived husband.

Another patient divided people into those with whom one could be silent and those with whom one could not. He counted the analyst in the second group. When he was silent the patient felt greatly tormented and heavily oppressed. Notwithstanding all other emotional determinants of this case, it can be said that silence in this analysis, while expressing an unconscious feeling of guilt, was also followed by a feeling of guilt. It is as if the patient's unconscious judged and condemned his own silence as a symptom of hatred, as a withdrawal of love, as if the silence was not only an expression of social anxiety, but was also followed by social anxiety.

Likewise, clarification is offered by analysis of the defiant and the insolent provocative behavior of the criminal. An over great need for punishment will in this case, too, be the explanation. It can even be said that, in such seemingly paradoxical behavior, a still more intense need for punishment pushes toward expression

than is the case in silence. Silence frequently is itself an indication
of the processes operating in the work of confession and is sometimes followed by the confession.

The phenomenon of defiance or rebellion approaches much
more closely the repetition of the deed. In its criminological form
of appearance, it is only a special case of the peculiar behavior
which some persons show to others toward whom they feel guilty.

One would expect a person who has wronged another to behave with a consciousness of guilt or with humility, with embar-
rassment or apologetically. A great many persons show, however,
the peculiar and unexpected reaction of insolent and unruly,
even hostile behavior toward the offended or injured person.
You find this peculiar behavior by no means in rough and crude
persons as might be expected, but in those who are especially
sensitive and shy. Sometimes one would even be inclined to assume a connection of some sort with these qualities.

A first explanation might be an actual unconscious or preconscious feeling of guilt that became excessively strong. In reaction
to this feeling, these people are thrown into the other extreme of
the swing of the psychic pendulum. Emotional processes of this
kind are not without analogy. I know of the case of an otherwise
tender, perhaps too tender, daughter who, as soon as her mother
falls ill, heaps upon her reproaches and accusations which devolop
into outbreaks of unbridled hatred. The tenderness, reactively
reinforced by the pressure of unconscious hostile impulsions, thus
turns into its contrary. The mother's illness has brought apprehension and tenderness to a climax from which the unconscious
tendencies of hatred can now surprisingly break through. This is
implied in the explanation the daughter was able to give for her
behavior, namely—that she is so sorry for her mother and so much
worried about her that she has to scold her. What are thus felt as
increased tenderness and apprehension are actually the contrary
emotional impulses of the tension of ambivalence.

We see again that quantitative factors contribute substantially
to the decision concerning the result of instinctual delusion, as in
cases that we described earlier. In clarification of this odd be-

havior, the role of a peculiar sense of shame that points to deeper
motives may be considered, as well as the simultaneous influence
of other emotional factors. Furthermore, we may believe those
people who, when they are insistently questioned, say they are
outraged by the calm of another person, the more so, the less
this other person moves to take revenge. His humility affects them
directly as a provocation, as if, by such a renunciation of natural
hostile responses of vengeance and punishment, he claims a superiority to which he is not entitled.

It isn't necessary to abandon our earlier explanation, but only
to qualify it more exactly and to supplement it. We observe that
the infliction of the first offense or wrong was engendered by the
need for punishment. It was an attempt to find a place for the
need for punishment and to satisfy it, in the expectation of being
scolded and wronged. The second reaction, the repetition of the
offense, indicates the failure of this attempt. It is as if the offender
took vengeance on the one he hurt because the latter did not let
him have the punishment that he unconsciously demands, and
as if he made the hurt person pay for the intense feelings of guilt
the perpetrator has to experience. He takes revenge on the hurt or
wronged person for having hurt him. That would, indeed, be absurd unless, as in this case, two conditions of an emotional nature
existed. We have already mentioned the first: it is the great intensity of a pre-existent need for punishment. We know that in
this case the need for punishment has become so great that it
drives impulsively toward new misdeeds. This is certainly the case
with certain delinquents who are driven from one crime to another and a worse one.

The need for punishment can reach this overpowering strength
also if one loves the offended person, if one feels the suffering
inflicted on him unconsciously as one's own. In other words—
under the psychological conditions of unconscious identification.
Repeated hurt or wrong would, therefore, be the repetition of the
first misdeed intensified under the compulsion of the need for punishment. But it is also the partial gratification of that need for
punishment, as the hurt is inflicted upon the person who was

drawn into the ego through introjection of the object. Repetition of the act and self-punishment by punishment of the other object coincide here in a compromise action. The second condition consists in that the repeated misdeed is of the character of an acted-out confession or rather that it replaces the confession through the act. I recall to you here only what has been said earlier about acting out in analysis.

The phenomenon here described, which exhibits perhaps its most conspicuous form in the unruly or defiant criminal in court, has, as yet, scarcely been made the subject of psychological investigations by psychoanalysis. Needless to say that, to non-analytical psychology, it has never yet presented itself as a problem. Perhaps the writers of fiction rather than the criminal psychologists are, in this matter, too, the ones who comprehend the complex development of displacements and reactions occurring in human emotional life. I shall limit myself to citing a single instance that originates in the genius for human knowledge of one of the greatest psychologists. Dostoevski characterizes Fedor Pavlovich Karamasov, father of the brothers Ivan, Dimitri and Alosha, thus: he wanted to take revenge on everyone for his own infamy. It also came to his mind how he had earlier been asked at one time, "Why do you hate this person so much?" and how he had replied in an attack of foolish shamelessness, "Why? You see, he hasn't done anything to me, that's true, but I have done something unscrupulously vile to him, and scarcely had it been done, when I hated him, just because of it." It strikes us that the criminal finds the characterization of his deed as unscrupulously vile to be self-evident and that he connects his hatred most closely with his misdeed as to time and cause. Obviously, he describes the connection as he feels it even though he is not able to find the unconscious links.

Returning to the problems of criminology: I believe we are all under the impression that criminal psychology will find it hard to answer the difficult questions posed by the psychic phenomenon of the crime, with the means and methods hitherto at its command.

The new points of view compel us to spend a little time on the history of criminal procedure. If an over strong need for punishment is an obstacle to the compulsion to confess, then we understand why such odd means were used in former times to make the accused confess. I wonder whether you know that several decades ago, the so-called confession cudgel was still in use in Switzerland. It was applied to the delinquent until he made a confession. This institution is a relic of tortures and means of coercion used in the Middle Ages, hence, of the external compulsion to confess.

Even considering all the barbarism and brutality, there must be some psychological sense, some method to this cruel madness of medieval criminal procedure. It is as if his pains would loosen the tongue of the mute or defiant criminal. This torture was a bit of anticipated punishment, so to speak, a partial punishment, followed by the other, the actual punishment. The measure of his suffering was then full for the criminal, his need for punishment was sufficiently satisfied for him to be ready for the confession. It could only have been that primitive unconscious comprehension of the criminal's emotional situation that would explain the use of a measure that fills us with abhorrence today. The transfer of this "compulsion to confess" from without to within, into the individual's inner life, has made it possible for us, as I've said earlier, to speak of an unconscious compulsion to confess.

We are guided then to the question of why such means were used to make the delinquent confess, as well as to another question, namely, as to where the high psychological and criminological valuation of the confession originates. The practice of the examining magistrate and the judge in criminal court shows that a confession is still sought from the accused by all the means that are permitted. The "question by torture," as it was called in the Middle Ages, has not yet disappeared completely. It has merely changed its form. The coercion has now become mild and subtle. It has been transferred to such an extent into the psychic realm that it can scarcely be called torture anymore. It is forbidden to take the accused by surprise or to outwit him in any way, but every effort is made to obtain an admission of guilt from him.

Can the value of the confession as evidence justify such great efforts? Certainly not, because the confession alone cannot serve as evidence, as we have heard. It has, of course, great value, but there are false confessions. On the other hand, there exist cases where testimony and circumstances constitute sufficient evidence allowing judge and jury to make a decision even if there is no confession. Judgment of this kind is, indeed, made in a great number of cases. Besides the factors mentioned by criminologists and teachers of criminal law, there must exist others that concede to confession a special psychological position.

We can guess what these factors are and we can clarify them to ourselves by visualizing what confession unconsciously means to the criminal and to the society that passes judgment. To the criminal, confession means that his conscience has acquired its voice. He becomes, through the spoken repetition, conscious of the significance of his deed. In his utterance he begins to transform his mute feeling of guilt, which was inaccessible to society, into one closer to the normal one. Having freely expressed part of his need for punishment, he has also declared himself deserving of punishment. Isn't confession thus the very preparation of the sentence? Indeed, isn't the criminal's own judgment on his own deed already secretly contained in it?

But in these features, there also must be concealed that, which for others, for the judge, jury and audience, is the emotional significance of confession. Society feels oppressed by the criminal's denials and by his silence as if by an enormous, sinister accusation. It is as if the right to sentence claimed by society were being questioned. The criminal facilitates the court's task and he even unconsciously anticipates it by confessing, since confession is itself an expression of his need for punishment.

There must be some psychological justification to the attitude of the court toward the confession, something that finds its hidden expression in that attitude. It has been said that in every accusation made by society because of a crime, a self-accusation is implied, as society has its own share of guilt in that the crime had been committed. This accusation against society is also expressed

in the confession against a society that allows the poor fellow
to become guilty and then leaves him to his agony.

The accusation of the criminal, aimed at the "collective guilt
of society," as the famous teacher of criminal law, Franz von Liszt,
expressed it, is implicitly contained in the confession. Confession
thus means not only a lessening of the unconscious need for punishment and at the same time its partial gratification. It also
gratifies and lessens the need for the punishment of society. It
satisfies this need of society in the same way as the tragic hero,
who, as he perishes, gratifies the collective need for punishment.

The cause of the atoning and cathartic effect of confession upon
the audience has to be sought at this point. No one who ever followed a trial by a jury attentively will consider this description
of the emotional processes in the audience improbable. It may be
said that both judge and audience wait for the criminal's confession to lift a heavy ban, as it were, as if to gain the possibility
of a comparison with one's own psychic life, the possibility of
unconscious identification with the delinquent. The confession,
which also formulates a concealed accusation against society, lifts
this ban and permits, for an instant, unconscious identification
with the criminal, the comparison of one's own psychic processes
with his, and the condemnation of his and our own instinctual
impulses.

We should at this time also remember a variation of confession,
which limits the possibility of this unconscious identification—
the affectless confession, the admission without any emotion. The
criminal confesses to his deed but shows no signs of remorse, no
indication as to what his deed means in his emotional life. How
can we fit this phenomenon in with our ideas? We can easily do
this by remembering the connection between repression and confession. As we know, the idea and the affective charge of an instinctual representative can have different fortunes. The idea can
be preserved while the emotion has been repressed. In the process
of confession, analogous circumstances can be seen. A criminal
who recounts his deed entirely without affect, like a police report,
may be compared to a neurotic who tells of the very essence of

his disturbance in such a manner that any indication of affect is missing. In such a case, the emotion is often found to be a displaced one. The need for punishment certainly is of determining influence in this displacement of affect.

Society also shows its gratitude for the confession, through which the criminal relieves it from its own unconscious feeling of guilt, by reacting to it with moderation of its judgment of his deed. Confession is, indeed, the criminal's first step on his way back to society. By confessing, he finds the first possibility of a return to the community after he had put himself, through his deed, outside its limits. The sentencing authorities react, too, to this rapprochement, to this first effort at reconciliation with society, by formally considering the confession as an extenuating circumstance. In this whole psychic process of which the process in court appears to us as the outward, crude form, the examining magistrate or the judge in a criminal court functions unconsciously as the typical representative of the father, who condemns and forgives, who judges and comforts.

In his confession, the criminal has admitted his misdeed to the community, as the child once admitted his naughtiness to his real father or to his substitute. As the confession of the child unconsciously represents a new wooing for love, an attempt at regaining the lost object, the criminal shows in his confession his intention to re-enter society by declaring himself deserving of punishment. The outsider is on his painful detour back to the family of man.

VI

The Psychoanalytical Theory of Criminal Law

LADIES AND GENTLEMEN: We pointed out earlier that the results of analysis confront us with new problems in criminology. We are not concerned with these new problems but with an important new point of view: analysis is in a position to prove that sentence and punishment also exist outside the courts, in their own right, as it were, making large numbers of officials and officers superfluous.

Criminal psychology has established the fact that some criminals punish themselves and that many a suicide has been committed as atonement for a crime. But this is not our concern. These are only single outward signs of emotional processes that do not always achieve as conspicuous an expression as that. Among the tasks of criminal psychology, there should also be the exploration of the congruities between the criminal's psychic life and that of those people who have not become criminals. Analysis of the emotional processes of neurotics offers one of the most rewarding opportunities, perhaps the best, and now, even the most accessible one, for such exploration.

The neurotic disturbance serves to a significant extent the need for punishment; the suffering from it clearly exhibits the character of punishment. But not only the symptoms of illness point to self-punishment—we know how smaller actions like parapraxes of everyday life, slips of tongue and pen as well as oversights (analogies to "negligence," which is a term used by jurists) reveal themselves as expressions of tendencies toward punishment. Persons

who are not neurotic also punish themselves unconsciously
through temporary privation or withdrawal of pleasures, through
injury to their capacity for enjoyment and for work. This kind
of inner punishment is by no means restricted to adult persons.
It appears in children, beginning at a certain age and a certain
stage of development. To mention one instance—an English patient reported about her childhood that, after having made excellent progress in her studies of the German language, she felt,
since a definite date, completely unable to continue in her studies.
It is important to mention that her father had been her German
teacher and that they frequently had had tender or humorous
conversations that her mother could not understand. After a certain event in the life of the young girl, she had become self-con-
scious because she had preconsciously recognized the deeper
emotional impulses underlying her tender relations with her
father. Her ability in German conversation immediately disappeared. The thought had occurred to her of comparing the German conversations with her father to those in a childish secret
language often used between children in the discussion of sexual
subjects. This secret understanding with her father seemed to her
to be directed against her mother who didn't know German and,
therefore, to be forbidden. She had punished herself through the
inability to learn German, just because conversation in German
with her father had been such a pleasure for her. It was as if
talking had substituted in her imagination for a far less innocent
activity together.

Now let us turn to the self-punishments of neurotic adults. I
have made it a habit to ask myself in every analysis of a neurotic
patient how and by what means that patient had punished himself. I dare say, that in every case, the answer to that question,
late as it often came, afforded me a valuable bit of clarification of
and insight into the psychic structure and the unconscious causes
of the neurosis. Keep in mind that the answer to this question reveals at the same time one of the most important hidden gains
from the illness.

I should like to tell you of some examples of these unconscious self-punishments which determined these persons' lives to their very depths. A patient spends his life in a painful isolation that makes social intercourse with people almost completely impossible. One might say he had sentenced himself to solitary confinement. Another patient works with the greatest intensity and persistence on certain tasks that mean nothing to him and cannot bring him any advantage. His internal sentence was obviously forced labor. He bore, as it were, a secret brand: "*travaux forcés.*" A masochistic patient suffers from the obsessional idea that an army of spears is directed at his eyes. Analysis shows that this idea originated in a chastisement for disobedience that the patient had, as a small boy, received from his father with an alpenstock to which an iron point was fastened. The symptom, in connection with fantasies that appeared later, left no doubt as to the blinding being the dreaded and desired punishment, easily recognizable as a substitute for castration. The connection between imagined deed or forbidden wish and the punishment, hence the "ground for punishment," as the jurists would call it, is almost always unconscious, yet it can always be uncovered when analysis is carried through. It follows the primeval principle that the punishment should fit the crime; in the case of the neurotic, the thought-crime.

A differentiation that forces itself upon the analytical observer of neurotic self-punishment is certainly worth mentioning. A certain measure of unconscious punishment can be found in all patients but, in many cases, the fear of punishment assumes the character of punishment. The fear has not only the character of a protective measure against the threatening self-punishment, but it eventually takes over all its functions. This we observe clearly in emotional dynamics of the phobias that cause such severe restrictions to the patient. The widespread compulsive actions, too, through which the neurotic protects himself from the forbidden action, assume the character of punishment. They force him to spend an astonishing amount of time and energy on these small actions and to punish himself through loss of psychic mobility. Certainly, we shall not underestimate the share of substitute gratification in the symptoms, but, also, the defense transposed into the form of punishment grows with the increasing temptation. The same can be said of compulsive thinking.

The difference between latent self-punishment interfering deeply with the life and fate of the individual, and its variation in the form of anxiety, is certainly worth noting. It must, however, be pointed out that it does not originate in any difference in the emotional intensity of experience, but that it mirrors the influence of certain external and internal determinant factors. Allow me to resort to a comparison. Balzac, like his great contemporary Napoleon, had the burning ambition to conquer and rule over the world, as shown in the conception of his *Comédie Humaine*. It was not a difference in the power of the drive but other circumstances that caused him to attempt to fulfill his ambition in another field. Once he actually wrote these proud words under a picture of Napoleon, "What he could not achieve with the sword, I shall accomplish with the pen."

Perhaps I may cite a good example of the character of punishment that anxiety possesses from the analysis of an obsessional neurosis. The patient suffered from the blasphemous idea that he had to slap God in the face. Usually when this idea emerged, he saw on the ceiling, like a vision, an old man's face which he compared to the face of God, and a hand approaching it about to strike. Much later and in another connection, as if by chance, he came to talk about a feeling that had been tormenting him for a long time, a kind of obsessional apprehension that could not easily be appeased and often assumed the character of panic, with all its physical sensations, like heart palpitations, trembling, perspiration. It was the fear that the ceiling might collapse and bury him. The connection between the fear and the obsessional idea had remained unconscious to him.

Another patient felt a heavy pressure on his chest and described this agonizing sensation to be like one caused by a heavy stone that had been rolled on his chest. It was easy to establish a connection between his sensation and the idea of his father's tombstone. In this case, the punishment had assumed the form of a physical sensation as in a hysterical conversion symptom.

The significance of the unconscious need for punishment for the psychogenesis of hysterical symptoms has scarcely been appreciated yet. In the following case, too, an organic sensation can be seen as the expression of punishment. A patient had peculiar sensations on the neck, difficult to describe; something seemed to strangle him. Once he came to talk about a play, *The Bells,* the performance of which with Sir Henry Irving had left him deeply impressed. In the play, an innkeeper, who years earlier had murdered and robbed a Polish Jew, constantly thinks himself persecuted by the chiming of the church bells that happened to sound at the hour of his deed and he hangs himself. At another time, the patient had spoken in an extremely uncertain way of the unpleasant feelings aroused in him when listening to church bells. Unconscious identification with the murderer of *The Bells* was obvious because of repressed death-wishes against the patient's own father, who, through his job, was connected with the church. The sounds of the church bells once had had great significance for the patient who had been urged to go to church and service.

We may wonder why the punishment inflicted unconsciously by the neurotic upon himself is not usually a simple one but extends in many directions. Thus, the patient just mentioned had punished himself not only with a whole series of symptoms but he also suffered greatly from his way of life unconsciously brought about by himself. This way of life tied him to a distant country and did not permit him to reveal freely his opinions and to develop his personality. He was thus not only condemned to stay far from his loved ones but also to dissemble time and again. Toward the end of his treatment, he once spontaneously described his fate as "a lifelong imprisonment like the man with the iron mask." I had a patient who forbade himself almost every sign of life, beyond breathing and thinking. He really was a "living corpse."

Those multiple punishments inflicted upon themselves, for instance, by obsessional neurotics speak loudly enough of their need for atonement. They may be likened to the combined punishments inflicted by our justice upon evildoers. They differ from them in several points. In their properties and mechanisms they are very closely connected to the forbidden impulses. A second point is the fact that, for a single impulse, multiple punishment is meted out, as if a judge were meting out imprisonment, loss of honor, fast on certain days and other added punishment for a theft. A neurotic will, for instance, punish himself for one proscribed wish with a washing obsession, with the execution of a certain cumbersome ceremonial, with isolation etc.

As we see, there are also penal codes outside the court and laws that inflict punishment scarcely less inexorably for every forbidden act, indeed, for every forbidden wish, laws that work with a cruel logic and an automatic precision that leave all earthly legislation far behind.

Now you will say that all this is very interesting for the psychological understanding of neurosis, but how can it further criminological discipline? There are, I think, several points to consider. First, criminology should take cognizance of the existence of an inner court of this kind, enacting its own laws and inflicting punishment of a special kind. It may be foreseen that this court will some time in the distant future strongly compete against the external court, indeed, that it will perhaps be able to replace it.

It may furthermore be a surprise to hear that analysis is regularly forced to trace back the punishment, in every case that it has the opportunity to investigate, to repressed wishes originated in the Oedipus complex. It is as if crimes originated only in that source. Criminal psychologists should see a challenge in the investigation of the extent to which this unconscious connection can be proved also in the criminal, of whether here, too, there exists an underground connection between the primal crimes of childhood and the deed of the adult criminal, of what influence the individual modification of the Oedipus complex had upon the development of the person who later became a criminal.

Indeed, I should think that the history of law or historical jurisprudence could learn much from the exploration of the unconscious processes in the neurotic. Because in the neurotic's psychic life some archaic features are preserved, here are sources of information about a period removed from remembrance, a time into which no historian of law can see. Analysis has taken the first steps in this direction through Freud's *Totem and Taboo* and Storfer's investigation *About the Exceptional Position of Parricide.*

Wouldn't the decisions of this inner court, after considering all the incisive differences, be better able to give information about people's views as to what crimes and transgressions they find deserving of punishment, and on what degree of punishment they decide? Shouldn't it be possible to reach certain conclusions from these decisions which, though they may have no influence upon penal law, could attain importance for future prevention of crimes, hence for criminal policy, as it is called in criminology? Of course, the important differences between criminal and neurotic will have to be carefully considered when the psychology of neuroses comes to be used for investigation in criminal psychology. These are the differences in the inhibitory institutions, in the prevalence of sexual impulses in neurosis as against egotistic and asocial impulses in crime, and there are other differences too. It seems, that, after all, certain neuroses are to a great extent a protection against crime. In any case, the results of analytical research make necessary a thorough revision of an old theory that is based entirely upon the psychology of consciousness and that is the basis of present-day criminology. To speak in more general terms, scientific progress, as well as humane considerations, both demand that teachers of criminal law, judges by vocation and lay judges, counsel for the defense and prosecutors, all should receive a thorough psychological training. The most intelligent among these functionaries complain that they are wanting in it to an embarrassing degree.

Allow me to leave now this topic and to return to our criminological discussions. The history of penal law informs you that, originally, society, the tribal community, had to sentence a criminal, while later the single judge functioned as the representative of the community. But it is not difficult to reconstruct a prehistoric condition in which the chief of the horde wielded all the power and controlled penal law, as did later, in Roman law, the paterfamilias over the members of his household. The transition to the penal law of the community occurred probably in the age of the brother-horde. It can be seen quite clearly in some neuroses how social anxiety and the feeling of guilt toward society or public opinion lead back to the fear of the father.

Transference in analysis sometimes proves itself to be an excellent means for the comprehension of other problems of penal law. One of my patients was a very intelligent jurist who had become ill with obsessional neurosis. He was strongly interested in the problems of his science. His analysis proceeded smoothly up to a certain point, when resistance set in in a special manner. He expressed himself in compulsive, brooding thoughts that seemed to have no connection with analysis. It was amazing how skillfully the patient unconsciously translated, in his compulsive thinking, questions that occupied his interest from the realm of transference into legal jargon. Soon it became clear that he expressed, for instance, resistances, aroused in him through a short interruption of the analysis, in the solution—in thought—of the vacation problem in employee insurance etc. We are interested here in the compulsive thoughts revolving about the problems of penal law. When he concealed something from me, the treatment of the crime of concealment of stolen property in penal law became the center of his brooding thoughts. The "dolus eventualis" had to serve in the representation of doubts as to whether some hostile or aggressive thought was conscious or unconscious. The legal problem of negligence was unconsciously the arena of his doubts concerning the determination of his slips of tongue and pen. He found expression for the extent of his need for punishment in the wide-ranging compulsive thoughts that followed the pattern of the sections of the Civil Code, thoughts about the question as to what punishment criminals should receive in certain cases imagined by him. Self-accusation and self-defense alternated in these compulsive considerations.

It was only when I succeeded, in several especially convincing instances, in making the connection between even the most insignificant details of his problems of penal law, which he took from his current studies, seemingly at random, and unconscious feelings and thoughts from the realm of transference, that he changed to more immediate expressions of resistance. The form of resistance in terms of penal law, the manner in which the scene of transference became a tribunal, made possible, regressively, a kind of representation of the evolution of penal law whereby a "crowd of two" had to replace society.

It cannot be without significance for the theory of penal law that the unconscious self-punishment of neurotics is based entirely upon the principle of talion, on the law "eye for eye, tooth for tooth." That part of submerged psychic life, which in the emotional processes of neurotics astonishes the observer time and again, can also be shown in the need for punishment. In surveying some of the unconscious self-punishments of neurotics, we find such strange kinds of imagined punishment not known to modern penal legislation as castration, burial alive, immurement, suffocation, being put in irons, and various other excruciating kinds of capital punishment. Physical sensations often represent various imagined tortures. A patient spontaneously compared his condition, which had become continuous, to the situation of the regicide Ravaillac who was torn apart by horses. The patient's father was actually connected with horse breeding and, as a little boy, he had often visited his father's stables. It was certainly not accidental that the patient likened his symptoms to the sensations François Ravaillac might have felt when he was torn to pieces by horses after he had murdered King Henri IV of France in 1610. The punishment for unconscious murderous wishes against the father had taken that medieval form of which the patient had read when he studied history in high school.

We see that the unconscious, having its own laws, is also in control of punishments that date from the childhood of mankind. At this point, it should be remembered that punishment is not a primary social institution and that its origin is seen in the more primitive vengeance. It should also be mentioned that the neurotic's fantasies of vengeance clearly exhibits an archaic character, as shown by the indeterminate nature of objects against which, according to Otto Rank, the actions of vengeance are directed.

We cannot be expected to prove to what extent these views still influence the penal law of our time and how many legal principles can be traced back to the principle of talion. That remains as a rewarding task for jurists who would do best to start by investigating the principle, "*Fiat justitia, pereat mundus.*"

We have arrived at certain points of view that make punishment appear to us as a psychological problem. The possibility arises for analysis at this point to make itself heard in the dispute among the theories of penal law. A theory of criminal law is understood to be the answer to the question as to the legal ground and the purpose of punishment. Again, we cannot go into the discussion of all the theories of penal law and we wish only to point out that the purpose of punishment is to protect important interests in the life of man and to exert an emotional effect upon the criminal.

It follows that every theory of criminal law which has no psychological basis is incomplete and inadequate. The purpose of punishment is mainly psychological, regardless of whether the punishment is meant to have effect upon the criminal or upon the community, of whether it should be a protection, deterrent, reprisal or something else. Therefore, psychology must take part in the decision.

Please do not consider this advice out of order. May I mention to you, as a horrible example, a famous theory of penal law that is still rather popular with some scholars? According to Hegel, punishment is the dialectic realization of the concept of law. Crime is in contradiction with itself and therefore naught. It is semblance, and it is in the nature of this semblance that it cancels itself out. Punishment is the revelation of the nullity of crime, the statement of its imaginary existence. The essence of Hegel's theory of penal law is summarized clearly and perceptibly in this sentence: "Punishment is negation of the negation of law, hence positing, restoration of the law." Not one of us will dare to deny the dialectic ability of the followers of Hegel among the teachers of penal law.

Turning to theories that should be taken more seriously, the older and now obsolete theory of legal reprisal will still attract the attention of the psychologist. According to it, reprisal is the paramount principle of criminal law. In the opinion of Kant, the most famous advocate of the reprisal theory, penal law is a categorical imperative. He who kills, kills himself. Hence, the principle underlying the determination of the extent of punishment in penal law is the talion. We know what this opinion means psychologically. In the form of a penal theory, it represents the deep-rooted legislation of the unconscious. All theories basing punishment upon an urge for revenge as an expression of the instinct of self-preservation belong here. The theories of indemnification and replacement that emphasize the effect of punishment as of a settlement, as well as the theories of agreement, can easily be recognized as outgrowths of the old theory of reprisal, intellectualized—if you like, rationalized—or adjusted to cultural progress.

We have seen that these theories are deeply rooted in the instinctual, in the unconscious of man. If there must be punishment and if it should really have the character of punishment, it can be instinctually based only upon the principle of talion. The reprisal theory has, therefore, the advantage of compactness and psychological consistency, but it contradicts all progress of culture and humaneness. Reprisal as the purpose of punishment is simply the representation of a powerful drive as a theory.

There is an essential difference between these theories and the theories of prevention. The theories of general prevention declare that punishment attemps to deter everybody through the threat of punishment. The famous theory of psychic coercion of Feuerbach, which dominated legislation for decades, is in this category. It establishes the threat of punishment and the execution of punishment as the emotional coercion that is expected to deter criminals. The theories of special prevention will aim essentially at the determent of the individual criminal.

Let us stay with these theories for a few moments. We can readily see that a new psychological purpose is being ascribed here to punishment. A second factor appears to be the role of society, of the community, upon which the threat of punishment is expected to exert a deterrent effect. Let us turn to this factor. The objection has been brought up that it was absurd to assume that punishment should not influence the criminal but somebody else, or society. The objection is, of course, justified as long as punishment is understood to be only the preventive to protect society. But does not the double function ascribed to punishment come here clearly to the fore? We see here the Janus-headed character of punishment. It is turned toward the criminal as well as toward society. Upon thorough consideration, it seems that the theory of general prevention concerns itself with the social task, the theory of special prevention with the individual task, but only both together form a whole. In the reprisal theory, the purpose of punishment was unequivoval. It concerned the criminal only and it was the reprisal for a committed deed, for a crime of the past. In the theories of prevention, the purpose of punishment lies in the future, being intended to be a deterrent in the future. What is the significance of the fact that the communiy figures here in the explanation of the purpose of punishment? Does not the punishment thus lose its original character as it turns into a preventive measure?

I believe that the penal purpose of determent from crime for everyone points quite clearly in the direction to which we should look for the reasons for society to figure in the purpose of punishment. It must be that people preconsciously recognized that no deep gulf separates them from crime, that we all carry in us latently all the germs of the criminal. That must be the actually effective motive for the change of the penal purpose. In other words, society begins to recognize its share in the guilt of crime.

Let us now turn to the effect upon the criminal, as it appears in the theories of special prevention. Clearly, the factors mentioned here are quite valid. Punishment has turned from a measure of reprisal into one of protection. Has it thus ceased to be a punishment? Criminologists usually admit the merely relative effectiveness of this measure and some experts even assure us that punishment neither improves criminals nor does it deter them.

Another impressive objection raised against the theory of prevention is that punishment cannot deter because most crimes are committed in the hope of concealment, hence of impunity. This argument is certainly justified for conscious psychic life, but we do not think as highly of its effectiveness as is usually thought, because, according to our assumptions, the unconscious does not know that much caution. The scrutiny of reality is, as we know, one of the tasks of the ego.

When you consider this situation, you will find that we are in a peculiar position. We had to admit that the theory of reprisal is in accord with the powerful unconscious ideas of man. The theory of protection, however, appeals more to our conscious concepts. It blurs, of course, the character of punishment and transforms it into a protective measure for the endangered social order. It perhaps implies the character of a merely transitory phase that replaces punishment through other and better protective measures.

All we can do is to look for a new basis for punishment. A necessary condition will be that it originate in the live observation of people and in human knowledge and that it use the new results of psychological research. This theory has been prepared through Freud's analytical results. We have to limit ourselves here to its basic features. The new psychological foundation of the purpose of punishment will originate in the analytical exploration of the pre-existent feeling of guilt, an exploration for which we owe thanks to Freud. We no longer doubt that, in the criminals, for whom penal legislation is intended, a powerful unconscious feeling of guilt existed even before their deeds. This feeling of guilt is, therefore, not a consequence of the crime. It is, on the contrary, its motive. It is only its intensification that causes man to turn criminal. Crime is felt as an emotional relief because it can connect the unconscious feeling of guilt to something real, actual. The deed serves the accommodation of the feeling of guilt that has become overly great. In other words, crime is committed

in order to grant the prescribed impulses a substitutive gratification and to give a cause and a relief to the unconscious feeling of
guilt. It is, so to speak, the peg on which to hang that pressure.

From those results of Freud's research follows a new psychological basis of punishment, a psychoanalytical theory of criminal
law. Punishment serves the gratification of the unconscious need
for punishment that drove toward a forbidden act. We know that
the roots of this pre-existent feeling of guilt can be found in the
Oedipus complex. In consideration of the double function of
punishment, we add that punishment also gratifies the collective
need for punishment through unconscious indentification of
society with the criminal. This cathartic effect of punishment and
the process of identification bring the emotional processes in the
criminal prosecution close to that of ancient tragedy. The hero's
tragic guilt and fall release the same feelings. It should be noted
that a psychological theory presented by Kohler, which refers to
the purging power of pain, stands closest to the opinion represented here, but still differs essentially from it. Whatever the
reception of my analytical theory by criminology may be, the
hitherto unheeded fact, discovered by Freud, that the pre-existent feeling of guilt drives toward the forbidden deed, will
have to be the center of future discussion of the purpose of punishment. If anywhere, this is the proper place to talk about the law
that was in us when we were born.

We should like to add a few remarks to the analytical theory of
punishment. Let us start by pointing out that the theory I presented to you is not expected to treat of the permanent or even
only of the temporary necessity of punishment, nor of its justification as an institution. There is no doubt as to the existence of
the need for punishment, but it cannot be proved that legal
punishment is the only or even an adequate means for its gratification. We could think of prophylactic measures that could restrain
the need for punishment from becoming all too strong, and of
therapeutic means to bring about the lessening of this need in
another way. The analytical theory of criminal law furnishes only
a psychological explanation of punishment, no norm. Develop-

ment of this theory is, as it were, implied in the development of penal law, which turned more and more from judging the deed to judging its motives. Transition to punishment of motives necessitates, however, a change in the motives of punishment.

The psychological connections between our point of view and the old reprisal theory are obvious from the way in which we not only acknowledge the conscious tendencies as determining for the purpose of punishment, but also take into consideration the unconscious processes. Our view differs from the reprisal theory, which was nothing but a scientifically formulated representation of the tendencies of the unconscious, by making not the talion itself, but the need for punishment, based on the talion, the center of its considerations. Unlike the reprisal theory, our idea is not based on a moral or legal principle, nor upon an ethical norm, but upon the psychic facts from which they derive. It considers thus the unconscious process, but only for psychological purposes, without making itself their captive and without becoming their docile expression.

In its modern disguise, we recognize in the old reprisal theory, the old taboo legislation of the savages, which works automatically on the talion principle. But the taboo law is in itself an unconscious confession of the community. Through the taboo law, the community shows that it feels the same impulses as the criminal and that, therefore, it frees itself from him. As Freud remarks in *Totem and Taboo,* the community often gives an opportunity through punishment, to those who inflict it, to commit the same wicked act on their part under the justification of atonement.

The same can be said of the theories of prevention. The contagiousness of taboo transgression appears in them more clearly and more unequivocally because they serve determent. They imply the strongest admission of the fact that the longing to transgress the taboo prohibition—now the statutes of the Civil Code—lives on in our unconscious and that people who obey the taboo, or the law, have an ambivalent attitude toward those marked by taboo, or as we would say, toward criminals. In its hypothesis of determent by punishment, the theory of criminal

THE COMPULSION TO CONFESS   295

law thus goes back to the primeval assumption of magic power that is ascribed to the taboo. Doing so, it admits that crime, the substitute for taboo transgression, is a contagious example, and it endeavors to protect itself against crime through threats.

The difference between the reprisal theory and the protection theory is not, you see, as great after all as we assumed that it was in the beginning. Our analytical theory of criminal law goes back to the unconscious motives of the legislation of taboo and leaves both those theories behind.

We can easily understand what the weak spots of the theory of determent are. It will scarcely be a reference to the conscious aim at impunity, which characterizes crime, that would help to uncover them, because the unconscious need for punishment opposes this aim energetically, if our theory is correct. But another consideration, heeding the analytical points of view, shows a more deep-seated flaw in the theory of prevention. It is the following: punishment considered the most effective deterrent against crime, according to prevailing opinion, becomes, under certain conditions which are extremely abundant in our culture, an unconscious and most dangerous incentive to crime. The forbidden deed, relieves, as you know, an overly great feeling of guilt. We see that, at its core, the theory of determent is insincere. The prospect of punishment does not deter the criminal, but unconsciously drives him to the forbidden deed. Even though the analytical theory may not justify punishment either, it is sincere in declaring that the purpose of punishment is the gratification of the perpetrator's need for punishment and that he demands unconsciously that which happens to him. Of course, for those criminals who never developed moral inhibitions, it will not be applicable, but, for them, punishment is not a suitable measure in any case, least of all, not one of determent.

We noted earlier that the theories of determent, and those related to it, fail to give punishment a penal character. All of them have, unknowingly, a trend in the direction toward a development leading to the entire elimination of punishment and inclining to replace it with preventive or prophylactic measures. We pointed

out before that the significance conceded to society in the purpose of punishment by the newer theories represents a kind of
admission of guilt, an unconscious confession on the part of the
community. The similarity of the forbidden impulses of the criminal and of the punishing community is clearly the basis of the
hypothesis of determent. This observation points to the direction
in which criminal law must develop—that of the eventual and
complete elimination of punishment.

We had an opportunity to study the development of the criminal laws. They were originally taboo prohibitions whose transgression was punished automatically, usually through the guilty
person's death. Only where this automatic punishment did not
take place did the tribe execute the punishment collectively. The
state which later took the place of the tribal community punishes
the criminal in the beginning according to the primeval and
sacred principle of the talion. The attenuation of punishment in
penal law and the extension of limits of the permissible testify
to a growing tendency toward elimination of punishment as
clearly as do the new theories of criminal law. This only means, of
course, elimination of the external punishment prescribed by the
law. Such a tendency implies that the individual's inhibitions
should be reinforced and that he should be left to his own conscience. This goal would be a return to the original legislation of
taboo, but on a much higher level. The external prohibition of
taboo legislation, directed against strong impulses, should become
an inner acquisition leading to their rejection or condemnation.
The development here again moves from without to within.

Our analytical theory of penal law endeavors to advance this
psychological development. It puts its main emphasis upon the
unconscious forces that drove the criminal toward his deed. This
makes evident the provisional character of our theory because it
can be valid only as long as an over strong pre-existent need for
punishment operates and necessarily and exclusively results in
the forbidden deed. Mankind will not lose this feeling of guilt for
a long time to come, but it may be possible that other channels of
discharge for it may be found for it. Even though one of the

strongest driving forces of crime still would not be eliminated, it would be led to another application.

Some researchers already maintain that, owing to the strong determinism of modern natural science, the basis of criminal law has collapsed. They say that the basis of the whole system of penal law, the tenet of the freedom of will, has been shaken and they predict that the concepts of guilt and innocence will disappear from the face of the earth and legal punishment will have the same fate. Courageous and sincere scholars like Dmitri Drill direct radical criticism against the social institution of punishment and compare the state, which controls the present-day penal system, to a person who expects to repair damage on a machine by adding new damage. In criminology we notice a growing tendency to consider and study crime not only in its significance as a cause for punishment, but also as an important phenomenon of social life. The progress of criminal policy that is concerned with the exploration of the individual and collective factors of crime, as well as the change of the borderline between criminology and criminal policy, as requested by criminologists, are signs pointing in this direction of development.

Extraordinarily incisive changes will certainly have to occur before this replacement of punishment through another measure is realized. Among these changes, society's compulsion to confess will surely play an important part. The growing courage to be sincere about one's emotional processes, to shed the conventional masks, and the extension of consciousness of the community cannot remain without influence upon the judgment over the criminal and upon the estimate of punishment as a social measure.

In the process of transition from punishment to another social institution, confession also will have an important function. We recognize this when we are tracing its growing significance within the criminal procedure. Replacement of the old by the new usually takes place in the following manner: the new first is leaning upon something established, appears to be welded to it, and then detaches itself in order to continue its existence independently and eventually replace the old. We can reconstruct a primitive legal procedure in which there was no place for confession at all, where punishment hit the criminal with the edge of the sword before he had any opportunity to confess.

When confession was taken into consideration later on, it was still most closely connected with punishment, as we see it in the external compulsion to confess, the medieval torture. The moderation of judgment through confession and the special position of confession within the criminal law suit will lead into a period of development in which confession will perhaps keep itself isolated and eventually be able to take the place of punishment. Confession would, of course, gain significance, especially as a most effective prophylaxis against crime, since it is the mildest kind of gratification of the need for punishment, while at the same time it grants the suppressed impulses a possibility of expressing themselves. We see that the unconscious compulsion to confess can still find important psychological utilization in the realm of criminology, too.

These are, of course, all dreams of the future, *"Zukunftsmusik"* as the German would say. It is merely a question of optimism or pessimism whether you can lend yourself to the belief that, at some very distant period, which will look back indulgently to our day, punishment will be abolished. Indeed, a time may perhaps come when the need for punishment will be less than it is now, and the means which will then be found for the prevention of crime will be to punishment what the rainbow is to the preceding devastating thunderstorm. This, however, belongs perhaps in the realm of Utopia. And I would not be in a position to contradict you seriously if you thought an outlook of this kind in a far future is little suited to console people for the inadequacy of our contemporary social institutions. The famous English scientist, Thomas Henry Huxley, once wrote this rather reasonable sentence: "What compensation for its sufferings does Eohippus (the primeval horse) find in the fact that millions of years after him one of his descendants could win the Derby?"

VII

The Compulsion to Confess in Religion, Myth, Art and Language

LADIES AND GENTLEMEN: If we have occupied ourselves perhaps too much with the psychological problems of penal law and criminology, I can promise you I'll be shorter in the clarification of the significance of the compulsion to confess within the other social institutions.

One of the great institutions within which the compulsion to confess becomes more and more victorious is religion. It is one of the strongest bulwarks built by mankind to protect itself from and to ward off those impulses that drive most strongly toward gratification. The forms of religious exercise and religious teaching: ritual and cult, dogmas and myths are full of unconscious confessions to sin. Rebellion and revolutionary impulses contradict the humility and blind submission demanded by religion and testify to the bitter fight the believer wages against the assault of his strong drives. From the hymns found in the Babylonian cuneiform inscriptions and the inscriptions on the memorial stones erected by the supervisor Nofer-Abu to an Egyptian goddess in Thebes, to the religious confessions of Tolstoi and Kierkegaard, one great confession rises to heaven that spans in stony silence all human suffering. In religion, mankind professes, in the form of penitence and atonement, to the eternal wishes by which it is stirred. The pious confess in their prayers and invocations that they are all sinners. In the realm of religion, too, there are commandments and prohibitions, punishments and penance, as in the realm of criminal law.

The phenomenon of confession in criminal procedure finds its counterpart in the confession of the sacrament of repentance. The origin of confession within religion is by itself a strong proof of the effectiveness of the compulsion to confess, as it developed along with the secular changes of the need for punishment. You know that I assume that confession is by no means peculiar to Christianity, but that it appears as the admission of sin as early as in ancient Babylon, in Persia, Egypt and Palestine, that Buddhism knows confession in our sense and that its beginnings can be found even in the religions of many primitive peoples.

Remember that confession is only a part of the procedure of penitence. Please do not think that the comparison of the sacrament of repentance with a court procedure originated in my imagination. The faithful themselves frequently make this comparison. To quote a good example, you find this sentence in *Catholic Moral Theology* by Professor Johann Pruner, "The sacrament of repentance has been instituted in the form of a court and with a court is associated an accusation. But it is an act of God's mercy that no one has the right to appear as the accuser in the court of repentance except the guilty alone." But also the great penal court at the end of time, which can be found in the religions from the Egyptian court of the dead down to the eschatological ideas of Christianity, is among these religious ideas that show how close law and religious life originally were to each other.

Through its reactive character, religious ritual generally testifies to the effectiveness of repressed revolutionary and hostile impulses. The confession is, however, the institution in which the compulsion to confess created its most unequivocal religious expression. Even the compulsive factor eventually found its representation and objectification in the obligation to confess. We clearly recognize here, too, the inner connection of the compulsion to confess and the need for punishment, as the confession is regularly followed by repentance or atonement. Those who confess are actually called "penitents" in ecclesiastical language and wherever religion still exerts its great power over souls, as in medieval Christianity, it inflicts heavy and oppressive punish-

ments upon the sinner after the confession. Even today, as its
mission on earth is changing, the Church recommends justified
strictness toward the penitent, as a psychic benefit to him, exceedingly deserving of thanks. Without such strictness, his salvation
would be in gravest danger. The emotional relief given the
faithful before confession as an indication of the displacement,
stood within its psychic framework from the psychological points
of view that we demonstrated for the compulsion to confess.

The role of the gratification of the need for punishment can be
shown here, too. We can easily conceive the anxiety of many
faithful before confession as an indication of the displacement,
from fear of punishment into fear of confession. Some priests and
neurologists tell about severe symptoms of anxiety in many faithful before the confession. Every analyst knows of these cases of
obsessional neurosis where the doubt of the patient, as to whether
he was unworthy when going to confession, stands manifestly
in the foreground. There are those other cases where the anxiety
as to whether he withheld nothing, confessed everything, can
grow to agonizing intensity.

You see that in the religious field, too, an excessive need for
punishment opposes the compulsion to confess. Luther prides
himself in his missive to those in Frankfort that he "delivered and
freed the consciences from the unbearable burden of papal law
in which it is ordered that all sins are to be told, and such anxiety
is stirred up in the stupid consciences that they despair, hence,
that the confession was a great, eternal torture." The duty to confess of Catholicism is, therefore, comparable to the external compulsion to confess in court of the Middle Ages. But in the form of
the exploration of conscience and of remorse, as the necessary
preparation for the religious confession, the Church has made
also the essential part of the work of confession obligatory. This
imperative character of the confession and of the exploration of
conscience still shows their original connection with penance or
punishment.

If you compare the severe punishments inflicted by the medieval
Church upon the sinner after confession with the present-day

penance prescribed by the priest, as for instance, to tell one's beads twenty times, the explanation that you will find for this change will be not the shrinking of the power of the Church, but the same line of development that we have traced in criminal legislation. In both instances, the psychic accent shifts from punishment to admission, from penance to religious confession.

A more thorough study of the history of the Church and her dogma actually shows, with all the clearness one could ask for, that of the three parts of which the sacrament of repentance of Catholicism consists, namely remorse (*contritio*), *confessio* and satisfaction (*satisfactio*) confession has become ever more important. Punishment is often completely omitted. The mild admonition of the Catholic priest or the simple formula told the sinner by the Buddhist monk after confession, "Watch out in the future!" if compared with punishments of earlier periods incisively affecting life, points to the provisional goal of the religious procedure of repentance, namely, to let confession take the place of penance. History of religion, in its connection with the results of psychoanalytical research, permits us to understand the place of confession within religious development.

From the automatically inflicted punishment for the violation of a taboo, the path of evolution leads by way of purging ceremonial to ecclesiastical punishment and finally to the confession, from without to within. Here, too, confession increasingly takes the place of penance. This development can best be recognized by considering the fact that, in its early period, the Church ordered the sinner to make a public confession as an exercise of penance. Modern Protestantism actually puts coming to terms with one's own conscience in the place of the external confession, thus unconsciously preparing for the future development that will go beyond confession and perhaps replace religion by other social institutions.

We were able to observe in penal law a growing tendency to direct punishment more towards the motives rather than the deed. The history of confessional practice offers an analogous phenomenon. The confession under Leo the Great in the fifth century still concerned only grave sins committed by the penitent. Now it concerns also sinful impulses and sins of thought.

Like confession in court, religious confession, too, is considered an attenuating circumstance, a ground for forgiveness on the part of the offended deity. *"Ego to absolve,"* says the priest, having thus not only declared his recognition of the penitent's intention to improve, but also the fact that now he is really "acquitted," absolved from guilt. We have seen that analytical procedure, so often compared to religious confession without regard to the differences, has a liberating effect largely because the repressed instincts are recognized and shown to a representative of the person against whom they were directed. You find an essential part of this psychic process, which remains, of course, unconscious, in religious form, in the confession because sin is a transgression against God and He or His earthly representative learns of the sins. Since you know analysis, you are not in need of my explanation of the incisive differences which show that the comparison of religious confession to analysis is unjustified. In another paper, I have tried to expose those differences and to appreciate their psychological significance. The priest knows as well, or rather, as little as does the judge why he ascribes so much value to the confession. The person who confesses abandons, in so doing, his isolated position. He replaces his unconscious feeling of guilt with a preconscious one. Only analysis warrants the transformation of the preconscious feeling of guilt into a conscious one.

You will even find the factor of hidden wooing for love in the religious confession or in the admission of sin and in the "open guilt" as Luther called it. The faithful say to God, "See how weak, how given to sin we are! Forgive us and love us in spite of it, as a father forgives his naughty children!" In my *Problems of Religious Psychology,* I attempted to demonstrate these psychic mechanisms in their effects with an example taken from Jewish liturgy, the Kol Nidre. In the religious confession, the sinner surrenders to divine grace as the criminal, in his confession, appeals unconsciously to the judge's benevolence.

The absolution of the penitent prepares his reacceptance into the flock from which he had gone astray, prepares the return of the lost son to his father's house, as the confession of the criminal prepares his return to the community. The admission of sin was, indeed, originally made to the community from which the sinner had been excluded, and it was considered the condition for his re-entry. The image of the father in heaven that the penitent, as well as the one who prays, addresses, in his admission of sin, gives testimony to the fact that religious confession originated in the confession made to the earthly father.

I know of an even more impressive proof of the growing importance of the confession in religious development. Have you ever observed that religion itself developed from the cult of gods to the confession made to them? There must be some significance to the fact that, in German usage, the word "confession" often denotes "religion," that religion is spoken of as "confession of faith." To indicate a person's creed it is sometimes said, "He confesses to the Catholic religion" or "He is of the Hebrew confession." Although customarily a differentiation is made between the words, "religion" and "confession," the fact that the words "confession" and "profession" are used to mean "religion" is not accidental. Is it not as if the Church had put profession, that is confession of the faith, in the place of the actual creed?

Theology will give you only an insufficient explanation. But if you study the history of religious development from analytical points of view you will find that profession to the creed, the credo, developed historically from the form of baptism in which the neophyte originally took a vow to renounce the devil and his works and to turn to God, to believe no more in the devils, as the Christians with little courtesy called the pagan gods, but in God. You can still find vestiges in Christian ritual of this original form of renunciation, which is testified to by liturgical history, but which later vanished. This seems to be a confession that one had previously been in the devil's services. You will also remember that the neophyte had to make a confession before his baptism, in which he had to admit all his "works of the devil." The denotation "confession of faith" then shifted to the positive part of the form only, but it may be understood that it is the religious confession of one's own sins which still appears in this designation. You see that here the compulsion to confess has shifted to the content of the creed, hence, has extended to the realm of thinking. The belief in the dogma has now become the object of the compulsion to confess, a phase that every religion experiences in its final processes. Protestantism has risen against this concept, which it calls "compulsion to profess," thus furthering the dissolution of religion in Europe.

Modern Protestantism rejects this external compulsion to profess and submits these processes of faith, too, to decision by inner factors. The development from religious confession into confession of creed thus offers us an example of the transferring of the compulsion to confess into the realm of the processes of thinking. The old professions of faith, as formulated in the great ecclesiastical synods, still contain the rejection of the contents of heretical creeds in the form *"Anathema sit."* They thus show their origin again in the condemnation of one's own sin of doubt and heresy. The counterpart to the religious phenomenon of the profession of heretical faith, whose last manifest form is no longer the confession, but only a positive statement, you may find in the confession which the ancient Egyptian has to make to the forty-two judges of the dead. In the Hall of the Two Truths the defunct has to declaim before Osiris, the master of the court, a kind of confessional litany which is in the one hundred and twenty-fifth chapter of the Book of the Dead, starting with these words: "O far striding one, who cometh from Heliopolis, I have committed no sin, O fire embracer, who cometh from Tura, I have not robbed. O long-nosed one, who cometh from Shmun, I have not stolen." The register of sins enumerates all possibilities of sin in the social and personal realm, in a way similar to that of the confessional litany in the Babylonian rites of penitence.

This kind of religious confession has been called "confession of innocence" or *"confession négative."* Analysis shows us many cases of negative unconscious confession. Just one example: A patient, seeking analysis because of symptoms of obsessional neurosis, starts the first session protesting that she is a decent woman, that she has never been guilty of sexual misconduct, never broke faith with her late husband, never gave in to temptations etc. Then she proceeds to recount her "absurd" obsessional doubts. She is tormented by doubts as to whether the chimney sweeper, the house painter, the baker's boy had not bumped into her or touched her when they happened to be in her house. Only to set her mind at rest about doubts of this kind, she wears drawers closed with an elaborate device, has a woman friend assure her time and again that no man has jostled her. Eventually, she has to have a watch and a piece of paper beside her in order to convince herself every few minutes, through certain written signs, that, meanwhile she had not been touched by any man. We have no reason to doubt her *"confession négative,"* but it includes a very positive unconscious confession. The character of her neurotic doubts and protective measures compels us to assume that she wrestles with unconscious fantasies of sexual temptations of various kinds.

In the profession of creed, as in the *"confession négative,"* the emotional emphasis shifts from the confession of a sinful faith to the profession of the true God. The fact of this transfer and the use of the words "confession" and "profession" of faith for "religion" seems to us to indicate that the confession in its positive form comes more and more into the foreground of religion.

Myth, which preceded religion, is less marked by the compulsion to confess. Indeed, its oldest forms are entirely free from the influence of this compulsion. They fall into a period in which repression of drives, as well as need for punishment, were still in their beginnings and hence, myth can afford to let instinctual impulses, later suppressed, freely express themselves. But frustration was already in existence and effective. According to Freud, the first myth originated with the single person who had detached himself from the mass, reformed reality in his fantasy in accord with his wishes and imagined himself in the role of the admired and envied father whom the gang of brothers had killed.

Along with the consolidation of the superego and the increase of the need for punishment under the influences of the feeling of

guilt and the longing for the dead father, the myth, too, is transformed. Besides the powerful dominant motive of accomplishment of the wish, the tunes of remorse and of the wish to undo the
deed appear now in crescendo. The myth of the hero becomes a
religious myth and shows signs of the transformations that obscure
its primary meaning through distortions, displacements and con-
densations. These transformations necessitate the reduction of the
latent content of myth through psychoanalysis. Its character as
a representation of wish-fulfillment or as a secular dream of young
mankind stays preserved, but, in addition, there appears also the
wish-fulfillment of the need for punishment reacting to these
tendencies in the features of the myth. The young, victorious
hero, god or demigod, now suffers a tragic fate. Oedipus fulfills
the strongest wishes of childhood. He kills his father and marries
his mother, but punishment follows the deed. In the course of
development determined by the secular progress of repression,
myth, too, is finally branded by the compulsion to confess. In it,
mankind professes its deepest impulses in the most unconcealed
manner.

Cultural history has shown that the origin of most arts is closely
connected with myth. Art, having first served magic purposes,
and representing one of the great compensations of mankind's
unfulfilled wishes, is not beyond the reach of the compulsion to
confess. Fiction, originating in the egocentric daydream and representing the fulfilled wishes of the ego, also becomes more and
more the representation of the emotional forces opposing these
wishes.

The turn, from the narration of purely material happenings to
the representation of those inner processes of the persons in the
drama and the novel, may be an expression of those counter-
currents, and modern fiction, psychologizing, shows in its representation the effectiveness of the compulsion to confess.

Writers always recognized and acknowledged this character of
the confession in their work. May I remind you of Goethe who
calls his works "Fragments of a Great Confession"? Ibsen pointed
with still stronger emphasis to the influence of the need for pun-

ishment in fiction with the words "Writing means to sit in judgment over one's own ego." Tragedy is an unconscious confession. The applause of the audience becomes a sign of the removal of the hero's isolation, of his absolution. Aristotle's catharsis is based essentially upon release from the latent feeling of guilt.

The psychological significance of a definite pleasure derived from confession within the "bliss of creating" and the artistic enjoyment has, to date, remained almost unnoticed. The transition from direct to indirect characterization in fiction is intimately connected with the restraint of free instinctual expression and with the breakthrough of the opposing tendency that manifests itself in the unconscious compulsion to confess. The situation in plays now mirrors life itself. Compare, for instance, the explanation given of themselves by the characters in the old plays, the "Voilà comme je suis" technique of characterization, as a critic called it rather appropriately, to that of Ibsen's characters. Njalmar Ekdal in the Wild Duck also occasionally talks about his own character, but shows only the way he sees himself, not the way the listener or reader would see him objectively.

Self-characterization contributes here even to the indirect representation of character, pointing to the difference between the self-concept of a figure and his objective, real character. We could say these statements are themselves expressions of the unconscious compulsion to confess, which require analytical interpretation. Today you smile at the stiff manner of primitive playwrights and narrators who let their persons characterize themselves and let them explain their own emotional processes. You prefer to recognize the characters yourselves from the unconscious indications in their words and actions. You want to guess the psychic processes taking place in these persons from sparse hints, and self-betraying gestures and intonations quite as you are accustomed to in life. There, too, as observers of people, we accept self-characterization in our stride, but we do consider it an objective portrait of the person, even though we assume that he remained unconscious of the essence of his character, which we look for behind his self-testimony and self-evaluation. In life we behave much as we do in analysis, trusting the other person's unconscious compulsion to confess more than his conscious self-representation. In life, as in fiction, we feel intuitively or try to guess essential features of the unconscious character from the details of conscious self-characterization.

Even though we cannot, in general, attribute objectivity to conscious self-concept and self-testimony, and use it only as a means to recognize the real character, we must, at times, acknowledge an exception to this rule. For instance, the persons in the works of the great Russian novelists like Tolstoi or Dostoevski, when greatly excited, occasionally give characteristics of themselves, confessions of what they think or feel, what they are driven to and by what inhibited, confessions that we consider sincere and that we recognize as holding a great deal of truth. It is significant, however, that these self-representations, in their often horrifying, self-tormenting sincerity, occur as a rule under the pressure of the need for punishment. They represent a kind of verbal masochistic exhibition, of self-punishment in words. When a person makes a confession of this kind, showing, as it were, his own ugliness naked before all, it can only correspond to an overpowering of the ego by the superego. Moral masochism has become overwhelming.

We believe these confessions which serve the purpose of releasing the person from an oppressing feeling of guilt. They tell the truth, but it is not the whole truth. The most deep-seated initial conditions as well as the most decisive motives of their confessions, are as unconscious to them as is their latent meaning. In these exceptional cases, too, we are therefore, left to seek the continuation of the confession into the unconscious and to search for its motives if we wish to see the character and behavior of these persons clearly. More deeply penetrating investigations will show, without difficulty, how the unconscious compulsion to confess determines also the development of painting and sculpture and music in their choice of subject and in their presentation.

I mentioned before that jokes and humor use special techniques in order to bring the repressed (even under pleasure—gain) back to the ego. The reproduction of a joke and our laughter at it are thus also among the unconscious confessions. Freud showed us that we know neither what we actually laugh at nor what suppressed impulses we confess to in the joke.

Language itself should have something to tell us about the nature of the compulsion to confess. If we expect this clarification of it, we must broaden the extent of the concept of language. It will be necessary for us to include not only the expression of thoughts and feelings in words, but also in gestures, countenance, peculiarities of the expression of the eyes and the voice and handwriting. This is the whole material with which we analysts work. Nothing else is at our disposal as a basis on which to build our scientific explorations. But is that not enough? Let us concern ourselves more closely with verbal language only. We have no doubt as to the fact that language was originally only a means for expression of human needs. This it has remained, more or less. If you travel through a foreign country, the language of which you do not speak, it will be your first endeavor to learn how to use and to understand all those expressions that concern your personal wishes and their fulfillment. It must be ascribed mainly to the effects of the powers of repression if, according to Talleyrand's remark, language, having been a means to express thoughts, preserved itself without being able to overcome the opposing tendencies, and developed into an expression of compromise, which endeavors to do justice to both emotional tendencies, to hide and to betray what we wish. It can fulfill this task through the occasional use of techniques of allusion, displacement, substitution, especially of modification and euphemisms, the more so as we use for its support glances, gestures and other means of nonverbal expression. The pictures of our bodies and their movements often speak louder than words.

With increasing differentiation, language is thus in command of all the means of fine play that revolves about expression and suppression, wise to our desire to say something and to conceal it. It even succeeds in the trick of expressing through demonstrative concealment that which ought to be concealed. Here, we approach the unconscious confession. The overt expression of our needs becomes their concealed admission.

This leads us to the peculiar change of meaning through which words like for instance the German *"gestehen"* or *"bekennen"* (both meaning to confess, admit, acknowledge) are going in the history of a language. This change cannot be without significance for the concepts behind the words. *"Gestehen"* originally means to say something with certainty, to vouch for what is said. In Goethe's *Faust* one reads: "You gentlemen, confess that I know how to live!" In Schiller's poem, Polycrates calls to his friend, "Confess that I am happy!" The word *"bekennen"* is used in a similar way, meaning originally to testify to, to say something giving it its full weight. Schiller's Demetrius says, "The Czar, whose son I confess I am," using the word *"bekenne"* and meaning merely, "I reveal myself to be the Czar's son or I assert that I am the Czar's son." Luther used the word *"bekennen"* with this old meaning: "As we recognize pure water in baptism."

In these applications, the words *"bekennen"* or "confess" have not at all that more special meaning which is given them today. And what about the German word *"Beichte"* (religious confession) which is used as a synonym for confession? The word comes from the old German *"pijehan"* meaning simply to talk. From the old high German *"pijiht"* there developed the middle high German *"begiht"* and *"bihte"* which may be recognized in the modern word *"Beichte."* The Latin word *"confiteri,"* from which the English "confess" is derived, like the German *"bekennen"* or *"gestehen"* originally meant merely to say something emphatically.

Thus, our excursion into the linguistic field brought us something of a surprise. All these words, *"bekennen," "gestehen," "beichten,"* "confess," which are used for the communication of something forbidden, of sin, originally had the meaning of emphatic speech, or simply of speech. This change of meaning is testimony to the secular progress of suppression. An expression, which primarily intended to serve the gratification of a drive, became a confession.

The more special meaning, as a consequence of the narrowing of the verbal concept, points to man's growing need for punishment in the development of culture. Speech as such, emphatic talk, gradually became identified with confession. But isn't this change of meaning proof of the way that, as we stated, leads from the tendency for expression to the compulsion to confess? We want to talk of the things which constitute our wishing and longing. If we cannot talk about these, what sense does talking make? This alone must be the meaning of the saying, "The mouth overflows with what fills the heart." If the heart is replete with unfulfilled wishes whose expression is forbidden, it unconsciously creates an expression—the unconscious confession. Speech is still mainly the expression of our needs, but the gratification of the need for punishment has joined our psychic needs and this factor transforms speech into confession. If we are able to be quite honest with ourselves, and I don't see why we shouldn't be, we should have to confess that actually we wish to speak only of that which we desire and of that which depresses us, and that we would prefer to be silent when an extreme feeling of guilt prevents us from talking and does not permit us even the confession of our impulses. "The rest is silence."

We have found the most extreme form of that silence in its latent meaning in the criminal. In one of those small observations that mark the outstanding psychologist, Dostoevski once described how most of the talk of the criminal aims at confession and the rest sounds false and empty to him. Raskolnikov says to his mother, who visits him soon after the murder, "We will have time to talk to each other freely." Having said that, he becomes embarrassed again and pale: "Again a short sensation of deadly cold passed through his soul, again it became entirely clear to him that he had just told a horrible lie, that he would never again be able to speak freely, that he must never again, never talk to anyone at all." One of my patients who developed a furious self-hatred, complained time and again that he couldn't bear to listen to his own voice, that it sounded to him false and mean, and he finally preferred to be silent for a long time.

But even when we are silent and do not care to say anything, unknown powers still force us to unconscious confessions. Even our silence is eloquent and becomes accusation and self-accusation. It is as if something in us protested against a tyranny that forbid us to express our strongest impulses, and as if this pressure engendered the opposite compulsion, which drives towards unconscious confession.

VIII

About the Origin of Conscience[*]

LADIES AND GENTLEMEN: The science of ethics cannot but be influenced by the fact that analytical theory has clarified the psychogenesis and development of the compulsion to confess and of the need for punishment. We now disregard established ethics, almost universally acknowledged to be questionable and limited to a certain period. We claim that analytical discoveries make the history of morals and some of their most important problems appear in a new light. More than this, the new insights resolve contradictions that appeared hitherto irreconcilable. One of them is the psychological problem of conscience. The long line of investigations into the nature of conscience shows the high value attributed to the significance of conscience as a psychological phenomenon. Disregarding monographs like those by Paul Rée and Ebbinghaus, conscience appears in every system of ethics from Socrates down to Paulsen and Wundt, in Catholic as well as in Jewish and Protestant moral theology.

We shall start here from verbal expression of which we find important disclosures in Wundt's *Ethik*. The word conscience (in German "*Gewissen*") points directly to shared knowledge. The German prefix "*Ge-*" was originally identical with the Latin prefix "*con-*." "*Gewissen*" is the direct translation of the Latin "*conscientia*" from which comes the word for conscience in English and other modern languages. According to Wundt, the expression "voice of conscience" definitely owes its origin to a mythological thought. The language, which called knowledge "shared knowl-

* Excerpts from this lecture were presented in my book *Myth and Guilt*, George Braziller, New York, 1957.

edge," originally meant by it, knowledge shared by the deity. Wundt says literally, "Affect and judgment, connecting themselves with the consciousness of the motives and tendencies of the one who acts, are not considered as his own psychic actions, but as processes originating in a strange power mysteriously affecting his consciousness."

How is this acknowledgment of the power of the gods to be explained? Wundt thinks that thought moves here, as it does so often, in a circle. Man first objectifies his own feelings and then tries to explain his feelings by the use of the objects so created. It is to be admitted that academic psychology has said everything that could be said on the subject but even that is still rather poor.

Now I should like to offer you an opportunity to compare this observation of old methods of psychological research with the observations of psychoanalysis. Favorable circumstances permit me to start from a concrete example that also shows important relations between the functions of conscience and the compulsion to confess.

My son Arthur, to whom the following contribution to the psychology of conscience may be attributed, is now eight years old.* He is, it seems to me, a quite normal child, intellectually good, but not especially gifted, impulsive and of happy temperament, without any particular inclination to meditation. He plays in a lively way and generally enjoys himself, is sometimes as naughty as other boys and reads only when he has to. He shows great trust in his parents and his conversation with them is frank. He represents, I think, a typical child of the big city, of a certain social stratum, without any noticeable peculiarities.

Once when he took a walk with me we met a gentleman whom I know, who joined us and in the course of our conversation said that an "inner voice" had restrained him from doing something. After the man left us, Arthur asked me what "the inner voice" was, and I replied absent-mindedly, "A feeling."

* This was written in 1923. The following discussion was for the most part published in an article "Psychoanalysis of the Unconscious Sense of Guilt" in the *International Journal of Psychoanalysis* (October, 1924).

The next day a conversation developed which Arthur started and which I shall reproduce here literally from written notes made that same evening,

"Papa, now I know what the inner voice is."

"Well, tell me!"

"I have already found out. The inner voice is one's thought."

"What thought?"

"Well, you know, for instance, sometimes I often go to the table without washing my hands. Then there is a feeling as if someone told me, wash your hands. And sometimes at night when I go to bed I play with my gambi. [He had kept this name for the penis from early childhood.] And then the inner voice tells me again, don't play!"

"Is that really a voice?"

"No, there isn't anybody there. It is memory that tells me that."

"Why memory?"

Arthur pointed vividly to his head, "Well, cleverness, the brain. When, for instance, you say on the day before, 'If the child runs and falls' and I run the next day, then the thought tells me, 'Don't run!' " [This example was associated with something that had actually happened. After having been often warned not to run so wildly, the boy had fallen a few days earlier and had hurt his knee so badly that a suppurating wound had developed and he was now wearing a bandage. His parents reproached him because of his disobedience.]

"But if you run in spite of it?" I asked.

"But if I run in spite of it and fall, then the voice tells me, 'Haven't I told you that you will fall?' Or sometimes when I make Mama angry, also when I make you angry, the feeling tells me, 'Don't make Mama angry!' "

Here we were interrupted. When I re-entered the room a few minutes later, Arthur began spontaneously:

"But now I know what the inner voice is! *It is a feeling of one's self and the language of somebody else*."

"What does that mean, the language of somebody else?"

Arthur looked doubtful and thoughtfully said, "No, that isn't true." After a little pause, he said vividly, "But it is true, though! What you said first! For instance, Mama once sent me to the grocer's and you told me, 'Watch out that no car comes!' And if I had not watched out, the voice would have told me, 'Watch out that no car comes!' Does everybody have an inner voice?"

"Yes."

"Isn't it true that the inner voice doesn't come to the outer voice? It doesn't? But it does, though! I can't say that because I don't know it. One of the two it must be. The inner voice, if one really has it, does not come to the outer voice, only if one talks about it."

The next afternoon he started again, "Papa, the inner voice is really when you have done something and then you are afraid. For instance, when I have touched the gambi I am afraid, I don't know what I am afraid of. But still I know I am afraid because I have done that. Well, it is a sort of a feeling!"

About an hour later he asked, "Isn't it true, Papa, that thieves have two voices?"

"Why two?"

"Well, one tells them they should steal, and the other tells them they should not steal. But no, only the one that says, 'Don't' is the real voice."

Since this conversation, about eight months had passed. The child had mentioned the inner voice only twice. Once he said spontaneously, "When Mama does not obey Grandma, she also has an inner voice that says she should always obey Grandma. And when she has not obeyed the next time, then she is afraid." Another time he asked, "Isn't it true, one doesn't always have an inner voice? Only when one needs it!"

I inquired, "When does one need it?" and he declared, "When one wants to do something bad."

Before we discuss these statements of a child, we should keep in mind what their significance is. From its beginnings, psychoanalysis acknowledged the emotional powers originating in the ego in their effect as factors of repression. Only lately has depth-psychology turned to the analysis of those repressing currents themselves.

The reconstruction of the history of ego-development produced results which appear, on first sight, scarcely less strange than the analytical theory about sexuality.

Those statements of a child seem to be valuable mainly because they offer an excellent proof of the correctness of the analytical assumptions concerning the origin and development of several ego-agencies. It can be shown here in *statu nascendi* what analysis had to reconstruct in tracing back emotional processes of the adult. A considerable part of these processes which later will be hidden is still able to exist here in conscious thoughts. Another part, however, has, at this phase, already been withdrawn from the conscious.

May I also recall to you the fact that in the child the separation of the conscious from the unconscious cannot be accomplished as sharply as in the adult. The region of the conscious has, according to Freud, not yet attained all its characteristic features in the child. It is still in the process of developing and is not yet able to transport everything into word presentations. The genuineness, vividness, and naturalness with which the boy makes his statements about his emotional life enhance their scientific validity as self-observations of an important phase of infantile development that otherwise eludes the attention of adults. Yet it should also be emphasized that these statements made by a child have certain limitations in their psychological applications.

These limits derive mainly from two factors. The child shows no general theoretical interest directed strictly at the understanding and explanation of psychic processes. He accidentally hears an expression ("inner voice") strange to him, wishes to understand what it means and then compares the psychic situation described by the gentleman, which the boy could understand certainly in part only, with similar emotional experiences of his own, of which he retained memory-residues.

His interest exceeds this limit, for the most part, only far enough for him to desire a clarification as to the workings of this "inner voice." His questions show that he wishes to compare that which he introspectively found in himself with that which I, the adult, can tell him about it. This psychological interest is, for his age, certainly remarkable, his gift of self-observation not ordinary, but he cannot be expected to pursue the leads systematically. His repeated return to the questions that stir in him, the emergence of the same problems after longer intervals, show, however, his endeavor to gain clearness about his psychic processes. It goes without saying that this endeavor has narrow limits. Still, I thought I should not direct his attention artificially to questions for which he is not ready and which had not spoken up in him. Therefore, I limited what I said (in a way similar to that in analysis) to cautious questions and encouragement to explain more exactly only what he had told me himself. This was also the only way to exclude suggestion.

We should evaluate the answers of the small boy as to the breadth as well as to the depth of the problems emerging here, taking this situation into consideration.

The second factor is a linguistic one. The child wrestles here with material that he can master only with difficulty. His vocabulary is limited and his choice of words cannot, of course, satisfy our demands for precision. For the difficult concepts that he wishes to discuss, his linguistic abilities understandably do not suffice. The limitations of language in this area cause many difficulties for us adults, too. You surely notice how uncertain he is in choosing words for what he wants to say, how he tries to comprehend the "inner voice" once as a thought, then as a feeling, and how he endeavors to express more precisely, in his definition of the expression "language of somebody else," that which I said first. It is, incidentally, surprising how the need for clarity drives him to ever sharper formulations. In the overcoming of the inadequacies of his childlike talk, he achieved a little stunt.

We try to accompany the small boy's statements with a kind of psychological commentary, which uses, as a comparison, the views about ego-development gained regressively in analysis. The child first explains to himself the "inner voice," which we may understand as the censoring agency of conscience, as the "thought of somebody." Characteristically, what comes to his mind when he searches for explanations are these two examples which concern washing and abstention from playing with his penis. The inner voice thus appears to him most conspicuous in its effect felt as an inhibiting factor in the realm of anal erotism and masturbation.

It cannot be coincidental that precisely these two examples come to his mind first. The close relation we observe in the analysis of adults, between the neurotic compulsion to wash and the infantile anal erotism as well as the masturbatory activity, is here confirmed in the initial emotional conditions of childhood. The other example shows how that censoring agency asserts itself in order to maintain the reality-principle face to face with the tendencies of pleasurable gratification. While the boy runs, the factor of self-criticism will interfere by warning him. His thought after the fall ("Haven't I told you that you would fall?") shows that he pre-consciously expected to fall, that the fall was the foreseen self-punishment for his disobedience.

At this point, he is able to identify the "inner voice" as the re-membrance of something he has heard, of a warning or admonition of his father's. This knowledge becomes sufficiently clear, during the few minutes that he was left alone in the room, to take the form of definition that the "inner voice" is the feeling of one's self and the language of somebody else.

This definition is psychologically quite correct and can be considered a translation, back into the language of a child, of the analytical theory about the origin of conscience and of the unconscious feeling of guilt. The child here has achieved a quite respectable psychological accomplishment. If you compare his definition with analytical theory you get this result. In his essay "On Narcisms," Freud described the genesis of a censoring agency which measures the actual ego by comparing it with the ideal ego. The incentive to the development of the superego from the critical influence of the parents, who communicate it through their voices, is followed later by the influence of educators, teachers and other people.

In his book, *The Ego and the Id,* Freud pursued this theme. In it he shows that the superego takes upon the primary identification of the child with his father. The infantile ego reinforces itself for the task of the control of his drives and the performance of repression expected of him by throwing up, in himself, the same obstacles which his father had put in his way earlier. He has borrowed, as it were, the strength for it from his father. The superego thus turns out to be the "heir of the Oedipus complex." The tension between the demands of the superego and the performance of the ego is manifested as a feeling of guilt.

In Arthur's case, we see this process in its first phases. We see the primary precipitate of identification with the father. We can observe how the tension between the continuing effect of the father's demands and the actual performances of the boy expresses itself as a feeling of guilt. We can observe how the vote of the superego develops from the father's admonitions and prohibitions. Here the categorical imperative of the superego can still be clearly seen as it originates in the father complex. The superego is, here, as it were, palpable in its genesis. The child, in tracing back his feeling of guilt, to a "feeling of one's self and the language of somebody else," chooses the correct regressive way. The "feeling of one's self" developed under the delayed influence of the criticizing, warning, forbidding "language of somebody else," namely, the father's voice—"what you said first."

A comparison comes to mind of the psychogenesis of the religious feelings of the masses with the formation of the individual conscience through inclusion of the judging father agency: "God is moral law itself, as it were, but thought of in personification."* The Church, too, declares conscience (this is Arthur's inner voice) to be "the voice of God in man," hence the continuing audible and effective voice of the exalted or deified father in the individual.

Through analysis, we have learned to understand the voices that play so clear a part in the symptomatology of the melancholics. As you know, those patients hear voices that talk to them in the third person and incessantly observe whatever they do or leave undone. This criticizing institution takes us back to parental criticism. According to Freud, the patients reproduce regressively the

* Kant's *Philosophy of Religion*.

development of conscience through reprojection of the voices into the external world whence they came. Characteristically, the voices which the patients hear speak about them in the third person. Here one may find traces of those people who took care of the infant and talked about him, the people who later are replaced by teachers and other authorities and eventually by society and public opinion. This symptom points clearly to the period when the observing ego-factor which developed from the primary identification with the father and established itself in the ego as the institution of conscience, originated. It must have been the time when the child still talked about himself in the third person, while the ego was already able, more or less clearly, to comprehend the contrast between his own instinctual life and the external demands for suppression of his drives.

The psychoanalytical explanation of the psychogenesis of the hearing of voices in states of melancholia and in paranoia takes us back again to the problems that emerged in the small boy. He asks himself whether "the inner voice comes to the outer one." That can only mean whether the inner voice cannot become an outer voice. After some doubt, he arrives at the conclusion that the inner voice does not "come" to the outer voice, hence, that the censoring agency does not manifest itself as an outer voice, "only when one talks about it." The voices of melancholic patients are another instance of this external audibility of the inner voice which was once really an external voice.

According to Freud, we can trace the significance of preconscious verbal presentations to the superego which betrays its origin from that which has been heard. These verbal presentations are as memory-residues of perceptions often accessible in isolation even to consciousness, from which the superego is withdrawn. We observe how often people remember and quote proverbs, comparisons, idioms used by their parents—"My father used to say. . . ." In the preceding lectures, you have recognized another significant instance of the "inner voice" becoming audible—the confession, secular or religious. In it, as in analysis, the "inner voice" actually comes to the "outer one," as Arthur says.

In the monologues that some people hold with themselves we can also, in part, recognize the censoring or criticizing institution as it becomes audible, to the extent that these monologues frequently contain more or less sharp self-criticism, self-observations, warnings, resolutions, etc. If we consider, regressively, the genesis of conscience and the role of identification with early love-objects, we recognize, in this kind of monologue, re-edited, as it were, new editions of earlier dialogues.

In the imaginary dialogues which some patients have with the analyst outside the analytical session you can trace this development. In doing so, you will notice, furthermore, how a now inner control station builds itself up in the patient. The mediating role of preconscious verbal presentations, as memory-residues, seems to extend much farther and to continue into the beginnings of the processes of thinking. The parents' significance for this development is obvious.

I quote here a remark of Feuerbach's from *The Essence of Christianity*, which seems to make the points of view of phylogenesis applicable to the development revealed by analysis: "Originally two were needed to think. Only on the level of a higher culture does man double, becoming able to play, by and to himself, the other's part. Thinking and talking are, therefore, one and the same in all old and sensuous peoples. They think only in talk; they think only in conversation. Ordinary people, not those educated to think abstractly, still do not understand the written word, even today, if they do not read aloud, if they do not pronounce what they read. How right is Hobbes, in this respect, in deriving man's intellect from the ears." You see how closely those remarks of Feuerbach's approach the psychoanalytical assumptions towards which we were driven in our investigations concerning the compulsion to confess.

The difference between that which is thought and that which is spoken is here clarified, a difference to which so great a significance is attributed in analytical therapy. Many a puzzling command and prohibition of obsessional neurosis, many apparently absurd compulsive ideas and many peculiar symptoms of hysteria will be traceable back to a paternal or maternal talk that has become unconscious or is used by the unconscious, and in this connection only find their analytical explanation.

Freud has explained that the emotional energy of these contents of the superego does not originate in the aural perception proper, but in the first relationship with the love-objects. These unconscious contents are of various kinds—warnings, prohibitions, orders, admonitions, as well as concepts and abstractions that have acquired special significance for ego-ideals of the individual and of society. It should be noted that the respect and high esteem which we have for certain moral opinions are not to be attributed to their absolute value, but to those unconscious first identifications with those love-objects, especially to the unconscious effects of the love which we early felt towards people who conveyed to us those opinions. Indeed, it can be said that the tenacity of certain moral concepts, which have become obsolete, depends on the immortality of that early identification with a beloved object.

Freud taught us to understand that early conflicts of the ego with those objects can continue as conflicts with the superego. In Arthur's case, we could observe early the signs of that conflict of the ego and the developing superego expressing itself in the "inner voice." The simplest and most general instance of a conflict of this kind is produced by the contrast between instinctual demands of the id and the demands of repression, which originate in the objects of the id. Conflicts of this kind develop at a time when the feeble ego seems to be helplessly exposed to the two institutions which oppress it. The ego is, so to speak, attacked from two sides and has trouble in keeping its balance.

Elsewhere, I told of a little scene from Arthur's life at the age of three, which shows the continuity of the contrast felt even at that time. In spite of admonitions, the child has been naughty and was punished by his mother. When he was reproached, he declared, sobbing, "Sonny wants to be good, but Sonny can't be good."

The conflict felt at so early an age and expressed so naïvely is the same which the Apostle Paul had in mind when he exclaimed in agony, "I do not what I wish to, but what I do not wish, this I do."

Almost sixteen hundred years ago, Augustine of Numidia whom the Church calls the Saint, wrote in his *Confessions* these noteworthy lines: "The spirit commands the body and finds immediate obedience, the spirit commands itself and finds resistance. . . . The spirit commands itself to be willing, the spirit which could not command at all, were it not willing, and still it does not do what it commands. But it is not entirely willing; therefore, it does not command entirely. . . . It was I who was willing, I who was not willing." Even as a youth, St. Augustine had implored the Lord, "Grant chastity, Lord, but, please, not immediately!"

While Arthur has earlier explained regressively, the "inner voice" as "a feeling of one's self and the language of someone else," he shows the next day that he is coming closer to the nature of the "inner voice." In his awkward way, he defines the censoring factor: "When one has done something and then is afraid." We see that he endeavors to understand his feeling of guilt, his moral anxiety. The example which he uses for an explanation is certainly most significant to him—the connection of masturbation with anxiety. Freud pointed out that behind moral anxiety hides the unconscious continuation of castration-anxiety. It is the core around which moral anxiety settles later. The fact thus becomes comprehensible that some analyses of neuroses create the impression that castration-anxiety may serve directly as a measuring device for the feeling of guilt. It is as if the feeling of guilt had found its adequate expression in the failure of the functions of the penis or in the ideas connected with it.

Following Arthur's further statements, we see that he concludes through analogy, that other people, too, must have an inner voice and that, if they do not obey their parents, they too, must feel fear. (His choice of the example of his mother in her relation to his grandmother is very likely to have originated in actual observation.)

In children's play the identification with the father, on which the establishment of the superego is essentially based, can be clearly observed. Arthur tried to train a dog, which we received later, to perform various little tricks and in his training efforts he used, preferentially, expressions of praise and reproof, encouragement and admonition that had been used towards him. The introjection of an object in its connection with the feeling of guilt could be traced much earlier in the child's play from various indications. When he was not quite five years old, the child had once been too lively in kindergarten and as a punishment he had had to stand in the corner of the classroom for a short time. After we had heard of this, we often teased him about it and called him jokingly by the nickname of "Arthur Stand-in-the-corner." He was very angry about it, protesting vigorously against that. We observed, however, that he used that same nickname for imaginary children in his play. It was as if he projected his quality onto an external object, imagined in play, and punished it now with the offending nickname. Through psychoanalysis, we have learned to understand the relief for the feeling of guilt through projection of this kind. It was clear that the child had identified himself, in his play, with his father or with the institutions representing him, and, thus, temporarily overcome the weakness and insufficiency of his ego.

From this time dates a note which says that, returning from kindergarten, Arthur played policeman in his room in the presence of his governess, and had, apparently, before him a considerable number of offenders whom he questioned. With a severe countenance, he asked an imaginary criminal, "What have you done?" Then he asked another one, "And what have you done?" and so on. Finally, he turned to the last of the evildoers present in his imagination, saying something to him that made the governess listen, "And you, Arthur Stand-in-the-corner? Ah, I know. You stole a gun. You will be locked up." Here the governess interrupted him, calling to him in surprise, "But, Arthur, you didn't steal a gun!"

"O yes! Here!" the little boy said spiritedly, and pulled from his pocket a small tin gun which he had taken from kindergarten that morning. We have never been able since to observe any such inclinations in the child. But it is indicative of the residual emotional effect of that experience that Arthur now inquired whether thieves have two inner voices. In this little scene, too, we can study the effect of these psychic agencies which contributed decisively to the establishment of the superego.

We have seen that the infantile ego later endeavors to resolve its conflicts between the demands for repression, which originally came from the outside, and its own drives. Through its own management, as it were, in the form of submission of the ego to the superego, Arthur's playing of the policeman's role, that of a typical representative of judging authority, the fact that he incriminated himself, is in accord with the derivation of the superego from the introjection of the father. The transition from identification with the object to the establishment of the censoring superego can here be clearly observed. From the phase already reached, the whole process is regressively reproduced in play, under the influence of an actual occasion.

In a similar way, as the policeman, represented by Arthur, confronts the ego, which in his play appears projected outward onto an imaginary object, the superego will later behave toward the ego. This psychic behavior at so early an age and the surprisingly alert self-observation, whose results we could observe three years later, could cause apprehensions in us lest the superego might not treat the ego with much tolerance later. That would mean that an increased disposition toward neurotic disturbance in Arthur's case might be anticipated. The derivation of the superego from the early object-cathexes justifies Freud's statement that the strength of the superego, which manifests itself as conscience or as an unconscious feeling of guilt, depends upon the greater or lesser intensity of the Oedipus complex and upon the manner and the time of its repression.

It is clear that the described scene in play anticipates the feared punishment, that it is inspired by the unconscious need for punishment, and that it pursues the same purposes which we would have to call "magic" in the psychology of peoples. Tendencies towards penitence and self-punishment also can be clearly recognized in the projection. The child plays the scene of questioning in order to rid it of its horrors. At the same time, the play satisfies the tendencies towards self-punishment. The most powerful motives appearing in the play are certainly those originating in the identification with an object. While the feeling of guilt corresponds to the fear of loss of love, the confession implied in the play is meant to prevent that loss, or rather, to restore the status quo.

In the analysis of this scene of childhood and of the confession contained in it, we again come across the fact that confession gratifies and relieves the need for punishment. No doubt, the effect of the play permits us to draw a conclusion concerning its motives. The play becomes a substitute for a confession that eventually is actually made. It seems certain to me that this latent significance of the play cannot be limited to this single instance. Observation would show that a lot of children's play unconsciously represents confessions. The "played confession," indeed, deserves the attention of psychologists and teachers.

This gives cause for a consideration leading us back to the essence of psychoanalysis. The characteristic processes of psychoanalysis can be represented by conceiving them as tracing back the conflict between superego and ego to its origin, the early conflicts between the ego and the objects of the id. These struggles which occur in higher regions are reduced to difficulties in overcoming the Oedipus complex. This is followed by the solution of the conflicts in the original realm through transference. We understand clearly that the psychic powers to which we appeal for help in analysis derive their own strength from the continuing effects of these early love-objects of the child. In analysis there appears a regressive reproduction of the psychogenesis of the super-ego. When the analyst gradually takes unconsciously for the patient the place of the superego, its strictness is modified through that very process of transference. Thus we arrive at a characterization of psychoanalysis as a method of overcoming the moral anxiety which originates in the Oedipus complex. That makes it transparent that the impulses which are effective in the patient on the basis of transference in analysis must be attributed to a revival of those tendencies, which, at the time, were used to overcome the Oedipus complex, but which proved to be inadequate. The child who experiences the anxious tension of the feeling of guilt will certainly first be inclined to conquer this tension by complaining to his parents and appealing to them for help. The peculiarities of infantile conflicts and the character of unconscious psychic processes, determined by them, make this natural way impassable, obliterated, as it were. It can be unblocked and made passable again only in the processes of transference of psychoanalysis. It is also understandable that the feeling of guilt acquired in the father complex resolves itself only in transference to a father-substitute.

In these lectures, I have tried to expose to you, from the perspective of the unconscious compulsion to confess, the reasons why the retransformation of the "inner voice" into an outer one—to use the terminology of little Arthur—can evoke emotional effects of such extraordinary depth and lastingness.

IX

About Child Psychology and Pedagogy

LADIES AND GENTLEMEN: If I express a bold assumption as to the fields in which the theory expounded here could attain practical significance, I would point out three in particular: analytical practice, criminology and pedagogy. The importance of the perspective that the conception of the compulsion to confess gives to child psychology and pedagogy results from the fact that the need for punishment, which is of such prominent significance, clearly develops its effectiveness in childhood. Teachers are certainly in a position to give interesting proof of this.

I'll limit myself to an observation that can easily be made in any nursery. There you sometimes see that children eating at table keep what is best, the food they like most, for the end of the meal. This habit seems first to represent a reliving of their education for reality transformed into the active and to be explained from the point of view of the compulsion to repeat. But the gratification of the unconscious need for punishment, too, can be clearly recognized in this action, which lies somewhere between play and habit. Reserving the best for the end is only the indication of a renunciation, because in case the need for punishment is increased, the final renunciation of the best can easily take the place of the reservation for the postponement of pleasure. This little habit is an apparently insignificant compulsive symptom of childhood. In the analysis of a case of severe obsessional neurosis, I came to understand the deep connection between that little habit of the child and the obsessional renunciation of the adult which eventually did not allow him any pleasure and made him unfit to live.

We sometimes see also how children refuse themselves pleasures, and reject love as if they did not deserve it. At the same time, they often show an increased need for love to pacify their feeling of guilt, but become naughty and defiant in order to receive punishment, entirely like adults, as if they hoped to be loved again after having been punished. In all these features we see unconscious expressions of the compulsion to confess. It should become the educator's task to understand these manifestations and to react to them in a manner corresponding to the aims of education. He should recognize the fact that the child becomes naughty because of his need for punishment, and he should not gratify that need, but resolve it. First of all, however, he should be careful not to produce unnecessary need for punishment in the child. August Aichhorn, in a fine essay, pointed to the therapeutic and educational value of free talk in the psychoanalytical sense, in the education of antisocial children in reform institutions. If you read Aichhorn's instructive discussions and study the examples he gives, you will find that the free talk of these children will always have the meaning of a confession. I take it for a confirmation of the theory here expounded that Aichhorn, with intuitive feeling, had the free talk, the confession, take the place of the expected punishment.

Confession (this time in the conscious sense) will, in education, attain ever greater significance as a preventive and therapeutic measure. It is, however, necessary that the psychic way to confession towards parents or educators stay open. The best and most natural means to make this possibility a precious reality in pedagogy is still the creation of an atmosphere of love and trust between parents and children. After all, it is still love, that great teacher of mankind, that overcomes even the unconscious need for punishment.

I regret that I have too little experience in pedagogy to be able to pursue the new perspectives which the educator receives by the theory of the unconscious compulsion to confess. I prefer, therefore, to tell you of features from the emotional development of a small girl, a development in which the compulsion to confess came to have special significance. This is by no means intended to be the reproduction of a child's analysis, only of single, selected features which are more or less typical. It was only after many years that the emotional processes of childhood were put in their proper places when the girl, who had become a mature woman, was in analytic treatment.

In her eighth year, little Lotte became ill with an obsessional neurosis. Every night before she went to sleep, she had to pray that something she was afraid would happen the next day might not come true. First one prayer, then two. Later the reasons why a prayer had to be said multiplied as did the number of prayers necessary to ward off the thing she was afraid of. Consequently, a severe insomnia developed. However, the main cause of these obsessional prayers turned out to be difficulties in the evacuation of the bowels. A severe constipation had caused a small anal lesion that produced severe pains during defecation. Later, the child retained the feces because she was afraid of the pain. The constipation became worse and worse and the lesion tore apart again during each eventual discharge. A vicious circle developed from which the child found, of course, no way out, so she began saying a special prayer at night that the discharge might not hurt her the next day or that it might not occur. Soon several prayers became necessary. Other causes appeared for which prayers had to be said. This situation ended when defecation was entirely impossible one day because hard fecal balls had formed that could not be discharged. The child felt nauseated. Manual reduction of the feces to small pieces was necessary, followed by the discharge of a large fecal ball accompanied by very severe pains. The lesion and constipation were then treated and the physical as well as the psychic symptoms disappeared.

The same year, our little girl attended a gymnastic course where she proved to be very skillful, especially at climbing high poles. In doing so, she had feelings of sexual pleasure and, after she discovered this, she always hurried to climb these poles at the start of the lesson. She pressed her genitals against the pole until an orgasm occurred. This deeply felt pleasure, almost bordering on pain, frightened her and she often wondered suddenly if this was not an illness. She was not able to explain the phenomenon to herself because at that time she did not remember having had similar feelings of pleasure before, nor could she make a connection between them and the masturbatory activity of her third and fourth years and the feelings of pleasure that had accompanied them. She had then masturbated by pressing both hands against the genitals, but that did not last very long. Her mother's prohibition put an end to those acts. She had never been caught while masturbating, but one day when she and her sister were leaving their mother to take a walk, the mother said, apparently abruptly, that they should make sure never to put their hands on the genitals because a person could be made severely ill from doing that and an operation could become necessary. This was stamped in Lotte's memory with particular clearness. The child felt fear at the time, masturbation occurred only a few more times, and soon was omitted entirely.

The mother's prohibition had a long lasting effect and evoked strong feelings of guilt even after masturbation had been given up. Then, after it appeared again, in the gymnastic course, the child was disturbed by the suddenly emerging thought that the intensely felt pleasure was certainly an illness. Her mother had threatened her not only once with illness and an operation, but had already suffered both these tragedies. A quite early memory contained the joy she felt at a reunion with her mother, who had been away for a short time. She had been told that her mother had been sick and had been operated on in the hospital. This memory was not even a single one. It was definitely established that later Lotte had had a similar reunion with her mother who had been again absent because of illness when Lotte was six years old. If her mother had suffered this punishment, with which she had threatened Lotte, she must also have indulged in that forbidden thing, the sexual pleasure, too.

It is clear from what Lotte's feeling of guilt received its intensity. Masturbation in childhood itself originates in the excitements following certain fantasies belonging to the area of the Oedipus situation.

I can give you an example that proves with what passionate ardor these fantasies are accompanied. The father of the patient who was a very busy physician had promised his little girl to bring her a doll when he returned from making his rounds. However, he found no time for buying the doll and postponed the gift from day to day until he finally asked the girl's mother to purchase it. The child, to whom the mother gave the doll, following a furious sudden impulse, threw it against the wall so that it broke. She wanted a baby from father not from mother.

Returning to Lotte, we need only to point out that she let the old threat of her mother concerning the consequences of masturbation come true. She actually fell ill and an operation took place. The child's need for punishment had found its gratification. The latent connection between the resumption of masturbatory actions in gymnastics and her difficulties in defecation becomes clear to us. It is as if the thick climbing pole had been substituted for an especially large penis, the paternal penis, and as if the difficulties in defecation had become the sign of the anal retention of that large genital. But the difficulties in defecation point also in another direction. Remember the infantile theories in which little girls imagine that children are born via the rectum. The anal theory of sexuality in early childhood here has a residual effect. The retention of feces assumes the significance of fear of a birth as a consequence of forbidden sexual activity.

The comparison and similarity of the difficulties in defecation with labor and of the last discharge, accomplished by operation, with a birth, has probably been noticed by you. Our reconstruction leads us to an unequivocal result. The little girl guessed the meaning of the illness and of the absence of her mother and connected it with the birth of a baby. Objective examination of the facts by a questioning of the mother actually showed that an abortion had been performed at the time. Through the trends of the Oedipus complex, identification with her mother had become the goal of the little girl's wishes. Attainment of this goal, however, was connected with pain.

Here I'd like to point out several features I consider significant in a larger sense than merely for little Lotte's psychic life, for instance, the delayed obedience toward her mother, which gratifies simultaneously the child's need for punishment through illness, pains and operation. The difficulties in defecation, which thus became simultaneously a confession and an expression of the need for punishment, show also the return of the old forbidden actions in the punishment itself, the infantile constipation and masturbation in its anal form. Incidentally, the masturbatory activity of that early time, too, exhibits the same traits of compromise, producing pleasurable and painful sensations. It appears quite probable that not only erotic, but also moral masochism accounts for the quality of pain. The fact that the unconscious factors of defiance and need for punishment frequently work both together and against each other, as gains from illness in neuroses of children, shows that our case can claim representative significance. Later, I shall discuss the compulsive character of prayer and its relation to anal compulsion.

We continue our study of Lotte's emotional development. Earlier, in elementary school, she had a tendency to commit little pranks, sudden, unprepared actions, similar to actions on impulse, which were followed by intense feelings of shame and guilt. She would, for instance, suddenly during class imitate the sound of an animal, drawing severe reprimands from the teacher. Or a year later, she would thumb her nose at the father of a little classmate, apparently without any motive, as she had never seen the gentleman before. She felt the impulse to thumb her nose at the next person who came through the door, even "if it were Teacher himself."

All these pranks were, at that time, equally unpremeditated, and of an impulsive character, and each such forbidden act was followed immediately by the urge to confess it to her mother. When she had performed the act, she immediately felt so tormenting, so urging a feeling of guilt, a fear that made her so breathless that, if the misdeed had been done at school, she often had to stop walking on her way home to catch her breath because she was afraid she would suffocate. Then she would say comforting and pacifying words to herself, as she well knew that all this torture would end the very instant she confessed her misdemeanor to her mother.

Fear of punishment could not play an essential part in this feeling of relief because the complete disappearance of all these urging, tormenting feelings of guilt and fear occurred immediately after everything had been confessed and before a reply, a scolding, let alone punishment, could be given. The last turned out to be so small, if it was meted out at all, that fear of punishment most certainly could not be considered as a motive for her anxiety.

We see, therefore, two years before the manifest neurotic disturbance of the child, a need for punishment at work, that derived from a strong, pre-existent feeling of guilt. These impulsive actions which we might call the naughtiness of a child were destined for the creation of a substratum for that obscure feeling of guilt, the cause of which had to be searched for. It is psychologically obvious that the misdeeds were undertaken with the idea of being punished, and served also the gratification of that need for punishment. These little actions, expressing at the same time defiance and the need for punishment, are furthered rather than inhibited by the civilizing tendencies of school and upbringing, once the need for punishment has become too great.

You should consider that the compulsion, which originated with the parents and developed into the inner prohibition later, sometimes displaces its intensity directly onto the countercurrents, becoming a compulsion to do exactly what is forbidden. In obsessional neurosis, this process of displacement can be observed frequently. The compulsion of the original prohibition becomes the compulsive countercommand of neurosis. One of my patients was persecuted by obsessional doubts about what he would do if, for instance, he were forced by his boss to have intercourse with the latter's wife, or if somebody forced him suddenly to undress completely, etc. You can see here how a forbidding "You shall not" changes into an imperative "You must."

This instinctual eruption, as you can see, was made obsessive by a reaction to an overpowering feeling of guilt in cases of compulsive masturbation and compulsive sexual intercourse. Analysis can prove that often in these cases a vehement violation of old, strong prohibitions occurred. The secret effectiveness of the superego and the need for punishment originating in it, can in this way often be recognized in the forced and compulsive form of instinctual gratification. Indeed, there are those who become playboys out of despair, out of being tired of life. Excess, too, develops as the liberation from a feeling of guilt that has become overpowering, the deferred effect of which can still be felt in the orgy. You remember that Freud characterized the feast as a demanded excess, as the solemn violation of a prohibition. We believe that not only does the temporary dispensation of the otherwise forbidden produce the festive mood, but that, connected with the feeling of guilt, the secret clinging to that prohibition, still resounding in the solemn demand for the celebration, reactively enhances the enjoyment of the feast. Analysis makes it clear that what was warded off, and is compulsively demanded, once was the object of prohibition and, in the reaction, became a command through inner countercompulsion. I believe that these psychic mechanisms explain impulsive actions to a large extent. The emotional relief resulting from those emotional breakthroughs has its source not only in the gratification of an aggressive or hostile drive, but also in the reduction of that dark pre-existent sense of guilt. The compulsive performance of what is prohibited again takes us back to the compulsive intensity of the need for punishment, which overcomes all conscious forces of defense.

The impulsive and compulsive character of the child's small forbidden actions is, therefore, explained not only by suppressed impulses of scorn or hostility, but also by their reactive reinforcement by the need for punishment. This may be compared to religious ceremonial where the forbidden is often demanded in the very name of religion. Furthermore, we may draw some conclu-

sions from certain compulsive experiences of the little girl. Their
performance can be characterized as acts lying between premeditated, prepared action and impulsive action. I mean here the
ideas to do certain forbidden things.

A comparison of those compulsive vows with the vows that appear in religion reveals certain facts which follow. The religious
vow generally consists in an extraordinary performance of suppression, wrested from the very strongest instinctual impulses, for the
love of God (vows of sexual chastity, abstinence from food, etc.).
There are, however, vows in religion that hold the prospect of
fullest gratification for otherwise suppressed instinctual impulses
and that demand the execution of the very thing that is otherwise forbidden, for instance, medieval vows to kill a certain number of heretics or pagans. You may compare Lotte's childish compulsion to thumb her nose at the next person who opens the
door to the tale in the Book of Judges where Jephthah vows to
God that he will sacrifice the first creature he meets on his return
home, and then sacrifices his own flesh and blood, his daughter.

We'll still return to the acted-out confession discernible in
Lotte's naughtiness. The turning point in little Lotte's life was
as follows. At the age of twelve, Lotte committed a theft which
took on great emotional significance for her. At that time, the
child, in the company of a small classmate, used to buy a snack
after school at a shop. One day on the way home, her classmate
said smilingly that she had taken a candy at the woman's shop
that day without her theft having been seen. Both girls were
greatly amused at the prank. This gave rise to Lotte's stealing.
From then on, she daily committed some small theft. She would
hide one candy in the hollow of her hand while showing the saleswoman a second one which she held between two fingers, then
she would pay for that second one only. Stealing was quite a
special pleasure for the child and even though, with her upbringing, it must have seemed to her an absolutely unheard of
crime, she had scarcely any feeling of guilt while she was doing it.
Lotte used as an excuse for herself a conversation of the saleswoman to which she had accidentally listened. The woman had

boasted of the many sweets she gave away. The child made this a welcome excuse. Lotte said to herself that it did not mean anything to the woman, since she did not care for the candy, etc.

The thefts came to an end when the saleswoman discovered them. Both girls were indescribably ashamed, never entered the store again and swore to each other never to tell anybody a word about it. This vow was kept meticulously, at least, on Lotte's part. Indeed, the vow would not actually have been necessary at all, as she felt, at the time, no urge whatsoever to admit the wrong she had committed.

After the period of thievery had ended, these compulsive impulses stopped at once, making way for pranks of an entirely different character. These were intentional, carefully prepared and well thought through pranks meant to anger the teacher as much as possible, yet with the smallest chance of being caught. Never again did Lotte feel a desire to confess any of those misdeeds at home. The thefts were the turning point because, even while she committed them, a feeling of guilt did not exist anymore. A contributing cause of the easing of her feeling of guilt was, in this case, probably the fact that Lotte had not been alone when the thefts were committed and that her little classmate was her accessory and even her leader.

Lotte's life, until the start of her analysis, took its course, as it were, under the sign of an increased need for punishment that, time and again, tended to push her towards inflicting damage upon herself. It was worth noticing that she permitted herself any enjoyment of life or use of a lucky break only after having first punished herself severely. This reversal of a familiar sequence, namely, instinctual gratification followed by punishment, into punishment followed by instinctual gratification, is by no means rare with neurotics. In these cases it appears as if punishment preceded every pleasure, as if permission to have some enjoyment of life were warranted only through the infliction of a punishment, pain or humiliation. The effectiveness of a strong pre-existent need for punishment is the explanation of such a strange attitude.

Among the numerous problems of child psychology, which

should be part of a discussion of this analytic fragment, we'd like to point out, in conscious onesidedness, only these problems in which the need for punishment and the compulsion to confess play a central role. Following little Lotte's development from an early age, we could observe how abandonment of masturbation, itself produced by the simultaneous effects of the pressure from the drive and from the need for punishment, mobilized old feelings of guilt. We saw, furthermore, how the resulting need for punishment drove towards gratification in these small impulsive actions. The people to whom these aggressive actions were addressed were basically the very ones—or substitutes—from whom punishment was expected or longed for, namely the parents or parent representative figures.

This point of view is important as it may claim a more general validity. Adults, too, in order to provoke punishment usually misbehave towards certain persons if they unconsciously feel guilty towards them. In analysis it is frequently found that a patient's conflict with a person represents the sign of a need for punishment from that very person. My conviction of the correctness of this statement has been so strongly fortified by frequent verification in analysis that I always ask myself, especially when the patient tells of conflicts or hostile impulses against close members of his family and friends, why he feels guilty toward that person. Even in aggression against someone, an expression of pre-existent feeling of guilt, an unconscious confession, can be perceived. Superhuman charity is perhaps needed to forgive all evildoers, in recognizing these hidden motives, because they do not know what they are doing.

A perspective on the unconscious need for punishment attains importance also in the critical examination of resistances in analysis. Certain forms of resistance, for instance, serve unconsciously to incite the analyst's anger, with the hidden aim of being punished. You probably know of the projection of the dissatisfaction of a·patient with himself onto the analyst, in resistance. It is as if the patient were becoming dissatisfied with the analyst because the latter made him dissatisfied with himself, or rather, made him conscious of a dissatisfaction with himself that he had not consciously felt before.

The impulsive actions of the little girl illustrate, in their compulsive character, traces of the effect of the unconscious need for punishment in various directions. Compare, for instance, the vows to perform some naughty prank with the vows of obsessional neurotics, also of obsessionally neurotic children. Vows of this kind are, as a rule, used to bar an obsessional instinctual impulse by an external compulsion that blocks the access to motility. The intention to punish oneself for a previous violation of a prohibition can also be clearly recognized in the vow. The reversed emotional process can be observed here in little Lotte's compulsive vows. The girl wards off the inner, over great pressure of the need for punishment by a vow to do something naughty. We know now that doing something naughty means relief from the need for punishment, but it is also clear that the latter substantially enhances instinctual gratification.

A general feature of moral masochism is gratification reactively enhanced by the need for punishment. This kind of gratification explains the pleasure which, in the black masses, in the leagues with Satan, becomes frenzy, "most painful pleasure." Violation of a prohibition, with the intensity driven high through the need for punishment, offers a gratification unattainable in any other way. This possibility of enhancing pleasure by a need for punishment shows the psychology of perversions in a new light. It is the deviation from the norm that is unconsciously used for instinctual intensification in the practices of sexual perverts because it is subterraneously connected with the need for punishment. Some of the fantasies and practices of perverts will easily be recognized as deriving from the unconscious feeling of guilt and representing what we call unconscious confession.

The instinctual processes of reversal into the opposite and of turning against the self, as you know them, are especially well suited to the purpose of hiding the concurrent factor of gratification of the unconscious need for punishment. You have come to understand the reversal of activeness into passiveness as a vicissitude of instincts. In addition, special significance for the unconscious feeling of guilt may be attributed to the reversal of activity, originally directed at the ego, into one directed at the foreign object. Think of the role played by those processes in the psychogenesis of homosexuality, of sadism and voyeurism.

These factors are important not only in the psychology of perversions. Criminology, too, must take notice of them. For too long a time it has ignored the fact that, in great numbers of criminals, the deed originated not in uninhibited yielding to instincts, but in eruption, out of a too strong psychic pressure that turns secondarily against a foreign object. Sometimes the particularly conspicuous and sordid details of a crime point in this direction. This is especially the case with crimes committed by juvenile delinquents.

If we follow the line leading from the first small actions in school, then the reappearance of masturbation, to the thefts and the pranks of prepuberty, we can connect two important observations. The first originates in the fact that the pranks and naughtiness of the early period were impulsive, in a sense, unconscious actions, while those of the later period were thoroughly premeditated and carefully prepared. This difference reflects another one, that will on first sight seem paradoxical. The little girl was closer to understanding the motives of her pranks as long as they were of an impulsive or compulsive character, than she was later when her pranks were premeditated and thought through. Later there appeared rationalizing and secondary motives that concealed the original motives which were based on instinctual tendencies and the need for punishment. The recession of the essential motives in the conscious was, therefore, closely connected with the pushing forward of new motives, with preparation and premeditation. Here arises a problem significant for criminology. It is the question of why the difficulty of comprehending, in their deepest psychic motives, crimes long prepared and premeditated for which the criminal can give quite detailed explanations, is greater than that in cases where crimes are committed in affect.

The same line, from harmless naughtiness at the age of six to the socially more serious thefts at the age of twelve, shows that the need for punishment, which remained without punishment, became ever more urgent, until it brought about more serious substitute actions. It appears possible to me that the psychology of certain criminals who proceed from lighter transgressions to more serious crimes becomes clearer in this perspective, however much other factors may exert their influence upon this course of events.

A dark need for punishment existed that sought a substratum and stayed there without gratification. It induced the temptation to commit the forbidden act again and again, or, rather, a substitute act which produced a new need for punishment—an ominous vicious circle which one could really call the "curse of the evil act." The force of a secret need for punishment has the character and power of an instinctual drive. Its pressure becomes recognizable in the increased gravity of the crime. The minor crime is no longer sufficient. As a substitute action, it neither gratifies the increased instinctual demands nor the dark need for punishment. The criminal must proceed to ever more antisocial acts and finally commit a crime, which, in its gravity, comes at least close to the sacrilege of the deed of Oedipus, justifying the unconsciously desired extent of punishment. As the result of the oppressive feeling of guilt, the forbidden action becomes secondarily its motive. This is no contradiction of the statement that the deed is an emotional relief because this relief is only a partial and short-lived one, yielding to a new feeling of guilt which drives again towards the forbidden action, if its intensity begins to exceed a certain degree.

Not only criminology, but also the theory and practice of education of children at home and in school, must make their own the new analytical insights into the workings of the unconscious need for punishment. There are only differences in degree between the naughty child and the one who has gone astray. The new results of research will be turned to good account in the difficult task of salvaging asocial and neglected children for society. The whole problem of juvenile delinquency presents new aspects from this point of view.

The analytic fragment with which we have occupied ourselves can convey to us also some general information about the effects of the compulsion to confess in the emotional life of the child. As we have heard, an extraordinarily strong compulsion to confess (in this case, in the sense of a neurotic compulsion) was connected with Lotte's first naughtiness in school, namely, the imitating of animals' sounds and making faces.

The symptoms of anxiety, increasing to become difficulties in breathing, show that what was to be confessed was not those small foolish tricks, but something hidden behind them, more serious things that justified the fear of confession. After confession, all driving and tormenting feelings of fear and guilt vanished immediately, as if gone with the wind. But the fact that the pranks were continued proves that the confession had brought only partial relief of the need for punishment. This is understandable, as the confession could only relate to those small misdeeds, the substitute character of which is obvious. The child could give no information about the deep connection of the small misdemeanor with those unconscious tendencies driving towards other goals.

In the same case, we recognize also the connection between the compulsion to confess and the urge to release the feces, a displacement of the compulsive factor felt by the child while defecating. The fear of defecation, the retention of the feces and the eventual deliverance from them correspond entirely to the fear on the way home after her first pranks and to the hasty tale and talk of the misdeed at home and the subsequent relief.

The compulsive prayer, centering about the apprehension because of the stool, has likewise taken over its compulsive character from the sensations of defecation, as Freud showed in his work concerning an infantile neurosis. In this example it can also be seen what the actual character of prayer is. It is an unconscious confession to God who represents the parents. Earlier we discussed the connection of the compulsion to confess and the compulsion to defecate, retention of the confession and anal obstinacy. It may easily be guessed that the compulsion to confess can be compared to a child's compulsion to defecate after retention of the feces. The ultimate roots of the fact that the compulsion to confess is a compulsion may have to be sought in this analogy. The child's pleasure and his anxiety in anal retention reappears in the psychic processes of the fear of confession and in pleasure in confession. May I remind you of the fact that the child values the release of the feces as an expression of love, and point to the unconscious purpose of the confession: to win back the approval and affection of society.

Analytic observation shows you, incidentally, that neglect of cleanliness, dirt itself, becomes an unconscious sign of a feeling of guilt, a sign that still retains its character of confession in compulsive washing, a neurotic form of reaction. The religious rites of ancient peoples, for instance of the Jews, which forbade the kin of the dead to take care of their own bodies, making uncleanliness a duty, confirm indirectly the psychological connection of cleanliness and the unconscious feeling of guilt which was found in the symptomatology of neuroses.

The significance of exhibitionist pleasure, so easily combining secondarily with masochistic inclinations, appears so clearly in the compulsion to confess that its discussion may be omitted in this connection. Mention of the works of Abraham about the oral character will suffice to remind you of the relations that result among certain character traits from processes of displacement in the oral realm and the compulsion to confess. The contrast pointed out by Abraham between the pleasure of retention and of discharge must be expected to become significant for the theory of the compulsion to confess.

A new point of view we gained from the analysis of the child's thievery opens up an outlook on new problems. We pointed out earlier that little Lotte no longer felt any urge to confess after her thefts, as she had in the preceding period. Several factors may have caused that change, one of which will have to be recognized as the decisive one: the company of her classmate. According to Freud's description, feeling of guilt is "social anxiety," and the fact that the friend knew of the thefts necessarily modified the compulsion to confess in the same way as the "mass of two" modifies the need for punishment.

From here a sequence of thoughts leads to the psychology of the gang of criminals. From analytical points of view, it can easily be understood that the need for punishment is greatly weakened through the effect of the gang—the community removing the feeling of guilt. It even occasionally orders the crime to be committed. The authority of the state—the police, the courts—otherwise functioning as the substitute for the father, is here replaced by the leader, to whom the individual member of the gang is tied in love and admiration. With the political criminal, the fact becomes reality, that the leader of the gang can, in his psychological function, be replaced by an idea, at least temporarily. The notorious reticence and secretiveness of the members of a gang of criminals and the difficulty encountered in efforts to make them confess and name the other members are caused by the unconscious homosexual ties of the individuals among themselves and between them and the leader. In psychological appreciation of this fact, it will be necessary to note that the need for punishment and, with it, the compulsion to confess is moderated, even removed by the merging into a community, regardless of what kind of community that may be. Mention should be made of the interesting psychological constellation in those criminals whose parents were criminals themselves and permitted their children to take part early in their transgressions. Here, too, a superego—a negative one—has established itself. In these criminals, too, indications of later attempts at identification with teachers, clergyman, etc. can be found, toward which the first introjections of objects, however, prove resistant. In these cases, several superegos are sometimes formed and a conflict occurs between the primary and secondary superego.

At this point, a few questions concerning collective life seem to invite discussion which we shall take up in the next lecture under the perspective of the compulsion to confess.

X

About the Social Compulsion to Confess

LADIES AND GENTLEMEN: We have noticed the psychic effect of confession upon the individual. Relief from the need for punishment and the hope for a new gain of love are not the only effects. The disintegrating of the personality is at least temporarily halted by the confession. The communication between the ego and that part of the ego from which it was estranged is restored. To use a picture that a patient once used in grim humor, the shady, under-ground-living lodger of psychic life, who had not been registered, had appeared at the police station and registered and been legally recognized there as a fellow occupant. Confession makes the individual perceive what he had not been willing to see in himself. We have said this involves a hurt to conscious self-regard, but can become a reinforcement of the unconscious ego-strength.

When we love ourselves, we continue and maintain on our own only what we have experienced from without since our childhood —the love that had once been given us. Unconsciously we are never alone, as the ego is itself the precipitate of our earliest and most significant identifications. If it is true, as the poets proclaim, that all suffering is loneliness, in endopsychic perception it orig-inates in one's own inability to love, which expresses itself as an unconscious feeling of guilt. It is easy to discover traces of such an unconscious sense of guilt, slightly disguised, but from the same source, in an everyday situation known to you all. You find it in the attitude of all women to whom a man declares his love, but who cannot reciprocate his feeling. The woman, as if she had to excuse herself, will feel almost apologetic, will assure the man that she respects or appreciates him, but cannot love him.

We may also search in this area for one of the reasons for occupational therapy, so frequently and emphatically recommended in neuroses. All work is a social activity and it also affords, besides the substitute gratification of unconscious impulses, a partial gratification of the need for punishment, allaying the feeling of guilt. Do you remember the tale from Genesis where Jahveh punished Adam and Eve after the Fall by toil, and where the toil was the tilling of the ground, hence a substitute for the forbidden incestuous act? Think of the universal symbolism of Mother Earth, a comparison to be found in all countries of the ancient Orient.

The character of this penance of toil implies, besides the sexual substitute gratification, the liberation from social anxiety which Freud described as the feeling of guilt. The serious inhibitions in work that occupy us so frequently in analysis, show unequivocally the displacement of a sexual disorder. No less clearly do they show that patients do not permit themselves to work as a form of an emotional overcoming of the feeling of guilt and that they cannot do so because of the depth of their need for punishment. It is meaningful that we psychoanalysts measure the emotional health of a person according to his ability to love and to work without too serious disturbance.

We started from the symptom of the neurotic. The symptom is essentially the unconscious confession of repressed urges and desires. In certain symptoms as, for instance, in hysterical seizures, in obsessional actions, in phobic anxieties, the character of the neurotic symptom appears particularly clearly as that of an acted-out, represented confession. The negative therapeutic reaction in analysis, as described by Freud, may be similarly classified.

The character of the symptoms of suffering invites their comparison with other phenomena known to us. You will remember that the same unconscious self-betrayal that finds expression in neurotic symptoms appears also in the manifold actions of self-inflicted damage, of self-sabotage and of working against the ego, that produce so many minor and major mishaps. The bicyclist who, meaning to avoid a certain obstacle, comes to fall just because of it, the applicant who deprives himself of the hope for

success through an "accidental" word, the young man who, wooing a girl, commits a fateful awkwardness, all of them have fallen
victim to the unconscious need for punishment. I like to imagine
that all these malicious, mischievous and malignant ghosts and
hobgoblins of our world of fairy tales (think of Puck in Shakespeare's gay play) are personifications of those secret, aggressive
tendencies redirected against the ego. You know that accidents
and "unintended" suicides are among those incidents in which
the mute death instinct makes successful use of that unconscious
need for punishment of the individual in order to achieve its aims.
Much more might be said on this topic but time presses and I'll
return to the discussion of the compulsion to confess.

The history of mankind's psychological development teaches
us what place in it we should give to the compulsion to confess.
Simultaneous effects of stimuli of outer and inner necessities have
brought about the suppression and repression of our strongest instinctual impulses. What once had been imposed from outside by
means of force has become, through the ages, an inner acquisition.
If we compare the original measures, which atoned for violations
of prohibitions of taboos, with our present-day laws, we find that
the punishments inflicted from outside were once of a cruel, barbaric, often life-destroying kind.

The external punishments have become milder but the inner
need for punishment has grown and become stricter and more
intense through secular repression. This need impinges upon
man's life today with exactly the same cruelty and destructiveness
to life as the external punishment of old. Confession is a psychic
process that developed in order to bring about relief from the
exaggerated and excessive pressure of mankind's unconscious need
for punishment.

As you know, there is a pre-existent feeling of guilt involved.
It was acquired at some point in the course of the remote pre-
history of mankind. Mankind's first reactions to the primeval
crime, to the slaying of the primeval father, represent themselves
as great unconscious confessions. The powerful social institutions,
which arose from those reaction-formations, show all the vestiges

of the same impulses exhibited much more clearly by those early confessions of the masses. They, too, are unconscious confessions of all mankind. Seen from this angle, the development of mankind shows itself as a great struggle to overcome the Oedipus complex and offers, thus, the collective analogy to the life of the individual, to the biologically determined process of development and maturation of the individual.

Great breakthroughs of drives like wars, revolutions, religious and nationalistic persecutions, and also feasts and orgies, bring powerful and violent instinctual interruptions and eruptions into the safeguarded realm of the secular progress of repression. The conduct of man in working at building culture can well be compared with that of the Jews who erected the second temple and who laid brick upon brick with one hand, while in the other they held the sword to ward off interfering enemies. In that long and troublesome ascent of man, the inner enemy, especially aggression, often succeeds in interrupting the cultural work. The significance of the ideal of the father and the idol of the mother, which I discussed elsewhere, as opposed to each other, grows to gigantic dimensions in this cultural process, because the demands of the need for punishment and the instinctual pressure are forever tied to it.

We might say that however as many and as powerful are the tendencies that may oppose the compulsion to confess, in the end it remains victorious and overcomes all of them. What is true in individual life is reflected also in the development of mankind. If we contemplate the three systems of thought produced by humanity in the course of time, we notice that, in the animistic period, an elementary tendency towards expression of the instinctual impulses is still dominant. In its later phases, however, the feeling of guilt and the need for punishment already appear, thus preparing the subsequent development towards religion. The projection of hostile and aggressive as well as cruel tendencies and the defense against demons testify to this on the level of the animistic conception of the world.

Myth and art, built upon animistic premises, represent strong wishes that were opposed by reality with its frustrations. Later, myth and art allow also the expression of the inhibiting powers, until these, too, themselves, become the subject of myth and art in the changed form of inner objections and emotional counter-currents. Religion is itself the unconscious confession of strong impulses, to ward off which, it came into being. In the final phases, however, development of religion invariably leads to the problem of the conscience, to the recognition of the great instinctual tendencies and the inhibitions opposing them, hence to confession. In the religious admission of the fact that we are altogether sinners and in the instinctual confessions, we have recognized the last result of the effect of the unconscious compulsion to confess.

Those religious confessions are joined and often replaced by the scientific confession in which the unconscious, instinctual currents and the unconscious conscience, themselves, become objects of research. We may in this connection say that analysis, as the newest scientific means, joins those great endeavors, which, in the course of human history, served the purpose of overcoming the pressure of the drives and the need for punishment, increased through the secular progress of repression.

Art, the law, social mores and religion have been unconscious social confessions. Seen in the perspective of cultural history, analysis is society's first confession, subjecting to psychological investigation the instinctual foundations, upon which rests the community itself. It is of no detriment to the value of analysis if we maintain that defense against demons in animistic cultural development and confession in religious development, using primitive means and means based upon feelings, have been concerned with those same tasks, which, by psychoanalysis, have been brought closer to their solution through scientific methods.

We should not wonder why it took humanity so long to recognize the deepest powers driving and inhibiting it, and the psychic foundations on which it rests. In the life of the individual and in the development of mankind appears the same typical process of very much belated understanding, a process once described by

Friedrich Hebbel in these psychologically true words: "He attained his goal before recognizing it."

Psychoanalysis reveals itself as a social confession mainly through the use of the unconscious emotional life as the actual realm of scientific psychology. Its work, which considers the psychic surface only insofar as it is the expression of deeper processes, differs from the old psychology, which treats only of the uppermost strata of psychic life, as modern taxidermy differs from old, obsolete taxidermy. I'd like to go into some details of this comparison. The old taxidermy was a primitive method of making likenesses of animals for zoological collections. The taxidermist stuffed the animal's hide with straw, hay or oakum and made the body stable with iron rods. The material was inadequate and the taxidermist did not need any knowledge of the animal's anatomy and biological properties. Little did it matter if the hide did not fit snugly around the material. The likeness of the animal was complete if its hide were filled with the stuffing according to the practice of the craft.

The modern taxidermist proceeds differently. He makes likenesses of animals after a careful study of the animals themselves. Minute study of the muscular system with its interplay and contractions, exact knowledge of the anatomy, of changes in the animal's shape in motion, of the structure of its bones and muscles, are nowadays indispensable prerequisites of his work. It goes without saying that, moreover, there must be a pronounced awareness of and memory for shapes. Exact models of the skinned animals are made, in fashioning which every tendon, every protuberance of the skeleton is considered. What is beneath the skin becomes more important for the modern taxidermist than the skin. Only in this way can likenesses true to nature be achieved and a new basis created for our zoological collections. Professor Leuckart once indicated, in drastic words in his inaugural speech, the result of the discord between intention and skill in the old, superficial method, when, many years ago, he took over the direction of the zoological museum in Giessen: "A zoologist can see miraculous animals in this museum, scarcely ever described even in old books of fairy tales, monkeys with sheeps' heads and goats' bodies, pigeons with looks of hawks are quite common here. . . . And with these specimens a student is supposed to be taught the purposefulness of the shapes of animals! As if it were important to demonstrate only the color and shape of hair and feathers!" Something like that we still find in our psychological museums, in many textbooks of psychology and psychiatry, which endeavor to describe the top layers as best they can.

Psychoanalysis, as a psychology in depth, creates the necessary initial conditions for deep reaching social and psychic changes. As a social confession, it shows to humanity the shape in which human instinctual life is and how mankind, refusing to acknowledge the underground power of its drives and impulses, is being guided by them. But it also shows how society judges its own concealed inclinations and tendencies and how it condemns them. Psychoanalysis leads up to the reduction of these repressed instinctual powers, as well as that of the need for punishment, and guides both into consciousness. *"Pecca fortiter!"* Luther urged upon the Christian of his time who was collapsing under the pressure of his conscience. Analysis offers no advice of that kind. It remains a science that does not have to serve immediately practical purposes, but it shows how the repressed instinctual impulses and the need for punishment operate and interfere with the aims of civilization.

Freud has pointed out that psychoanalysis has the significance of a great narcissistic hurt to mankind. Psychoanalysis proves that man is by no means unrestricted boss in his emotional household, that he is not "master of his soul" as he flattered himself. It must hurt his false pride when he learns that he is mastered to a great extent by impulses, wishes and desires entirely unknown to him. Yet deep down he has a pre-knowledge of this strange state of his emotional situation. Every day shows you that humanity is full of false self-esteem contrasting curiously with its unconscious feelings of inferiority. Man's self-righteousness contrasts conspicuously with his secret judgment of himself, with his concealed self-concept. The social confession of analysis has a cultural mission the goal of which is a mankind that dares to see the truth, to face the music. It does not appeal to moral reason. It rather shows the psychotherapeutic effect of truth.

The unconscious compulsion to confess proves disguise and falsehood to be a burden and a longing for the truth to be effective deep in human psychic life. One would hope that, through the scientific confession of analysis, the moral courage to be sincere might grow in the community. To attain that goal, it is, however, necessary to acknowledge freely one's strongest drives and the forces of conscience that oppose them, to recognize oneself and to accept oneself. If analysis prevails, we should see the end of the emotional make-believe of the individual and of society as well.

For the first time, analysis consciously submits to mankind's hidden compulsion to confess. You know about the affective obstacle trying to prevent the compulsion to confess from prevailing in the individual. It is mainly the increasing need for punishment that refuses to be contented with the suffering hitherto experienced. Analysis has, as a collective confession, found this to be the strongest resistance in the world. Freud would have been justified in saying that psychoanalysis touches on the too great need for punishment of a humanity which is not yet willing to allow itself the relief of confession.

But analysis will make people more modest in another way, too. It convinces them of the fact that no conscious counterdrive measures up to the hidden powers of emotional life. It confirms anew the deep meaning of that Latin saying, *"Fata ducunt volentem, trahunt nolentem"* (Fate leads the willing, drags the unwilling) by new insights, among which we may count also the theory of the unconscious compulsion to confess.

LADIES AND GENTLEMEN: Once again, I should like to point out that not only is the compulsion to confess, as we see it, unconscious, but that it also remains in its deepest motives unconscious. This situation is similar to that of conscience, the unconscious function in ourselves which Freud has shown us. Yet conscience is something we should be able to boast of as being that which is best known to us in life. It is no longer a mere coincidence of language that the word "conscience" contains the root "science." The fact points to hidden psychological connections. The concept of knowledge itself becomes questionable in analysis. Analysis sees here problems which were only faintly thought of or, at times, not thought of at all, by the psychology of old. I believe that analysis has convinced you of the fact that there are actually two kinds of knowledge, namely, a conscious one with which we are accustomed to work, and an unconscious one which often produces surprising effects in our emotional life and which, through analysis, can, to a large extent, be made the conscious possession of the individual.

A profound difference exists, therefore, between the knowledge acquired in learning, hearing, reading, and that acquired through experience. Strictly speaking, only this second kind deserves to be called knowledge that cannot be taken away from us, because it is closely connected with our experiences. Freud has emphasized the fact that to have heard and to have experienced are two entirely different things, as far as their psychological character is concerned, even though both have the same content. I told you, earlier, something about my small son. Permit me to quote him again. Once when Arthur was in the first year in grade school, I asked him teasingly how he came to know so definitely that two and two were four. In fun, I did not accept the answer that he knew it from his teacher and from his arithmetic textbook, but pointed out to him the possibility that even these absolute authorities might be in error. Pressed by my question for reliable sources of his knowledge, the little boy finally exclaimed impatiently, "But I know it in myself!" Here the difference between knowledge from outside and inner conviction was characterized in a childishly awkward but realistic manner.

I have not intended to put before you anything finished and complete, only to make suggestions which you may perhaps digest, to communicate to you experiences which strongly adduce certain views, and to ask you to scrutinize in your own observation the theory of the unconscious compulsion to confess, which I have been advancing. I have reminded you, furthermore, of the fact that knowledge based only upon what one has heard is worth little. I hope, therefore, that you will compare what you have here heard with your own impressions and experiences. I should be happy if your own experience were to bring you to the point where you "know it in yourself."

PART THREE

The Shock of Thought

Introductory Note

THE following essays, dating from the years 1924 through 1927, contain new contributions, additions and revisions concerning a psychoanalytical theory which I published in a work of larger size, *Compulsion to Confess and Need for Punishment*, in 1926.* These essays, too, center about the relations between the powers of human drives and that inner agency which psychoanalysis calls the superego. I am aware of the fact that the individual essays contained in this volume are not all of the same psychological depth. I have no intention of denying their fragmentary and one-sided character.

* Part Two of this volume.

Berlin, October 1928

I

Fright

1

AFTER Abraham, Ferenczi, Jones and Simmel had made important contributions concerning the problem of traumatic neuroses in the discussion during the Fifth International Psychoanalytical Congress,* Freud took up this topic again in 1920 in a larger context.** He sees in the traumatic neurosis a consequence of an extensive instinctual eruption through the protective barrier against stimuli, which is the primary function of our mental apparatus. He points out that it is not merely the intensity of the stimulus arriving at the protective barrier which brings about the traumatic neuroses. The condition of the ego-strength must be considered another important factor. If this threshold is low, the psychic apparatus will be less capable of receiving an influx of energy. In that case, the consequences of an eruption through the protective barrier must be more violent than in a case with a higher strength of its own, which possesses a greater binding force. Recognition of this second factor implies a warning to us not to overestimate the pathogenic power of an external injuring or traumatic factor. The particular pathological result will depend on the combined effects of both factors. There will again result a supplementary sequence analogous to the one Freud postulated for the cooperation of constitutional and accidental factors in the etiology of neuroses.

Confronted by the theories about traumatic neurosis which

* *About the Psychology of War Neuroses*, International Psychoanalytical Library, Volume I, Vienna, 1919.
** *Beyond the Pleasure-Principle*, 1920, Collected Writings, Volume VI.

attribute the greatest etiological significance to fright and to the endangering of life, Freud's conception appears first to be a return to the old doctrine of the effect of shock. But contrary to it, the essence of shock is seen in that eruption through the barrier that protects the layer of the cortex which receives stimuli. The fright retains its significance also in the frame of Freud's theory because its determinant is the absence of anxiety-preparedness. This determinant implies a lower resistance of the systems first receiving the stimulus. Because of that low cathexis which cannot bind the oncoming quantities of energy, the consequences of the eruption through the protective barrier take place much more easily.

Freud's concept seems to me to require an analytical supplement and extension. The course it should take was indicated in other explorations of Freud's, but not pursued by him, nor by other analytical authors. The following attempt at a modification is necessarily of a hypothetical character, the more so, as there is only scant experience available in this field to support it.

This attempt is restricted essentially to the diligent observation of traumatic neuroses during the war. I had ample opportunity to study many cases at and behind the front, but none to analyze them. The following hypothesis originated, therefore, in the comparison of impressions and clinical observations of traumatic neuroses, on the one hand, with experiences from analysis of nontraumatic neuroses on the other. My thesis should not, however, be denied justification in advance because of the fact that adverse circumstances prevented analytical investigation of accident-neuroses from being carried through. It is, after all, in the nature of a hypothesis that it can be verified and proved only when arrived at by more routes than one.

It should, furthermore, be noted that other, nonanalytical observers have not profited so much as might have been expected from the possibility of utilizing clinically this material on hand for examination, and that they have not come nearer to a psychological understanding of traumatic neuroses. We therefore see, between breadth of experience and its intellectual use, a supplemental relation similar to that between intensity of stimuli and degree of ego-strength in the traumatic neuroses themselves. The emphasis placed on the hypothetical character of the following discussions is meant merely to indicate that they treat of anticipatory ideas which should be verified in special investigations. While entirely convinced of the provisional nature of all scientific concepts, one may still consider that a certain piece of research has come closer to the hidden connection than another.

Furthermore, the publication of this paper appears to me to be justified, in spite of its hypothetical character, because it is the attempt at an explanation whose analytical verification is equally desirable on theoretical as well as on practical grounds.* The nature of the special stimuli that have traumatic effect in the neurosis from shock has been investigated and clarified in so many ways that our analytical investigation can scarcely hope at this point to be able to penetrate more deeply into the understanding of the disturbance. Freud characterized the intensity of stimuli as the factor etiologically most significant. Emphasis on the second factor, the individual degree of ego-strength, makes it, however, also according to this theory, understandable that relatively small intensities of stimuli in many cases produce traumatic effects, hence, that they are able to erupt through the psychic protective barrier. The stimuli objectively known are, in the genesis of traumatic neurosis, the sources most exactly determined and explored. Not only laymen refer to them exclusively in explaining the disease. Scientific investigators, too, have recognized their significance time and again. Undoubtedly, the special stimulus is in definite causal relation to traumatic neurosis, but this relation is by no means unequivocal and exclusive of other factors, as can be seen from Freud's theory. Research will need to ask why one stimulus produced such different effects, and why the particular effect was produced in the individual case.

* I have gone carefully through the medical literature concerning traumatic neuroses, but neither there nor in general textbooks of nervous diseases, could I find an approach to my hypothesis. This essay was written in 1924, before the publication of Freud's *Inhibition, Symptom and Anxiety*. Freud's paper has shown the many points in which the ideas here advanced are in need of modification and the many in which they coincide with his ideas.

2

In looking over the situations from which traumatic neuroses develop, and considering critically the effectiveness of objective stimuli in producing the individual neurosis, we are reminded of another problem, even though at the same time soberly evaluating all differences in the two, a problem in which psychoanalysis had to be interested at an early time. That is the relation between the objective stimuli of a dream and the subsequent dream. The significance of the objective stimuli of the senses in the psychology of dreams has been found by careful observations and has even been confirmed by experiments. The correctness of the theories which state that excitations of the sense organs are inciters of dreams has never been doubted by psychoanalysis. The problem was, however, how to prove the connection between the external, accidental stimuli of dreams and their contents.

Freud proved the inadequacy of the theory of dream stimuli from the fact that it leaves two points unexplained, "first, why the external stimulus is not recognized in its true nature in the dream (compare with the arousal dreams, page 18) and second, why the result of the reaction of the perceiving mind to this misunderstood stimulus can be so unpredictably variable."*

I use here the dream of Maury, the French psychologist, which has become famous as an example of a dream the content of which is definitely causally connected with an external stimulus. The dreamer sees himself transported into the time of the Revolution's Reign of Terror, experiences gruesome scenes of murder, is taken into custody and put before the Tribunal. There he sees Robespierre, Marat, Fouquier-Tinville and other prominent men of that time, whose questions he answers. He is sentenced after many incidents and then taken to the place of execution, accompanied by a vast multitude. He mounts the scaffold, the executioner ties

* *Interpretation of Dreams, Gesammelte Schriften,* Vol. II, p. 222.

him to the board, it topples, the blade of the guillotine drops. He feels his head being severed from his body, wakes in the most frightful anxiety and finds that part of the head of the bedstead had fallen and struck the vertebrae of his neck, much as does the blade of a guillotine.

There are two factors that interest us here which seem to be helpful in building a bridge to the psychological comprehension of the traumatic neurosis. The first one is the connection between the somatic external stimulus appearing in the dream-formation and the actually produced dream. The second concerns the particulars of the relation in time. The second factor gave rise to a spirited discussion in the *Revue Philosophique*.* Maury is struck on the back of the neck by a small board and dreams in the extraordinarily short time between the fall of the board and his waking caused by it, a whole novel of the time of the Revolution, a dream that releases a lively affect of anxiety. A special acceleration of the succession of ideas seems to be a property of dream-work, as is shown in other examples referred to in Freud's *Interpretation of Dreams*. We remember, however, that this is a specialty not only of the dream. People in danger of drowning or of falling from great heights see run off before them in a few seconds many scenes from their lives, like films following each other swiftly.

Freud gave an explanation of Maury's dream, which seems to give us a possibility of understanding the other factor concerning the modification of the external stimulus. He believes the French psychologist's dream represents a fantasy that had been stored intact in his memory for years and that was stirred (one might say touched off) the instant the sleeper received the arousal stimulus. This view would also help to eliminate the first difficulty, namely, that of the shortened time. It was, as Freud says, "tapped lightly," as if one were to play only a few measures of a familiar piece of music on the piano and the whole piece then emerged from memory. Something in its entirety is thus at once set in excitation from a point of eruption. "Through the arousal stimulus the

* *Revue Philosophique*, 20. *Année*, 1895: Egger, *La durée apparente des rêves;* Le Lorain, *Le rêve D. . . . L'appréciation du temps dans le rêve.*

psychic station is excited, which opens the access to the whole fantasy of the guillotine. This, however, is not lived through in sleep, but only in the memory of the wakened. Awake, one remembers in all its details, the fantasy, which only as a generalized whole, had been touched on in the dream."

What do the psychic processes in these arousal dreams have to do with the situations which we make responsible for the origin of the traumatic neuroses? The connection seems on first sight to be a very loose one. As in the arousal dream, an external stimulus acts which then evokes physical sensations and mental processes. The short interval of time between the unconscious perception of the sensation and the waking can be compared easily to the interval between the perception of a stimulus, as in a railroad accident, and the first reaction of the person involved in it.

If we think of the temporary clouding of consciousness in the case of the accident, a condition which is like a blackout of a few second's duration, after the eruption of the stimulus, we are reminded of sleep. Another factor for comparison is surprise. The dreamer experiences a stimulus for the occurrence of which he was not prepared. Likewise, the patient in accident-neurosis. The significance of the surprise factor in the psychogenesis of the accident has been recognized in Freud's theory.

If we take dreams of the type of Maury's dream of the guillotine, which are by no means rare, another point of comparison appears, namely, the release of strong affects of anxiety. What interests us psychologically in this comparison is: "What happens in our emotional life in dreams of this kind and in cases of accidents in the short time between reception and pre-conscious comprehension of the stimulus? In other words, what psychological process takes place in the time between the arrival of the stimulus at the cortical substance receiving it and the first reaction to its reception?"

Freud has explained that the oncoming stimulus in Maury's dream of the guillotine, as in other dreams of that character, excited a whole fantasy which had already been complete and available. Is the somatic stimulus, as such, reponsible for the vehement anxiety with which the dreamer wakes up? The answer is, of course, "No." The intensity of the affect is justified by what the stimulus means in its emotional modification. If a similar stimulus were to impinge on us while we were awake, we certainly would not feel any anxiety. But is this so certain? Changing the picture only slightly, we can easily come close to one of those situations that could adduce a traumatic neurosis. Supposing Maury wakes, then takes a walk one day and is suddenly hit by a small piece of board that may have fallen from some scaffolding. Only a few elements are changed in this situation, but in place of a healthy person starting up frightened from stifling dreams, who soon calms himself, we have the picture of a victim of accident-neurosis with all the classical symptoms.

One could easily argue here that the accident-neurosis occurs only as a consequence of too strong a rush of stimuli, that a collision, a vehement blow, a violent electric storm is the cause. But the clinicians also report time and again about stimuli of small intensity that are responsible for the occurrence of traumatic neuroses. On the other hand, they often show us numerous instances of strong stimuli endured without any damage. Readily conceding the fact that, beginning from a certain intensity of stimulus, everyone is bound to fall victim to a traumatic neurosis, I shall concern myself here exclusively with those cases which, though not showing a special intensity of the stimulus, still lead up to this form of disturbance, and I emphasize this limitation. It is easy to point to a certain psychic and physical constitution (we indeed acknowledge its significance) but emphasis on the constitutional factors does not relieve research from the task of investigating the special psychic processes in the case of the accident.

Other objections appear and require consideration. The dreamer is able to tell us something about the psychic happenings in that short interval of time, namely, his dream. But the traumatic patient can report only a very little about his physical sensations during the seconds when the accident struck. To invalidate this seeming contradiction is not so difficult as it may seem at first. In the first place, it is not correct that the dreamer always knows about his dream. Frequently, objective sensory stimuli release an affect of anxiety in the sleeper, which can be noticed from his meaningful signs, while the dream that gives notice of the emotional modification of the stimulus is not remembered. On the other hand, analysis of the traumatic experience could show us unconscious material that we did not expect.

We have said it was not the somatic stimulus as such that justified Maury's anxiety, but the fantasy released by the stimulus. The importance of the stimulus, as the releasing factor, is undoubted, but it is comparable to that of the spark that falls into a powder keg. We say that Maury's old fantasy, "wakened" by the sensory stimulus, is a typical one, the core of which anyone familiar with psychoanalysis will recognize as a castration fantasy. It is this latent meaning of the fantasy that justifies the extent of anxiety. The perception of the stimulus has caused the conjuring up of an old fantasy which, while it originated in infantile complexes, made contact with the reading of the adult.

Only the fantasy of the guillotine, however, is admissible into consciousness, while the castration fantasy, which lies behind it, explains the intense fright. One might say that the idea of being guillotined had once, while he was awake, made momentary contact in Maury with the unconscious castration idea of the child and the anxiety connected with it. It is this anxiety that reappears in the dream.

The physical sensation as the small board struck was only the "stimulus" that mobilized this old unconscious anxiety. The stimulus then caused a psychic modification that brought up thought-material which shows this infantile anxiety in analytically transparent covering, indestructible and effective in the emotional life of the adult. The fright is only in part explained by the sudden influx of stimulus. It is really a "fright in thought" as Freud called it in *Interpretation of Dreams.** This intensity of anxiety can be understood by the fact that the dreamer has gone back to old, repressed material. It is as if the small board, in striking the body, reminded him of that unconscious fantasy, as if it were its realization.

* Collected Works (*Gesammelte Schriften*), Vol. II, p. 385.

There is no doubt as to the significance of this unconscious fantasy for the degree of affective intensity. I can use the report of an English physician, Dr. Brunton, of one of his cases, rather than numerous examples explaining this role. In this report, the shock and the fright effect of a weak somatic stimulus stands out boldly because of an anticipatory thought.* The students at an English college had come to hate one of the assistant instructors. They decided to frighten him and prepared an execution block and hatchet in a dark room. Then they seized the instructor and led him before a group of black-robed students who posed as judges. When the assistant instructor saw this arrangement he thought it was a joke. But the students assured him that they were quite serious about it. They told him they were going to decapitate him on the spot. They blindfolded him, pressed him to his knees and forced his head onto the block. One of them simulated the sound of a swinging hatchet; another dropped a wet towel on the instructor's neck. When the blindfold was removed, he was dead.

3

Returning to our earlier example and a description of its consequences, we find that Mr. A. Maury was a twenty-three-year-old student of jurisprudence and medicine, who took a walk in the year 1840 on the Rue Rivoli, not expecting any surprise attack or accident, but feeling in good spirits. Suddenly a small board fell from a scaffold, striking the back of his neck and he dropped to the ground. He did not suffer any major injury, but there soon appeared the symptoms of a traumatic neurosis. Accelerated pulse, abnormal excitability of the system of the cardiac nerves, increased blood pressure, hypnalgesia, abnormalities of secretion, differences between pupils, disturbances of locomotion and vision, etc., were

* From Dr. R. Liertz, *Harmonien und Disharmonien des menschlichen Trie bund Geisteslebens*. (Harmonies and Disharmonies of Human Instinctual and Mental Life) Leipzig, 1925, p. 196.

found beyond doubt by the *Médecine des Hôpitaux*. There is no reason why we should not assume that myotonoclonica tropidans and Oppenheim's akinesia amnestica were present in classical completeness.*

It is easy to prove in this example the significance of the fright factor of the surprise. It seems to me that merely pointing to it is not enough to make more understandable the eruption through the protective barrier in this case of traumatic neurosis. There must be something specific in this fright to help explain the pathological reaction. Let us again compare psychologically the situation of Maury as he was struck by an arousal stimulus in the dream and by an accident. The stimulus had the effect of reminding the sleeping man of something—the complete imaginary picture. This turned out to be—it can hardly be said any other way—a novel with the strong effect of castration as the dominant theme.

In the arousal dream of Napoleon as quoted by Freud, and in similar dreams known to every analyst, there is found the peculiar effect which Egger, in his discussion of Maury's dream, characterized as "l'effet rétrospectif et rétroactif de la sensation." We found that an old anxiety, in becoming a present one, was the especially frightening factor in the arousal stimulus. That old anxiety was, in this case, the castration anxiety which was aroused by a sudden external stimulus.*

* The special literature about traumatic neuroses offers numerous examples of similar situations in which the disease originated. We take from Oppenheim's *Textbook of Nervous Diseases*, Sixth Edition, Second Volume, Page 1938, just this statement: "but any other injury, even those concerning only a peripheral part of the body—neck, feet, etc.—engender the disease. . . . For instance, several times I saw serious neuroses after a violent plunge, or blow against the tip of a finger or, also, after a finger had been squeezed for some time." The biographical data concerning A. Maury, I found in the article *"La durée apparente des rêves"* by Victor Egger in *Revue Philosophique,* 1895. This author reports on page 45, *"le rêve de la c'était l'epoque ou il étudiait simultanément le droit, la médecine et en général, toutes les sciences."* Unfortunately, I have not been able to find more exact biographical data of significance about Maury, in spite of a diligent search in the libraries of Paris.

* The significance of castration anxiety for the development of the traumatic neuroses has already been described by Sadger. Simmel's experiences, too, testify to this connection, not easily recognizable to the non-analyst.

We believe that something of that kind occurs in the situation of the group of traumatic neuroses we are discussing. The specific character of the fright consists in the impression of an old unconscious anxiety suddenly becoming a present one, even though this specific character may afterwards turn out to be part of a more general psychic attitude. It is not a dreaded situation that becomes entirely clear materially, but a sudden real impression which has the capacity of reawakening through memory all of the unconscious anxiety. An insignificant material stimulus (as in a dream of the type of Maury's) has sufficed to revive certain old thought-content and to make affects tied to it reawaken in their full force.

That no material realization of an old unconscious fantasy takes place, but only one in thoughts should be emphasized because it implies a psychically reinforcing effect. This may be compared with the fact that an illusion frequently releases stronger emotional effects than a direct and exact representation. This character of illusion is peculiar to the situation. A traumatic situation of this kind presents itself, therefore, in the following manner: it is as if (I emphasize, as if), suddenly, in an unexpected manner, something we once dreaded and then disclaimed and banned from our thoughts became real. The dark disaster, which we unconsciously expected, is suddenly at hand.

Take the case of an unforeseen railroad collision. The content of the unprepared traveler's fright would be an old unconscious expectation of disaster in his own life becoming actual. The strong impression of the shake-up in the collision has been left to unconscious modification for a matter of seconds. There it has reactivated those old apprehensions which had been rampant in the dark. Something unknown, suddenly impinging as a threat in one's life, had been known unconsciously for a long time, but was estranged. Something that had been unconsciously expected seems to become reality at the very moment when one was not thinking of it. We understand this to mean that a submerged psychic reality with the character of anxiety is suddenly transformed into a present reality, a process comparable to the sudden removal of a resistance due to repression. Cause and connection of this psychic process are supplied by a material occurrence, namely, the traumatic event. This piece of undoubted reality gives the character of reality to the whole experience. A certain unconscious process has returned unexpectedly. This return is not tied to an instinctual process, but to an external event. The traumatic event appears like an unconscious confirmation of the justification of that old anxiety.

How did the expectation of disaster evolve, the confirmation of which we unconsciously comprehend as the traumatic event? It appeared in each of us as an emotional reaction caused by unconscious impulses. The expectation of disaster had been caused by the repression of these strong tendencies. It was later, along with its psychic motivation, drawn secondarily into the unconscious. The fact that the dark, apparently irrational, feeling of imminent disaster could not be reconciled with normal human intelligence, with common sense, which had consciously long ago discarded the belief in a mysteriously punishing power, may have contributed to that result.

It is now as if that punishment we unconsciously dreaded were suddenly at hand. It stalks us in an unprepared moment. A day like any other has transformed itself suddenly into a *"dies irae, dies illa."* But from where did the dreaded disaster come? It is easy to answer this question, if we remember that our psychic life reverts in the traumatic moment to obsolete, animistic ways of thinking. We have been accustomed to consider ourselves the masters of our will. Our motions have obeyed our intentions. Suddenly we sense unexpectedly the working of an unknown force without recognizing where it originates. It is suddenly here as if a powerful hand lifted us, shocked us, pulled us or threw us down however it pleased.

A primitive psychic reaction, which we never overcome completely, causes us to trace back unconsciously to higher powers, originally to parents, everything overwhelming that happens to us, that we experience passively. A similar reaction forces us to consider unconsciously everything threatening and horrible we experience, as a punishment coming from those sources. As we know, we later acknowledge natural forces or fate as our masters, but in the background of our unconscious there still stands the father or the mother whose will impinged upon our life in early days. We had felt that we were the masters of our ego and now suddenly we come to feel a power which causes us to recognize, with the speed of lightning, our entire impotency and helplessness.

The connection of fright and self-confidence and narcissistic libido now becomes clear. In the experiencing of the shock, the established ego has suddenly come to feel a threatening power of fate, as that of a father-substitute. It has been overpowered by the superego reprojected into the external world. Shock appears as the result of an expression of force or rather of will, of that mysterious power with paternal character. The adult who, otherwise, would certainly look back at his childhood beliefs half compassionately, half contemptuously, reacts to this sudden overthrow like a surprised, intimidated child who, conscious of guilt, waits for the sudden appearance of his strict father from whom he expects punishment.

4

We have found reason to supplement in a certain direction Freud's evaluation of fright as a factor in the etiology of the traumatic neuroses. We believe that in many cases a definite fright is released when an old repressed expectation of disaster seems to become actual. The factor of surprise remains fully valid also in our hypothesis. It undergoes, however, a displacement and now concerns something once dreaded by us which suddenly seems to become a reality in changed form or under changed circumstances. This may perhaps be the general psychological nature of fright.

A second, though small, revision of Freud's concept appears necessary. He points out that fright is the condition that takes hold of us when we face a danger without preparation. The absence of anxiety-preparedness is the characteristic of fright. This certainly seems correct. But it seems to follow from our description that preparedness for anxiety cannot be completely absent. How can this description be reconciled with Freud's concept? We feel that there is truth in Freud's characterization of fright through the lack of preparedness for anxiety, but we have seen in fright all the traits of a resumption of an old unconscious anxiety. If our opinion does justice to the actual psychic processes, then in most cases an over-powering anxiety is suddenly aroused. This anxiety is by no means justified by the real incident, at the moment of the accident. The external impression is subjected to an unconscious modification.

The difference of opinion is certainly not unbridgeable. Freud's description concerns conscious preparedness for anxiety. This preparedness is certainly absent in a traumatic situation. But it is possible that an unconscious, a free-floating anxiety, so to speak, lives in almost all of us which has nothing to do with an expectation of immediately imminent actual dangers.

A differentiation that occurred to me elsewhere seems to be of possible use here. I thought I should generally keep apart fore-anxiety and end-anxiety, these expressions being used in analogy to Freud's fore-pleasure and end-pleasure.* Fore-anxiety is the psychic preparation for an approaching external or internal danger, not merely a warning sign, but a primitive attempt at a first conquest of the danger. Fore-anxiety might also be called a rehearsal of the dreaded situation for conquest. End-anxiety is the reaction in squarely facing the situation of danger.

Fright has, it seems to me, the character of end-anxiety, which through the absence of fore-anxiety, assumes special intensity and emotional power. Preparedness for anxiety is really absent in fright insofar as the present unexpected situation of danger is concerned. In its place, the old anxiety-preparedness has suddenly become present, having originated not merely as a psychic reaction to actual intense hostile impulses. This free-floating anxiety readily interprets the sudden shock as the beginning of approaching punishment. We see here fore-anxiety has a special function. It seems to alleviate the end-anxiety and aims at protecting the indi-

* *Compulsion to Confess and Need for Punishment*, 1926. (See Part Two of this volume.)

vidual from the full impact of the anxiety-preparedness of former times. It refers him only to the present situation of danger.

Its double function would, therefore, be this: to eliminate and overcome psychically as much as possible the old anxiety-preparedness and to limit or reduce it to a present one. The limitation of anxiety to the present situation is, thus, equivalent to a reduction of its intensity. It is as though we had deprived it of a sounding board. Regression to the old, free-floating anxiety has the same effect as an increase of intensity. It is, therefore, not a minus but a plus anxiety that breaks through in the traumatic neuroses. The force of the external factor does not alone cause this abundance of anxiety, but also the regression to early anxiety released by this factor, the anxiety that brings fear of castration or of death at the hands of the father.

In addition to the other factors, this one is of decisive importance for the quantity and quality of the individual's reaction to the traumatic situation. The lack of fore-anxiety engendered a psychic short circuit, as it were, connecting the oncoming stimulus immediately and directly with the deepest emotional strata. It seems really as if all of us were provided with a larger or smaller measure of free-floating anxiety connected with our unconscious feeling of guilt, as if the fear of danger could, in certain cases, take recourse in moral anxiety, the core of which we know to be castration anxiety. A certain part of this anxiety is released when danger is imminent, and it appears as fore-anxiety, situated before end-anxiety.

Fore-anxiety gives, in a way, a warranty or security against the end-anxiety's becoming too intense, or, if you will, against the impetuous, ego-overpowering emergence of that deep unconscious anxiety of our childhood. Besides the intensity of stimuli, it is the time factor that modifies the normal course of anxiety in the traumatic experience. The suddenness of the eruption of the stimulus prevents the development of fore-anxiety, and, therefore, of protection against an encroachment on the realm of unconscious anxiety. It also causes the swift interpretation, or rather comprehension, of the invading stimulus as if by instinct, in the sense of that old expectation of disaster. It has already been pointed out

by psychoanalysis that symptoms are formed in order to retrieve
and master anxiety, to convert it into small change, as it were.
From our discussion, we are forced to conclude that anxiety re-
trieved in the symptoms of traumatic neuroses has the character of
fore-anxiety.

We can see that by this roundabout way we have arrived at a
supplement to Freud's theory of traumatic neuroses, which leaves
its core intact, but which modifies its husk at a certain point. The
theory of the protective barrier against stimuli in traumatic neurosis is intact, but in many cases the protective barrier seems to us to
be of a special kind, as it gives protection from the primal anxiety.
The mechanisms of anxiety form the protective barrier here,
which, in the traumatic neuroses, is broken into. In an indefinite
number of cases of this illness, the ego suspects the other menace,
as it were, behind the external danger, as if the danger implicit in
the external situation gave cause for a reactivation of the ego's
hidden fear of the superego. In the depth of these cases, it makes
no difference in the development of a fear of death whether or not
there is real danger to life in the traumatic situation. In many
cases, fear of death develops even though there is no sufficient
cause for it in reality. According to Freud, fear of death occurs
between ego and superego.* For an instant, the ego sees itself
abandoned by the superego. The security of being loved and protected, which has unconsciously accompanied us since childhood,
has disappeared. Metaphorically and often literally, the ground
has been pulled out from under our feet and that allows us, for
moments, to plunge into emptiness.

5

It follows from the preceding discussion that in the traumatic
situation, a sudden disturbance of the narcissistic libidinal situation takes place. The shock has suddenly broken through the relatively great independence from the superego which the ego had

* *The Ego and the Id. Gesammelte Schriften,* Vol. VI.

attained. It is as if the ego were unexpectedly, and in a drastic way, reminded of the superego's power, projected outward as fate. This reminder, however, has a definite direction: that of punishment. This sudden disturbance of the narcissistic position of the ego has been especially emphasized by Abraham.

We see similarities and differences between these arousal dreams that end in anxious waking, and those situations in which traumatic neuroses originate. There takes place, in both, a resumption of old impressions that have become unconscious. This resumption marks an act of emotional return and is called "*régression enforcée*" by the French psychologists. In the arousal dreams, the somatic stimulus is used for modification in the dream, reactivating old, imagined anxiety situations. In the situations engendering traumatic neuroses, it is also the external stimulus that causes resumption of an unconscious anxiety.

The differences are determined mainly by the decisive circumstances of the external situation. The wish to sleep undoubtedly functions as a reinforced protective barrier if the stimulus is not too strong when a waking is then forced. In this case, the wish to sleep can cause, at least, a delay of the anxiety effect. This factor coincides with the injection of a fore-anxiety, although abbreviated. Furthermore, it seems likely that the sleeper's doubt as to the material reality of the stimulus may have an effect which would cause him to ask if he were conscious: "Am I asleep or awake? Am I dreaming or is it real? Do I have to wake up because of it or can I go on sleeping?*

* No ghost needs to rise from the tomb of the old psychology of the conscious to remind us that these forms of expression are foreign to the dream. We know that, strictly speaking, we are using the wrong language, taken from the realm of consciousness, in characterizing the function of the dream as that of wish-fulfillment. Actually, we should repeat this every time: if it were possible to describe, in the language of the conscious, the psychic processes of the dream, we should have to state that something goes on in the dreamer's emotional life that we can only comprehend as this or that wish. But the objection made by philosophers cannot touch at the essence of the analytic theories. The psychoanalyst can no more be made responsible for the inadequacy and scantiness of human language than for so many other inadequacies with which he is taxed.

We should turn here to an objection which seems seriously to endanger our hypothesis. Most authors who have published their observations about traumatic neuroses have noted that the reactions of the victims of accidents quickly set in and fulfill their purpose. We cannot ignore the significance of this argument by pointing to the fact that in some cases this quick and adequate reaction is missing, that a paralyzing horror seems to prevent the individual from all action. In the majority of cases, it has been shown convincingly that the reaction sets in quickly and purposefully. Of course, it is possible that flight or other appropriate measures are resorted to as a reflex, similar to the way animals behave when confronted by sudden danger. That reflex would set in without necessarily excluding the great anxiety affect.

We should see clearly that this does not concern the essence of the question. This we understand when we keep in mind the importance of the time factor. There may be only seconds between the perception of the stimulus and the individual's reaction, but this is enough time for a preconscious recognition of the true nature of the stimulus, enough time for the stimulus to be, as it were, tentatively put in its proper place, according to individual experience, and perhaps for appropriate measures to be taken reflexively. The continuing effect of anxiety in depth is thus by no means excluded. It takes place as though on another psychic plane. It may be that recognition and evaluation of the real situation or its comparison with analogous situations known by the individual occur in the pre-conscious system, while the unconscious clings to the infantile affective comprehension of the situation. The judgment adjusted to reality would, thus, leave untouched the affects due to deeper causes. In this way, the anxiety affect would be cut off only as far as the upper strata of the emotional life are concerned. This process would be comparable to one of defense in the face of vital necessities. Here a strong affect is really squeezed in, as it would be expressed in Breuer-Freud's old theory of hysteria. It cannot be discharged emotionally. Its effects will, however, come to the fore later.

6

Once more I shall discuss the fright factor in the etiology of traumatic neuroses, in order to make a few remarks on the side, as if to show some paths branching off at this point. Considering again our attempt to explain the specific fright in the situation in which this neurosis originates, we recognize this fright as related to another, a fright felt in the face of impressions we call sinister or uncanny. Or rather, there is a sinister element contained in experiencing traumatic impressions that lead to accident-neurosis.

The uncanny factor of an experience evolves, according to Freud, from the revival of repressed infantile complexes either through an impression, or from an apparent, renewed confirmation of obsolete primitive beliefs. Freud points out that these two species of the uncanny cannot always be precisely separated because primitive convictions are rooted in infantile complexes. It seems to me that here the outlines of a bridge can be recognized, unclear at first, a bridge which leads from the analytic explanation of the uncanny experience to the exploration of the fright, so significant a factor in the origin of traumatic neurosis. We have recognized the revival of repressed infantile complexes and the apparent confirmation of obsolete views in the regression to unconscious anxiety and its hidden meaning. These features, it seems, are common to both kinds of experience.

We know, however, that there are special differences between the experience of an uncanny impression and that of impressions that can lead to a traumatic neurosis. It is easy to see that even though there may be an uncanny element in the traumatic situation, it is not essential. Likewise, the experience of such impressions may often be followed by traumatic neuroses, but it need not necessarily have this result. Therefore, the thought-contents of the uncanny element and of those impressions that lead to traumatic neuroses are, as such, independent of each other. They coincide, however, at a certain point.

I have shown that the disparity between the impressions coming from outside determines the kind of emotional reaction. This answer, being too general, can scarcely satisfy us. We merely emphasize two factors in order to appreciate the psychological differences, factors essential for the formation of traumatic neuroses, but not for the appearance of the uncanny element. They are the impression of danger immediately threatening our life and the suddenness, the surprise of the traumatic experience that excludes anxiety-preparedness and fore-anxiety.

Only in a very few cases is an imminent danger or a threat to life connected with these impressions we call sinister or uncanny. When, at twilight, we think we see a picture come to life and step towards us out of its frame, it still does not mean, beyond doubt, that our life is in danger. Even if it seems to threaten us, we still do not feel a bodily thrust, slap or hit originating from the mysterious picture, and the testing for reality helps us to overcome the anxiety. In experiencing something sinister, the doubt as to the material reality of the content of the experience is a protection against the traumatic effect. But a person who feels in the traumatic accident a severe shock to his own body cannot doubt the reality of his experience, of his sensation.*

When the uncanny element appears suddenly, and has beyond any doubt the character of reality, seems to cause real danger to life, and is, possibly by accident, connected with a strong mechanical shock, then, indeed a traumatic neurosis can develop with all its clinical characteristics. In that case, the experience of something sinister has assumed a traumatic character. This is shown in many

---

* One of my patients reports that soon after his father's death, when he woke at night from deep sleep, he had the extraordinarily lively impression of his father in a vagabond's clothes, standing at his bed. At the same time his knowledge of his father's having died was present. In interpreting this report, I assume it was the echo of a dream. When the patient was still a wild and obstinate boy, his father often called angrily to his mother, "Throw out the little vagabond!" That hallucination was certainly an extraordinarily uncanny impression to which the patient reacted with strong anxiety, palpitations and trembling. Although the patient stressed time and again the liveliness of the vision, a doubt as to its reality must have remained, because the patient

instances in neurological literature. Mechanical shock seems to be an essential factor in an accident with traumatic effect. Freud pointed out that mechanical shock must be recognized as one of the sources of sexual excitation. The mechanical power probably frees that quantity of sexual excitation which becomes traumatically effective because of the absence of preparation for anxiety. As I said earlier, the directness and the character of reality in the experience are enhanced by the mechanical shock.

The other factor, which causes a difference between experiencing something sinister and experiencing the details of an accident, is that of suddenness, of surprise. A stranger, who spends the night in a castle that he is told is haunted, is psychically prepared for the emergence of uncanny sensations. If, in the night, he hears a peculiar knock on the wall, or thinks he does, he is, possibly through fore-anxiety, protected against a traumatic effect. In other cases, a general emotional atmosphere with a sinister effect is sufficient psychic preparation for experiencing a special sinister impression or feeling its effect. All this is, of course, true only where a special psychic disposition does not exist to conceive of something as sinister.

I do not intend to state all the differences between both qualities of experience. What has been said is enough for our purposes. We find that experiencing an uncanny impression under certain rare conditions such as suddenness, mechanical shock or imminent danger to life can bring about a traumatic neurosis. It is more important to keep in mind that the experiences which evoke a trau-

---

pinched himself hard on the cheeks and pulled his hair to convince himself as to whether he was asleep or awake. A doubt of this kind, which still requires confirmation through one's own bodily sensations, is excluded in a traumatic accident because of the evidence of the bodily sensations. But the doubt can appear afterwards. The assumption is perhaps justified that the unpleasure of mechanical shock came about through the reversal of effect of the pleasure which the child feels when passively moved, as when lifted, put down, etc. In tracing this psychological development, one may perhaps be led back all the way to the intrauterine condition. *Beyond the Pleasure-Principle,* Gesammelte Schriften, Vol. VI, p. 222.

matic effect in accident-neurosis would not have this power over us if we did not unconsciously perceive something uncanny in them. I believe that I characterized the essence of this sinister element in the discussion of the specific anxiety in traumatic neurosis.

It seems doubtful to me whether a traumatic neurosis could have come about if this element were missing. It may, on first sight, appear strange or even absurd to assume that in accidents of everyday life, on the level of a high civilization and of world-dominating technical achievements, there should exist such a thing as an uncanny experience. However, we say that they are percéived by the people concerned only in such a manner as to release in the unconscious the well-known *reaction* to something sinister or uncanny. Technical progress is of very little importance to the unconscious in man. The recognition of the force of hidden powers may manifest itself in an accident caused by a machine or in a railroad crash, as well as in an event caused by earth tremors or other natural catastrophes. What we maintain is that those traumatic experiences have a character peculiar to them which we would consciously call uncanny. This is experienced so, regardless of whether a soldier has been buried by a grenade, or a traveler thrown from his seat in a train collision, or lightning has, out of the blue, struck close to somebody taking a walk. As times are, it may not be superfluous to note here that the word "sinister" is meant to describe the emotional reaction of the person concerned in the traumatic situation, not at all to signify an acknowledgment of higher powers at work.*

* Psychoanalysis has described how these higher powers are psychologically conceived. Questions concerning a conception of the world (*Weltanschauung*) are not the business of scientific research. We have nothing to do here with metaphysical problems. It is only the statement of facts which we pointed out, that continuance of our psychic dependence deep into maturity, strictly speaking, until the end of our lives. A statement of this kind can hardly be used to consider those old beliefs eternal or unshakeable. If an opinion may be expressed here, it should rather give cause to wonder how little the crown of creation, as man likes to call himself, has outdistanced the rest of the mammals.

7

Everywhere in the discussion of the original causes of traumatic neurosis we come across the importance of the factor of suddenness and surprise. It would, no doubt, be bold, but by no means hopeless, at this point, to try to comprehend the nature of surprise in general. Fright is, of course, only a special case of suprise. But one could be justified in considering an expectation that has become unconscious to be a surprise, an expectation that we face in reality at an unexpected time, under changed conditions, or in a form not easily recognizable.* Then the surprise would be the expression of a difficulty in recognizing something long known that has become unconscious. It might even signify the degree of emotional expenditure required for the identification of something that has become unconscious. Strictly speaking, surprise should be defined as a defensive reaction directed against the suggestion to forget about what is habitual and to rediscover the oldest in the new.

It is clear that in this way the psychology of the reception of new impressions gains a changed aspect. Perhaps there is, according to the words of the sage, really nothing new under the sun—that is, psychologically speaking, and that we would not be able to grasp and understand anything absolutely new. Only in making a connection with something long known, but not necessarily conscious, can we absorb it at all, making it our own.

The long known does not have to be limited to ontogenesis. The strongest impression of early acquired or inherited fragments of knowledge can be gained in the analysis of certain traits of infantile experience. Freud, in the discussion of a case of childhood neurosis, arrives at the opinion that some kind of knowledge, difficult to determine, something "like a preparation for the understanding in the modification of early experiences in the small

* There exists also a "joyful" fright. That is the emotional reaction felt when something we once hoped for, but in which we can no longer believe, suddenly becomes reality.

child" must have some effect. (*Gesammelte Schriften,* Vol. VIII, page 566.)

In the sexual enlightenment of the child, for instance, one can scarcely escape the impression that, in a way, it always comes too late. This reminds one of something a Viennese lady, well-known for her malapropisms, said after she had attended the opening night of a drama: "The play is very beautiful, but it is not suitable for a première." The resistance psychoanalysis has found in the world is based mainly on the rejection of repressed knowledge, a reaction which comes from well-known affective sources.

The bewilderment with which we face new insights is an emotional reaction which consists in the difficulty of recognizing something known long ago that has become unconscious. This concerns new scientific truths as well as errors. All learning is, in a way, an anagnorisis of an unconscious kind. It only seems paradoxical, but really is not, when Goethe says, "Everybody learns only what he can." A psychologically oriented pedagogy would certainly come to practical conclusions from a well-considered conscious use of these analytic insights.

Along similar lines, I attempted to explain the emotional reactions to foreign deities, cults and rites in *"Der eigene und der fremde Gott,"* published in 1923. Exploration of the psychological nature of surprise should become fruitful also for the science of esthetics, widening in a definite direction our understanding of artistic creation and enjoyment. A narrative keeps us in suspense if it arouses our unconscious anticipatory ideas and fulfills them in an unexpected manner or under unexpected circumstances. It has certainly been observed that in a play we feel that surprise is unnatural and uncalled for if we have not been unconsciously prepared for it in some way. Suppose that in a realistic play, at one point, one of the main characters is suddenly stricken by a heart attack during a bridge party, but the audience has not been prepared in any way, through preceding remarks, for the illness or the occurrence of such an event. If there is any dramatic effect here at all, it certainly will be only a superficial one, similar to one we feel when a picture falls from the wall. The effect would be deeper if the audience, in an inconspicuous way, had been informed of a previous illness or earlier fainting spells of the person. This technique of allusion has an even deeper effect than if the audience has been prepared for the possibility of the dramatic moment in a clumsy and conspicuous way.

We generally say that the death of a relative or a friend has a less shocking effect upon us if we have been prepared for it, perhaps by a long illness. That is correct. But the shock is the greater and more lasting if we had once thought of that possibility, repressed the expectation (or wish) and then suddenly receive, "unprepared," the news of the death of the person who was close to us. From this angle, too, light is shed upon the psychological problem of shock and fright.

8

Returning to the heart of our topic, we should like to emphasize once again that it is a definite fright which frequently makes its psychic effectiveness felt in traumatic neurosis. It is the fright that we feel when a danger, which we once unconsciously expected and which we thought we had escaped, suddenly becomes reality. We believe that in many cases this effectiveness would be far from so great were it not for a deeper resonance it receives from our unconscious feeling of guilt.

In support of this opinion, I shall mention several factors pointed out by those authors who have studied traumatic and war neuroses. The fact is emphasized that an injury or wound suffered at the same time as the traumatic event occurred, tends, in most cases, to prevent the development of a neurosis. It is actually as though a wound, hence, a punishment, the equivalent of castration, had replaced the fright that was psychically modified only later, and had gratified the person's unconscious feeling of guilt or his masochism. This is comparable to cases in which people are spared neurosis if they fall ill organically, or if they enter an unhappy marriage, etc.

In this manner, the euphoric mood, which can be considered maniacal, exhibited by many war-injured persons after shock, may also be explained, without excluding the strength of other ideas like that of returning home, safety from renewed danger of death, etc. These people have paid their tribute. Now nothing more can happen to them. They have escaped, as it were, with a black eye. Our conception would also explain, in part, the conspicuous fact that, in contradiction to the analytic dream theory, the dream takes the victim of an accident-neurosis back, time and again, into the traumatic situation. Freud said that these dreams retrieve the mastery over stimuli and develop the anxiety, the omission of which was the cause of the traumatic neurosis.

These dreams help in this way to fulfill the primary task which must be fulfilled before the pleasure-principle can dominate. This view is not contradicted when we mention, as a more special addition, the fact that these dreams represent reactions to the re-awakened feeling of guilt. They are actually the wish-fulfillment of unconscious feelings of guilt reacting to repudiated, sadistic instinctual impulses.* This would compel us to consider the dreams of victims of accident-neurosis close to the punishment-dreams that gratify the masochistic tendencies of the individual.

We intended to treat here of only one of the psychoanalytically comprehensible aspects of shock and fright. But we should remember that there exist, besides it, other emotional factors not discussed, the significance of which we should not underestimate. It should, I hope, be accepted without objection if the attempt is made here to trace one single thread in a multicolored fabric.

It will be kept in mind that there are, in addition to it, many others and that the total impression results only from their simultaneous effects.

---

* Freud himself had already considered this concept possible when he said, "if we have not become uncertain of the wish-fulfilling tendency of the dream through the dreams of the victims of accident-neurosis, we could still resort to the assumption that in this condition, the function of the dream has been shaken as so much else, and deflected from its intentions. Or we would have to remember the mysterious masochistic tendencies of the ego."

II

Sexual Desire and a Feeling of Guilt

Recently two psychoanalytic authors had a scientific discussion in the columns of the *International Journal of Psychoanalysis* concerning "Need for Punishment and the Neurotic Process." In a clear and unequivocal manner, Wilhelm Reich pointed out the significance of an accumulation of libido in the etiology of neuroses in contrast to the secondary demands of the need for punishment. His presentations were so lucid that in several points they appeared to be irrefutable statements of facts, almost to the degree of banality. Take, for instance, the sentence that "man's morality is never on so firm a foundation as his immorality, and that one thinks one is moral where basically one is merely afraid of the consequences of a deed." This statement is true beyond doubt and not only the analyst, but any somewhat introspective young teen-age girl is more than capable of saying something about the confusion between morality and "fear of consequences."

Franz Alexander, in his perceptive and justified defense against Reich's attacks, found himself goaded into making several statements that arouse our protest. He points out as one of his fundamental ideas, that the morality of the neurotic superego is a "corrupt and formal one" and that in condemning it he does not mean "genuine morality." It is rather difficult to discriminate between corrupt, formal morality and genuine, strong morality. I would refrain from daring to speak with certainty in these matters in a world in which no evaluation is in the least comparable to the certainty that, in a foreseeable time, green grass will grow over our graves.

My small contribution towards the solution of these problems will start from this discussion, without joining it. I do not intend to do so because, among other reasons, I do not believe the contrasts to be irreconcilable. The primacy of the damming-up of libido is maintained even if the significance of the unconscious need for punishment is recognized. The small segment of the body of problems which I am trying to delimit here is highlighted by a statement of mine that concerns the problems discussed and that, since it was made, has evoked strong protests. This statement says that in a number of neurotic cases the influence of the feeling of guilt increases the libido and deepens the instinctual gratification.

Some psychologists argue that the facts do not bear out this process and that sufficient instinctual gratification exists without the feeling of guilt. I had meekly to agree, but I also reminded them of the possibility that what they protested had perhaps once in the course of the history of science been stated by somebody, but certainly not by me. If somebody says that there are also brown horses and that they, too, are used for riding and pulling, he does not, by saying this, dispute the existence and usefulness of white, black and dun-colored horses.

Some of my physician friends objected to my statement that libido is a border concept between the somatic and the psychic and that my assertion of an increase of libido defies all physiological laws. This, of course, was a realm where I could not follow them. I could not follow them, it is true, but, alas, neither could they lead the way. What is known about the physiology of libidinal processes is of little use for the explanation of the problem from this angle. Much of what I have gathered about the nature of libido from physiological points of view has certainly left a strong impression with me, but this impression was not always unequivocal. Some of the statements of this science which is so proud of its precision have exhibited a wealth of imagination that would have shamed our greatest poets.

Following Freud's lead, we have all found that the feeling of guilt inhibits instinctual gratification. Every day of our analytical practice shows us again that, as Alexander expressed it so well, "all that reduces moral anxiety enhances instinctual gratification." We know that accumulation of libido, primarily deriving from the influences of the external world and of the ego, can be determined simultaneously also by the factor of a feeling of guilt. But it seems to me that in analytical literature we have not sufficiently emphasized that in many cases damming-up of libido has a reactive effect upon the feeling of guilt.

One would really expect the reverse to be true. A person who was able to ward off the onrush of his instinctual impulses to an unusually large extent should feel in full possession of his self-confidence or of satisfaction with himself and his energy, since he is free from guilt and fault. This happens sometimes when ability to sublimate is especially great and libidinal economy extraordinarily good. In the majority of neuroses, however, and in most character deformations which we see, we observe something peculiar: repression does not succeed, yet the feeling of guilt grows, and under certain circumstances, it assumes an emotional power which combines with that of the repressed drives. Even though the symptom has the character of a substitute gratification, it does not gratify to a sufficient degree.

The analytic explanation of this situation is simple. The feeling of guilt does not concern the action, but concerns the endopsychically recognized danger of temptation and it grows with that danger. The accumulation of libido enhances the unconscious temptation which is stronger than that in actual gratification of a drive. The temptation on one hand, the anxiety connected with it on the other, and the feeling of guilt become more urgent and more impetuous. Reich and Alexander each pointed out another aspect of this psychic process. Actually, both factors, the accumulation of libido and the feeling of guilt, work together. Their motto might be expressed, "March separately and unite to hit the ego."

In many cases of neurosis, we can see that both factors unite while still on the march, as it were, for the common aim. The ego fights the damming-up of libido and resorts to the superego for help. To the increased demands of the superego again correspond increased instinctual demands which are to be held down. These instinctual demands provoke punishment from the superego, until finally, as in obsessional neuroses and in masochism, both demands are gratified simultaneously. There results, then, the seemingly paradoxical psychological connection in which, for instance, the feeling of guilt concerning sex, of the ascetic who lives in chastity in the desert, is by far stronger than that, say, of the habitué of the Moulin Rouge. It would be definitely wrong to derive this difference only from that between the different moral demands of the two types, and to consider only the divergencies between the philosophies of life responsible for this difference.

Another determinant is, indeed, the difference between the expenditure of repression and the extent of instinctual gratification. Sometimes, however, it seems that the person who yields lazily to his instincts develops a far lesser feeling of guilt than the one who resists them. Repression creates the semblance of a dangerous and sweeping power of instinctual impulses which had not been felt originally.

Absence of gratification shrouds the love-objects with magic and endows them in our imagination with a dangerousness that is by no means their attribute otherwise. For the priest, a woman's embrace may be compared to a hunter's trap—"*laqueis venaterum*" —and he warns us urgently that any wickedness is small compared with woman's—"*brevis omnis malitia super malitiam mulieris.*" To a ladies' man, the arms of a woman are simply parts of a human body slightly fragrant with "*Nuit de Noel,*" and woman's "wickedness," a matter of course which arouses in him neither resentment nor astonishment. Warnings of the power and dangerousness of women can be found less in night clubs, where they might be appropriate, than in monasteries where women are considered "*instrumenta diaboli.*" Nature has endowed sex with greater power over St. Hieronymus, who flees from his fantasies into the desert only to succumb to them there, half starved and parched, than ever she endows the admirer of the ballerinas. The great service of culture and religion to sexuality is still not enough acknowledged. They have enhanced sexual gratification by their having marked it as sin. Remove girdle and veil and the pleasant illusion is gone. Girdle and veil are, therefore, eminently erotogenic means.

Modesty, then, not only represses the sexual impulses. It also preserves them, indeed, deepens them.

"This sherbet is good. How good it would be if it were a sin to eat it," says the Neapolitan woman. This remark reminds us again of the statement which emphasizes strengthening of libido and deepening of sexual gratification by the influence of the unconscious feeling of guilt.

Our experiences so far show that reduction of the unconscious feeling of guilt opens the path to instinctual satisfaction, as pointed out recently by both Reich and Alexander. That certainly is correct and of decisive significance but it comprises only part of the psychic processes hitherto recognizable. In a considerable number of cases, I have observed that this overcoming of the unconscious feeling of guilt soothes and reduces the excessively driving force. It is as though the dynamics of the analytic process have set in on two opposite sides, as though they create changes and displacements on various levels. The liberation from a feeling of guilt weakens the libidinal instinctual force. This effect can be explained, particularly in those cases in which the feeling of guilt contributes to the intensification of sexual desire. Does that imply a contrast to our experience according to which everything that reduces moral anxiety enhances instinctual gratification? By no means, as this remains true in all cases, and is confirmed time and again by the recuperative process.

It is a contrast insofar as it can be shown that in certain cases an increase of moral anxiety can force sexual gratification. In the analysis of the cases discussed here, it was found that certain sexual experiences of early childhood and of puberty were kept in such pleasurable memory because, in addition to all other factors, they showed the influence of the feeling of guilt. This sexual play and experimentation, again and again reproduced in the imagination, often led to masturbatory activity and gratification. They were described as pleasurable in tone, especially when they concerned strictly forbidden activity or actions in situations where there was danger of being exposed to discovery.

I shall point out here only a few cases of this kind. A young girl "tried out" men in her sexual fantasies, imagining now one man, now another, in certain love scenes, in order to find out which fantasy would afford her the greatest excitation. At that stage of her imagination, she also changed the sexual situations. She recalled having found the greatest pleasure in a sexual situation with a man while her mother was in the next room, so that she was forced to fear being disturbed by her mother at any moment. Never before had she felt so deep a sexual satisfaction. The second case concerns a man who, as an officer in enemy country, had a date with a nun in a convent at night. Time and again, his fantasies returned to that scene in which the nun's habit, the cell, the hard bed, the crucified Jesus on the wall played a great role. Sexual desire and the gratification felt had never been greater than in that situation.

I shall briefly point out other similar cases. For instance, an otherwise cold woman was capable of sexual orgasm only when she knew her husband was near by while she betrayed him with her lover. A man attained full potency only when his sexual partner pronounced obscene words during the act. To this category belongs a great number of frankly detailed cases with special conditions of love-making, for instance, those characterized by Freud as demanding the condition of the betrayed third person, also those female types pointed out by him, whose sexual anesthesia is removed only by a secret relation. In all these cases, the latent influence of the unconscious feeling of guilt can be demonstrated in the enhancement of desire and the deepening of satisfaction.

At this point, we should reply to various objections which attempt to shake our conception. The most important one will assert that the phenomenon we described as a strengthening of gratification by the breakthrough of a prohibition is of a secondary nature. This objection will especially stress the fact that it is the significance of fixation and regression that is decisive for the intensified urge and the deepening of gratification. I am of the same opinion and I go even farther than that in this direction. I believe that, in studying these cases, we could contribute something to our understanding of the nature of fixation and regression, namely, the possibility of a complication which we have not yet sufficiently appreciated.

One can discriminate between a primary fixation on the infantile objects of incest or on their substitute persons and the secondary one. In the former, the biological necessities of the sexual drives have created their expression. In the formation of the secondary fixation, which strengthens the original one, the condition of the prohibition is one of the determining factors. It is the same in the regression. Thus, the natural incestuous tie is not dissolved by the feeling of guilt, but, often enough, deepened and strengthened. It can be shown in many analyses that this condition of prohibition, which originates in the incestuous choice, influences reactively the later choice of object and is one of the factors in its determination.

There are certain configurations in the love life of men and women whose common features are the violation of infantile prohibitions; for instance, the type of man who finds his fulfillment only in the humiliated love-object, the other kind who requires the condition of a betrayed third person, the type of woman who insists on secrecy in her sex relations and many other special conditions in the love relations of normal and perverted persons. We know the origin of this prohibition, these external and internal influences which opposed the infantile sexual gratification. These influences can, as we see in the psychology of neuroses, be so lasting that they still reverberate in the allowed and legal sexual gratification. The connection of sexuality and the feeling of guilt has, under present cultural conditions, become so intimate that even marital sexual intercourse often enough means, unconsciously, the violation of a prohibition. It could be said that through these influences the realm of sexuality has been so much saturated with a feeling of guilt that it cannot be imagined any longer without that feeling.

I should like to emphasize once more the decisive factor from which we started. The disappearance or reduction of the feeling of guilt is one of the most important initial conditions for sexual gratification. But its increase or its influence also brings about instinctual eruption which then appears as a mixed form of gratification of both needs. I should even say that, in innumerable cases of emotional eruption, in the triumph over the superego, the forced and violent character of this conquest still gives evidence of the aftereffect of the unconscious feeling of guilt. If I may draw a conclusion from impressions gained in the observation of only a few cases of manic-depressive patients, I should dare to say that the manic phase corresponds by no means to a pure and simple triumph of the superego. The turbulent, violent, highly stimulated nature of the manic personality still shows that the unconscious feeling of guilt is present under the surface at the very moment of its subjugation. Children's boisterousness may perhaps be best compared to manic behavior, that demonstration of the violation of a prohibition still showing the continued effect of the prohibition even in its violation. It might be said that mania is the emotional state, the intensity of which is determined, among other factors, by the depression which is latent and which continues below the surface. Even in the mood of the drunkard who is "high," there are traces of the grief or sorrow which he tries to drown.

We gain, at this point, a number of insights that deepen our concepts in a certain direction. The orgy is an instinctual eruption, whose extent is characterized not only by the removal of the accumulation of sexual urges, but also by the secretly continuing effect of the feeling of guilt. Its violence, its excessiveness is determined also by the fact that the prohibition remains unrecognized in existence in the background.* This factor of a never completely mastered feeling of guilt, not mastered even during the act, explains certain features of the psychology of the criminal. There exists an emotional mood of despair, originating in the repeated and futile effort to master the instinctual urge. There exists another one resulting from the effort to resist the attacks of the powers of conscience.

Both factors may have an indeterminate share in the psychogenesis of the type of crime which we call affective. Tired of fighting on two fronts, the criminal is simultaneously overpowered by his instinct and by the powers of his conscience. Sometimes

* A Rumanian proverb says, "What you run away from, runs after you."

we see a similar process in the neurotic who, between instinctual urge and pressure of feeling of guilt, succumbs to the conditions which the Church, with fine psychological feeling, calls "sin of despair" ("*la tentation de désespoir*"). The Church, and rightly so, considers overstrictness, the rigid, fanatical clinging to asceticism and penitence sinful. The Church knows that an exaggerated feeling of sinfulness must lead to the very sin of despair. He who knows himself to be damned needs no more renunciation, he comes not only to sensual enjoyment, but to frenzy, to orgy. Religion, thus, really demands sin, since without it, there could be no remorse, no fear of God and no piety.* As one can see, the ways of the Lord are mysterious and not always direct.

As Freud characterized it, the feast is not only an allowed, indeed, it is a required violation of that which is otherwise forbidden. The celebration also presupposes that the prohibition continues in existence, having been overcome only for the moment. The intoxication is followed by the hangover which, however, had been there before, otherwise no intoxication would have been necessary. One might say that the intoxication shows what efforts it takes to overcome the depression.

It would be wrong and unjustified to expose only one side of the problem. In analytic observation, the fact can be demonstrated that sorrow and melancholia are not only reactions to a loss, but that they signify the relentless fight against the impulses that wished for this loss. Here a neglected factor appears. The feeling of guilt, which is of such great significance in the psychogenesis of neuroses, is by no means a psychologically simple phenomenon. It is not only the moral reaction to forbidden activity, but also to its repetition. Analytically speaking, the feeling of guilt also receives its intensity by the unconscious repeated enjoyment of a forbidden gratification.

Though it may certainly sound paradoxical, one is nevertheless psychologically justified in saying that as long as the unconscious feeling of guilt lasts, the temptation to repeat a proscribed

---

* Therefore, the faithful may sing fervently of the fall of man as of "*Felix culpa.*"

activity is near. One would expect the reverse to be true but the complex psychological constellation justifies this conclusion. The analytically comprehensible nature of remorse fits into this connection. He who repents too much is in danger of doing again that which he repents of. One speaks of the gnawing character of remorse, thus indiacting its self-tormenting, autocannibalistic character, but its essence is the continuing appetite. Incidentally, there exists also remorse over not having committed "sins," regret for lost, missed utilization of opportunities for gratification of our drives.

In the final phases of the obsessional neurotic process, often that which was earlier forbidden becomes an impulsive demand and request. Its omission releases moral anxiety. A young man whom I treated for psychic impotency showed great feeling of guilt in the last quarter of his analysis whenever he did not satisfy a woman sexually, while earlier it had been the sexual satisfaction that he considered forbidden. Furthermore, he was now driven, as if by a compulsion, to have too frequent sexual intercourse.

There are numerous analogous examples in the history of the religions. Out of their abundance, only one will be selected, from the time of the Katharers, the heretical sect which damned any carnal intercourse. The monk Gervasius tells of the time that William of the White Hands, Archbishop of Reims, once rode on horseback outside the town with his clerics. One of the monks of his retinue noticed a beautiful young girl in a vineyard. He approached her and, in a most gracious way, made an amorous proposal. But she replied that once her maidenhood was lost, she would irrevocably be given to eternal damnation. Now the monk suspected that the girl adhered to the godless teaching of the Katharers. The Archbishop, having heard that the girl treasured so highly that which belonged to her earthly body and deserved so little reverence, had her seized. When, in spite of all persuasion and promises, she insisted on her frightful aberration, she was given over to the hangman. In her delusion, she could not see that one had to despise earthly things and obey the Church, outside of which there is no salvation. *"Extra ecclesiam non est salus."*

We cannot ignore, either, that this repression, too, has a double character. Freud determined the nature of repression as something between flight and condemnation, a preliminary step to condemnation. Not in contrast, but as a supplement to this description, one can add that repression also preserves the situation of temptation, that it not only fights off the forbidden pleasure, but also holds it fast. This aspect of the repressive condition is shown clearly through the processes of the return of the repressed from the middle of the repressive. In them, the repressed instinctual impulses, or the repressed thoughts, apparently abruptly break through the defense and receive some gratification.

It would perhaps be practical to discriminate between these processes and another one we have just characterized. In it, the feeling of guilt fights the repressed impulses until it becomes their ally. I call this the submersion of the repressing into the repressed. Certain measures of defense had been erected against the proscribed ideas, but they proved themselves too weak. The fought-off instinctual impulses have become too powerful and have pulled over into their realm also all those factors that had been destined to fight them. It is as in certain actions to save drowning people. The rescuer is pulled down by the endangered person. Similarly, the moral feeling of guilt often facilitates instinctual eruption and enhances the intensity of gratification.

This point of view should have significance for analytic therapy because it reveals the nature of certain difficulties in our therapeutic efforts. These difficulties are caused by the fact that the gratification that was intensified and deepened by the feeling of guilt is less easily accessible to reduction and sublimation than the normal, even though antisocial one. I have earlier pointed briefly to the significance of this point of view for the psychology of the criminal. Schiller, whom Nietzsche rightly called "the moral trumpeter of Saeckingen," announces emphatically that it is the curse of the evil deed that it must procreate evil. It would be by far truer to change the emphasis in that sentence and to say that it is that very curse directed at the "evil" deed that produces these effects.

The present cultural situation is responsible for the fact that man is unsatisfied in following his instincts, because moral demands object, and he is unsatisfied in resisting them, because of the deep down unchangeable animalistic nature of man. He is unsatisfied in accepting the pricks of flesh, and unsatisfied in kicking against them. In view of this situation, pervailing in this most magnificent of all worlds, the deeply refreshing optimism of certain philosophers is, indeed, to be admired.

I believe there is little hope for any essential change in the emotional life of people. They remain poor, miserably suffering creatures, suffering even where they cause suffering. It is perhaps already a consolation to state such comfortlessness rather than to prettify it, to give it an optimistic interpretation, to make it appear nice and to hush it up.

III

Some Unconscious Connections
of Hatred and Anxiety

THE impulses of hatred, which should be considered representative of the destructive tendencies, are as mysterious as those of love, as far as their origin and their dynamics are concerned. The man who is filled with hate makes just as pathological an impression as the one who is in love. Until we ourselves experience hate, we are hardly better able to understand the psychic motives and aims of the hater, than those of that other monomaniac, the person who is love-struck. We cannot see that the love-object of one is an angel on earth and we do not understand why the other insists on considering a certain object a devil in human form.

But we do know that hatred, as related to the object, is older than love, and that part of the riddle resulting from the strong admixture of hatred with the love impulses is explained by the fact that hatred is love's precurser. Another part of the riddle becomes understandable through the defensive reaction of certain ego-drives which, in turn, can point to the almost unavoidable conflicts that result between ego-interests and love-interests.

But where does hatred come from? Freud teaches us that it originates in the primeval rejection by the self-loving narcissistic ego of the external world with its stimuli. The prototypes of the relation of hatred originate in the struggle of the ego for its assertion and maintenance. The ego hates, therefore, all objects that become sources of unpleasurable sensations. Taking this statement of Freud's biologically, one may say that the ego hates all objects exerting stimuli and capable of endangering its exist-

ence. The ego reacts with anxiety to the approach of an object
of this kind, which means danger to its preservation, and it tries
first to remove itself from the source of stimuli by the suitable
action of escape.

Anxiety is preformed phylogenetically in the individual. Freud
characterized its nature as a signal of danger. It can point to
experiences of the forebears, which had traumatic effect. Where
reflective flight is not possible, the individual will take other measures in order to cope with the dangerous stimulus. He will, for
instance, endeavor to remove the source of stimuli, primarily by
incorporating it, by devouring it.

Hatred may be described as that relation to the object which
announces a preparation for one of these two reactions, or as that
relation which is caused by their delay. In later development,
hatred will, indeed, be moving between these two opposite actions,
and will either remove itself from the hated object or destroy it.
Even in the development of love relations at a later period, which
exhibit a mingling of intense hatred, both tendencies thus performed through the relation of hatred, become clearly recognizable. They stand out more strongly when love impulses regress
to the sadistic-anal level of organization.

Here I shall state the fact that hatred stands biologically and
psychogenetically in intimate connection with anxiety or, in other
words, that hatred is one of the impulses which derive from the
affect of anxiety. It is not necessary to emphasize the fact that
anxiety is capable of transposition into emotional impulses of
other kinds and of causing other object reactions. What are the
special conditions from which this special genesis of hatred results?
I have indicated one of them—hatred can arise only if spontaneous
suitable reaction to the approach of a dangerous object is impossible. Motor action would be the expression of a mastery of
anxiety and would make it unnecessary for hatred to arise. This,
of course, is true only for a primary situation of the kind that has
been described, while later on, hatred becomes the instinctual
pre-condition for the possibility of that reaction.

A comparison of these conditions with those of the opposite

emotional representative suggests itself. Originally, love evolves from an instinctual inhibition, that is, the postponement of the immediate gratification of the sexual instinct. All the idealistic attempts at extenuation, all the poetic transfiguration and all the metaphysical depth of the philosophers cannot bring about the disappearance of the psychological fact that originally love can develop only where immediate and direct sexual gratification is impossible.

Analysis cannot truthfully say much about the nature of the mysterious and extolled feeling, glorified by the religions and celebrated in poetry. The scant clarification which psychoanalysis is capable of supplying shrinks essentially to a single sober result of research, the origin of love in sexuality. The primary and most important condition for these overwhelming feelings certainly turns out to be, whatever may be said, the ungratified sexual need. Whether this feeling, which has given people so much happiness and so much more misery, comes from heaven or the other place, whether God in His kindness has given it to mortals, or whether the devil has afflicted them with it—"*virtus diaboli est in lumbis*"—its origin in the gross, socially disowned sexual need is beyond doubt.

Postponement of immediate and direct sexual gratification is the primary pre-condition for the psychogenesis of love. Postponement of object annihilation is the pre-condition for the beginning of hatred. This can be recognized also regressively by drawing conclusions from the intended effect to the motive of the action. If the obstacles causing these feelings to arise are removed, the gratification of the primary instinctual needs follows immediately. The lover aims at union with the object, the hater at its annihilation.*

The sagging of feelings of love after sexual intercourse corresponds to the subsiding impulses of hatred after the annihila-

---

* It is noteworthy that hatred seeks the proximity of the object, as does love. As traces of the tendency to approach the object can be found even in platonic love, so they can be found in the most sublimated impulse of hatred. And it seems that hatred "par distance" is entirely out of favor with people.

tion of the object. Both phenomena are the result of never completely achieved mastery of the stimuli. Both leave the impression of "unfinished business."

An object from which danger threatens, fear of the object, the impossibility of mastering this anxiety by escape or the annihilation of the dangerous object immediately, or in an adequate way —these are the features that comprise the essential conditions for the release of the reaction of hatred. These cannot, of course, be the only ones.

This will be made clear in the answer to the obvious question that follows. Why does hatred result from the described situation rather than a continuation of anxiety? This cannot be easily answered. The sincere answer can only be that we do not know. We are tempted to assume that this differentiation takes place under the influence of quantitative factors. We seem to have found with some certainty that hatred is a kind of defense against anxiety, a primitive attempt at mastery of anxiety. A deeper insight into the question of how the transmutation of anxiety into hatred can come about will probably result from the contrast of death-instincts and life-instincts shown in Freud's conception. But the nature of anxiety, originally perhaps a reaction to the primary pleasure in letting the ego perish, has not yet been sufficiently clarified.

From this derivation, the clarification of several factors of the impulses of hatred results. It is most important that the anxiety, for the mastery of which hatred is mobilized, clearly continues within the experience of hate. The impulse of hatred is aimed only at objects one fears, objects from whom the ego expects external or internal endangerment. Whenever this factor of fear drops out, feelings of contempt, aversion, indifference result, but in no case hatred. The factor of unconscious anxiety is immanent in the impulse of hatred and can not be detached from it. It is in accord with the law of the rebound of affects that fear of an object can transpose itself into aggression once that feeling has attained a certain strength. This mechanism is, incidentally, not at all limited to people. Dogs frequently attack people because they are afraid of them, and they desist from aggression when they feel they have nothing to fear. The rat, when cornered, attacks people furiously.

From impressions gained in the psychoanalysis of neurotics, the insight may dawn on us that there is more to these dynamics of the transposition of anxiety into hatred and into resultant aggressive tendencies than we have recognized so far. Certain experiences of analytic practice suggest the conclusion that sudden actions of aggression or hatred frequently result from attempts to fight off anxiety which has become excessive. Impulsive acts of this kind exist not only in hysteria. Also, the symptomatology of obsessional neurosis and, in the shape of instinctual eruptions even more, that of manic-depressive disorders, furnish numerous examples of this special form of defense against anxiety.

I should think in this connection that a psychological explanation may be found of aggressions in psychotic cases. In cases of paranoia, the aim is to master the threat coming from the object, or seeming to do so, by threatening the object.

Of still greater significance is the exploration of these defense mechanisms and of this process of transposition in the psychology of the criminal. Criminal psychologists, judges, prosecutors and defense counsels would do well to study these difficult emotional processes with the help of the analytic method. A large number of otherwise unexplainable crimes are clarified in the psychic process in which an aggressive action is used to reduce the tension of anxiety. Certain cases of suicide have no other explanation than that, under the influence of too great anxiety, hatred had been turned against the ego, driving it into death. It may be said that the ego prefers its own annihilation to anxiety which has grown too intense and has become inescapable. It executes the aggression against the object introjected into the ego, the object which had threatened it with danger.

We are back again, then, to the problem of the transposition of hatred into anxiety. It is impossible to fathom its depth without considering the contrast of life—and death—instincts. Anxiety is a phenomenon of reaction to the instinctual desire of the individual to achieve death by the shortest route. The resistance of the ego against this instinctual challenge effects the reversal of affect, which transforms the primary pleasurable character into anxiety. As a logical supplement to Freud's conception, it should be said that anxiety is the expression of the struggle against the longing for death, in other words, of the struggle against the temptation to revert to the quietude of inorganic development. Hatred would, hence, be the expression of defense of the ego against the object which arouses in us this wish, a reaction of the life-instinct against the goal of the death-instinct.

This protesting reaction, which owes its strength to Eros, can achieve its effect only with the means used by the older death-instinct. Indeed, it retains the old instinctual aim and changes its course only in that it displaces the pleasure onto another object. Hatred is, therefore, a drive which, through displacement onto another object, aims at gratification of the death-instinct. Displacement is the process that saves the ego from ruin, while still permitting it the enjoyment of part of the old gratification via the foreign object. We pointed earlier to the case where an over increased anxiety can drive the ego into death. This can be expressed also in a positive way. The ego desists from struggling against annihilation and succumbs to the temptation of the death-instinct.

Clearly, hatred has assumed, as it were, only the executive power of the death-instinct, while the choice of object—a foreign object or the ego—has only secondary significance. Suicide because of unhappy love can be explained by the regression to which the life-instincts are subject. The ego annihilates itself rather than destroy the beloved person. There is no hate without an object. There is, however, a readiness to hate, which is originally as little discriminating in its choice of an object as is love. It is a free-floating hate, as it were, representing the attempt at mastery of a latent anxiety.

In the analysis of a number of neurotic patients, one can observe that hatred also has another significance of an emotionally dynamic and affectively economic kind. Hatred frequently helps in sparing a person intense affects of anxiety and prevents him from the development of over great feelings of unpleasure of this kind.

The significance of this economic factor in the genesis of hatred deserves deeper psychological appreciation.

At this point, a certain sequence of psychic processes, which I described earlier, may be seen in a more comprehensive aspect. In *Compulsion to Confess and Need for Punishment,* I expounded a theory to the effect that, in a considerable number of cases, neurotic patients as well as healthy persons had intense feelings of hatred against the very persons who showed them a well-meaning and friendly attitude. The psychological fact that many persons have this attitude of increased hatred toward the very objects to whom they have caused damage or offense seems here bewildering. In the former book, I attempted to explain that this seemingly paradoxical reaction derives from the effect of the unconscious feeling of guilt, and to show the way in which it does so.

This is where that special psychological case fits into a more general complex of facts. The castration-anxiety, whose representative we found in the unconscious moral anxiety to be, has continued as hatred. It seems, indeed, that the increase of that moral anxiety can bring about impulses of extreme hatred and frequent outbreaks of hatred.

In many cases of neurotic patients or neurotic characters, I was able to convince myself of the effectiveness of this mechanism. One of my patients would not be satisfied until she had most deeply offended every person close to her, relatives and friends. Once, when she had hurt her best friend in this manner, she gave this description of her psychic processes during analysis. "I was horrid to R. because I had been horrid to her before. But being horrid makes me hate her." The hatred appears here clearly as the attempt at freeing herself from the stifling pressure of the feeling of guilt which has become overwhelming and which urges repetition of the act. This is, therefore, a special case of anxiety, unconscious moral anxiety from which emerges the impulse of hatred. But we know that here, too, a realistic anxiety is primarily in the picture, an anxiety which Freud has shown to be the core of moral anxiety.*

* The analysis of relations of love sometimes gives the impression that hatred against an object originates in the anxiety which reacts to the antici-

The process of the psychogenesis of hatred deriving from a definite attempt at mastery over anxiety appears quite clearly in cases where the object of anxiety is also the primal image of the superego. In the case of a certain young girl, the impulses deriving from the Oedipus complex assumed a peculiar form. As their motivation, as far as it was conscious, it was stated that the patient hated her mother because the latter caused her to hate herself, meaning to say that she was forced to hate herself because of the education given her by her mother. It could easily be guessed that the qualities that caused her to develop this self-hatred were intimately connected with the impulses of her sexual instincts, and that the anxiety concerned situations in which there were temptations of this kind.

It can be frequently observed in the transference-situation in analysis that the patient becomes aggressive in thought and talk when anxiety similar to a feeling of guilt has reached a certain intensity. This psychological derivation necessarily leads to a conclusion that is confirmed by analytic observation of the individual: hatred becomes the more intense the stronger the unconscious anxiety is, in defense against which it was produced. It seems sometimes that the greatest intensity of hatred is reached under the impression of impulses of stifling anxiety. We cannot decide here whether and to what extent realistic anxiety is deepened through moral anxiety in cases of this kind. I consider it probable, however, that the pressure of the feeling of guilt contributes decisively, together with other factors, to this development of the impulses of hatred. Supported by unconscious feelings of guilt, hatred attains

---

pated dependency of the ego upon the object. Hatred, in this case, seems to be a psychic phenomenon of reaction to strong masochistic tendencies. In some cases it can be seen that the hatred with which some women react to the approach of a certain man originates in the anxiety—among other sources—which accompanies their anticipation of much suffering in the relation with him. A motive of this apparently unfounded hatred is the anxiety concerning the preservation and maintenance of the ego, originally, fear of being overwhelmed. Compare the earlier, deeper explanation of anxiety originating in the struggle against impulses of the death-instincts, with this explanation.

sinister dimensions. In these cases, it is interesting to observe that annihilation of the hated object is the goal not only for realistic reasons of instinctual gratification, but also because the removal of the object is expected to give liberation from the stifling pressure of moral anxiety. The aggressive outbreak has, therefore, the purpose of flight from an intense anxiety.

I should not like to conclude the discussion of this analytical theory without emphasizing a problem that presents itself here. It concerns the impulses in the typical constellation which, in analysis, we call the Oedipus complex. This situation is of great significance for the development and maturation of the individual. In it, the small boy shows clear signs of sexual and jealous impulses towards his mother and betrays no less clearly his hostile impulses towards his paternal rival. This psychological connection between hatred and unconscious anxiety appears to be of far-reaching and lasting significance in the development of this situation.

The rather longlasting, frictionless coexistence of contrasting tender and hostile feelings towards the father as well as other features of the psychic process suggest a certain assumption that appears to be worthy of consideration. Does the impulse of hatred in this situation, too, develop only under the influence of anxiety? In other words: I believe the boy's primary rejecting and hostile attitude, which initially does not at all conflict with his tender feelings for his father, develops into hatred only later through the defense against his castration-anxiety. This hatred, I believe, is then increased under the influence of the closeness of temptation, and later reactively strengthened through moral anxiety. In this situation, too, it seems to me that hatred is an attempt at mastering the unconscious anxiety.

I must refrain from pointing to some aspects that result from the clarification of the connection between hatred and anxiety. I may, however, without being accused of rashness, say with assurance that from this point, more than one path leads into hitherto scarcely entered realms of ego-psychology.

IV

Forgiveness and Vengeance

1

IF WE may believe the psychologists of the conscious, there is nothing problematic or questionable in the fact that we forgive someone who has offended or hurt us. It is for us to decide whether we choose this or another reaction to an act that was directed against us. Of course, we can seldom refrain from commenting on our choice and pointing out how much more noble it is to forgive than to take revenge.

However, the very fact that the reaction of forgiveness seems to be something psychologically quite simple, elementary and self-explanatory, might arouse our distrust. The processes which appear to official science as self-explanatory usually are those least understood by it. Is it really a foregone conclusion that we forgive? On the contrary, it is a very unnatural reaction.

Nothing could be more plausible and natural for people than to take revenge. The moral reaction which, for several thousand years, has accompanied our strongest and most elementary instinctual impulses to an increasing extent, brought about the suppression of the deep, truly unquenchable need for vengeance that lives in us. It is a peculiar fact, though not surprising to the psychoanalyst, that society proscribes this need for the individual while satisfying it for itself in so many fields.

Punishment in education and in legal procedure and penitence imposed upon the sinner by religion, war and other social institutions are, in origin, manifestations of revenge. The individual's need for revenge, suppressed in our social order, has been preserved in the unconscious, strong and vigorous as on the first day and none of the intensification of moral prohibitions affect it at all.

For the unconscious there exists neither forgiveness nor negation.* In the analysis of neuroses, we observe the deep and decisive extent to which the individual's unconscious drives to take vengeance for wrong suffered, and the inexorability with which the unsatisfied need for revenge can turn against the ego. On certain occasions it can be observed that a particularly strong, vengeful impulse, a trend towards retaliation and revenge to a large extent destroys the individual's life. One finds (with the customary regret or without it) how little the Christian principles of clemency and forgiveness can do in the face of such strong emotional impulses.

Only fools, hypocrites or sick people deny the deep and voluptuous satisfaction adequate revenge can give, deny the extraordinary feeling of liberation, indeed, redemption from stifling psychic pressure, which follows successful revenge.** That femininely sentimental remark of Mme. de Staël's that to understand all is to forgive all reveals its profound untruthfulness also in analytical practice. The understanding of the motives and instinctual forces of our fellow men may sometimes—I say sometimes—cause us to judge them more kindly but it is remarkable how small is the influence of that understanding when we ourselves are offended or hurt by their actions. Scholars have good reason to wonder at our illogical and peculiar attitude when we

* Compare Freud, *Negation. Gesammelte Schriften,* Vol. XI.

** In contrast to all humanitarian talk so eloquently proclaiming man to be good, and showing enthusiasm about his progress, Heinrich Heine's upright and morally courageous admission may be quoted here, "My frame of mind is most peaceful. My wishes are: a modest hut, a thatched roof, but a good bed, good food, milk and butter—very fresh, flowers in front of my window, beautiful trees outside my door and, if the good Lord wishes to make me completely happy, he lets me have the joy of seeing hanged on those trees about six or seven of my enemies. Deeply moved, I shall forgive them before they die, all the wrong they inflicted upon me in their lifetime. Yes, one must forgive one's enemies, but not until they are hanged." From *Thoughts and Notions (Gedanken und Einfälle).*

forgive more quickly and readily the wrong inflicted upon another.

It is clear from the start that psychologically we must discriminate between forgiveness extended to us and that we extend to others. Psychoanalytical investigation reveals, however, these two kinds of forgiveness to be by no means so sharply different, so independent from each other as we should expect.

If it is true that there is no forgiveness for the unconscious, then traces of the original tendencies should still be discernible in the reaction-formation. This is so, indeed. Forgiveness, to be conceived of as reaction-formation to intense tendencies towards revenge, has become the most sublimated and sublime form of vengeance. To forgive somebody has come to be an expression of tendencies towards the deepest humiliation of the person forgiven. That deep reaching, almost irrepressible human impulse to pay back in the same coin only seems to have yielded to the reactive tendencies. We are in reality ready to forgive only after we have taken revenge. Where revenge is impossible for external or internal reasons, even forgiveness becomes revenge. When we help our enemy we heap "fiery coals" upon a guilty head, thus taking revenge. Behind a transparent mask, what has been warded off has taken the place of the powers of defense, like a usurper with the royal insignia on the throne of the legitimate ruler. Even the Church, though condemning vengeance, makes a point of paying back in the same coin. "In these sacred halls vengeance is unknown," Sarastro proclaims in the *Magic Flute,* but it is taken anyway.

"Mine is vengeance," saith the Lord. One may wonder why God does not claim the privilege of forgiveness with the same decisiveness, and why he challenges us poor humans to accomplish that prodigious feat of forgiving one another. That feat, incidentally, joins the others which He demands of us and for which He has, in His inscrutable way, equipped us likewise inadequately.

Religion adds to the postulate of forgiveness a weighty reason. It demands that we forgive others so that we, too, may be forgiven. Doing so, it has touched on the motives of forgiving more deeply than did the psychology of the conscious. We are all sinners at all times. We, too, have inflicted evil upon others and must, therefore, fear punishment. Religious teachings, introducing this argument, intend to make us decide for this special kind of instinctual renunciation by appealing to the social anxiety, and to the moral anxiety, that live in all of us.

The conscious effect of this suggestion is undeniably strong. We are more inclined to forgive somebody if we are conscious of the same or a similar guilt. But we said this concerned only the conscious. If the decision of the conscious prevailed, we would not suddenly feel resentment and desire for revenge long after we had forgiven an offender or enemy. Nor would we suddenly have feelings of guilt or anxiety, were we certain that we have long been forgiven for a past wrong. The psychology of the conscious, of course, says that these feelings originate in the fact that forgiveness in either case has not been complete, that the anxiety and the thirst for vengeance, respectively, correspond to this very imperfection. We cannot contradict, as in this world everything is imperfect. We should, however, prefer to assume that these unexpected feelings, so strongly contradicting our conscious attitude, are outgrowths of repressed impulses that try to force their way back into consciousness. In any case, everyday experience teaches the analyst that the idea of forgiveness belongs entirely in the realm of consciousness and that the repressed impulses of vengeance and retaliation are everlasting, are really eternal.

2

I shall not discuss the numerous neuroses where those unconscious vengeful tendencies had an essential influence upon the determination of the severity and extent of the illness. It seems better to me to go back to a number of observations that show us the problem under discussion from an unexpected angle. During the last few years, I have had a chance to study in analysis several people whose conscious vengeful tendencies were unusually intensive and lasting. This thirst for vengeance was, as a rule, directed against members of their family, former friends and people close to the patient. It expressed itself in variegated, often elaborate daydreams and fantasies that frequently exhibited the most refined cruelty.

It was not always mere fantasy. In a few of these cases, actions took place either of an impulsive kind or as the result, apparently, of long premeditated plans. In many cases, one could easily see that the people upon whom revenge was taken were merely substituted persons and that the revenge had been displaced onto them from the primary objects. In one of these cases, the patient's thirst for vengeance could best be compared to the mood of one who has run amuck. The looseness of object-choice in vengeance was amazing. The slightest cause, scarcely perceptible to others, was enough to arouse a whole sequence of vengeful fantasies. I was much impressed by the vengeful fantasies of a man to whom an elderly gentleman had once addressed a harmless jesting remark which caused him to feel deeply hurt. Eleven years later he struck the offender with exquisite cruelty where it hurt most. He professed to the maxim, "Revenge is to be enjoyed cold." He postponed the execution of his plans to a time when circumstances were most favorable for him.

In the course of the psychoanalysis of people of so clearly and lastingly vengeful a type, astonishing discoveries are arrived at. They are in decisive contradiction to the concepts of vengeance and forgiveness, otherwise so willingly and universally adhered to. It is easy to see that these detailed situations of revenge, time and again elaborated in fantasy, could develop only on the basis of inhibitions of action. In most cases, it was possible to reconstruct psychologically a definite phase without being particularly arbitrary. This phase made its effects felt during the time between the offense or hurt and the emergence of plans for revenge. In these people, an especially intense urge for reprisal or revenge had arisen immediately after the offense had been inflicted upon them. This urge was originally warded off, probably for external reasons, because their own power was not sufficient, or because certain circumstances prohibited an immediate reaction. Only later, internal inhibitions set in, among which the demands of culture have an important place.*

The deepening of the cultural requirements has unquestionably increased the intensity of the unconscious tendencies. Their effect equals that of an accumulation of affects. The transmutation of external punishments and deterrents into feelings of guilt leads to emotional consequences no less cruel than the barbaric measures of ages past. The psychic effect of mourning, which is felt between the ego and the superego, is scarcely less cruel than the mourning rites of ancient peoples and of the primitives of our time, with their cruel self-tortures. Part of us, too, dies with the beloved persons, even though this occurs in other, less conspicuous forms. The psychic effect of the deepening of the moral demands appears also in the realm of vengeance, on both sides. The principle of talion which prevailed in early antiquity does not seem to correspond to our advanced humanitarian demands, nor does it satisfy the instinctual impulses intensified by the processes of repression. To make a comparison, the advantage in saving capital is an increase of interest, while the privations forced by economy seem to justify expectations of a still bigger amount. People's vengeful tendencies, too, grow stronger and more sophisticated.

Suppression of the primary impulse had the effect of psychic frustration, and that in a special sense. The person who inflicted the offense or injury was unconsciously taken into the ego, introjected. This introjection initiated the turn of the instinctual impulse against oneself. To the process of defense and object-introjection corresponds the deep unconscious feeling of guilt in the ensuing time. It comes from two sources. It is borrowed from the

* Freud shows us a similar psychic situation in the psychogenesis of the tendentious joke. (*The Wit and Its Relation to the Unconscious. Gesammelte Schriften*, Vol. IX.)

introjected object and it relates to one's own suppressed hostile impulses.

In this phase, a peculiar internal tension develops that is sometimes unbearably painful. Its mood ranges from depression to depersonalization and extraordinary disquietude. The retroactive transmutation of this self-tormenting attitude into one of sadism towards the external world·is especially significant within the typical emotional sequence. This transmutation occurs under the pressure of the psychic tension which has increased to the extreme, and it has the effect of psychic relief.*

It is difficult to look into the special dynamics of this process. They may best be described as two different processes which combine their effects. The instinctual impulse turns back against the object while a regression to an earlier phase of libidinal development occurs. In turning back, the instinct hitherto directed against the ego, an ego changed by the introjection of the object, drives towards eruption against an external object, hence, towards revenge. The difference between this phase and the earlier one is clear enough and can be dynamically well determined. In the first, the ego is treated like a hated object. In the second, the object is treated like a hated ego. The historical development explains this peculiar change. But it also implies the possibility of regression from the second phase of development to the first.

Both reactions exhibit a distinctly archaic character. A fine example of the first kind has been given by Freud in his analysis of Michelangelo's Moses.† In the scene described by Freud, when Moses expresses his furious anger at the idolatrous Israelites by tearing at his beard, the ego is treated like a hated—and loved—object. An external obstacle, the distance, prohibits action of revenge against the object.

---

* The moods here described, which follow the defense against motor reactions of revenge and the object-introjection, can be found also in fiction, for instance, in the figure of Hamlet. This particular play is for the analyst an example of the psychic effects of warded-off tendencies for revenge. Seen from this angle, the prince's melancholia and feeling of guilt become better understandable.

† *The Moses of Michelanglo (Gesammelte Schriften)* Vol. X.

I give an example from the life of a compulsive neurotic who wished to show a new card game to an elderly relative. While playing, his pupil was extremely awkward and unreasonable. Soon afterwards, my patient behaved in a very unusual way. He began not to understand simple things, stared stupidly in front of himself and behaved altogether like a fool. This, too, could be compared with Hamlet's attitude for instance, in the scene with Rosencrantz and Guildenstern.

The course and effectiveness of the psychic process here described can easily be traced in the analysis of certain types. This is undoubtedly an interesting process. The original offense and hurt had the same effect as certain forms of frustrated love. Its psychic consequences were similar to those often observed in those frustrations of love when the object, as such, was consciously given up, but introjected into the ego. Several conspicuous features reveal this origin of vengeful tendencies also to those not familiar with psychoanalysis. The extraordinary gratification through the suffering and torment of the objects that are the targets of revenge, is, in fantasy, enjoyed as if the object's suffering were simultaneously one's own. The frequent sexual excitation combining with the fantasies and the self-tormenting remembrance of the offense or hurt which caused the fantasies, point to homosexual and sadistic impulses as the origin of those scenes, as is the case in fantasies of beating.

The special gratification in fantasies of revenge can best be understood in comparison with another psychic phenomenon. Freud showed, in the analysis of certain masochistic fantasies of children, a phase of development in which the child experiences in fantasy, clearly with sexual satisfaction, the idea of a child being beaten.* In these fantasies, homosexual tendencies and impulses from the unconscious feeling of guilt are simultaneously gratified. Fantasies of various kinds can take the place of indeterminate ideas about some child being beaten or chastised. The fantasies may vary in the detailed circumstances and kinds of

* A Child Is Being Beaten (Gesammelte Schriften) Vol. V.

chastisement. They may combine with something read or heard and frequently assume features of a novel.*

During his puberty, one of my patients became intensely sexually excited when he imagined the Christian martyrs being subjected to various tortures by the Roman legionnaires. Another was led to masturbatory acts whenever he imagined the horrifying punishments that the revolutionists in his country had had to suffer. When this patient first entered analysis, his person did not figure consciously in these fantasies. He experienced them as an onlooker, as it were, on an imagined stage. Later, however, he put himself in the place of the commanding person, the judge or executioner. Still later, he played in his imagination the parts of the torturer and the tortured together.

The connection of this kind of fantasied beating and plans and fantasies of revenge, which we have described, is obvious. We need only to put real persons in the place of invented—or transformed—ones, to let a hurt appear as the real or rationalized cause of the imagined punishment. We must continue, in a certain direction, that phase of the fantasies of beating in order to arrive at a fantasy of revenge of a pleasurable character, as described before. Often those fantasies of revenge, too, have the character of a novel. Sometimes they are daydreams of the accomplishment of revenge in definite elaborately depicted situations, showing the preparation and the details, and preferably dwelling upon the pain and suffering of the victim. In these features, too, the fantasies of revenge prove to be the counterpart of those typical scenes in which a child is being beaten.

Our derivation has shown that the deep thirst for revenge draws, in these cases, its special intensity from various sources. The original impulse for retaliation, not manifested because of special emotional conditions, has turned against the ego and was strengthened in doing so.†

* Compare Anna Freud, *Phantasy of Beating and Day-Dream* (*Schlagephantasie und Tagtraum. Imago* VIII. 1922, p. 317 f.).

† There are reasons for me to assume that the special kind of cruel self-irony in the jokes of the Jews about weaknesses and shortcomings of their own peo-

The suppressed aggressiveness, which now can only turn against the ego, gradually adduces an extraordinary tension that could achieve the destruction of the ego. As soon as this aggressiveness attains a certain intensity, not determinable by us, the ego succeeds in warding it off. It is again turned back outward, a new object-cathexis takes place, a fantasy of revenge and sometimes actual revenge action. Clearly the turning back to sadism is an attempt of the endangered ego at self-rescue. The ego would have perished had it not succeeded in throwing the aggressiveness outward. Analytic investigation of those eruptions can show that they owe their vehemence and explosive power also to the pressure

---

ple originate in a similar attitude. The impossibility of taking revenge on their enemies was caused by external circumstances and was a decisive cause of that attitude. This is the example of a phenomenon, concerning the psychology of peoples, borne out by the psychic dynamics here described. The offense or hurt from outside, the suppression of revenge caused by the adversary's actual superior power, the introjection of the hated object into the ego and the rage against it. The peculiarity of this interesting phenomenon is the fact that the aggression against the ego creates its expressions in those jokes which mercilessly castigated its own weaknesses and faults. Compared with them, the derision of the Jews by the people among whom they lived appear like clumsy or brutal farces. The suppression of vengeance is one of the causes of the special sharpness and unerring aim of the Jewish joke against the Jews, as this vengeance is secretly contained in it. The Jewish joke against its own people strikes at the heart. The attack, coming from the peoples among whom the Jews live, does not injure any vital organ, however brutal and violent the attack may be. Only seldom is this second phase of aggression followed by the third in which not the changed ego, but, again the external object, the offender, is attacked. The object's continuing superior power is the cause of this inhibition, too. However, it cannot be denied that the aggression of the Jewish joke against its own people hits also the people among whom the Jews live, in a latent way, but recognizable to the unconscious. This particular kind of joke betrays the suppressed rebellion even in the self-humiliation and self-parody. It hits, in its turning against the ego, the object absorbed into the ego, as if to say, "See what has become of us through you and your guilt! See what miserable, weak and terrified creatures you have made of us!" Without an understanding of the psychic mechanisms here described, and revealed only by psychoanalysis, the psychology of the Jewish joke would never go below the surface. (Compare my paper "About the Psychoanalysis of the Jewish Joke" in *Imago*, 1929, issue 1.)

which has been exerted on the warded-off tendencies. This investigation is comparable to a geological examination of erupting, destructive masses of lava which show their power to have been increased by silent struggles in the earth's interior.

3

It may be worthwhile to point out a few more features of this special reaction of vengeance. In cases where real actions of revenge ensue from the described psychic constellation, they rarely cause serious damage to the object. They contrast noticeably with the extremely cruel, sophisticated and variegated tortures invented for their victims by the individuals in their pleasurable fantasies. It is as though one or more definite emotional factors prevented extensive damage to the object. One might surmise that this feature is connected with the one that earlier caused an inhibition of the aggression against the ego. In one case it was the extreme of damage to the object which was avoided, in the other, the extreme of damage to the ego, entirely in accord with the previously mentioned assumption of acts of revenge against formerly beloved persons. It is as if the transitory phase leading from the hostile impulse, via introjection of an object, to the turning again against the object, could offer effective protection against too severe damage of the object. The fantasies have in the meantime taken on, as it were, the function of a buffer. In them, partial gratification is anticipated and does not have to be sought any longer in reality. In several cases, it could be seen that the actions of revenge had a harmless and infantile, sometimes almost clownish character, contrasting conspicuously with the cruel nature of the preceding fantasies. In one of these cases, the patient, who had a serious dissension with his family, came to visit his parents following a sudden impulse. He listened accidentally when his family, assembled in the next room, made some unfavorable remarks about his behavior. He seized a large cake prepared on the table for the whole family, ran away without saying a word, and ate it up at high speed.

Perhaps I should point out the part apparently played by the *word* in the fantasies of revenge. I do not mean the insults and curses used by these people at the appropriate point in their revenge fantasies towards their objects.* What I mean is the expression of the vengeful tendencies in verbal presentations, or rather, the imagined details of the action of revenge described in special, quite definite words frequently repeated in the fantasies. I was, thus, astonished at the stereotyped phrase which a neurotic used in his fantasies of revenge, "To tear the jewel from his chest." He borrowed this sentence from the description of an ancient Peruvian or Aztec sacrificial feast where the heart is torn out of the human sacrifice.

In another case, a strong, clearly sexually-colored gratification appeared in the person as soon as he imagined, in his fantasies, his use of a certain insulting expression in a particular situation. All this is in complete accord with our experiences concerning the psychology of sadistic and masochistic perversions. In a considerable number of cases of this kind, the word or a certain sequence of words is of definite significance. A masochist became thus sexually excited only when his partner spoke to him in a particular way or said certain words that had emotional value discernible only to him, originating in infantile experiences. In other cases, a whole ceremonial of words developed, enhancing the

* The psychologist can understand why verbal eruptions of this kind constitute a verbal substitute for action. They are, so to speak, actions in words. They approach magic action and they are apt to associate themselves with it. It suffices to point to many old customs of folklore of this kind, which pertain to the realm of "black magic." It is not surprising if occasionally the same phenomenon can be found in persons of a very high cultural level. Thus Disraeli says about himself that he never took revenge on an offender. He would only write that person's name on a slip of paper and bury it in a drawer. It is remarkable, he says, how soon the bearer of that name sinks into oblivion. (According to A. Maurois, *La vie de Disraeli*. Paris, 1928, p. 264.) Psychoanalysis will easily recognize in this practice a symbolic action equivalent to a burial in which the drawer containing the enemy's name is substituted for his coffin.

sexual desire and containing insulting or humiliating expressions. The significance of this verbal masochism has not yet been thoroughly explored and its study seems to hold great promise.

I said earlier that, in the type observed, serious damage to the object through revenge came about rarely. In a few cases, however, such actions were accomplished and revenge fully took its cruel course. But it was noteworthy that these actions turned out to be almost more damaging to the person's own ego, which happened either simultaneously with the action or as its consequence and could have easily been foreseen. This looks like a reaction in two directions, as if the ego would readily pay the full price of its own ruin if only the hated object would perish at the same time. The conditions, emotional and otherwise, conducive to this kind of revenge do not seem to have been clarified completely yet.

A particularly intense unconscious feeling of guilt will have to be considered in the study of these cases. It is the same as that sense of guilt which finds its place and relief in the accomplishment of the forbidden deed. At this point, we approach the psychology of criminal types first pointed out by Freud—of those who became criminals through unconscious feeling of guilt. The perpetrator of the deed is shown to be its second victim, unless one would call him its original, primary victim. The deed has perhaps cast its shadow over him in advance. A number of observations and analytic experiences might be inserted at this point, which could furnish far-reaching and bewildering revelations about the motives and psychogenesis of a special type of criminal. A great number of the cases of those we call juvenile delinquents belong to this group. It has not yet been said that the unconscious feeling of guilt, preceding the crime, behaves like any other repressed material. It can be demonstrated, through its outgrowths admissible into the conscious, that the same processes of condensation, displacement, generalization here take place as in the symptomatology of neuroses. Below the surface, the criminal's associations pursue their way via his deed. His associations of sound do the same.

We do not deny the fact that the part of criminal psychology, revealed by psychoanalysis, derives mostly from analogy with neurotic psychic life where criminal tendencies emerge as veins occur in rock, and that it concerns only certain types of criminals. These are two instances of associations in which the repressed aggressive tendency returns from the center of the repressed: the father of an analysand talks to him about a projected trip to Egypt. The son says, "You must buy a tropical suit. Linen would perhaps be best." This very moment he recalls having once seen the body of a person who had died on board ship, as it was lowered into the sea, shrouded in linen. In another analysand's dream, he tells his mother that he wants chicken, but she brings him beef and he wakes up in anxiety. The interpretation in part was facilitated by the fact that in American slang of this time "chicken" connoted young girl. Beef, taking the place of chicken, connoted the flesh of his father who had been killed.

For the type discussed here, the crime is a shock which can be overcome only through long emotional work. Its effect is that of a trauma and it often produces the same psychic phenomena. The return to the scene of the deed, so frequently an obsession with the criminal, represents perhaps one of those attempts at overcoming the deed psychically, comparable to the phenomena in victims of accident-neurosis. They, too, try to free themselves from the emotional pressure, in reliving the deed so that the latter appears to be a passive experience. Thus we find a surprising connection between the psychology of a certain criminal type and that of the victim of accident-neurosis. The remembrance of the crime is interrupted by attempts at annulment, by conscious flashes of doubt in the nature of an assertion such as, "I can't have done that," that hold against the certainty of the accomplished deed. As in obsessional neurosis, this doubt is often displaced onto a minor detail, for instance, whether or not a lantern was lighted at the scene of the crime, etc.

Considering the ground I have to cover, I am obliged to abandon this interesting topic and to return to the strictly limited subject of this investigation.

4

I started with the unequivocal statement that the unconscious does not know the concept of forgiveness and that this concept belongs entirely to the conscious mind. The preceding presentation has shown how the process, resulting from a psychic hurt and originally concerning the relation between A and B, subject and object, can become a conflict within the ego if certain circumstances cause this development. In that phase, the original offense, directed at the object, will turn against the ego which comes to feel all the aggressiveness and strictness of the superego. The defense against the aggressive tendencies causes reactively their unconscious increase and, thus, an accordingly deepened feeling of guilt. The postponement of revenge has definitely a part in this development as the endopsychically recognized aggressive tendencies are subjected to strict evaluation by the superego. As in analytic investigation of other emotional processes, we recognize the fact that it is often much more cruel to make a person his own judge than to have him judged by another. The Church recognized this intuitively and made use of it in the institution of confession.*

* The deepening of the unconscious feeling of guilt through postponement of revenge can be clearly seen in Hamlet's psychology, as well as the turning of the vengeful tendencies against the ego, the destruction of which is aimed at. "To be or not to be . . ." This heavy feeling of guilt of the prince leads him, indeed, to his ruin simultaneously with the annihilation of the object. The postponement of revenge causes a sense of guilt in him as does the omission of the originally forbidden action in the final phases of obsessional neurosis. The expression "sicklied o'er with the pale cast of thought" used by Hamlet in describing how "enterprises of great pith and moment lose the name of action" clearly points to the death-wishes directed against the ego. Paleness is unconsciously conceived as a sign of death. The inhibition of the action of revenge also means, to Shakespeare, the tragic guilt of Hamlet and is regretted by him. Even at the end, Fortinbras declares that this inhibition prevented him from ascending the throne, saying "For he was likely, had he been put on, To have prov'd most royally."

In consideration of the correlated conscious processes, a conclusion suggests itself from the insight into this psychic process, a conclusion that sounds paradoxical. It is impossible to forgive another unless one forgives oneself first. Even if expressed in another way, it still sounds paradoxical: we can forgive only if we meet our own vengeful tendencies and drives for reprisal with a certain tolerance. From that it would follow that forgiveness is impossible if introjection of the object has taken place because then the aggressiveness turns against the ego.

In other words, we can forgive only after having taken revenge on the object or on the ego changed through introjection of the object. Revenge is, unconsciously, unavoidable. If it does not strike the external object, it strikes the object introjected into the ego.* We recall here how frequently the course of the second vengeful reaction, which I called archaic, can be observed in *statu nascendi* in children when they have no other possibility of reprisal. "You will cry, Mother, when I go out on the terrace and catch cold," said a small girl threateningly when she felt hurt by her mother. The revenge taken on the ego or, rather, on the introjected object can, in its emotional effectiveness, be observed well in the analysis of adult neurotics.

I received my first impression of the intensity of the psychic forces effective here, when I analyzed an elderly lady who had been living with her sister, and for many years quarreling most bitterly with her. She was completely bald from the crown of her head down. She had torn out her hair in terrible rage in scenes of quarrels through many years. When invited in the first session to say what came to her mind, she stayed silent and for many sessions I could not move her to express those thoughts. All urging was futile. She could not decide to say what she had been thinking of. Finally she gave in and against most intense resistance, she disclosed the first thought of the first session. Lying on the sofa in my office, she had seen some dust under the bookcase and, be-

* Compare the hara-kiri of the Japanese, committed in front of the enemy's door.

cause of it, she bitterly criticized the qualities of my wife as a housewife. My wife was, in this case, a sister-image.*

I believe I have shown that, for the unconscious, only reprisal can be an adequate form of reaction to offenses, hurts and damage, and that the concept of forgiveness has no validity for the unconscious emotional life. I have hitherto traced the psychic process only in the hurt or offended person. He will, I said, feel hurt or offended until he has taken reprisal upon the adversary or upon himself. His vengeful tendencies will, in a certain emotional constellation, turn against the ego, the more intensely so, the less he takes revenge on the other person. He will take revenge upon himself for everything that he wanted to inflict upon the other person. Or, more correctly, he will take revenge upon himself for everything the other person has done to him. That would not make sense unless the ego, changed through identification with the object, were concerned. The raging of the ego against the object is continued in the raging of the ego against itself. Thus continues also the rage against the introjected object against which the motor reaction did not take place. The single event is reproduced, as it were, on one's own and re-enacted continuously. Here it can be seen clearly how much more deeply the analytical ego-psychology penetrates than the ego-psychology of Adler who explains these same phenomena much more simply and in a way better adjusted, of course, to popular comprehension.

No less significant and interesting is another part of ego-psychology, not yet investigated by psychoanalysis. That is the emotional process in the offender, the person who inflicts damage, after he has perpetrated his action. I refer here again to a certain type which is neurotic or close to the neurotic character, a type whose special psychic attitude I attempted to describe in *Compulsion to Confess* and *Need for Punishment*. I attempted to show the psychic mechanisms that cause certain persons to turn aggressively

---

* My analytic technique of urging was entirely wrong in this case. Only loosening of the feeling of guilt would have allowed expression of the thought which was engendered by hatred. This observation sheds significant light on various problems of analytic technique.

against those toward whom they feel guilty. This peculiar phenomenon goes further. Many people show particularly strong hostility and hatred toward those very persons who offer them only good will, friendliness and even love. These, it should be noted, are not the often discussed cases of lack of gratefulness, at least not only these.

To the unconscious, gratefulness is as foreign as is forgiveness. Love takes its place. The paradoxical phenomenon, consists, however, in the fact that a special vengeful tendency is directed against the very persons toward whom one has an especially good reason to feel gratefulness and appreciation. In the theory of the compulsion to confess, I tried to explain that this peculiar attitude originates in the unconscious feeling of guilt and that it means to say, as it were, "I am not worthy of this kindness or friendliness. I am not deserving of so many favors." The observation is noteworthy and psychologically consistent that this peculiar vindictiveness increases the more, as the other, the attacked person, continues to show more love, patience and friendliness.

Under these psychic circumstances, a peculiar emotional cycle evolves. If the offended person does not take revenge but remains composed and friendly, this attitude is felt to be somewhat humiliating. It incites a still more intense desire to hurt or to offend, to be aggressive toward the patient object. It is as though the offender feels the renunciation from revenge to be an especially sophisticated and sublimated form of revenge or scorn. This is entirely in accord with what I said earlier about the impossibility of unconscious forgiveness. It seems as if this odd attitude endeavored to show how impossible it is to renounce the gratification of revenge. It seems as if the offender or the enemy, as we may call him, sensed it to be inhuman not to take revenge, and that the injured person must unequivocally feel strong vengeful tendencies in himself whether he shows them or not.

It is an uncanny feeling for the enemy if his deed—or misdeed, if you will—does not drive the injured person into natural hostile or retaliatory action. He will try to provoke this action through accumulation or increase of the offense, because his unconscious moral anxiety tells him that revenge cannot fail to appear, that there is no final renunciation of revenge. He is outraged by friendly or forgiving behavior on the part of the offended person because he also senses in it revenge of a special kind. This is the way the Romans may have felt about the attitude of the first persecuted Christians. Their renunciation from revenge drove the Romans to humiliate them still more deeply, in fact, drove them to orgies of hate. They felt unconscious arrogance in that renunciation and they sensed that this was a new, special kind of revenge against which there existed no protection, and they were driven to fury.* The enormous moral anxiety of the Romans is one of the most important motives of the persecutions of the Christians. Their anxiety was justified. Today Rome is Christian, the city of *"senatus populusque Romanus"* exists no more and that slender, despised Rabbi from Galilee has had his frightful and most sublime revenge.

Using a case of neurosis, I shall elsewhere discuss more thoroughly this bewildering part of ego-psychology. It will suffice here to point to the fact that this special unconscious mechanism can be demonstrated by no means only in the emotional life of neurotic patients. Traces of its effectiveness can be found also in persons who would be called psychically healthy. A man who is furious with his tailor to whom he owes money is subjected to its influence no less than the pupil who drops his teacher, to whom he owes much, surprisingly fast and turns against him. This mechanism of sadistic aggression, originating in the unconscious feeling of guilt, dominates the defiant criminal as well as the children who show off a kind of demonstrative naughtiness.† The wife who comes home with a dress that is too expensive is especially apt to reproach her husband for having dropped ashes on the tablecloth. The husband, returning from a little extramarital adventure, unconsciously reproaches his wife because he feels

* The analytical way of thinking can deepen the psychological explanation, given by Nietzsche, for the origin of the feelings of resentment, through the mechanisms of introjection of an object.

† Compare *Compulsion to Confess and Need for Punishment.*

guilty towards her. He is very much exposed to the temptation to provoke a quarrel or a marital scene if his unconscious feeling of guilt exceeds a certain limit.

I repeat, what has been discussed here concerns only a certain psychological type, a group of people whose number, of course, increases steadily under the influence of our cultural conditions. Analytic investigation of these cases reveals that the representatives of this type cannot forgive their fellowman the hurt which they inflicted upon him and hate the object offended or injured by them the more deeply, the less the object is prepared to take revenge. The quintessence of the body of observed psychic facts concerning this type can be expressed in two formulas—revenge on one's self for the hurt not inflicted upon the other person, and revenge on the other person for the hurt inflicted upon him. These persons do not forgive themselves for what they have not done to the other and they do not forgive the other for what they have done to him.*

It is clear from the preceding how little emotional significance there is in forgiveness from outside compared with the criticism and hardness of the superego within these people. Frequently, external forgiveness is accepted only by the conscious mind while the superego drives the ego the more relentlessly and mercilessly towards destruction. The religions have analogies to this psychic phenomenon. The Catholic Church discusses it in the difficult chapter of scruples. The sinner, for instance, does not feel redeemed through the confession, but the more guilty, even unredeemable. Then Catholicism expects *gratia,* grace, to redeem the miserable penitent, to loosen that stubborn feeling of guilt, which turns against the ego and aims to judge and destroy the object with it.

Forgiveness may be considered an attempt at conscious cancel-

* Women frequently behave in this way which only seems illogical. A patient appeared for her analytical session in bad humor declaring that she was furious with me. "It is as if you have given me grounds to feel guilty towards, you." That same patient expects other people to be especially nice to her when she treats them badly and brutally. Her demand is psychologically justified as it seems to say, "How unhappy I must be to behave so badly."

lation, a felt disclaimer of a fact whereby the essence of the emotions stimulated by the fact remains in the unconscious. Its character as a reaction-formation does not exclude, but rather includes, this continued existence of the original tendencies. It has been said that it is inhuman and unnatural to turn the other cheek if a person has been struck on one. But the fact has not been taken into consideration that this Christian teaching concerns a reaction to the unconscious tendency to answer by striking both cheeks of the person who struck on one cheek. It hence teaches meekness as a reaction to particularly strong fury and thirst for revenge.*

5

Even though forgiveness can be recognized as reaction-formation of the conscious only, the milder judgment of people, of their tendencies and actions, is quite possible. The most important prerequisite for this attitude is a reduction of the ideal demands. He who makes excessively high demands of this kind on himself is compelled to become cruel and vengeful. The great reformers and moralists became bloodthirsty as soon as they came to power over people because they expected too much of them. Robespierre's faith in human virtue was unshakable. He had, therefore, to have several thousand French heads cut off.

Little confidence in the possibilities of human perfection is one of the most essential pre-conditions for the love of people and for tolerance.** It may sound even stranger that tolerance to-

---

* Analysis of this reaction-formation shows again that repression of aggressive tendencies brings about their intensification. Two examples of the described contrasting reactions may be given here. A patient refuses to give me her hand declaring that she is angry with me because she had to masturbate the night before. It is as if her hand were taboo. Another patient cannot make himself get up early in the morning, becomes furious with himself and lets himself fall out of bed, injuring himself seriously.

** "I always thought the worst of people, especially of myself, and I have rarely been wrong yet." (Nestroy)

wards the ego is one of the prerequisites of mild and just judgment of one's neighbor. One must be able to forgive oneself in order to forgive others. He who is too strict towards himself will be resentful and vindictive toward others. This may be contrary to accepted ethics, but it has the advantage of being psychologically true.*

At this point I return to the sentence, "To understand all is to forgive all." To suggest that one can understand all implies monstrous arrogance. To consider understanding all to be the same as forgiving all, implies a no less monstrous psychological error. It is not given to us, ephemeral beings on this small planet of ours, to understand everything, and if we could do so, to take revenge would be just as senseless as to forgive, because then every intense emotion and action of this kind would be senseless. The very fact that we love and hate and that, following our ambitions, we are ever making efforts, is the result of an illusion—"*L'illusion c'est tout.*" Even science is only a small, faint light in the deep darkness around us and while we proudly call ourselves explorers, we are comparable to a few daring moles, who for several minutes emerge from their burrows, blink their aching little eyes at the world, and then imagine they can impart to their fellow moles a comprehensive idea of the earth. Under closer scrutiny, the demand implied in the second part, as well as the first, of that remark about understanding and forgiving is presumptive, too. What gives us frail and miserable ephemeral beings the right to forgive each other? Tolerance of galley slaves chained together toward each other is no virtue nor can it be demanded with great moral aplomb.

* This is no contradiction of Freud's remark that he who restricts aggression towards the external world becomes stricter towards the ego (Gesammelte Schriften, Vol. VI), but rather supplements it. When this strictness has become too great the ego tries to save itself, aggression turning back against the external world. As always, analytical research faces here, too, eventually, a problem of instinctual quantities. I believe I have shown elsewhere that forgiveness towards oneself, tolerance towards the ego, is a prerequisite for our understanding of certain things in ourselves and in others. Compare my book *Wie man Psychologie wird*, Internat. P. A. Vienna, 1927.

Generally it should be remembered that the practical value of
maxims like that of Mme. de Staël is as small as that of other moral
statements. Similarly, the exhortation for tolerance, for mutual
forgiveness, has little prospect of success in the face of the unchangeable human psychophysical constitution. Christ called
Himself meek and praised the peaceful. His teachings have offered
peace to the world forever. Since then, there has not been the
smallest piece of land in Europe that has not been soaked with
the blood of murdered people.

V

Success and Social Anxiety

A Contribution to the Analytic Exploration of Fate

1

IN its early stages, psychoanalysis had been occupied exclusively with the etiology of neuroses, but soon was compelled to divert its attention from the symptoms of the patients to other topics. Actually, a surprisingly large part of the patients' lives, their whole emotional development, the essence of their biography found its expression in a language not restricted to the inadequate medium of conscious verbal presentation alone. Nervous illness proved to be part of the person's fate, a rather important part, as it absorbed the suffering patient's interest and severely restricted the possibilities of his work and pleasure.

It was not so important, however, as it appeared to the patient in its displacing of everything else, because the disturbance represented the result of complex psychic processes which had for a long time preceded it. All that was emotionally effective and essential occurred before the onset of the illness. The illness, its etiology, its course and prognosis, its basis and aims as far as the drives were concerned, represented that fragment of the patient's fate which had first revealed itself to the analyst in the most conspicuous and obtrusive manner and attracted his close attention. This fragment was not the only one. The really decisive events in the individual's life, as in that of nations, are usually not very conspicuous nor obtrusive. The quietest, not the noisiest, hours determine our fate.

431

It seems to me that Freud led science closer towards comprehension of this obscure concept of fate, closer than anybody else in many generations. He started from, and then, time and again, returned to the postulate that natural tendency and experience, disposition and accidental causes, all form a mutually complementary whole. The tracing back of individual constellations to the psychosexual constitution and the experiences of submerged years of childhood, the consideration of instinctual disposition and development of the libido, the influences of the family and of education, the observation of the coexistence of inner demands and those of the external world, and of their mutual conflicts show psychoanalysis to be one of the essential paths toward revelations concerning the individual's fate.

It would certainly be wrong to grant too much validity to Friedrich Schiller's emphatic statement that the stars of our fate are in our hearts. At any rate, these stars come out and fade away in some cases, as for example, in that of a cripple or of a child with congenital syphilis. Exploration of constitution and heredity, a consideration of biological, social and economic factors, show how little the purely psychological aspect takes account of the complexity of the entire picture. But analysis has, in its investigation of human instinctual life and of the unconscious processes, revealed the great extent to which psychic processes determine the fate of the individual. Analysis is able to point out and to describe, in its effects, one of the most important and hitherto not appreciated determinants in the play of forces of all the exogenic and endogenic factors resulting in the human fate.

Analysis is destined to make one of the most essential contributions to an investigation which should be called research into fate. Analysis does this at the point where it joins efforts to find the laws of events and to uncover the relations that exist among all individual happenings. While other disciplines reveal facts concerning the manifold, determining exogenic factors like climate, natural surroundings, race, etc., psychoanalysis offers hitherto unseen, hitherto not exhausted, possibilities for the scientific comprehension and appreciation as to their effects in depth, of psychic determinants of an unconscious kind.

I do not mean to lay claim in what I have said to have opened a new aspect for the psychoanalyst, but to have formulated a hitherto not defined task of research. I should add, at once, that many unsystematic attempts have been made at an analytic exploration of fate. Various analytical publications build bridges to this new field of research, although not aiming in the same direction. They are detailed histories of patients, analytical biographies of great personalities, various attempts at a systematic explanation of character. It is not difficult to point out in what way these contributions differ from those I have in mind and to what extent they follow the same direction.

The essential points of view for analytical research into fate should be able to show the decisive (at least nearly decisive) significance of unconscious factors in the life of the individual, as far as they determine illness and health, success and failure, choice of the love-object and way of life, ascent and decline, etc. The role of coincidence which has, not altogether incorrectly, been called "fate traveling incognito" would be further reduced if individual experiences, their mutual connection and their general course were to be considered from this analytical angle. Its role would be reduced, but not entirely eliminated.

Man of western culture is accustomed to acknowledge only the facts of external reality. Analytical research into fate, however, would suggest with mild but increasing insistence that he recognize and acknowledge the hidden but decisive realities of emotional dynamics. This way of looking at the individual's fate and at the fate of many individuals is no more suited up to this time to furnish an answer to the futile question of the meaning of life than any other way. It can, however, perhaps show much of what happens in life according to a law, possibly a senseless law. If seen from this angle, the pattern of psychosexual life would unequivocally emerge as a determining factor for all the rest of a person's being, and this not only for pathological individuals.

Undoubtedly this analytical research into fate would have its share in the incompleteness, inadequacy, and discontinuity of all human comprehension. It will mean merely a tiny alteration of our limits towards the recognizable. It will shed faint, often flickering light upon a strip of the darkness around us and within us. It would be wrong to be ashamed of this limitation of scientific work and to tend to conceal it timidly. Research does not acknowledge horror in discovery nor any horror in a vacuum.

2

These are tasks for a generation of psychologists, for *"le grand. psychologie de demain."*

One of the most fascinating topics of analytical research into fate will be the problem of success and failure. Here, too, Freud was the first, the "prodromos" of future research, to point to a part of the problem, but perhaps the essential one. Although he did not later emphasize the psychological significance of this particular phase of that research, Freud has shown that failure following success, typical in the cases he described, can be explained by the underground effectiveness of the powers of unconscious conscience. It can be proven by analysis that this effectiveness originates primarily in the Oedipus complex. It is as if every success later in life were tied by secret threads to the paramount success at which we aimed in our childhood, as if, unconsciously, success in later life, however distant it may be from its origin, was significant in the accomplishment of those early proscribed wishes. From this origin, the reaction of conscience receives its strength and lasting quality. This success, however, is abandoned the moment it has been achieved.

Another type of character formation should be pointed out here, which at first looks like a variation of that analytically described by Freud. While the latter type of individual fails as soon as success has been achieved, the type I shall describe now never permits himself (unless under definite internal conditions) to achieve success. This concerns a great number of people who, time and again, manage unconsciously to put new obstacles between the determination of a goal and its achievement, and so never, or too late, see their wishes fulfilled. The semblance of fate in a life of this kind appears most clearly in all those cases where the goal is almost reached and suddenly there is a seemingly altogether external obstacle that cannot be overcome. In analysis, the fact is often discovered that these persons, as the invisible managers, arranged for the unexpected obstacle or at least have made use of its existence with extraordinary unconscious skill. They are especially gifted stage managers, as it were, in this play of fate which they seem to attend as spectators only.

Over and over, the impression is gained in the analysis of these people, that a great effort is wasted at the very moment when it should find its justification. One cannot deny that success and failure in these cases do not only depend upon the effect of unconscious factors. Often enough, actual external factors, circumstances of material reality play along in a tragic, more often tragicomic, fate of this kind. But sometimes it is entirely clear that these people who suffer under their fate behave like a mischievous demiurge (he may be called God, as well) who, in an elaborate and carefully planned way, produces these very turns of fate. These people are not conscious of the fact that they are imitating so exalted a model. Every analyst knows of a large number of cases where, whenever success approaches, these unforeseen obstacles pile up.

With another type, the desired success is attained, but satisfaction in it is wanting. I know of the case of a very intelligent man, an artist, in whose life a typical situation keeps reoccurring. He feels a strong urge for the enjoyment of life, often is even obsessed by it, but indulges in it only seldom. Again and again, he postpones the gratification of his wishes until he shall have achieved this or that goal. But when the goal is attained, it does not seem to him to be enough and the gratification of his wishes is again postponed. When he pauses in his work, he has lively daydreams of how he will enjoy life, after first having completed this or that piece of work. These fantasies are his best consolation in the strong depressions to which he easily falls victim in his aversion against the work and in his struggle with his brittle material. After the work is completed and critically examined by him, it does not seem to him to be a success any longer, compared with the image he had in mind, but he sees it now as full of flaws and mistakes. It does not seem to satisfy his demands now. A new plan emerges and he is forced to postpone the fulfillment of his wishes until after its execution. Time and again, he repeats to himself, "I am going to go to Cairo or the Riviera, associate with beautiful women and finally enjoy life, once I have finished this accursed work." In this cycle he never attains the longed-for enjoyment.

An idea of the significance of this ever increasing, never fulfilled wish may be gained in the analytical consideration of certain features in the biography of Giovanni Segantini. The artist's birthplace where he spent the first five carefree years of his childhood was Arco. His mother died then and the small boy had to leave home. He never saw his birthplace again. The wish to return to Arco arose in him over and over when he was alone in the mountains of the Engadine, where he painted in later years. While he worked, this was one of his most urgent wishes. Always he wanted to see the beloved town again and eventually he set the date for this trip as the time when he would complete his great triptych of the Alpine World. "As a reward," he wrote, he would fulfill his long-cherished wish when he had attained that goal. He died a few weeks before he attained it.*

In a case which was under my observation, the typical postponement of wish-fulfillment was combined with a definite anal factor. A business man kept planning for his retirement from work when he could, *procul negotiis,* enjoy his hard won savings in a pleasant and leisurely manner. But the date of retirement for

---

* It is peculiar that Dr. Karl Abraham overlooked this significant feature in his beautiful study (*Giovanni Segantini,* 2nd edition, 1925, Leipzig) in which so much emphasis is rightly put on the artist's relationship with his mother who had died early.

which he longed was postponed again and again because the available financial means always seemed to him to be too small to warrant a comfortable, carefree life, although an objective observer would have considered them ample. Whenever he thought he had provided for everything, he found he possessed too little to cover his needs. He was, as it were, a Tantalus in an industrialist's garb.

Analysis of cases of this kind leaves no doubt as to an unconscious secret anxiety that deprives these persons of the fruits of their work, forces postponement of gratification and prevents them from fulfilling their wishes. What seems to be an increased, strict demand, posed by reality, is actually a secret prohibition on the part of the superego for which a rationalization has been found. The analyst does not find it difficult to discover the analogy to this peculiar behavior in the symptomatology of obsessional neurosis. What is shown in obsessional neurosis, by the various compulsive traits in pathological distortion and in exaggerated forms, is generalized, displaced and demonstrable in a form closer to reality in the way the lives of these persons, namely, their fate, develop.

The victims of obsessional neurosis renounce instinctual gratification for mysterious or obscure reasons, or they permit it only upon the fulfillment of definite, very complex and extensive protective or safety measures. In the course of that disturbance, the conditions to be fulfilled will multiply, become more complex and weigh down the ego more heavily and oppressively. Ever more elaborate obstacles will be thrown in the way of the gratification of impulses, which becomes less and less possible and is postponed until all those conditions are fulfilled in the most exact way and in every detail. Obedience to the conditions, often time consuming and pedantic, will gradually fill the whole life of the patient or the best part of it.

Another feature of symptom-formation in obsessional neurosis, as observed in analysis, comes to mind here for comparison. First and foremost, in the psychogenesis of obsessional neurosis there is involved a definite, for example, a sexual, instinctual gratification, while the net thrown by the compulsion is then extended farther and farther. Now every enjoyment is postponed as though it were the representative of that prohibited sexual gratification. In almost all cases of obsessional neurosis, we find instinctual gratification postponed until all protective measures are fulfilled, or we find it prevented by an inner prohibition.

One of my patients, who suffered from a washing obsession, had to follow an extraordinarily complicated ceremonial before he could even allow himself to go to the theatre, for instance. Ever new conditions originating in the system of the washing compulsion opposed the lively urge for this pleasure, until the visit to the theatre had eventually to be given up. Long before all compulsive actions prescribed by the precept of protection against dangers of infection were executed, the theater performance was over. In this case, as in an abundance of others, a pleasure harmless in itself had obviously been treated psychically, as if it were a dangerous undertaking that could be ventured upon only after the accomplishment of definite safety measures. The postponement and all the conditions that caused it find their explanation in the defense against an unconscious anxiety connected with the instinctual gratification which is followed originally.

The analysis of the cases described here can be fully understood if they are compared with the emotional dynamics of these compulsive symptoms. A secret anxiety exerts its influence, an anxiety that opposes fulfillment, especially, of the strongest wishes. The analyst need not be particularly ingenious to arrive at a conclusion concerning the motives, which results from the psychic effect. If the postponement has the meaning and the effect of defense, it clearly follows that attainment of the instinctual aim, or fulfillment of those wishes, implies a situation which for obscure reasons the ego opposes. There evolves, therefore, a situation desired and dreaded at the same time, desired on the part of the drives of the individual, dreaded on the part of his ego.

The anxiety originally concerned castration, became fear of death and continued as unconscious moral anxiety. It became less distinct, more stifling, withdrew from the conscious, but was none the less powerful. Whether, in approaching the desired instinctual goal, it will then express itself as indistinct discomfort, or whether it will be completely silent, or hide behind a reactively increased self-confidence, the anxiety will still be there and be the stronger the less the way into consciousness is open to it. The obscure threatening punishment now originates in uncontrollable powers, and is feared to be approaching from fate or from God.

The closer the goal is, the stronger grow the inner voices delaying or forbidding its attainment; the more strongly powers seem to intrude into sober everyday life, powers which we thought we had overcome long ago. Into the modern world of electric lights, of automobiles, of dynamos, of radio, a power feels its way that comes from primeval days and exerts greater coercion than all the technical upsurge and all the so-called progress of a civilization that believes it has freed itself from God, while it merely has been abandoned by Him. On that wall there appears, ghost-like, next to the electric advertising signs, the newest dispatches about the formation of trusts, stock value, entertainment advertisements, a *mene tekel* written by an invisible and strong hand.

In tracing back the psychic processes of the described type, psychoanalysis, again and again, arrives, via some intermediary stations, at the same situation in childhood, a situation that is like a germ cell of this later, peculiar phenomenon. An instinctual impulse emerged, imperiously ordered gratification and came into conflict with the demands of the external world. It could be gratified only if that obstacle in the external world were eliminated. This was for certain reasons the first condition against which the ego struggled. The simplest and certainly primary instance of an emotional situation of this kind is shown in the conflict of the child's sexual drive and the prohibitions from outside.

The boy who wishes to follow his sexual impulse, must, in his fantasies, come across the image of the forbidding and admired father. This inhibiting authority must be removed if the sexual gratification is to be permitted. From the original fear of castration as punishment for a violation of the prohibition, fear of death developed on the part of the ego as a reaction-formation to repressed death-wishes against the father. The fear of death, in its more subdued, less outspoken form, appears as moral anxiety. If the father's death is the condition *sine qua non* for uninhibited instinctual gratification, the ego will endeavor to fend off those strong wishes. The conflict between those urges and the forces of defense has been declared permanent. After that, there is no peace, only shorter or longer truces in the ego.

Later on, the pattern which originally concerned only the sexual conflicts is displaced onto all pleasures unconsciously connected with the grossly sexual ones. For instance, in obsessional neurosis, everything that promises enjoyment for the ego can enter into unconscious connection, through thought, with the father's death or that of a substituted person, and, in this connection, can become the unconscious motive to inhibit the enjoyment. This can best be expressed by defining the enjoyment as the representation of the forbidden, every success as the representative of the longed-for and dreaded overcoming of the father. From here a path opens to the first comprehension of that peculiar attitude towards enjoyment and success which interests us here.

Fear of death is now unconsciously put before the instinctual gratification which it followed earlier.* Now it throws its shadow

---

* This unconscious connection was especially clear in two cases. In both, there existed the wish to see a certain town, and the two people were full of an uncertain fear that something would happen if they were to fulfill that wish. In one case it was the fear of dying. In that case an old prophecy played a role which had been interpreted in this way by my patient. In the other case the patient referred to the saying, "To see Naples and die," which itself may perhaps owe its existence to a superstition of this kind. The psychological affinity of these premonitions and apprehensions to compulsive phenomena comes to the fore if we recall a thought, which started a patient of Freud's on many a brooding thought. Several years after his father's death, this idea forced itself upon the son's mind when, for the first time, he experienced the pleasurable sensation of sexual intercourse, "this is magnificent; for that one could murder one's father." (Freud, "Remarks about a Case of Obsessional Neurosis." Coll. Writ, Vol. VIII. p. 311.) Analysis was able to supply similar explanations in several cases of a stifling fear of the attainment of a certain age. An obsessional patient was tormented by the fear that he would die in his fortieth year. This was the age that his father had reached.

over the bright image of fulfillment. If, for instance, in puberty, severe measures of penance and expiatory practices followed masturbatory activity, the psychic sequence is reversed later. The execution of ever more extensive and complex protective measures is expected to ward off anxiety. Depending upon this execution is the decision of whether or not gratification is to be permitted. During one patient's puberty, each relapse into masturbation was followed by a vow of abstinence for ten days. If that did not succeed, if, for example, an emission occurred during the night, he had to double the vow and postpone the time to permitted masturbation for twice as long, later for three times as long and so on. Afterwards, gradually every pleasure was drawn into the realm of this type of postponement. He forbade himself to visit a theater, to read interesting books, to enjoy stimulating company and conversation, even to read the newspaper until he had remained sexually abstinent for a definite time. Later, this whole procedure became more complicated by the addition of certain protective measures enforcing abstinence. Many little activities had to be accomplished, certain demands of a special kind had to be complied with before he would permit himself even the smallest pleasure. As the intrusion of those satisfactions he fought off disturbed the execution of his compulsive actions more and more, the defensive measures multiplied and the gratification of his wishes had to be postponed more and more.

The reversal of the sequence of gratification to protective measure, into the sequence of protective measure to gratification, is the psychological spot from which a primary insight can be gained into the described portentous constellation. Work or performance frequently takes the place of the protective measure the closer the neurotic situation comes to a socially better adjusted one. Work or performance itself takes on the character of penance, as if in fulfillment of that primeval curse of the tale from Genesis. Analytic observation, however, will not overlook the fact that the longer this process of transformation lasts, the more comprehensively and energetically the work has taken the place of the forbidden gratification. The instinctual component overpowers the

reactive character of the symptom in the final phases of obsessional neurosis. The very expiation slowly becomes sin, one might
say in the theological vernacular.*

In the type here discussed the broadened, socially better adjusted effect in a later phase of this described dynamic course can
be demonstrated in the whole formation of the life, in the development of the fate of the persons concerned. That which had been
there early, reappears late; that which once happened in the nar-
rowest limits is reflected in far reaching relations. We find here
again the condition which had to be fulfilled before the wish is

* In this direction, too, the Church has demonstrated her sure psychological
instinct by repudiating exaggerated self-castigation, calling it a sin. She knows
from experience that in repentance there is still a delayed enjoyment of the
repented deed, and that the desperate attempt to wipe out something that has
happened, often signifies its happening again. The psychology of the flagellant
and of the penitent, in which expiation of carnal lust becomes itself lust of
the flesh, was known to her. An analogous phenomenon is to be found in
the final phases of obsessional neurosis where eventually the illness itself and
the reaction-formations against the fought-off impulses are felt as guilt. There
occur all phenomena which I summed up in the expression, "Expiation becomes sin." This whole process is explained not only through the instinctual
tension, the damming-up of libido, but also through the definite simultaneous
influence of the over great feeling of guilt. Too intensive repentance produces
depression that can be relieved only through perpetration of a new proscribed
deed. The reactive hatred against the person who burdened us with such strong
feelings of repentance is certainly also active in this situation.

Something should be said here about the differentiation between the feeling
of guilt concerning the ego and that which is borrowed. This differentiation
made by Freud is very significant, theoretically and practically, but it does
not erase the fact that primarily there exists only a borrowed feeling of guilt
or that every feeling of guilt is a borrowed one. This can be understood ge-
netically, as well as from the point of view of emotional dynamics. In the very
feeling of guilt somebody else is accused, the one who was responsible for the
rise of that feeling of guilt. Even in the unconscious feeling of guilt, the object in the ego is the target. That which thus accuses itself accuses others, the
parents or their substitutes. Goethe reproaches the gods: "You push us into
life, you let the miserable become guilty." In other words, the feeling of guilt
concerning the ego is a differentiation which derives from the primary, borrowed feeling of guilt. Let us assume a billiard ball, capable of human feelings,
pushes another hard, on the same table. Isn't its feeling of guilt, because of
the damage caused to the other ball, a delusion? Hadn't it been pushed itself?

permitted gratification, and postponement of gratification, which eventually tapers off into its renunciation or, rather, into its substitution.

But in the background, the analyst still recognizes the secret anxiety that unconsciously intrudes between wishful impulse and its gratification. Between the emergence of these wishes and their renunciation, that painful approach and retreat continue which make up the content of a human life, of every human life. "In between, there is left just enough space for the dream of happiness and love to burst and vanish." (Hieronymus Lorm)

3

Analytic consideration of these cases sheds new light upon the psychogenesis of the concept of duty. Duty is originally the fulfillment of the conditions which must be met before one may allow oneself instinctual gratification, hence, it is primarily an effect of social anxiety.* The defensive or protective character of duty cannot remain hidden from deeper psychological insight, even if it aims later to acquire a positive purpose under the influence of the increasing share of gratification. Little does it matter that this concept of duty seemed to detach itself, gradually but completely, from its origin and that, subsequently, the functional relation to the following satisfaction of a drive was dropped. This later phenomenon is psychologically connected with the fact that the

* Freud characterized the feeling of guilt as social anxiety. This determines the origin of the feeling of guilt. The instinctual factor within this still obscure reaction perhaps gains significance, if Freud's explanations are supplemented by the addition of the statement that the feeling of guilt can be traced back to two remembrances, namely, that of the satisfaction of a drive and that of the expectation of punishment. The feeling of guilt may, therefore, be determined as social anxiety in the face of the emergence of a forbidden instinctual impulse. This characterization helps also to understand how there is, in the feeling of guilt, the influence of the memory of the forbidden instinctual gratification, and how the process of repentance still includes its unconscious renewed enjoyment in fantasy.

performance of duty has, itself, annexed some instinctual gratification, has, itself, unconsciously become a partial gratification, in complete analogy to the character of the compromise of neurotic symptoms.

It is difficult to deny that some psychological features here described are also part of the concept of ethics. The greatest emphasis in morality is still on its imperative and prohibitory factor. Instinctual renunciation is still its essential trait, so much so, that a tragicomic *quid pro quo* is possible, namely, that sometimes what is psychically felt as unpleasure is, for that very reason, felt to be ethical. Shaw once wrote the seemingly paradoxical sentence: "An Englishman considers himself moral as soon as he feels uncomfortable." The factor of time in the concept of morals can be traced clearly back to its origin as a reaction and as penitence. From this point of view, morality may be defined as the waiting time which has to be observed until that which was formerly immoral is permitted.

The fateful, unconscious connection of success and a feeling of guilt, as described here, could easily be confused with the relations between success and the overcoming of all the external difficulties of hard and pitiless reality. Certain special factors in the fate of these people, however, cause to disappear any doubt of the fact that emotional powers of an unconscious kind are here at work. Often all external obstacles seem to vanish as by the stroke of a magic wand when success is no longer cherished or when it has been dearly paid for in another field, when, indeed, there no longer remains a motive for the development of anxiety. It is as though success were being bought only by suffering or by the performance of a severe penance. To the psychologist, the inner relation of this phenomenon with the nature of a vow is clear. What is a vow? A promise given to the higher powers to renounce an instinctual gratification in order to see another one, a more highly valued one, fulfilled.

The experience, originating in reality, that success can be achieved only through toil or suffering, that the gods have demanded sweat before granting it, is brought to its extreme in the cases under discussion.* Inversely, success often appears no longer to be valued because not enough sacrifices have been made for it. The pleasure often appears incomplete or empty because it has not been paid for dearly enough. In several cases that I observed, the attainment of success was, unconsciously, so intimately connected with the condition of the father's (or the older brother's) death, that a little anticipated, unconscious mourning had to be recognized in the deep depression preceding the success. The skeleton in the closet seems really a part of the necessary furnishings of every successful and esteemed citizen.

In other cases, psychoanalysis finds that intense effects of anxiety are the emotional payments for success. This was the case with an actress who suffered from extreme stage fright which often grew into attacks of anxiety. The anxiety supplied, as it were, a guarantee for success on stage. Whenever she appeared on stage full of self-confidence, or assurance without anxiety, artistic success was denied to her.

The unconscious moral anxiety before success, or more generally speaking, before happiness, is definitely not limited to neurotics. The religions and the customs of all people testify to the universally human existence and effectiveness of these unconscious feelings. The belief in the evil eye suggests itself in this connection as do the libations which the Romans offered to the gods of the netherworld, to the *diis inferis,* before their banquets. The great significance of the deep-reaching conception of hubris, in Greek faith and tragedy, may be ascribed to the psychic effect of that unconscious moral anxiety.

It often seems as if people were seized by a feeling of uneasiness when they see happiness or success that has not been counterbalanced by pain. "I have paid my debt to happiness," says the wise king in Schiller's poem. He who has observed the always happy man shudders at the envy of the gods, namely, at the feelings of guilt at work underground. These feelings of guilt demand their

* A masochistic patient frequently expressed apprehension that his analysis did not proceed satisfactorily when he felt relatively comfortable, was not tormented by his symptoms or did not feel very depressed.

sacrifices before they allow man to attain the miserable bit of gratification he calls happiness. "Not one have I yet seen to end in
happiness." It is as if the gods, the deified fathers, first lull their
victim into deceptive safety by spreading their gifts with "never-
tiring hands," only to remind him the more frighteningly of their
monstrous, cruel power. Psychoanalytically speaking, the warded-
off feeling of guilt will prevail the more triumphantly, the greater
the energy that has first been expended to ward it off.

In analysis are occasionally found special fateful features which
may appear like a confirmation of the old belief in fate, and which
give an indication of the secret emotional powers at work. The fate
of a certain man, whom I observed, will not easily vanish from my
memory. Time and again, the father had risked a substantial fortune by gambling in stocks. Finally, in the firm hope of regaining
what he had lost, he wagered everything, buying a large number
of certain securities. He lost almost his whole fortune. The son
had reproached him again and again most severely because of his
gambling. A serious conflict developed; their relations were completely severed and the father died while he was traveling abroad,
unreconciled. The son had earned considerable standing for himself by his strenuous work, and slowly he also acquired a fortune.
Under the most difficult circumstances, renouncing many comforts of life, he overcame all obstacles with extraordinary cir-
cumspection and energy. Apparently, he was able to overcome
adverse and hostile circumstances which would have stopped anyone else, and to remove difficulties which seemed insurmount-
able. Several years later, as a mature person, he once felt tempted to
gamble in stocks. He kept winning until he bought certain securities which were almost out of circulation and then suffered severe
losses by this purchase. At the same time that his interest in this
gambling increased, his neurotic symptoms set in and increased
in severity. I could find in analysis repressed facts that showed
the very same securities in the picture, the purchase of which had
ruined his father financially. A similar situation had developed
as that which had caused the breach with his father.

In several other cases, it seemed like an ingenious coincidence of fate when success was spoiled by the very means that had served in its pursuit. Here, too, the accident had been arranged unconsciously or, at least, made use of unconsciously. In these cases more than in others, the impression is clear that success depends not only upon the external conditions and the drives of the ego, but also upon the relations between ego and superego.* At the same time, we come to see the dimension in depth at which the attainment of success is determined by the formation of the individual Oedipus complex which finally crystallizes in the establishment of the superego. The analyst daily has the opportunity to convince himself of the fact that the fight with the external world is not always the most difficult, but that its continuation, the fight between ego and superego, sometimes is the hardest. While man may face a thousand enemies outside himself, in the time of maturation the ego will know none more dangerous than the superego. Not so, when life nears its end. Then death appears as the only real enemy until it, too, becomes the "mildest form of life" to the now tired eyes.

4

If, in this section, a similar type of character is taken into analytical consideration, the limits of this discussion will be exceeded only to a small extent. This concerns only a special case, a particularly obvious variation of the one described earlier. In its fate, appears a peculiar constellation with a tragic note. Coinciding external and internal circumstances, the combined effect of several factors, make the long aimed-at or ardently wished for success take place just when it has become senseless. They permit an intensely desired satisfaction to come near enough to be grasped when it can no longer be enjoyed. This tragic trait is apparent in the fate of some of the great people whom we admire. It is the

---

* Compare Napoleon's remark, "Happiness, too, is a quality." (*Bonheur est aussi une qualité.*)

more tragic when those people feel deeply how much they would have been helped by their success, how much this satisfaction would have meant to them had it been achieved earlier or under other circumstances. When Hebbel lay dying, he said, "First the cup is missing, then the wine." He said this in a concise and eloquent way of his own tragic fate. Lord Beaconsfield, the omnipotent English premier, who had once been a pale, derided and deeply intimated Jewish boy, the son of Isaac d'Israelis, said to his friends who congratulated him when he reached the peak of his career, "For me, it is twenty years too late. Give me your health and your youth." He clearly recognized that success which comes too late scarcely longer deserves the name and said, "that means to reach death and immortality at the same time." One can hear him, at the age of seventy-six, venerated like a god, murmur again and again, a little poem sent him once by a friend who had early become wise.

> "What is life? A little strife
> Where victories are vain
> Where those who conquer
> Do not win
> Nor those receive who gain."

We find often enough the prototypes of such tragic fate in a distorted, pathological form in the analyses of some neurotic patients. There, as well as in many a fate which does not owe its development to neurosis, it is clear how the superego managed to prevent success long enough, until it meant enjoyment no longer, or until it did not offer the dreamed-of satisfaction. The tragicomic character of these fates, which seem to be determined only by external circumstances, becomes apparent when these people recognize how much suffering they have inflicted upon themselves. How futile were many sacrifices, privations and renunciations, how senseless (making sense psychologically only) were so many struggles and such pain, and how much more easily these people could have obtained that overvalued success, that gratification which had been exaggerated in fantasy! Everyone who has studied the fate of many neurotic or of many healthy persons from analytical points of view knows how many "unheard of human sacrifices" have been made to the over severe superego. In retrospective contemplation of these fates, there arise complaints and accusations that eventually sink into silence, complaints and accusations that clearly testify to the grotesquely comical talents of that demiurge called Jahve.*

While the unconscious feeling of guilt was not powerful enough in many of these cases to prevent success entirely, it still made its effect felt by postponing success until it no longer meant what it once did to the individual. In some cases, the fulfillment of wishes of long ago, which now have lost their meaning, is like tragic irony, as it takes place just in time for the hearts not yet to be too tired to recognize this fact. The deep reaching, pre-forming significance of the development of the Oedipus complex is noticeable also in this connection, and the influence of the individual psychosexual life upon the other realms of human existence can still be recognized here, too. The remark, *"Si jeunesse savait, si vieillesse pouvait,"* reflects some of that melancholy knowledge.

The reports of explorers and missionaries about some savage tribes of central Australia seem almost to imply a psychological correlation in ethnology to this development of an individual's fate in which all of us have a greater or lesser share. In some tribes in Australia, the young men are, commencing with puberty, subjected to extensive restrictions concerning the time of marriage and the consumption of certain foods highly valued by primitive people. During their best years, the men of the tribe are not permitted to marry nor to eat of these prized foods. The older they grow, the less strictly are the prohibitions respected. When enough white hairs appear on the chin, the man is allowed to marry. When their teeth threaten to fall out, consumption of these delicacies is permitted the men.

* It was he, who in ancient times, first gave an example of that peculiar fate, when he caused Moses to lead the Israelites to Canaan, and then ordered him to climb Mount Nebo so that he could see the promised land. "Because," said he, "you shall see the land before you, but you shall not set foot on the land that I shall award the Israelites."

For those poor cousins of ours who still are spared culture's blessings, and for us who are endowed with them, there remains, in our common misery, after all, the illusion of a just world order and of this comforting certainty: up there, above the stars a benevolent father must dwell.

VI

Faith in a Higher Justice

Is THERE something akin to a principle of talion in nature? That was the question a renowned naturalist recently attempted to answer in a brochure. He believed he could replace Darwin's theory of selection, the hypothesis of survival of better adjusted species, by the application of this point of view. A species, which, with its superior physical strength, oppressed a weaker one for a long period had to yield gradually to the latter which developed in the struggle a special means of defense. The victors eventually succumbed to the vanquished. The verification of the scholar's postulates must be left to experts of natural science. The first impression of this combination of teleological and moralistic contemplation of the process of coming into existence and passing away is not favorable to this theory. But perhaps the third, fourth or nth impression may be decisive. Still, this explorer energetically advances the view that happenings in nature are dominated by the principle of a higher justice.* As I said, the first impression

* While reading the scientific paper of this scholar, an ancient tune sounded in my memory, a tune I had often heard from my grandfather when I was a child. It is the song "*Chad gadjo*," sung to a melancholy Jewish folk-tune:

> "A little kid, a little kid,
> God judges the world and all that's His,
> All that is good, all that bad is.
> To give the killer death He willed
> As he the son of man has killed,
> For he has guided to the slaughter
> The ox that swallowed all the water
> Which had put out the fire quick
> That took revenge upon the stick

451

is not decisive. One should not even yield to the much stronger impression that happenings in nature are arranged by a higher injustice.

Perhaps human fate seems better suited to bring problems of this kind nearer their solution. But it is not better suited, since it is, itself, part of that unrecognizable process which, through the influence of psychic factors, grows still more complex and more difficult to penetrate. Because we are not privileged to solve the old questions, it is perhaps better to turn our attention to the newer psychological question, as to how faith in a higher justice could arise, a faith that is so deeply rooted in the human soul. Do we not still secretly believe that after a time of suffering there come better days, that he who always tries hard can be redeemed? And do we not still struggle against the fact that this redemption takes place only at that special time, when, according to the word of the Greek sage, man is to be praised as being happy, namely, when he is dead? We still unconsciously share the illusion that success awaits the good, failure the bad, even though from an elevated view are seen neither good nor bad people and even though both success and failure are tiny waves in the sea of universal transitoriness.

Psychoanalysis can make an important contribution to the psychological problem of the genesis of this kind of belief in fate. About this problem, Freud has already said what is essential, starting from the psychology of compulsive thoughts. What I shall say here, as a supplement, likewise originates in analytic practice, starting, however, from the analysis of moods that sometimes get

---

> For rushing without any right
> To slay the dog quite dead on sight
> Which limb from limb the cat had rent
> That bit the kid so innocent.
> The little kid, belonged to Dad,
> Two farthings for it paid he had.
> A little kid, a little kid!"

To me it seemed that the unknown author wished to symbolize in this fateful chain of events the Talmudic comment (Sabbath 32 a), that no one escapes his fate and his merited punishment.

hold of the ego. There are, therefore, captured and analytically interpreted impressions of pensive moments in which a belief of the described kind arises in people and in which they feel as if touched by the fatefulness of certain turns of events which they feel to be, in a way, predestined.

I had best start from isolated features that look like arabesques of a type described in an earlier essay. An impression of this kind was produced by a certain situation in the life of a man in whose youth the wish to own and to read many interesting books was predominant. At that time, he was without means and had few possibilities of satisfying his increasing interests. Now a mature man, he was recently sitting at his desk and looking pensively at his large library containing many unread books that covered all the walls of his study up to the very ceiling. In these moments, in a pause of life, as it were, the memory of many hours of his boyhood came back in almost painful clearness, of the time when his deepest longing concerned the possession and the reading of books. The old wish was still strong in him, but with many duties, overburdened with great and responsible tasks, he could now scarcely find the time and occasion to indulge in the pleasure of reading any longer. A similar aspect results from the constellation in the life of a patient, a constellation which seems to represent the artful incongruity of human existence. As a child, the patient especially liked a certain dish of meat. His parents were poor and this expensive dish appeared very rarely on the family table. Now he could easily afford to eat this favorite food every day, but a serious organic stomach disease forbade him to have it.

In some, not in all cases, analysis can give psychological insight into the genesis and structure of individual features of this kind, which seem to reflect turns of fate of a tragicomic nature. It shows how the combination of actual, external factors with unconscious determinants can frequently lead to a result exhibiting features of fate. As an example, I am thinking of the analysis of the following little scene described by a patient. One evening he sat at his desk finishing a task he was obliged to complete and which had caused him much effort. In the next room his small son was play-

ing, jumping about rather noisily. First, the man found himself
slightly distracted and disturbed, but he endeavored to return to
his calculations. The longer the noisy play went on, the more impossible it became and the more impatient and irritable he became. He wanted to hurry into the next room and scold the
"naughty" child roughly and to reproach him severely for his lack
of consideration. Restraining himself in a moment from yielding
to that strong impulse, he was surprised at the vehemence of his
impatience which almost took on the character of blind fury. At
the same time, he felt a curiously stifling pressure near the heart,
combined with breathlessness. Suddenly, apparently without any
connection, he felt forced to think of his own father as he had
seen him in his last years. He saw clearly before him the aging
man's image opening the door to the nursery and looking at him,
then a little boy, with a severe expression.

In the analysis of those feelings which impressed my analysand
strongly, the significance of the emergence of the effective and
stressed thoughts became clear. When the patient was still a small
boy, as old as his son, he had often played just as noisily and
thoughtlessly and was often vehemently scolded by his father.
Often he wondered about and was hurt by the intense and incomprehensible wrath displayed by his father on these occasions
and, in thought, had reproached him for unjust treatment. Only
later did it become clear to him how strongly his father's seizures
of excitement had been influenced by his rapidly progressing heart
disease. During the scene when he heard his son jumping about in
the next room, feelings similar to those of his father had arisen in
him and all those painful memories of his hostility, of early death-
wishes against his father must have unconsciously awakened in
him. That moment was, therefore, dominated by his recognition
of how emotionally similar to his father he had grown, and it was
filled with unconscious anxiety and fear of death. The astonishment at himself and at his unusual vehemence and fury looked
like the beginning of human understanding of his father's attitude, the importance of which exceeds by far that of intellectual
comprehension, because he had experienced it. The pain near the

heart and the breathlessness were actually sensations of which his father had complained. Later medical examination indicated the probability that these sensations of the patient were early signs of the same affliction.

Speaking retrospectively of the feelings in this scene, the patient was somewhat horrified, as if he had heard the roaring of the wings of fate over his head. His impression was that somehow in that scene something mysterious had taken its course, something which he called "higher justice." The same vehement effects, the very emotions for which he had once reproached his father so severely, had suddenly appeared in him, who otherwise thought so much of his self-control and gentleness. Suddenly he had felt the urge to behave in the same rash and unjust way as his father, to behave in a way that had once appeared so incomprehensible, even unforgivable to him. His shock was, in a way, an apology to the long dead father.

Parents may thus become educators from beyond the grave, parents who never were distinguished pedagogues here on earth. The influence of a fear of reprisal and of the unconscious feeling of guilt shows unmistakably in the affective stress and in the character of the described sensations. For the belief in a "higher justice" to which the patient professed, it may also have been decisively significant.

A mood reported by another patient may have resulted from a similar psychological constellation. The previous day, she recounted in her analytic session, she had suddenly experienced a lively feeling of *déjà vecu* which was accompanied by mildly melancholy sensations. She had reposed on her sofa half-reclining and looking, "thoughtlessly," as she said, at her four children at play. She realized she was looking rather inattentively at the children. Suddenly she became conscious, in a peculiar way, of her position on the sofa, of the light falling into the room, of the playing children and the whole situation. She described her feelings as though she had had a thought absence for seconds, while at the same time embracing with her eyes the whole room with all that was happening in it. It was as if she had been, somehow, observing herself in doing so. It was not, however, a state of depersonalization because she felt an odd sadness, like a mood of farewell, while she was looking at her children at play. She now admits she might have had some thoughts during that time but she could not say anything about their kind and content. She could only say that she must have once before experienced a quite similar situation with similar feelings.

Afterwards, analytic investigation showed that the special mood, this constellation of feelings she pointed out, lost its mysteriousness, once it was assumed that an unconscious remembrance emerged in her. All the thoughts coming up in later associations suggested the reconstruction of a remembrance of the patient's mother. Eventually she was, indeed, able to remember a scene in which she had once observed her mother. This scene had, for reasons not known to her, impressed her deeply. Her mother had been lying on a sofa, as she had been now, and had been looking at her children playing in her room, with a special, peculiar expression in her eyes. The patient's age was at that time approximately the same as that of one of her children. From certain circumstances determinable in time, the fact could be reconstructed that her mother had by that time been suffering from cancer of the uterus. In that scene, the patient must have identified herself intensively with her mother. Furthermore, a faint understanding must have arisen in her of what her mother felt at the time, while she was perhaps thinking of an early death and looked sadly at her children's play.

The whole recollection, however, was unconscious during the situation proper. This is indicated through the feeling of *déjà vecu* as well as in the feeling of looking at herself, which is a reverberation of her attentive observation of her own mother in that forgotten scene. Certain traits will, to the analyst, point the way into long forgotten childhood, as, for instance, the situation of the mother and the children at play, the melancholy glance which observes and at the same time looks inward. Also the knowledge, that has become unconscious, has made possible an intuitive comprehension of the little scene. During the preceding few days, the patient happened to have suffered from abdominal pains and it was easy to guess that she was unconsciously afraid of an imminent affliction of the uterus, even though her physicians had made another, less serious diagnosis.

In both cases, an unconscious identification, based on a remembrance, had developed in the two scenes. The process of identification enabled these people to understand better the particular mood of the object with whom they identified themselves, in a similar situation, and to appreciate it psychologically. This beginning human comprehension, this intuitive understanding of emotional processes in the old objects toward whom there was an ambivalent attitude, cannot be something entirely new. Even though the approach to the same situation and increasing age enhance identification and the deepening of understanding, there must also be other unconscious factors exerting influence in the psychic genesis of those special moods, those evanescing and still impressive moments.

The empathic understanding cannot originate primarily in the similarity of the situation. Rather, there must be involved a kind of regression to childlike understanding which at the time comprehended, perhaps still without adequate verbal presentations, the emotional situation of the parents. The observing child had already possessed at that time something that adult intellect might fail to grasp. Besides all their affective wondering, there must have been in the children, even then, a certain budding psychological understanding of the meaning of the father's inexplicable vehemence, and of the reason why the mother's glance rested so full of graveness and melancholy upon her children.

It is difficult to determine this pre-knowledge and understanding of children at its best. One may compare it to an instinctive insight. Also, the special psychological interest on the part of many children must be acknowledged. It often makes them sense with remarkable accuracy connections that are not comprehensible to their intellect. Sometimes their beginning interest enables them to recognize intuitively the innermost motives of human action, the understanding of which so often eludes adult comprehension. We find, therefore, not new knowledge, but a renewed recognition of psychic processes. This recognition is made possible by several factors, of which unconscious anxiety is of special significance. From the unusual kind of feelings in those scenes and from the whole situation, we can conclude that this understanding originated in the memory of the parents' illness and death, and that one of its sources is one's own fear of death. Here Thanatos becomes a teacher. The reaction to fear of death opens secret, hitherto closed passages. By unconscious powers of conscience, this understanding has been prepared and helped to break through. Now it dawns on us that in the establishment of the principle of a "higher justice," a psychological, rather than a metaphysical, fact was concerned.

This impression is strengthened by examples like the following, from the life story of a neurotically disturbed woman. As a girl, Mary was often invited to the house of an older married friend with whom she had been at school. This friend's husband was increasingly attractive to Mary, and the more she struggled against it, the more deeply she felt her interest in him. He reciprocated with the same intensity. Mutual interests and tasks enhanced this affection. After a long emotional conflict, Mary agreed to enter into secret love relations with her friend's husband. The divorce of the married couple ensued and the old friendship was severed. Happy and full of glad hopes, the girl entered into marriage after her long time of suffering. In the beginning, the harmony of this marriage seemed unruffled. After a certain time, Mary met a young girl whose peculiarly confident and gay nature exerted a special attraction upon her. She drew her into their circle, was able to win her over to her and her husband's special interests and became close friends with the girl. The fact, that for many months she was unaware that her husband was falling under this girl's spell and was unaware of the girl's being in an inner conflict exactly like the one she had experienced, appeared definitely to be caused by an emotional blindness. So Mary was destined to experience all the painful feelings that the first wife of her husband, her conquered rival, had once experienced, to suffer the same effects of jealousy, defiance and repudiated love that she had caused her friend. Even to a superficial observer, it was only too clear that the old game repeated itself, but with roles exchanged. The victor of yesterday was the vanquished of today. Having first conquered, she now succumbed. She who suffered now, had earlier caused suffering to others. She broke with her friend, and her husband left her to follow the younger and more attractive woman, as he had done before. Consequently, Mary had a nervous breakdown that finally brought her into analysis. The analysis had to be interrupted prematurely but apparently it helped her to find new happiness or at least a new illusion that she called happiness, after such severe vicissitudes.

In following that whole course of fate, the first impression is, that with all its ups and downs, its glamor and misery shown here only in very much abbreviated form, this course has somehow been contrived. Here, a believer could really find a confirmation of the figment of a law of higher justice. He would be satisfied that anything arbitrary, unpredictable, irrational has receded and that an element of symmetry or equalization in fate has seemed to come forward. The line followed by this and many another fate seems no more to be an indecipherable zig-zag, disorganized and confused. Yet this impression would be wrong.

In analysis, anything recognizable as being in accord with a causal law definitely leads to the discovery of certain childhood impressions reverberating in the depths, to peculiarities of the libidinal and ego-development, to influences of education and of the external world. Was it, for instance, by accident that Mary drew the girl ever more closely to herself and that she introduced her to her own husband, and was there not a bit of hidden homosexual inclination effective here? Was it fate coming from outside, a lot imposed by dark powers that, in turn, she had to experience all the suffering she had caused to the other woman? Was it not rather the identification, gradually asserting itself, with her older friend whom she had loved so dearly, that was operating in the unconscious depths? Didn't the frequently recurring memory that Mary's father had left her mother to follow "the other

woman," a memory of a short stay of the child with the latter, of
her vacillation between mother and father have some influence
upon the way in which Mary's fate developed? Didn't a similar
situation in the home of the parents of her husband perhaps have
some emotional significance which could have determined his
fate?

We can then see how the semblance of a transcendental, higher
justice scatters and vanishes. Whatever remains of that semblance
can be reduced, in analytic consideration, to the effects of psychic
dynamics. That which seems to indicate metaphysical effects in
the fleeting events we call human fate, appears in analysis as
simultaneous external circumstances, and unconscious factors.
The drama of destiny of a playwright would, of course, be well
justified in trying to see rise, fall and catastrophe in Mary's fate
or in that of other people. The playwright would look for a trans-
cendent meaning or significance in it—with somewhat less justification. What meaning can be seen there is, however, not a metaphysical connection, but a psychological one. In the place of the
metaphysical thinking that, after the manner of the old philosophers, clouds the water to make it appear deep, metapsycho-
logical thinking, according to Freud, must set in. The vicissitudes
of the drives and the formation of the superego, the effects of the
instinctual powers and of the powers of conscience that can be
traced to them, assume greater importance here than the works of
supernatural, incomprehensible powers. The veil is not so much
to be removed from the transcendental, as from the minds of
men. It is not guilt or innocence that expresses itself, for instance,
in the development of the fate described above and of so many
that could be described, but the effects of an unconscious feeling
of guilt, once acquired by the still weak and undeveloped ego in
childhood, a feeling of which it could not rid itself.

We should best refrain from any final statement about the
events of the world. Even the impression of a pre-established
disharmony, of a contrived disorder, of predestined utter chaos,
may be inadequate. In any case, nothing can be noticed of a higher
justice except for that childhood belief present in our uncon-

scious psychic life. The time has come to give that up, too. "Away with the holy parables, the pious hypotheses!," to speak with Heinrich Heine. What we are left with, after an attempt to solve forthwith the "cursed questions," is an inkling of how deep the unconscious forces of our emotional life are, which contribute to the determining of our fate, and how much we still depend upon the ideas of forgotten forefathers who have been dust and ashes for a long time. The believers, the majority of whom can be found today outside the Church, recognize, in special whims of fate, the influence of a higher justice. They can tell guilt from innocence. Those with more insight know of the simultaneous effects of exogenic factors and of inner impulses and of the fact that, in the process, often an old figment, an illusion never completely overcome, has gained the upper hand in the psychic life of the individual. Pure joy in faith is left only to the saints and to some professors of the exact sciences.

About the Genesis of the Superego

THE genesis of the superego has been clearly described by Freud. The significance of the concept of this factor in psychic life, and its psychological effects, has by no means been appreciated fully as yet. I believe that such appreciation requires the discussion of certain essential points that need clarification. This discussion cannot, however, be expected to afford a complete explanation. Its character will be, rather, that of a psychological consideration. He who knows that complete darkness prevailed until recently in these passages of the emotional underworld will not expect the first light that penetrates to illuminate everything. Certainly, there will result many erroneous or inexact observations, but that does not absolve us of the duty to explore. Jakob Grimm once said, "We must have the courage to make mistakes, too."

The formation of the superego, the taking of the father into the ego, can occur only when the conflict between the anxiety and the impulses originating in the Oedipus complex has attained a certain intensity and a certain form. There is some truth in the statement that the formation of the superego is a psychic consequence of castration-anxiety, but it does not seem to be sufficiently exact. The original identification of the small boy with his father is continued in the emotional incorporation of the father into the ego in the form of the superego. Formation of the superego is an attempt to overcome the fear of the father, an attempt which was preceded by others. It has been too little noted, as yet, that the establishment of the superego shows, in itself, that it is a phenomenon of reaction to a fantasied overcoming of, and doing away with, the father. While it establishes the father's power forever, it also replaces it to some extent, making the effects of his presence superfluous to a certain degree by taking over his sphere of influence. He who has erected those prohibitions in himself is no longer so much in need of the external veto that still remains in existence in the background.

The comparison of this development with the formation of the reality function preceding it is revealing. The ego, facing the perceptual world, experiences external stimuli that leave traces of memory and that enable the ego later to recognize gradually which of these stimuli may be expected to give pleasure and which unpleasure. This remembrance then functions upon the approach to the stimulus as a signal, as an indication of something familiar. Little by little, the ego spares itself the trouble of having the same unpleasurable experience over and over again, of being warned by remembrance. Its emergence is, as it were, an abbreviated, probational reliving of the previously felt sensation of unpleasure. The external experience comes to be a possession of the ego through memory, and thus, its repetition becomes superfluous.

There exist also intermediary links between this acquisition of the sense of reality and the formation of the superego. I shall select the most important one, the parents' warnings of the possible dangers of reality, their pointing to injuries, their exhortations to postpone an immediate instinctual gratification, etc. Later, these warnings and exhortations are pushed into the background and eventually made superfluous by two factors, the growing experience of the ego and the introjection of the parents as warners. In the analysis of pampered children, or children educated with special care, we can often see that the external warning has been transposed into an internal one, its origin frequently staying unconscious. The parental warning or reminder has now changed into an inner reminder of the ego. Now the independence of the growing child will often turn angrily or indignantly against the mother's or father's warning of possible dangers and say, "I know that myself."

As in this building up of the reality function, the parental share in it gradually becomes an internal, unconscious possession that makes the warnings of the parents themselves superfluous. The parental authority is done away with to a certain extent in the building up of the superego and of morality. The same phenomenon that testifies to the internal gain of power on the part of parental authority, shows the decline of its external power. That which achieves internal victory, had first to be thoroughly conquered. The reactive character of the superego reveals itself in this enthroning of the father after the revolution.

In analytical circles, too little notice has been taken as yet of the psychological fact that in establishing the superego, the ego seizes power over the father. What has been emphasized is the fact, more important, of course, that the father takes possession of the ego in this process. Now it is no longer the father himself who is feared and loved. It is part of the ego that arouses fear. The superego, a part of the ego, now says, "You shall not"—no longer the father in reality. The actual father may appear much less significant than this inner factor, and the small boy can even criticize him sharply on occasion. It is the super-father in the ego who gives orders and who forbids.*

I must say once again that the psychogenesis of the superego represents an attempt to overcome the fear of the father. Also, it should be noted that in the same period the father, transformed in the superego, is assigned a much greater power and importance than the father in reality. The formation of the superego might best be likened to an act of preservation. The prerequisite is that the object be dead. Then it may last in its changed form for thousands of years and arouse shudders and anxiety. The formation of the superego signifies, therefore, simultaneously, the dispatch and the exaltation of the father, indicating the point at which his fall became the transition to his greatest triumph.

---

* The super-father, projected outward, is now called God. This psychogenesis of the belief in God from the idealization of the father is possible only when the figure of the father joins the ranks of the idealized forbears:

"I, as an idol, joined him, the idol.
I waste away, becoming my idol, myself."
(Goethe, Faust II)

It is because of the difficulties encountered in the psychological explanation of individual development that we seem to be justified in taking into consideration the analogy in collective psychic life. This is the more so because, according to Freud's explanation, the superego reflects all that the evolution and the fate of man have created and left behind in the id. The primal father of the primitive horde had been a powerful, violent and dreaded tyrant. His fall became, hundreds of thousands of years later, the condition for his rise. The first legends about him were certainly created while he still lived but their development reached its peak long after his death. In memory he grew again into the primal image of an omnipotent authority. Never was his superior force so unrestricted and magnificent before his sons until long after they had convinced themselves of his powerlessness. As the time since his disappearance increased, the brighter became his image.

The more profound the certainty, the security of his being dead, the more alive he grew in them. What, little by little, detached itself from the earth and moved towards heaven, had first to be sunk deep down in the earth. Out of the process of his decay, a new world arose and out of the dark into which he sank ever more deeply, a brightness grew which illumined the world.

Here again is a repetition of the development in which fall and rise constitute an event complete in itself. I have made an attempt to comprehend the projection of the totem animal upon the sky, as the typical case of its psychic "dispatch," in a paper concerning the psychology of religion, "Oedipus and the Sphinx."* There I show that, at the time when that projection occurred, religious development had already progressed via the totemistic phase to other concepts of the deity. "Now it could throw the totems that had become obsolete into the celestial lumber room." I mentioned in my paper that the rise of the deity meant not only

---

* "Image," VI (1920), p. 95 f. On page 110 of this issue, this statement can be found, "The Egyptian gods were mortal, but while their bandaged and well-wrapped bodies lay in their earthly graves, their souls shone as bright stars in the firmament."

an advancement, but, unconsciously, also a removal and, as seen from earth, a kind of secret dispossession.

In this new concept of religion, the old psychic dynamics still prevail which are generally effective in the formation of religion. The respect, love and esteem for the deity have reached their highest point. Simultaneously, however, the revolutionary unconscious wishes that aim at its removal break through. This process represents a second or third edition of a similar one that preceded it long before. Totemism was one attempt to overcome the fear of the father, accomplished through the mechanism of displacement. Likewise, the displacement of anxiety in the infantile phobias concerning animals can be understood as an attempt to master anxiety.

The formation of the superego is only the last link joining this chain. It continues the killing of the father in the form of incorporation into the ego. It commemorates his victory, but also his ruin. It is a token of the immortality, but also of the transitoriness of his power. It eternalizes him, repressing him in reality. It is the representation of an emotional *"le roi est mort, vive le roi,"* where the new king is the ego enriched by the superego.

There must be a connection between the features described here and the fact that the superego usually attenuates its strictness as the individual grows older, though there are, of course, exceptions to this general rule. The emotional attitude towards the father is changed by the partial achievement of the goals desired in childhood. The drives of the id have become less urgent and the ego has become more similar to the father. The absolutistic reign changes gradually to a democratic one that exhibits the tolerance and weakness peculiar to all democracies. The pressure of the id and the tyranny of the superego give way to more temperate trends. The technique of non-violence has achieved victory in emotional life.

This process of gradual assimilation with the father and of declining strictness of the superego can sometimes be observed in the analysis of neuroses. In the fates of many neurotic persons there appears with advancing age something akin to a late peace, a peace in which all emotional crises and struggles lose in intensity. This peace signifies psychic attrition rather than a victory over the power of those much resisted instinctual impulses. It signifies an asylum for the emotionally homeless rather than a home. Still, the decisive fact cannot be overlooked: this self-adjustment and subordination, often after the superego along with the cruel id-impulses had led the ego to the brink of disaster, is due also to the decline of the strictness of the moral, self-destroying factors of the ego.

One of those pensive sayings, melancholy even in their gaiety, which live on in my people, comes to mind here: "How fortunate that not only the hunted tire, but the hunters, too!" That may offer comfort to those who are still being chased. The dead are left cold by this and any other wisdom of the world.

Freud's View on Capital Punishment

Postscript

Freud's View on Capital Punishment

THE following paragraphs form a contribution to a symposium *For and Against Capital Punishment,* edited by Judge Emil Desenheimer of a German Superior Provincial Court, and published in Frankfurt in 1926. The judge had asked prominent people to express their opinions on capital punishment, a subject intensively discussed in public at the time. Contributions by Martin Dibelius, Arthur Drews, A. Forel, Thomas Mann, Jacob Wassermann and others are contained in the brochure. After he had discussed with me the three questions asked by the judge, Freud asked me to answer them in his place.

Question One:
Have you ever given thought to the nature, reason and purpose of punishment and written and published something about it?

Question Two:
In particular, have you ever anywhere taken a stand concerning capital punishment?

Question Three:
As you know, capital punishment can be evaluated from the points of view of law, ethics, religion, politics, sociology, medicine and economics. Would you be kind enough to express yourself concerning capital punishment from these points of view or from one of them and then to state by way of résumé whether you are an adherent or an opponent of capital punishment?

Professor Freud has asked me to reply to your inquiry, which I have received from him. I believe I should, in accordance with your purpose, describe briefly the contributions which psychoanalysis can, at this time, make to the solution of the questions as you posed them.

Answer to Questions One and Two:

According to its sphere of work, psychoanalysis can make statements about the nature of punishment only from psychological points of view. This limitation is, however, by no means meant to concede that the point of view of psychology is of lesser significance than that of law, sociology, religion, etc. We believe, moreover, that the purpose of punishment is mainly a psychological one, regardless of whether the punishment has an effect upon the criminal or the community, whether the purpose of punishment is to be sought in protection, determent, retaliation or in some other manner. Psychoanalysis must, therefore, be here heard as a psychology in depth.

Our science started from the psychology of neuroses and, only gradually and in continuous contact with experience, approached the task of finding satisfactory answers to more general questions. It has not yet been in a position to offer final judgements about the psychology of punishment. It could, however, offer new and significant points of view for the solution of these problems. Essential insights into them are contained in Freud's *Totem and Taboo* and in his short essay "Criminals from a Sense of Guilt." Their appreciation should, and thinking of a not too distant future, we may say, will, contribute decisively to a revision of our views about the nature of the criminal, as well as to important reforms in the administration of criminal law. In a recently published, more comprehensive book, *Compulsion to Confess and Need for Punishment,* I attempted to apply the results of Freud's research to the problems of criminology and of the theory of criminal law and to show the fruitfulness and significance of the analytical points of view in that field.

Answer to Question Three:

Crime was originally violation of a taboo. The law of taboo, the oldest of the world, was based upon the principle of the talion: an eye for an eye, a tooth for a tooth. He who kills shall be killed, or in the version of paragraph 21 of the official outline of a general German criminal code of 1925: he who kills another person will be punished by death. Very intensive and untamed impulses of mankind, vengefulness and demand for retaliation, have found their expression and their instinctual gratification in that primitive law. As Freud remarks, punishment not infrequently offers, to those who execute it and who represent the community, the opportunity to commit, on their part, the same crime or evil deed under the justification of exacting penance. Only the fact that mankind shrinks from facing facts, from acknowledging the facts of unconscious emotional life, delays the victory of the concept of capital punishment as murder sanctioned by law. My attitude concerning the problem of capital punishment originates, therefore, not in humanitarian reasons, but in the appreciation of the psychological necessity of the general human prohibition: thou shalt not kill.

This attitude is, furthermore, determined by the new results of research, which psychoanalysis has offered concerning the psychogenesis of the criminal and the psychology of punishment. The surprise implied in those statements gives us reason to expect that society will resolve only slowly and hesitatingly to appreciate it according to its significance. However, even though those results may be delayed in prevailing, they cannot be prevented from doing so. Freud has shown that, in the criminals at whom criminal legislation is really directed, a powerful unconscious feeling of guilt exists even before the deed. Psychoanalysis finds this pre-existent feeling of guilt in the repressed impulses of the Oedipus complex. It is hence not a consequence of the deed, but its motive.

Actually, it is only the increase of the unconscious feeling of guilt that causes a person to become a criminal. The crime, as an action that substitutes for the fulfillment of the strongest uncon-scious wishes of childhood, is felt as a relief because it can connect the pressing instinctual feeling of guilt to something real and present. The deed serves the purpose of finding a place for this feeling of guilt that has become too great. Or, in other words, the crime is committed in order to grant the proscribed drives a sub-stitute gratification and to give the pre-existent feeling of guilt reason and relief. As a result, punishment, according to accepted views, the most effective deterrent against crime, becomes, under certain psychological extremely common conditions in our cul-ture, the most dangerous unconscious stimulus for crime because it serves the gratification of the unconscious feeling of guilt, which presses toward a forbidden act. Suicide, for instance, ulti-mately satisfies the murderer's unconscious need for punishment with active assistance from the judiciary.

The results of psychoanalysis reveal possibilities of allaying, channeling and often psychically overcoming the overpowering unconscious feeling of guilt, the real, the underground motor of crime.

If permitted to take the liberty of modifying somewhat your main question, I should, in concluding, answer it thus: "I profess to be an opponent of murder, whether committed by the individ-ual as a crime or by the state in its retaliation."

EXHIBIT 1

Notes on Part 1

Exhibit 1

Notes on Part One

1. Julius Glaser, *Handbuch des Strafprozesses*, 1883, Bd. I, S. 738.
2. Erich Anuschat, "Spuren in der kriminalistischen Praxis," *Die Polizei*, April 1931.
3. Edmond Locard, *Die Kriminaluntersuchung und ihre wissenschaftlichen Methoden*, 1930, S. 26.
4. Bercher, *L'oeuvre de Sherlok Holmes et le Police scientifique*, 1926.
5. *A Study in Scarlet*.
6. Weingart, *Kriminalistik*, 1904, S. 109.
7. The chief of the detective service of Lyons, Dr. Edmond Locard, has drawn a sharp distinction between similarities and differences in the two methods in his interesting study, *Policiers de roman et de laboratoire*, 1930.
8. Quoted by Hans Gross in *Handbuch für Untersuchungsrichter*, 5. Aufl., 1908, Bd. I, S. 310.
9. Weingart, *Kriminalistik*, S. 157.
10. New York, 1926. P. 231.
11. Partly from Weingart, *Kriminalistik*, S. 120, 181. Many similar cases may be found in the well-known handbooks by Gross, Nicefort-Lindenau, Reiss, Ottolenghi, etc.
12. Dr. W. Schatz, "Hilfsindizien," *Kriminalistische Monatshefte*, 1928, S. 271.
13. Compare Dennstedt, *Die Chemie in der Rechtspflege*, 1910; Jeserich, *Chemie und Photographie im Dienste der Verbrechensaufklärung*, 1931; also papers by Popp, Schütze, etc., in *Archiv für Kriminalanthropologie*, and Look, *Chemie und Photographie bei Kriminalforschungen*, contain a multitude of such examples.
14. Edmond Locard, *Die Kriminaluntersuchung und ihre wissenschaftlichen Methoden*, S. 125.
15. The archæologist Fiorelli found in the ashes of Pompeii traces of garments so well preserved that the design and texture of the materials used could be reconstructed.
16. Weingart, *Kriminalistik*, S. 111.
17. "Zur kriminalpsychologischen Bedeutung des Verbrecherwerkzeugs," *Archiv für Kriminalanthropologie*. Bd. 52, S. 249. The author says: "The tools

and their quality enable one to guess pretty accurately the psychological premises of the deed. Very often investigations into the crime confirm the deductions made from the tools used."

18. Henze, quoted by Weingart, *Kriminalistik*, S. 87.

19. This example, like some of the preceding ones, is taken from "Spuren in der kriminalistischen Praxis," *Die Polizei*, 1931, by the Berlin magistrate, Erich Anuschat.

20. Erich Anuschat, *Die Gedankenarbeit des Kriminalisten*, 1921, S. 44.

21. Gross, *Handbuch*, S. 187.

22. "The progress of criminology means less trust in witnesses and more in real proofs." Hans Gross. (Preface to the third edition of the *Handbuch für Untersuchungsrichter*.)

23. "Your peculiar facility for deduction," as the faithful Watson calls it. ("The Greek Interpreter.") Holmes himself boasts of these "faculties of deduction which I have made my special province." (*The Adventure of the Copper Beeches*.)

24. *Kriminalistische Denklehre*, 1927. Locard and Anuschat also point to the example given by Sherlock Holmes.

25. S. Bernfeld has recently drawn attention to the resemblance between analytic interpretation and criminological work. "Die Krise der Psychologie und die Psychoanalyse" (*Internationale Zeitschrift für Psychoanalyse*. Bd. XVII, Heft 2.)

26. Edmond Locard maintains that the criminologist recreates the criminal from traces the latter leaves behind, just as the archeologist reconstructs prehistoric beings from his finds. (*Die Kriminaluntersuchung*, etc., S. 200.)

27. D. F. Krüger, "Begriff und Grenzen der kriminalistischen Kombination," *Krim. Monatshefte*, Bd. I, 1927.

28. Lothar Philipp, *Kriminalistische Denklehre*, 1927.

29. Anuschat, *Die Gedankenarbeit des Kriminalisten*, S. 7.

30. Lothar Philipp, *Einführung in die kriminalistische Denklehre*, S. 84. This sentence does not, incidentally, invariably hold good; the value of the clues and all they mean must be taken into consideration.

31. Compare Schopenhauer's wise remark: "No one with common sense runs a risk of forming false conclusions, but he runs a great risk of making false judgments. False judgments abound, but false conclusions, drawn in earnest, are very rare; they may be the result of haste and are then rectified on reconsideration. The difficulty and the danger lie in establishing the premises, not in drawing conclusions from them; the latter follows necessarily and as a matter of course. But to find the premises, there lies the difficulty."

32. Goddard, *The Hupa*, quoted by Th. Preuss in *Archiv. für Religionswissenschaft*, Bd. IX, S. 102.

33. Polizeidirektor Tenner, "Kriminaltaktische Grundsätze," *Kriminal. Monatshefte*, Heft 12, 1930.

34. *Die Gedankenarbeit des Kriminalisten*, S. 28.

35. Compare the able discussion of the experts' reports in the Halsmann case by W. Gutmann, *Das Fakultätsgutachten im Falle Halsmann*, 1931.

36. We may choose one example out of a number of cases. (Many others can also be found in the books of Sello, Alsberg, Hellwig, etc.) Otto Götz was sentenced to death on December 5th, 1919, for the murder by poisoning of his betrothed. The sentence was based principally on the expert opinion of a chemist, who maintained that potassium cyanide as a means of bringing about abortion was unknown. He did not know that all poisons, cyanide of potassium included, are used for that purpose. After Götz had served nine years penal servitude his case was reopened. The second sentence, on February 27th, 1929, at Augsburg, was four years penal servitude for criminal abortion and manslaughter.

37. *Kriminalpsychologie*, S. 157.

38. *Kriminalistische Monatshefte*, I. Jg., Heft 5.

39. In this argument the psychological considerations were hardly more convincing than the logical inferences. The counsel argued: "If only thieves frequent the Humboldt park at night (as the public prosecutor says) why should a man intending to steal go there, since he would only find colleagues?" The manifold motives contributing to human actions are as little considered in such a remark as the possibility that thieves might steal from each other.

40. Albert Hellwig, in his article, "Kriminalistik als Lehre von den Spuren der Tat" (*Monatsschrift für Kriminalpsychologie*, Bd. 12, 1921–22, S. 345), must admit that "the establishing of facts is a psychological process, when all is said and done."

41. Philipp, in his *Einführung in die kriminalistische Denkarbeit*, Berlin, 1927, S. 82, says "The remaining possibilities have to be judged by their psychological possibility. It is necessary, however, to think oneself into the mind of the suspected man."

42. Compare Reik, *Geständniszwang und Strafbedürfnis* (*Internationaler Psychoanalytischer Verlag*, 1927).

43. At the Prison Congress in London in August 1925 the Lord Chief Justice said that we must not forget that half of the harsh sentences originate in lack of understanding, in the inability of the judge to think himself into the mind of the culprit. The demand for psychological training for criminologists has been voiced lately so often and so urgently that one might think— judging by results—that the demand takes the place of that training. To quote only one opinion out of many, E. Sello, in his *Die Hau-Prozesse und ihre Lehren*, 1908, S. 133, etc., says "Any judge, public prosecutor or counsel who considers an empirical everyday psychology sufficient had better give up his job. No other profession requires such serious, scientific psychological training, both theoretical and practical, for no other profession has to solve such difficult and responsible problems. Paradoxical though this may sound, it would be easier for a criminal lawyer to dispense with jurisprudence than with psychology."

44. *The Brothers Karamazov.* In *Crime and Punishment* it is said of Porphyri Petrovitch that there was nothing in his delusions; "nothing at all, no facts, nothing positive, nothing except this feverish delusion, nothing except psychology, which has two sides to it."

45. Compare Albert-Hellwig, "Zur Frage der Befangenheit des Angeklagten," *Archiv für Krim.-Anthrop.*, 57, S. 274; and "Befangenheit als Verdachtsgrund," *ibid.* 37, S. 377.

46. There are in existence only a few incomplete notes to the fourth volume of Zola's *Les quatre Evangiles,* which was to be called *La Justice.* If it had been finished it would certainly have furnished an excellent psychological study of the examining magistrate.

47. Compare the following examples from recent criminal proceedings: in the Frenzel case in Potsdam the public prosecutor characterized the erotic connection between two adolescent girls (who were present) as "obscene behavior." In the Vienna murder case against Gustav Bauer, where the decision depended mainly on character clues, the public prosecutor addressed the following sneering remark to the accused: "So you are the man who can love two women at the same time." Not everyone can answer such questions in the quiet way that Dr. von Hirsch-Gereuth did. He was a witness in the perjury suit against Kolb and was asked: "Have you noticed that the accused says things when he is excited for which he cannot be held responsible afterwards?" "That I have noticed in everybody," replied the wise physician.

48. *Der Verbrecher und seine Richter* (Internationaler Psychoanalytischer Verlag, 1929).

49. "Analysis has penetrated into the law courts and will not disappear from them." (Hugo Staub, "Einige praktische Schwierigkeiten der psychoanalytischen Kriminalistik," *Imago,* Heft 2, 1931.)

50. Freud, *Das Fakultätsgutachten im Prozess Halsmann;* also Erich Fromm, "Oedipus in Innsbruck," *Psychoanalytische Bewegung,* Heft 1, 1930.

51. Delivered June 1906 at Professor Löffler's Seminar, University of Vienna. (Gesammelte Schriften, Bd. X, S. 197 *et seq.*)

52. Erich Fromm, "Zur Psychologie des Verbrechens und der strafenden Gesellschaft," *Imago,* Heft 2, 1931.

53. It seems to me necessary to oppose the opinions cited above, because they resemble the mistaken views of some criminologists and exponents of criminal law. A dispassionate and reasonable judge of psychoanalytical contributions to criminology, Prof. C. Bohne of Cologne, agrees with psychoanalysts who say that their science will have a distinct influence on criminology and penal law. But the basic reform of criminal law, with which we have made a beginning will not, he says, consist in the substitution of punishment by safeguards, nor in freeing judges from the letter of the law, but rather in a complete revolution of the methods of proof, in the collaboration of psychological and scientific research in the establishment of facts. This procedure will not be limited to external events and material evidence of the deed, but

will, above all, be extended to the state of mind of the culprit and to immaterial psychological evidence and will thus influence the meting out of punishment. ("Psychoanalyse und Strafrecht," *Archiv für Strafrechtswissenschaft,* 1929, S. 445.) We agree with Prof. Bohne when he says that the penal reform made necessary by psychoanalysis will begin with the establishment of proof and not, as many analysts suppose, with the system of punishment or with the psychological view taken of the culprit, etc. Personally, I believe that this reform will attack first of all the system of proof. Of this there are many indications. This book, dealing with the proof by clues, the strongest kind of evidence in the penal procedure of the present day, is one of them. The arguments brought forward by the judges, the significance of which should not be underestimated, cannot deceive us. It is not a question of a "change in our inadequate law of proof" (Bohne), but of its disappearance. In contradistinction to Prof. Bohne and to my analytic colleagues (E. Fromm and others), I hold the view that psychological evidence must not claim a place in the establishing of proofs. A. Hellwig has also admitted that psychoanalysis may attain importance in many branches of criminal law, especially in penology. ("Psychoanalyse und Strafrechtspflege," *Juristische Rundschau,* Heft 3, 1930.) The same author expresses his indignation that recently psychoanalysts "who sometimes are not even physicians, let alone psychiatrists, have been invited as experts." ("Psychoanalyse und Strafrechtspflege," *Juristische Wochenschrift,* 23 May, 1931.) He points to the analytic criminological group of workers in the Berlin Psychoanalytical Institute, which was established "to win over judges, prosecutors and defending counsels and to induce them to invite psychoanalysts in every suitable case, instead of psychiatric experts." We have grave doubts whether this was the aim of the group of workers in question. Hellwig claims to have discovered yet another of their aims: "In the end they hope so to train the executives of criminal law in psychoanalysis, that we may be able to dispense not only with a psychoanalytic expert, but also with a psychologist or psychiatrist." I do not think so. I prefer to think that their aim was to train the representatives of criminal law so highly as to be able to dispense with those representatives and eventually with the law itself.

54. French criminal-psychologists have understood this psychological constellation better than their German colleagues. Edmond Locard (*Policiers de roman et de laboratoire,* 1929, p. 145) observes that an obscene anonymous letter hardly ever comes from a prostitute or a "fast" man, and rarely from a man or woman with a normal sexual life. To those officials who are astonished that such indecent letters are written by "chaste" young girls of good families, one might say, "*L'anonymographie est un brevet de virginité.*" Naturally, it is here only a question of bodily chastity, which may, however, very well be combined with fantasied orgies. The eminent criminologist adds: "*Et je ne crois pas qu'on puisse trouver de meilleur illustration à la thèse de Freud, sous le nom de psychoanalyse, que cette prédominance de l'idée sexuelle dans*

les lettres ou la personnalité s'exprime en se dissimulant." A case given in detail by Locard (p. 251, etc.) shows his great gifts of observation.

55. Freud, "Dostojewski und die Vatertötung" in *Die Urgestalt der Brüder Karamasow,* 1930.

56. The temptation to transgress those limits exists not only for the psychologist but also for the judge, the public prosecutor and the official. Lately we have again seen attempts to use psychological methods of proof in the problem of finding the culprit, as for instance in the pathetically naïve endeavor of C. Leonhardt ("Psychologische Beweisführung," *Monatsschrift für Kriminalpsychologie und Strafrechtsreform,* 22 Jg., Heft 3, March 1931.)

57. *Kriminalpsychologie,* S. 228.

58. Weingart, *Kriminalistik,* 1904, S. 123.

59. The following report is by Egon Erwin Kisch, *Der Fall des Generalstabschefs Redl,* 1924.

60. Hans Gross, *Handbuch für Untersuchungsgefangene,* Part I, S. 21.

61. Wulffen, *Kriminalpsychologie,* S. 249.

62. *Handbuch für Untersuchungsrichter,* S. 21.

63. Weingart, *Kriminaltaktik,* S. 165.

64. "For murder, though it have no tongue will speak with most miraculous organ," Hamlet, Act II, Scene 2.

65. Reik, *Geständniszwang und Strafbedürfnis* (Internationaler Psychoanalytischer Verlag, 1925).

66. Recently Pollke quoted a similar case in *Kriminalistische Monatsschriften,* Heft 2, 1928, S. 205: A Polish workman, Michael Wolca, who was employed on a building in the Duisburg Forest, had spent his week's wages on drink and gambling with his boon companions at the local inn. On leaving the inn he went to the foreman's shed where all the workmen's working clothes were kept, meaning to steal them. The lock withstood all his efforts. He climbed a stack of wood in front of the shed, wedged a lever about two yards long between the roof and the wall of the hut. By dint of this he lifted the roof far enough to get his head and right arm through. He had just succeeded in grabbing some of the clothes hanging inside, pulling them through and throwing them on the ground, when the stack of wood tipped over and he lost his foothold. The roof slipped back into its original position, leaving him dangling between the roof and the wall. He was found there dead next morning.

67. "There is something of the worst in the best of us, there is something of the best in the worst of us."

68. *Kriminalpsychologie,* S. 265.

69. A strange superstition among thieves in Europe and Asia. Cf. *Archiv. für Kriminal-Anthropologie,* 1908, S. 302 *et seq.*

70. "Neues zur Kotuntersuchung in Kriminalfällen," *Archiv für Kriminologie,* Bd. 84, May 1920, S. 14 *et seq.*

71. Freud, *From the History of an Infantile Neurosis*, Collected Papers, Vol. III.

72. Hellwig, "Die Bedeutung des grumus merdæ für den Praktiker," *Archiv für Kriminal-Anthropologie*, Bd. 23, p. 188 *et seq.*

73. *Kriminalistische Aufsätze, Archiv für Krim.-Anthrop.*, 1908, S. 302.

74. *Kriminalistische Aufsätze*, S. 310.

75. *Kriminalpsychologie*, S. 235 *et seq.*

76. Wulffen, *Kriminalpsychologie*, S. 237.

77. *Kriminalpsychologie*, S. 238.

78. Compare Freud, *Beyond the Pleasure Principle*, 1922.

79. Dostoevski has recognized these unconscious tendencies much better than modern criminal psychologists. Petrovitch in *Crime and Punishment* describes the strange behavior of the criminal shortly after the deed. ". . . . he thrusts himself forward, giving his opinion unasked, talks continuously of things best left alone, revels in parables and asks why he is not arrested. . . ." This description applies, of course, only to a certain type of criminal.

80. Petrovitch reasons thus: "I leave such a man entirely to himself. I do not arrest him or worry him, but every hour and every minute he must suspect me of knowing everything, his whole secret. I have him watched ceaselessly, and if he is conscious of suspicion and in constant fear—then, by Jove, he won't know what to do; he will come and give himself up. . . . ; this is as certain as that twice two makes four; it is, so to speak, a mathematical fact. . . ."

81. From A. Gleichen-Russwurm, *Weltgeschichte in Anekdoten und Querschnitten*, 1929.

82. *"Dort drängt die Menge sich zum Bösen,*
    Da muss sich manches Rätsel lösen." (Goethe's *Faust*.)

83. People who think this opinion exaggerated had better read the contribution of an eminent jurist to this question. "The history of law is still too one-sided. It is a history of institutions; it describes the organization and rules of justice. . . . In a word, the history of law is too much a history of institutions and too little a history of the mind. If it continues on those lines it is in danger of merely accumulating and describing a mass of material; but material without a deep and firm mental basis is lifeless. If the history of law is merely treated as an accumulation of material it will interest a smaller and smaller circle of people, and at last only the historian of the law. Instead of contributing to the knowledge of human nature it will contribute only to the knowledge of material law." (Hans Fehr, *Gottesurteil und Folter*. Special edition on the occasion of Rudolf Stammler's seventieth birthday, 1926, S. 231.)

84. Punishment may here be traced back to a ceremonial repentance. This deserves exhaustive investigation.

85. Ch. Keysser, "Aus dem Leben der Kaileute" in R. Neuhaus, *Deutsch-Neu-Guinea.* Bd. III, S. 62 *et seq.*

86. An analogy to this may be found in the symptoms of obsessional neurosis.

87. Frazer's *The Belief of Immortality and the Worship of the Dead* supplies comprehensive information on this subject.

88. M. Dobritzhoffer, *Historia de Apibonibus,* 1784, Bd. II, S. 92, 240.

89. C. Gay, *Fragment d'un Voyage dans le Chili et au Cusco,* 1848, p. 25.

90. K. von den Steinen, *Unter den Naturvölkern Zentral-Brasiliens,* 1894, S. 344, 348.

91. E. F. im Thurn, *Among the Indians of Guiana,* 1884, pp. 330, etc.

92. J. I. Monteiro, *Angola and the River Congo,* 1875, Vol. I, p. 65.

93. H. M. Bentley, *Pioneering on the Congo,* Vol. I, p. 275.

94. Father Abinal, "Astrologie Madagasce," *Missions Catholiques,* Vol. XI, 1879, p. 506.

95. From Erich Sello, *Die Irrtümer der Strafjustiz und ihre Ursachen,* 1911, Bd. I, S. 397 *et seq.*

96. Malinowski, *Crime and Custom in Savage Society,* p. 87 *et seq.*

97. Rev. J. H. Bernau, *Missionary Labours in British Guiana,* 1847, p. 561.

98. R. Neuhaus, *Deutsch-Neu-Guinea,* Bd. III, S. 134.

99. George Brown, *Melanesians and Polynesians,* p. 197.

100. Stanbridge, "On the Aborigines of Victoria," *Transactions of the Ethnological Society,* Vol. 1, 1861, p. 299.

101. G. Taplin, *The Narrenyerie Tribe,* pp. 19–20.

102. George Brown, *Melanesians and Polynesians,* pp. 385–6.

103. A. W. Howitt, *The Native Tribes of South-East Australia,* p. 448.

104. J. Dawson, *Australian Aborigines,* p. 68.

105. W. Bosman, *Voyage de Guinée,* 13e lettre, p. 227.

106. W. Plehn, "Beiträge zur Völkerkunde des Togogebietes," *Mitteilungen des Seminars für orientalische Sprachen,* Bd. III, S. 97.

107. Cf. K. Lehmann, *Das Bahrrecht, Germanist. Abhandl. für Konrad v. Maurer,* 1893, S. 23 *et seq.*

108. Rudolf His, *Der Totenglaube in der Geschichte des germanischen Strafrechtes,* 1929, S. 15.

109. K. Lehmann, *Das Bahrrecht,* S. 42. A relic of the trial at the bier still survives in par. 88 of the German code of criminal procedure, according to which the corpse must be shown to the accused for recognition. The occasion is naturally made use of to attempt to obtain a confession from the accused.

110. *Richard the Third,* Act II, Scene 1.

111. The Kpelle, a Negro tribe in Liberia, bury a sharp knife with the dead man, so that he may kill his murderer. (See Dietrich Westermann, *Die Kpelle,* 1921.)

112. In the old German penal law the murdered man was carried to the law court accompanied by his relations, who walked with drawn swords in-

toning the funeral chant. The inference is that the dead man himself was originally the plaintiff, and the relations appeared later as his representatives. Brunner (*Deutsche Rechtsgeschichte*, Bd. I, 1906, S, 252) puts forward a similar view: "In this way only can we summarize under a single heading the different functions of the dead man, such as in the mourning with the dead, the conjuration of the dead, the dead man as guarantor, bondsman and witness, and the part he plays at the trial at the bier." (Compare also his *Der Totenglaube*, S. 18; and Hans Scheuer, "Das Recht der Toten," *Zeitschrift für vergl. Rechtswissenschaft*, Bd. 34, 1916.)

113. *Handbuch für Untersuchungsrichter als System der Kriminalistik,* I Teil, S. 183.

114. It may be noted that in Schiller's poem the unconscious confession of the criminal is prepared by the scene on the stage.

115. This original form is of course hypothetical; it is the foundation of the reports of Schiller's poetical inspiration which have come down to us. The poet has taken his subject from Suidas and made use of one passage from Plutarch and one from the Greek anthology.

116. J. Dawson, *Australian Aborigines,* p. 68.

117. A. Oldfield, "The Aborigines of Australia," *Transactions of the Anthropological Society,* Vol. II, 1865, p. 246.

118. Compare Ludwig Hopf, *Tierorakel und Orakeltiere in alter und neuer Zeit,* 1888.

119. G. P. Steinmetz, *Rechtsverhältnisse von eingeborenen Völkern in Afrika und Ozeanien,* S. 278.

120. Compare Wundt's *Völkerpsychologie;* also Rudolf Kleinpaul, *Die Lebendigen und Toten,* 1898, S. 12 *et seq.*

121. The myth of the death of Ibycus of Rhegium has a German parallel in the tale of St. Meinrad and his ravens. The birds pursue the murderer of the holy man. Making a terrific noise they cluster round his head, thus solving the crime and bringing him to justice.

122. For Hector the flight of the birds is of magical importance (*Iliad* XII, 229). "Whether they fly to the right, to the day and the sunshine;
Or whether they turn to the left, to the coming night and the darkness."

123. The fly belongs to these animals. The brood of the flesh-fly (*sarcophaga mortuorum*) feeds on corpses. In the Philistine town of Ekron there was a fly oracle which the Israelite king Ahazia consulted. (II Kings 1.) Beelzebub is the lord of the flies and is used as an oracle. The Scandinavian tribes of the old Germans had flies, besides horses and birds, among their animal oracles. (Hopf, *Tierorakel und Orakeltiere,* S. 115 *et seq.*)

124. André Siegfried, *Les Etats-Unis d'aujourd'hui,* 1928.

125. It is not relevant to our purpose to examine the correctness of the deduction. The reconstruction of the psychological process is the only important thing here.

126. Compare A. Hellwig, "Verwendung von Polizeihunden," *Preussisches Kommunal-archiv*. Bd. II, p. 398 *et seq.*; also Friedo Schmidt, *Verbrecherspur und Polizeihund*, 1910, and *Polizeihundeerfolge deutscher Schäferhunde und neue Winke fü Prolizeihundführer, Liebhaber und Behörden*, 1911.

127. We will quote one example of the work and success of police dogs. It is taken from Hellwig (*Moderne Kriminalistik*, Leipzig, 1914, S. 33). On the Dallmin estate in West Priegnitz a nine-year-old girl had been enticed into a wood and killed; the body was found the same night. Next morning two policemen with their dogs, Prince and Bołko, came to Dallmin where, in the meantime, another dog from a different police district, had tried in vain to follow the scent. The child's clothing was given to the dogs for the scent. It was snowing hard, but Prince followed the scent through the wood to the coachman's house and there, owing to the deep snow, he lost the scent. There was, however, reason to believe that the murderer was one of the servants on the estate. Two people were suspected, a workman with scratches on his face, and a sixteen-year-old gardener's helper whom the father of the murdered girl and the magistrate both believed to be innocent. This boy was told to stand among the other employees and then the lower part of the girl's apron (rape was suspected) was shown to the dog. The dog searched round the room and when he came to the apprentice he barked and looked from him to his master. At first the boy protested his innocence and said the dog had barked at him because he had lent a hand in removing the corpse. He only abandoned this attitude when he was reminded that the lower part of the girl's apron had given the dog the scent; he then confessed and said that he had thrown the knife with which he had killed the girl into the wood. The next day the other dog took the scent from the boy's hands and in a short time returned with the knife, which he had found under a fir tree.

128. This fairy tale was made use of by Gustav Mahler in his *Klagendes Lied*.

129. Grimm, *Kinder-und Hausmärchen*, No. 28.

130. Monseur "L'os qui chante," *Bulletin de Folklore*, Vol. I, pp. 39, 89, II, 219, 245, III, 35 *et seq.*; S. Mackensen, "Der Singende Knochen," *Schweizer Arch. für Volkskunde*, Bd. 25, S. 147.

131. Anton Mailly, *Deutsche Rechtsaltertümer*, 1929, S. 195.

132. A. Schiel, *Drei-und-zwanzig Jahre Sturm und Sonnenschein in Süda-frika*, 1902, S. 228 *et seq.*

133. S. Pinto, *Wanderungen quer durch Afrika*. (Translated by H. von Wobeter), 1881, Bd. I, S. 121, 123.

134. W. E. Roth, "North Queensland," *Ethnograph. Bulletin* 9, No. 13.

135. K. W. Schmidt in J. D. Lang, *Queensland*, pp. 360–1.

136. R. Salvado, *Mémoires historiques sur l'Australie*, pp. 332–3.

137. L. Levy-Bruhl, *La Mentalité primitive*, 1922, p. 194.

138. Hugh Low, *Sarawak*, pp. 262–3.

139. Albert A. C. Le Soulf, "Notes on the Natives of Australia," in R. Broughmith's *Aborigines of Victoria*, 1878, Vol. II, p. 289 *et seq.*

140. Similar examples may be found in Rudolf His, *Der Totenglaube in der Geschichte des germanischen Strafrechts*, 1929, S. 16.

141. E. Hesselink, "Ein verräterisches Eichenblattstückchen," *Archiv für Kriminalanthropologie und Kriminalistik*, Bd. 80, 1927, S. 55.

142. Lorimer Fison and A. W. Howitt, *Kamilaroi and Kurnai*, 1880, p. 250.

143. Freud, "Notes upon a Case of Obsessional Neurosis," 1909, *Collected Papers*, Vol. III, and *Totem und Tabu*, Gesammelte Schriften, Bd. X.

144. Hubert and Mauss in *Année sociologique*, Vol. III, 1904.

145. Frazer, *The Magic Art*, pp. 120, 122 *et seq.*

146. A. E. Crawley in *Encyclopædia of Religion and Ethics* (Vol. VI, p. 507) observes that the limit of a period of this kind can be approximately determined by two facts: (a) Australian Negroes, who are on a primitive cultural level, have no ordeal, and (b) the peoples of Europe gave up Divine judgment (*Gottesurteile*) toward the end of the Middle Ages.

147. A. H. Post, *Afrikanische Jurisprudenz*, 1887, Bd. II, S. 149.

148. E. Peschuel-Loesche, *Volkskunde von Loango*, 1907, S. 112.

149. *Die Gottesurteile ei den Bantuvölkern, Sudannegern und Hamiten* Weida i. Th., 1909.

150. The "Bread Trial" (*Judicium offae*) belongs to this group, too. In this, the morsel had to be swallowed without chewing; if it stuck in the throat guilt was proven. Felix Dahn (*Studium zur Geschichte der germanischen Gottesurteile*, 1857) believes that the Communion was turned into divine judgment on the analogy of the heathen ordeal of trial by eating. He calls attention to the word "*communicare*," used by the officiating priest as well as by the suspected man who swallows the bread and cheese. A famous historical example of Communion taken under the threat of immediate death is the case of Pope Gregory the Seventh, who took the Communion and invoked sudden death upon himself if he had committed the crime of which the royal faction accused him. Concerning Communion as an ordeal compare also the saying of Radbertus that, whoever ate the Body of Christ and drank His Blood unworthily would call judgment down upon himself. (Benno Hilse, *Das Gottes-Urteil der Abendmahlprobe*, 1867, S. 50.) The accused received the Host after he had said, "*Si aliter est quam dixi et juravi tunc hoc Domini nostri Jesu Christi corpus non pertranseat gutter meum, sed haereat in faucibus meis, strangulet me suffocet me ac interficat me statim in momento.*" (F. Dahn, *Bausteine*, 1879, Bd. II, S. 16.)

151. Muller in *Globus*, Bd. 81, S. 280.

152. De Compiègne, *L'Afrique Equatoriale*, Paris 1875, p. 309, 320.

153. J. H. Johnston, *The Congo*.

154. *Encyclopædia of Religion and Ethics*, Vol. IX, p. 526 ff.

155. Compare Frazer, *Pausanias*, 1898, Vol. IV, p. 175.

156. From the *Encyclopædia of Religion and Ethics*, Vol. IV, p. 508.

157. *Encyclopædia of Religion and Ethics,* Vol. IX, p. 526 *et seq.*

158. *Gouvernement Général de l'Afrique Occidentale Française. Notices publiées par le Gouvernement Général à l'occasion de l'Exposition Coloniale de Marseille. La Côte Ivoire.* Corbeil, 1901, pp. 570-2.

159. *Calabor and its Mission,* 1901, p. 34 *et seq.*

160. "A Journey in West Issu-ch-uan," *Royal Geographical Society, Supplementary Paper,* 1886, I, p. 70.

161. Peschuel-Loesche, *Volkskunde von Loango,* 1907, S. 434 *et seq.*

162. Nausea, that is, the giving back of what has been eaten, is the forerunner of confession. It is, so to speak, a primitive form of repentance. The man who "keeps" the portion of corpse he has eaten is guilty.

163. Psychoanalysis can interpret many forms of ordeal, hitherto unexplained, by the factor of symbolism. Thus, for instance, the Latuka in Africa make a woman suspected of adultery grasp a red-hot spear-point. (Fr. Stuhlmann, *Mit Emir Pascha ins Herzvon Afrika,* 1894, S. 781.)

164. According to ancient and primitive thought, divination (by means of which the priest-magician finds an unknown murderer) is accomplished by touching. The dead man's ghost descends into the priest; the magician is possessed.

165. The Babylonian word for "oath," *mamètu,* may also be used for "curse." Lack of space makes it impossible to adduce examples in confirmation of this point in these pages.

166. Hermann Kurz in *Germania,* Bd. XV, S. 235.

167. American criminologists still call a certain kind of examination "the third degree." A slang expression denoting the questioning of the defendant is to "put him on the grill."

168. As I have shown elsewhere, the same phenomenon may be studied and described in the genesis and development of another social institution. When belief in dogma as an eternal truth began to wane, it was defined all the more precisely, its official importance increased and the "proofs" became longer and more subtle. (Reik, *Dogma und Zwangsidee,* Internationaler Psychoanalytischer Verlag, 1930.)

169. I have not met with such an indication in any accessible book on the history of law and comparative law.

170. *Deutsche Rechtsaltertümer,* Halthaus, 172, 1,607 *et seq.*

171. "The decision as to the meaning of the evidence rests on the free conviction of the court, derived from the essence of the trial." (Par. 261.)

172. Albert Hellwig, *Moderne Kriminalistik,* 1914, S. 89.

173. Charles Keysser, "Aus dem Leben der Kaileute," in R. Neuhaus, *Deutsch-Neu-Guinea,* III.

174. Erich Sello, *Die Irrtümer der Strafjustiz,* 1911. Albert Hellwig, *Justizirrtümer,* 1914. Theodor Rittler, "Der Indizienbeweis und sein Wert,"

Schweizerische Zeitschrift für Strafrecht. Jg. XLIII, 1929. Compare further the rich material provided by the works of Max Alsberg, Gross, etc.

175. *"Was ist das Allgemeine? Der einzelne Fall. Was ist das Besondere? Millionen Fälle."* (Goethe).

176. In the report of the case, made by the prosecuting counsel Nemanitsch, in Gross, *Archiv*, Bd. VI, S. 272 *et seq.*, only the Christian names of the persons concerned are given. The surnames used here are fictitious and are only added in order to make the narrative more vivid.

177. Dr. August von Nemanitsch, counsel for the prosecution, who described the case in *Archiv für Kriminalanthropologie*, Bd. VI, 1901, says: "Juliane had the reputation in her village as a daughter of *Venus vulgivaga*." Of Gregor however he says that "he could easily have made a living if he had not been so devoted to Bacchus and Venus." That was the mythological way in which counsels expressed themselves in the last century when passing judgment on accused persons.

178. As an example of the clamorous *vox populi* we may quote the aged Franz Pürnagl: "I cannot help voicing the conviction that it was Gregor Adamsberger who killed Juliane Sandbauer in order to escape her everlasting demands for money and to get rid of the only person who knew his secret. This conviction is shared by the majority of people in Finkbrunnen. I cannot imagine anyone except Adamsberger having an interest in Juliane's death, since she had no money whatever." There is no doubt about the sincerity of his opinion even though it may surprise us that the peasants of Finkbrunnen should talk perfect juristic German.

179. It was the charge of arson, on which the jury had found him guilty, that saved him from the inevitable sentence of death. Penal servitude for this crime might be looked upon as an aggravation of capital punishment, which is forbidden according to Austrian law. Gregor had committed more than murder, which justified the extreme penalty, and so he was not sentenced to death. Strict logical adherence to the law sometimes has useful consequences.

180. Gross. "Anmerkungen," *Archiv für Kriminalanthropologie,* Bd. VI, S. 290, etc.; also "Ein fataler Indizienbeweis, Gegenbemerkungen zu den Bemerkungen in diesem Falle," *ibid.* Bd. VII, S. 323 *et seq.*

181. Stooss, "Ein fataler Indizienbeweis," *ibid.*, Bd. VII, S. 312 *et seq.*

182. *Archiv*, Bd. VI, S. 290.

183. *Archiv*, Bd. VII (1901), S. 327.

184. Bierling (*Juristische Prinzipienlehre*, 1911, Bd. IV, S. 117) lays down two empiric propositions as the basic rules of circumstantial evidence. The first is that no absolute inference may be drawn from one single positive fact to another positive fact, even if that fact is so unique as to possess great evidential value. The second is that a number of independent facts, each unimportant in itself, may under certain circumstances prove the very strong probability of another fact, not yet established.

185. In a Congress of German teachers of Public Law, held in 1926, Erich Kaufmann, in a paper about equality before the law, said of judicial technique that it was no better than a prostitute, willing to serve anything for anybody. The same may be said with certain reservations about circumstantial evidence.

186. A patient of mine remembered that at an age corresponding to that of the girl in question, she had read *Sündfrüchte* instead of *Südfrüchte* ("fruits of sin" instead of "fruits of the south"). The mistake is determined by an unconscious recollection of the expression "fruits of sin," used in many bad novels.

187. In everyday life, too, we interpret the gestures and tones of voice (which we do not consciously perceive) of other people in the sense of their unconscious feelings. In this way we make lines of communication between their unconscious and ours.

188. The counsel Neuda has described it in Katscher's *Schuldlos verurteilt*, 1895, S. 74. Also Sello in *Die Irrtümer der Strafjustiz*, S. 212 *et seq.*

189. Dr. Neuda appealed against the sentence.

190. Sir George Grey, *Journal of Two Expeditions of Discovery in North-West and West Australia*, 1841, 11, p. 238.

191. J. G. Frazer, *The Belief in Immortality and the Worship of the Dead*, 1913. Vol. I.

192. S. Nachtigal, *Sahara und Sudan*, Berlin, 1879, Vol. II, S. 686.

193. Eduard Pechuel-Loesche, *Die Loango-Expedition*, 1907, 3 Abt., 2 Hälfte, S. 335.

194. "The law is, and will remain, a relatively coarse instrument, an axe, not a razor or microtome." (J. J. Anossow, "Tat und Täter," *Monatsschrift für Kriminalpsychologie und Strafrechtsreform*, Jg. XXII, Sept. 1931, Heft 9.)

195. J. J. Anossow's excellent paper, "Tat und Täter" (see above), opens up such perspective of future practice in penal law.

196. Professor Meiner, quoted in W. Gutmann, *Das Fakultätsgutachten im Falle Halsmann*, 1931, S. 59.

197. "Explain, if you can, how Dreyfus could have been so unpopular if he had really been a traitor. Had he been a traitor he would have been on very good terms with his colleagues. . . ." (Sept. 1889.)

198. The psychological effect of the belief in the omnipotence of thoughts is also proved by all kinds of self-accusations. Their investigation by psychoanalysis would be a special task and would be amply repaid.

199. "To pronounce judgment is not a purely juridic-technical art; it is also an act of will, indeed, more the latter than the former." Deinhardt, *Erfahrungen und Anregungen zur Kunst der Rechtspflege*, 1909, S. 43.

200. Max Rumpf, *Der Strafrichter*, 1912, S. 98.

201. *Handbuch für Untersuchungsrichter*, I. Teil, S. 34.

202. In four years Calvin had more than fifty people executed on theo-

logical grounds as the result of the most subtle logical reasoning. On this occasion Luther said that "Hangmen were not the best doctors."

203. No less a person than Emile Zola has described how an examining magistrate may form a fixed opinion as the result of small suspicions and how this conviction may be proof against all arguments, even against absurdities. If accidents do not fit into lines of thought, they are ruled out. The strength of this conviction makes improbabilities probable and reinterprets conflicting evidence on its own lines. (*La Bête Humaine.*) Zola shows how an examining magistrate disbelieves the confession of a murderer, because certain details in his tale do not fit in with his system. The magistrate follows his own false theory with the shrewdness and unconscious passion shown by monomaniacs. The crime must have happened in *this* and in no other way; here again, the belief in the omnipotence of thoughts proves fateful.

204. Other people who have been influenced by the doctrines of psychoanalysis have drawn attention to the effect of these unconscious impulses. (Max Alsberg, *Das Weltbild des Strafrichters*, 1930.) Sello in *Psychologie der cause célèbre*, 1910, quotes an experienced counsel for the defence in a sensational murder trial: "the case is going badly; there is too much blood in it." This "too much" refers to the judge; his imagination has tasted blood. King Lear realizes that the identical impulses that find satisfaction in the crime are latently effective in the judge when coming to his judicial conviction. "*See how yon justice rails upon yon simple thief. Hark, in thine ear: change places; and handy-dandy, which is the justice, which is the thief?*"

205. The defending counsel, Max Alsberg, observes that the superstition is not rare among German judges that "To admit inability to gain the necessary evidence for a conviction would be to discredit the whole institution of criminal justice." The same counsel adds: "There are judges who look upon an acquittal as a sign of inadequacy and this engenders the bitter feeling of having damaged the cause of criminal justice." (Quoted from Rudolf Olden and Josef Bernstein, *Der Justizmord an Jakubowski*, 1928, S. 6. This is a book which may be recommended to all interested in the question of circumstantial evidence.)

206. They say that a lion who has missed his spring abandons his victim shamefacedly. A little of this shame survives unconsciously in the judge who has to acquit a defendant because the circumstantial evidence was not quite strong enough. Against this assumption of unconscious feelings in judge, prosecuting counsel, etc., there will certainly be great opposition. Some observers also deny, it is true, the behavior of the lion in the circumstances described, but few will maintain that he goes away happily after his miss, glad to be able to spare his victim.

207. Hirschberg gives many examples of this resistance against a justifiable demand to reopen proceedings. ("Zur Psychologie des Wiederaufnahmeverfahrens," *Monatsschrift für Kriminalpsychologie*, XXI, Jg., Heft 7, 1930,

S. 407.) See also Sello, *Die Irrümer der Strafjustiz*, Band 1, 1911, S. 462. Alsberg expresses his opinion in the same way (*Justizirrtum und Wiederaufnahme*, Berlin 1913, S. 47 *et seq*.). The judge regards it as a moral defeat when he is "forced to admit that the State has annihilated an innocent man."

208. I think it was Alfred Polgar.

209. In February 1911 the butcher Eduard Trautmann was found guilty of the murder of Emma Sander. Counsel for the prosecution asked the jury to bring in a verdict of guilty on the basis of faultless circumstantial evidence, using the words "Annihilate this brute in human form." Sixteen years later, after having served *sixteen* years of penal servitude, Trautmann was acquitted. It turned out that Sander had been a victim of the mass murderer, Karl Denke, who had committed twenty murders before criminologists got on to his track.

210. As has already been indicated, it is probably a rationalized return of that aspect of the clue when the criminal police forbids touching the clues in order to "keep them intact."

211. Sometimes it takes the form that we *might* have killed someone without knowing it. When a reality-test is blotted out in connection with these thoughts, delusions of a very resistant kind appear. Schnitzler has given an excellent description of the overpowering strength of such thoughts in his last novel *Die Flucht in die Finsternis*, 1931.

212. The haste with which we try to elucidate a crime is not explicable on rational grounds alone; it testifies to the unconscious operation of such affective tendencies in the criminologist. At the beginning of one of Conan Doyle's stories, *The Naval Treaty*, this unconscious connection is noticeable. Sherlock Holmes, when working on a crime, exclaims: "I suspect myself . . ." —"What?"—"Of coming to conclusions too rapidly."

213. Freud observes that it cannot be an accident that three masterpieces of world literature—Sophocles' *Œdipus*, Shakespeare's *Hamlet*, and Dostoevski's *The Brothers Karamazov*—treat of the same topic, namely, parricide. It may be added that the discovery and proof of the unknown murderer's guilt form (again not accidentally) an essential part of their external and internal plot. It is worth considering what means of solving the crime are employed in these works (oracle, ordeal, circumstantial evidence) and how different are the tactics employed to discover the author of the crime. An exhaustive psychoanalytical investigation should be able to show in what form the belief in the omnipotence of thoughts expresses and hides itself in these three authors.

214. The emphasis I have laid on the problem which these three masterpieces have in common proves that I do not share the usual contempt for detective fiction. I believe this opinion to be the result of certain unconscious factors. These masterpieces are not alone in showing that the theme of crime

forms the center of many of the greatest works of literature. A theme of this kind is, moreover, also often another way of presenting important problems, when a forbidden act has been committed and the question arises: "Who did it?"

215. In this hidden expectation we behave like savages who have to admit that a crocodile killed A., but maintain that the magician B. ordered the crocodile to commit the wicked deed.

216. The dead *do* tell tales.